THE NEW MIDDLE

BONNIE WHEELER, Series Editor

The New Middle Ages is a series dedicated to pluridisci
particular emphasis on recuperating women's histor
This peer-reviewed series includes both scholarly mor

PUBLISHED BY PALGRAVE

Women in the Medieval Islamic World: Power, Patronage, and Piety
edited by Gavin R. G. Hambly

The Ethics of Nature in the Middle Ages: On Boccaccio's Poetaphysics
by Gregory B. Stone

Presence and Presentation: Women in the Chinese Literati Tradition
edited by Sherry J. Mou

The Lost Love Letters of Heloise and Abelard: Perceptions of Dialogue in Twelfth-Century France
by Constant J. Mews

Understanding Scholastic Thought with Foucault
by Philipp W. Rosemann

For Her Good Estate: The Life of Elizabeth de Burgh
by Frances A. Underhill

Constructions of Widowhood and Virginity in the Middle Ages
edited by Cindy L. Carlson and Angela Jane Weisl

Motherhood and Mothering in Anglo-Saxon England
by Mary Dockray-Miller

Listening to Heloise: The Voice of a Twelfth-Century Woman
edited by Bonnie Wheeler

The Postcolonial Middle Ages
edited by Jeffrey Jerome Cohen

Chaucer's Pardoner and Gender Theory: Bodies of Discourse
by Robert S. Sturges

Crossing the Bridge: Comparative Essays on Medieval European and Heian Japanese Women Writers
edited by Barbara Stevenson and Cynthia Ho

Engaging Words: The Culture of Reading in the Later Middle Ages
by Laurel Amtower

Robes and Honor: The Medieval World of Investiture
edited by Stewart Gordon

Representing Rape in Medieval and Early Modern Literature
edited by Elizabeth Robertson and Christine M. Rose

Same Sex Love and Desire among Women in the Middle Ages
edited by Francesca Canadé Sautman and Pamela Sheingorn

Sight and Embodiment in the Middle Ages: Ocular Desires
by Suzannah Biernoff

Listen, Daughter: The Speculum Virginum and the Formation of Religious Women in the Middle Ages
edited by Constant J. Mews

Science, the Singular, and the Question of Theology
by Richard A. Lee, Jr.

Gender in Debate from the Early Middle Ages to the Renaissance
edited by Thelma S. Fenster and Clare A. Lees

Malory's Morte D'Arthur: *Remaking Arthurian Tradition*
by Catherine Batt

The Vernacular Spirit: Essays on Medieval Religious Literature
edited by Renate Blumenfeld-Kosinski, Duncan Robertson, and Nancy Warren

Popular Piety and Art in the Late Middle Ages: Image Worship and Idolatry in England 1350–1500
by Kathleen Kamerick

Absent Narratives, Manuscript Textuality, and Literary Structure in Late Medieval England
by Elizabeth Scala

Creating Community with Food and Drink in Merovingian Gaul
by Bonnie Effros

Representations of Early Byzantine Empresses: Image and Empire
by Anne McClanan

Encountering Medieval Textiles and Dress: Objects, Texts, Images
edited by Désirée G. Koslin and Janet Snyder

Eleanor of Aquitaine: Lord and Lady
edited by Bonnie Wheeler and John Carmi Parsons

Isabel La Católica, Queen of Castile: Critical Essays
edited by David A. Boruchoff

Homoeroticism and Chivalry: Discourses of Male Same-Sex Desire in the Fourteenth Century
by Richard E. Zeikowitz

Portraits of Medieval Women: Family, Marriage, and Politics in England 1225–1350
by Linda E. Mitchell

Eloquent Virgins: From Thecla to Joan of Arc
by Maud Burnett McInerney

The Persistence of Medievalism: Narrative Adventures in Contemporary Culture
by Angela Jane Weisl

Capetian Women
edited by Kathleen D. Nolan

Joan of Arc and Spirituality
edited by Ann W. Astell and Bonnie Wheeler

The Texture of Society: Medieval Women in the Southern Low Countries
edited by Ellen E. Kittell and Mary A. Suydam

Charlemagne's Mustache: And Other Cultural Clusters of a Dark Age
by Paul Edward Dutton

Troubled Vision: Gender, Sexuality, and Sight in Medieval Text and Image
edited by Emma Campbell and Robert Mills

Queering Medieval Genres
by Tison Pugh

Sacred Place in Early Medieval Neoplatonism
by L. Michael Harrington

The Middle Ages at Work
edited by Kellie Robertson and Michael Uebel

Chaucer's Jobs
by David R. Carlson

Medievalism and Orientalism: Three Essays on Literature, Architecture and Cultural Identity
by John M. Ganim

Queer Love in the Middle Ages
by Anna Klosowska

Performing Women in the Middle Ages: Sex, Gender, and the Medieval Iberian Lyric
by Denise K. Filios

Necessary Conjunctions: The Social Self in Medieval England
by David Gary Shaw

Visual Culture and the German Middle Ages
edited by Kathryn Starkey and Horst Wenzel

Medieval Paradigms: Essays in Honor of Jeremy duQuesnay Adams, Volumes 1 and 2
edited by Stephanie Hayes-Healy

False Fables and Exemplary Truth in Later Middle English Literature
by Elizabeth Allen

Ecstatic Transformation: On the Uses of Alterity in the Middle Ages
by Michael Uebel

Sacred and Secular in Medieval and Early Modern Cultures: New Essays
edited by Lawrence Besserman

Tolkien's Modern Middle Ages
edited by Jane Chance and Alfred K. Siewers

Representing Righteous Heathens in Late Medieval England
by Frank Grady

Byzantine Dress: Representations of Secular Dress in Eighth-to-Twelfth Century Painting
by Jennifer L. Ball

The Laborer's Two Bodies: Labor and the 'Work' of the Text in Medieval Britain, 1350–1500
by Kellie Robertson

The Dogaressa of Venice, 1250–1500: Wife and Icon
by Holly S. Hurlburt

Logic, Theology, and Poetry in Boethius, Abelard, and Alan of Lille: Words in the Absence of Things
by Eileen C. Sweeney

The Theology of Work: Peter Damian and the Medieval Religious Renewal Movement
by Patricia Ranft

On the Purification of Women: Churching in Northern France, 1100–1500
by Paula M. Rieder

Writers of the Reign of Henry II: Twelve Essays
edited by Ruth Kennedy and Simon Meecham-Jones

Lonesome Words: The Vocal Poetics of the Old English Lament and the African-American Blues Song
by M.G. McGeachy

Performing Piety: Musical Culture in Medieval English Nunneries
by Anne Bagnell Yardley

The Flight from Desire: Augustine and Ovid to Chaucer
by Robert R. Edwards

Mindful Spirit in Late Medieval Literature: Essays in Honor of Elizabeth D. Kirk
edited by Bonnie Wheeler

Medieval Fabrications: Dress, Textiles, Clothwork, and Other Cultural Imaginings
edited by E. Jane Burns

Was the Bayeux Tapestry Made in France?: The Case for St. Florent of Saumur
by George Beech

Women, Power, and Religious Patronage in the Middle Ages
by Erin L. Jordan

Hybridity, Identity, and Monstrosity, in Medieval Britain: On Difficult Middles
by Jeffrey Jerome Cohen

Medieval Go-betweens and Chaucer's Pandarus Choreographing Lust and Love
by Gretchen Mieszkowski

The Surgeon in Medieval English Literature
by Jeremy J. Citrome

Temporal Circumstances: Form and History in the Canterbury Tales
by Lee Patterson

Erotic Discourse and Early English Religious Writing
by Lara Farina

Odd Bodies and Visible Ends in Medieval Literature
by Sachi Shimomura

On Farting: Language and Laughter in the Middle Ages
by Valerie Allen

Women and Medieval Epic: Gender, Genre, and the Limits of Epic Masculinity
edited by Sara S. Poor and Jana K. Schulman

Race, Class, and Gender in "Medieval" Cinema
  edited by Lynn T. Ramey and Tison Pugh

Allegory and Sexual Ethics in the High Middle Ages
  by Noah D. Guynn

England and Iberia in the Middle Ages, 12th–15th Century: Cultural, Literary, and Political Exchanges
  edited by María Bullón-Fernández

The Medieval Chastity Belt: A Myth-Making Process
  by Albrecht Classen

Claustrophilia: The Erotics of Enclosure in Medieval Literature
  by Cary Howie

Cannibalism in High Medieval English Literature
  by Heather Blurton

The Drama of Masculinity and Medieval English Guild Culture
  by Christina M. Fitzgerald

Chaucer's Visions of Manhood
  by Holly A. Crocker

The Literary Subversions of Medieval Women
  by Jane Chance

Manmade Marvels in Medieval Culture and Literature
  by Scott Lightsey

American Chaucers
  by Candace Barrington

Representing Others in Medieval Iberian Literature
  by Michelle M. Hamilton

Paradigms and Methods in Early Medieval Studies
  edited by Celia Chazelle and Felice Lifshitz

The King and the Whore: King Roderick and La Cava
  by Elizabeth Drayson

Langland's Early Modern Identities
  by Sarah A. Kelen

Cultural Studies of the Modern Middle Ages
  edited by Eileen A. Joy, Myra J. Seaman, Kimberly K. Bell, and Mary K. Ramsey

Hildegard of Bingen's Unknown Language: An Edition, Translation, and Discussion
  by Sarah L. Higley

Medieval Romance and the Construction of Heterosexuality
  by Louise M. Sylvester

Communal Discord, Child Abduction, and Rape in the Later Middle Ages
  by Jeremy Goldberg

Lydgate Matters: Poetry and Material Culture in the Fifteenth Century
  edited by Lisa H. Cooper and Andrea Denny-Brown

Sexuality and Its Queer Discontents in Middle English Literature
  by Tison Pugh

Sex, Scandal, and Sermon in Fourteenth-Century Spain: Juan Ruiz's Libro de Buen Amor
  by Louise M. Haywood

The Erotics of Consolation: Desire and Distance in the Late Middle Ages
  edited by Catherine E. Léglu and Stephen J. Milner

Battlefronts Real and Imagined: War, Border, and Identity in the Chinese Middle Period
  edited by Don J. Wyatt

Wisdom and Her Lovers in Medieval and Early Modern Hispanic Literature
  by Emily C. Francomano

Power, Piety, and Patronage in Late Medieval Queenship: Maria de Luna
  by Nuria Silleras-Fernandez

In the Light of Medieval Spain: Islam, the West, and the Relevance of the Past
  edited by Simon R. Doubleday and David Coleman, foreword by Giles Tremlett

Chaucerian Aesthetics
  by Peggy A. Knapp

Memory, Images, and the English Corpus
Christi Drama
   by Theodore K. Lerud

Cultural Diversity in the British Middle Ages:
Archipelago, Island, England
   edited by Jeffrey Jerome Cohen

Excrement in the Late Middle Ages:
Sacred Filth and Chaucer's Fecopoetics
   by Susan Signe Morrison

Authority and Subjugation in Writing of
Medieval Wales
   edited by Ruth Kennedy and Simon
   Meecham-Jones

The Medieval Poetics of the Reliquary:
Enshrinement, Inscription, Performance
   by Seeta Chaganti

The Legend of Charlemagne in the Middle
Ages: Power, Faith, and Crusade
   edited by Matthew Gabriele and Jace
   Stuckey

The Poems of Oswald von Wolkenstein: An
English Translation of the Complete Works
(1376/77–1445)
   by Albrecht Classen

The Poems of Oswald von Wolkenstein: An
English Translation of the Complete Works
(1376/77–1445)
   by Albrecht Classen

Women and Experience in Later Medieval
Writing: Reading the Book of Life
   edited by Anneke B. Mulder-Bakker and
   Liz Herbert McAvoy

Ethics and Eventfulness in Middle English
Literature: Singular Fortunes
   by J. Allan Mitchell

Maintenance, Meed, and Marriage in Medieval
English Literature
   by Kathleen E. Kennedy

The Post-Historical Middle Ages
   edited by Elizabeth Scala and Sylvia
   Federico

Constructing Chaucer: Author and Autofiction
in the Critical Tradition
   by Geoffrey W. Gust

Queens in Stone and Silver: The Creation of a
Visual Imagery of Queenship in Capetian
France
   by Kathleen Nolan

Finding Saint Francis in Literature and Art
   edited by Cynthia Ho, Beth A.
   Mulvaney, and John K. Downey

Strange Beauty: Ecocritical Approaches to Early
Medieval Landscape
   by Alfred K. Siewers

Berenguela of Castile (1180–1246) and
Political Women in the High Middle Ages
   by Miriam Shadis

Julian of Norwich's Legacy: Medieval Mysticism
and Post-Medieval Reception
   edited by Sarah Salih and Denise N.
   Baker

Medievalism, Multilingualism, and Chaucer
   by Mary Catherine Davidson

The Letters of Heloise and Abelard: A
Translation of Their Complete Correspondence
and Related Writings
   translated and edited by
   Mary Martin McLaughlin with
   Bonnie Wheeler

Women and Wealth in Late Medieval Europe
   edited by Theresa Earenfight

Visual Power and Fame in René d'Anjou,
Geoffrey Chaucer, and the Black Prince
   by SunHee Kim Gertz

Geoffrey Chaucer Hath a Blog: Medieval
Studies and New Media
   by Brantley L. Bryant

Margaret Paston's Piety
   by Joel T. Rosenthal

Heloise and the Paraclete: A Twelfth-Century
Quest (forthcoming)
   by Mary Martin McLaughlin

ON FARTING

LANGUAGE AND LAUGHTER IN THE MIDDLE AGES

Valerie Allen

palgrave
macmillan

ON FARTING

Copyright © Valerie Allen, 2007

All rights reserved.

First published in hardcover in 2007 by PALGRAVE MACMILLAN® in the United States – a division of St. Martin's Press LLC, 175 Fifth Avenue, New York, NY 10010.

Where this book is distributed in the UK, Europe and the rest of the world, this is by Palgrave Macmillan, a division of Macmillan Publishers Limited, registered in England, company number 785998, of Houndmills, Basingstoke, Hampshire RG21 6XS.

Palgrave Macmillan is the global academic imprint of the above companies and has companies and representatives throughout the world.

Palgrave® and Macmillan® are registered trademarks in the United States, the United Kingdom, Europe and other countries.

ISBN: 978–0–230–10039–8

Library of Congress Cataloging-in-Publication Data

Allen, Valerie
    On farting : language and laughter in the Middle Ages / Valerie Allen.
    p. cm. — (The new Middle Ages)
    Includes bibliographical references and index.
    ISBN 0–312–23493–7 (alk. paper)
    1. Flatulence—Social aspects. 2. Flatulence—History. 3. Flatulence in literature. I. Title. II. Series: New Middle Ages (Palgrave (Firm))
GT2840.A45 2007
306.4—dc22   2006046360

A catalogue record of the book is available from the British Library.

Design by Newgen Imaging Systems (P) Ltd., Chennai, India.

First PALGRAVE MACMILLAN paperback edition: May 2010

10 9 8 7 6 5 4 3 2 1

Printed in the United States of America.

Transferred to Digital Printing 2010

CONTENTS

List of Plates and Figure	xi
Acknowledgments	xiii
List of Abbreviations	xv
Introduction: The Midden Age	1
THE BEGINNING	9
Old Farts	9
For the Edification of Copious Shitters and Costive Maidens Whose Hours at Siege Should Be Profitably Employed	15
"Sometimes I Sits and Thinks, Sometimes I Just Sits"	20
Hard Lessons	22
Logic 101	25
The ~~Music Album~~ Musical Bum	27
Butts and Instruments: Nature versus Art	30
The Musical Universe	33
Canticus Canticorum [Song of Songs]	35
Broken Air	38
The Nose Knows	42
I / Thou	45
One Flesh	53
Pneuma	62
A Short Excursus on Wind	66
Till Death Us Do Part	68
Inspiration	76
Stuck in the Lavatory	80
"There was an old lady who swallowed a fly. . ."	87
Farting at the Devil	90
Filthy Lucre	94
Shitting Ducats	97
Duck-Rabbit, Face-Bottom	106

IN BETWEEN	115
In the Beginning was the Word	115
The Silver-Tongued Butt	116
The Grammar of Farts	118
Potent Words	123
Legitimate Etymology	127
Rebuilding Babel	131
Bastard Laughter	146
Better Out Than In	153
Spend A Penny, Save a Penny	155
Flatus of the Voice	159
DIE AFTERWISSENSCHAFT [END-KNOWLEDGE, PSEUDO-SCIENCE, BUTTHOLE-SCHOLARSHIP]	163
The Mystery of Roland	163
Fartprints of Roland	170
M. Roland le Pettour	
Hemingstone	
Suffolk	174
The Color of the Balloon	179
Notes	183
Bibliography	219
Index	237

LIST OF PLATES AND FIGURE

Plates

1	Luttrell Psalter, f. 185b, first half, Fourteenth Century English	109
2	Beinecke MS 229, f. 147r. Old French Prose Lancelot, Thirteenth Century	110
3	Romance of Alexander, MS. Bodley 264, f. 90v. French and English, Fourteenth–Fifteenth Centuries	111
4	St. Helen's Church, Brant Broughton, Lincolnshire Thirteenth–Fourteenth Centuries	112
5	Gargoyle (from front), Angel and Royal Hotel, Grantham, England, Fourteenth Century possibly Fifteenth Century	113
6	Gargoyle (from beneath), Angel and Royal Hotel, Grantham, England, Fourteenth Century possibly Fifteenth Century	114

Figure

1	The division of music according to *Summa musice*	31

ACKNOWLEDGMENTS

All translations of Latin, Middle English, and French are either mine or lightly edited ones from published translations. To my colleagues at John Jay College of Criminal Justice: thank you for tolerating my researches with humor and help. Special thanks to: Bill Coleman, Kirk Dombrowski, Carol Groneman, Jacob Marini, Larry Sullivan, Marny Tabb, Richard Zeikowitz, and Gary Zaragovitch, my most generous reader, unstintingly helpful. To medievalists who kindly shared their learning: Alison Beringer, Elaine C. Block, Joyce Coleman, Jeffrey Cohen, Mark Cruse, Morgan Davies, Nat Dubin, Jody Enders, Carol Everest, Martin Foys, Bruce Holsinger, Simon Horobin, David Porter, Nancy Regalado, John Scattergood, Michael Sargent, Al and Judy Shoaf, Jeremy Smith, Ilicia Sprey, Jocelyn Wogan-Browne; most particularly, Ruth Evans (thanks Ruth for reading the manuscript), Alan Fletcher, John Thompson, and Michael Uebel. To Anthony Axiotis, Charles Fantazzi, Malcolm Knapp, Eric Rabkin, Jonathan Sawday, Samantha Schad of the OED, Rupert Willoughby, and the editorial staff of Palgrave, whose patience surpassed Job's. And to Gary Zaragovitch once again for his pen-drawings. Mistakes, alas, are mine. This work was supported in part by a grant from the City University of New York PSC-CUNY Research Award Program.

Work from various sections of this book previously appeared in "Broken Air," *Exemplaria* 16 (2004): 305–22. For helpful reviews, acknowledgments to Jeff Persels, Russell Ganim, Danuta Shanzer, and C.W Woolgar. Some of the material in the expanded introduction was originally published as part of a response to a review of this book, appearing in the Institute of Historical Research's *Reviews in History* online journal, <http://www.history.ac.uk/reviews/paper/shanzerdresp.html >.

Finally, this book is dedicated to two people: Arthur the Mathematician, who will spot at once that Molloy cannot divide his farts correctly.

> I can't help it, gas escapes from my fundament on the least pretext, it's hard not to mention it now and then, however great my distaste. One day I

counted them. Three hundred and fifteen farts in nineteen hours, or an average of over sixteen farts an hour. After all it's not excessive. Four farts every fifteen minutes. It's nothing. Not even one fart every four minutes. It's unbelievable. Damn it, I hardly fart at all, I should never have mentioned it. Extraordinary how mathematics help [sic] you to know yourself.

(Beckett, *Molloy*, 39)

—and to Ares, named after the god of war, but in my pantheon, your gifts have always been invention and laughter.

LIST OF ABBREVIATIONS

CT	*Canterbury Tales*, in Chaucer, *Riverside Chaucer*
EETS E.S.	Early English Text Society, extra series
EETS O.S.	Early English Text Society, original series
EETS S.S.	Early English Text Society, supplemental series
Etym.	Isidore of Seville, *Etymologiarum libri xx*
Fr.	French
Gr.	Greek
Inf.	*Inferno*
Inst.	Priscian, *Institutiones grammaticae*
L.	Latin
ME	Middle English
MED	*Middle English Dictionary*
NRCF	*Nouveau Recueil Complet des Fabliaux*
OE	Old English
OF	Old French
OED	*Oxford English Dictionary*
OLD	*Oxford Latin Dictionary*
PF	*Parliament of Fowls*, in Chaucer, *Riverside Chaucer*
PFA	*Proverbes Français Antérieurs au XVe siècle*
PL	*Patrologiae Latinae*
PRO	The National Archives: Public Record Office, Kew, London
SE	Sigmund Freud, *Standard Edition*
ST	St. Thomas Aquinas, *Summa Theologiae*

INTRODUCTION
The Midden Age

Here is a book about the body's detritus, the wind, water, and solids that our intestines throw out daily. Beyond farts, its general preoccupation is with what people throw out. Worthlessness sustains the project throughout. Most irresistible of all garbage is scientifically obsolete bodies of knowledge: a geocentric universe, four humors, the doctrine of sympathies, alchemy, astrology; and what better repository for such rubbish than the Middle Ages? Itself the waste lot of redundant knowledge and "false" etymologies, the Middle Ages provides a vantage point from which to rethink modernity's preoccupation with accumulation. Waste reveals more about those who threw it out in the first place than about the nature of the revolting. In dirt, observes one anthropologist, there is system.[1]

We might think of this book as "drutling," a term that, according to John Jamieson's *Etymological Dictionary of the Scottish Language*, applies to a "dog or horse that frequently stops in its way, and ejects a small quantity of dung at intervals." It farts around, its progress nonteleological, visiting topics as the wind blows, spending too long on some ideas, returning to spend even longer on them, allowing disparate texts to rub alongside each other without respect for historical system, and undoubtedly omitting more than it digresses upon. This book is a bum, a word that means "buttocks" in Modern and "anus" in Middle English[2]; its "introduction" offers no reduction of thought and only lengthens the task of reading. The fart, which disposes of the body's waste gases, is the sign par excellence of the futile endeavor: we fart around when we do nothing useful.

Drutling or bumming around refines the idea of *flânerie*, that fashionable loafing of nineteenth-century Parisians, who, around 1840, apparently took to taking turtles for a walk and letting the turtles set the pace.[3] It was a momentary, if unsuccessful, protest against the speed of urban progress, for "down with dawdling" won the day and the turtles became soup. The bum, however, is no Baudelairean aesthete, no Monet who circles around the cathedral to paint it in differing lights, no gentleman of independent means with leisure to take life slowly. Unemployed, the vagrant has nothing to do and thus everything; homeless, nowhere to go and thus everywhere. Where the *flâneur* is inevitably a man, enjoying the civic and locomotive freedoms of maledom, this bum eludes conventional topographies of gender and desire, the "he" an accident of grammar. Now he stops to meditate on the fresh dog-doo on the pavement in front of Notre Dame, walks around the cathedral, stops to rummage in a trash can, but no cigarette, so he circles back to find the dog-doo disintegrating in the rain, while the medieval gargoyles perched above, keeping vigil on the present, dump their gutter-waste onto his bare head. Had he been standing beneath Saint-Lazare cathedral in Autun, France, or the front of the late medieval Angel and Royal Hotel in Grantham, Lincolnshire, it would not have been a mouth emptying down on him, but a bottom.[4]

Everyone else in the crowd has an appointment to make except the bum, for whom anything might happen because nothing is planned. The signposts by which one orders a day or a book become redundant if there is little progressive sequence to connect the parts, which—whether ideas or events—juxtapose randomly as merely contiguous. Synchronous with the present yet not, the vagrant moves between past, present, and future, never quite belonging to any. It is the way we might speak of the Middle Ages, the age median between classicism and renaissance, different from modernity and yet its origin.[5] This is how we also speak of a fart, which does not exist qua fart until it passes the anal threshold. A fart *in futuro* is just trapped wind. A fart long past no longer exists. A fart comes into being in the moment of transition, in between inside and outside, in between cheeks.

In between people, the bum drutles alone. His is the special kind of loneliness experienced in a crowd, the solitude of the outcast. Engels repudiated the alienated condition of the modern urban crowd, its intimacy without community, where bodies of strangers press together. The bum, haloed by smell, sits alone on the park bench, strangered twice over, unable to share even mutual alienation with another. We identify alienation as the special condition of modernity, yet the archetypal image of Christian medieval selfhood is the pilgrim, the peregrine, the *homo viator* [traveling man], as Aquinas calls him (*ST*, 3a 86.1 corp). The medieval pilgrim may think he knows where he is going, just as Beckett's tramps were sure they were waiting for Godot, but his final, anagogic destination is always on the far side of attainment, and his certainty as fragile as the epistemological contingency that modernity claims as signature. Need we point out that the fart is, by definition, an outcast? Passing gas or solid matter is a personal act of ostracism, where the body discards through the backdoor what Galen calls its "alien load" [*achthos allotrion*].[6] Long before it offends another, a fart has become unwanted within the body of its owner, and been banished from the presence of the innards. As sixteenth-century Laurent Joubert describes it, the anal sphincter muscles discharge their superfluities when "they become disgusted with them" [*se facher*].[7] Partaking in the general nature of filth, the loathsomeness of a fart "is not a quality in itself but it applies only to what relates to a *boundary*, and, more particularly, represents the object jettisoned at that boundary, its other side, a margin."[8]

A fart is something one may hear, smell, feel, or, God forbid, taste, but it is never visible (lit farts notwithstanding). Refusing the shapes and colors with which we cut letters, the fart is unclaimable for the empire of the eye, which has dominated Western epistemology since Plato. The eye allows us to theorize (Gr. *theōreō*, "I look at"), to be voyeurs at a safe distance, to read dead words, and snoop uninvited; but the nose requires immediate participation and proximity, and the transient fart can only be performed, never archived. Invisible but audible and smellable, the fart draws us away from the economy of the eye to explore knowledge that one cannot apprehend at a safe distance. Where the eye theorizes, and by claim to objectivity styles its knowledge as critique, sound and smell require closer involvement. Hearing, it is true, occurs also at a distance, yet the noise of a fart violates the distance between subject and object. Medieval sound is an ethical mode, a principle of internal balance and being.[9] Even more so does smell involve intimacy for it alone among the five senses requires both distance and direct contact with its object. Smell makes an impossibility of the punctual subject, for it breaches that critical space between subject and object upon which subjectivity depends; in doing so, it calls into question the very grounds of medieval selfhood.

Farts supplement shit as does living speech to the archive of writing. Medieval illuminators understood the pictorial elusiveness of the fart and devised ingenious ways to suggest its presence: bellows and wind instruments are regular devices, and turds provide an ideal synecdoche for wind. With finger for pen, shit for ink, and farts for speech, the unscriptured bum daubs his stories, which, resistant to all précis and chapter division, can only be endured until he stops. For the artist Philip Guston, paint, the medium of expression, is "only colored dirt."[10] The filled diaper is the first picture we make. Homer, it is said, was blind, and so instead of fighting, he did his bit by singing. Tiresias, also blind, had the gift of foresight. His debility becomes a *felix culpa*, a happy fault that brings more good in its wake than the loss it originally represented. This is the lesson of human waste. Though excrement be the mark of incontinence, weakness, shame, decay, and death, and marks our finitude, in it lies wisdom. It is an ancient truth that wisdom should lie within what is rejected, yet also a deeply modern aesthetic that art originates in rubbish. "The only objects that interest me are the worthless ones, the scrap," said Picasso,[11] *flâneur* of dumpsites, who saw the potential in something so intrinsically free of design or purpose. The aesthetic of waste introduces us into an arsy-versy, nonteleological world in which detritus is precious, the fart, sign par excellence of nothing, assumes the deep meaning of speech, and laughter becomes the proper *responsio* of reason.

The great thing about garbage is that you never know what is coming next. Its promise is a surprise, sometimes of gold, sometimes of much worse. One can only be sure that the desirable will be mixed up with the repulsive, for this is the character of the midden. *Disjecta membra*, loose parts, nestle alongside each other, discontinuous but juxtaposed. What gets placed on the garbage heap? Whatever is unwanted, unusable, and broken. Brokenness is a recurring idea throughout this book. We encounter it in the division of the fart (especially with reference to Chaucer's *Summoner's Tale*); in the theory of sound as air broken forcibly by farts, speech, laughter, and all sound; in the theory of smell as the breaking open of a body; in alchemical degradation of matter prior to transmutation to something nobler; in the digestive process; and in humor as iconoclasm or desecration. While violence is involved literally in iconoclasm, it conceptually inflects any kind of making unholy, which is what desecration means. As we see from the Old English, what is holy (*hāliʒ*) is whole (*hāl*). What desecrates, therefore, fragments. Paradoxically enough, sacrifice, which requires wholeness in its victim, breaks open the body. Desecration lies very close to holiness, especially when it occurs in the sacrificial breaking of Christ's body. In the division of a body—as in the breaking of the deer after a hunt—the goodness within is released. Thought theologically, breaking makes transcendence immanent, for when the sacred is violently broken open it becomes real.

The sacred and the profane relate to each other less as juxtaposed contraries than as domains that reflect each other antisymmetrically. It follows then that in medieval dirt should lie purity, or pace Mary Douglas, that purity is dirty matter in its place. Innocent III's heightened rhetoric of purulence illustrates just how fascinating the repulsive could be, how it could occasion edification, how much at home excrement and farts are in the medieval symbolic order. Poking through a midden and etymologizing—one of this book's maggots—are both acts of archeological excavation. In the midden, one finds the most unlikely bedfellows and is constantly surprised by the connections between different things, finding analogies that freewheel between objects rather than any coherent whole that depends on an internal connection of deductive reasoning. In the etymological midden explored in the book's middle part, we investigate the backside of the family tree of meanings, unearthing connections between words revealed in puns, word play, the word-origins of medieval etymologists, and other such verbal dross thrown out, perhaps understandably, by modern linguistics, which, in occasionally being parodied here, is parodied with affection, and with a view to thinking more deeply about its guiding assumptions. By unraveling the lines of demarcation between legitimate meanings and those born out of wedlock (some possible, some unlikely, all for play), we ponder the meaningfulness of the ludic. Words are broken apart to release their inner truth. It has long been known that medieval etymologies are, by modern philological standards, wrong, and by consequence are not often taken seriously as a discursive practice. In an effort to take them seriously, we temporarily suspend the truth-value of the derivations and ask what word-genealogies look like to medieval etymologists. Upon examination, they look increasingly like rhetorical device and grammatical division, exegesis, word play—like puns both serious and playful, in which the universe of language is tied down to one word, puns momentarily making visible the ligatures and disfigured kinships. They are happy faults, rich examples of analogical thinking that posit correspondences between dissimilars without recourse to chronology or historical method.

All acts of breaking presuppose a body to be broken. To that extent breakability and materiality are co-terminous. Farts, speech, and laughter break open bodies, and acts of the mind such as *anagnoresis* can themselves be 'broken' down into bodily acts: intention to stretching, inspiration to breathing in, ideation to seeing. Medieval writers on grammar, logic, rhetoric and word derivations—a motley list that includes Dante, John of Salisbury, Isidore, and Priscian—give words bodies and break them apart in a variety of ways. All believe in the human being as a grammatical animal, in the material presence of words, and in the ethical obligation to use them rightly. We generally assume that medieval philosophy of language represents words as labels stuck after the fact onto prior *realia*. The 'linguistic turn' articulated in poststructuralist thought, where we speak of language as actively constitutive of reality rather than passively reflective of it, is not ordinarily considered a medieval phenomenon, yet in the discredited viewpoint of Roscelin's extreme nominalism, we see the possibility of a kind of medieval linguistic turn that posits concepts as inextricable from the bubbles of air in which they arrive, of content that has no being independent of its form. If ideas cannot be completely separated from the words in which they are expressed, if combinations of words really do matter, if even a dactyl is ethical, and if apprehensions—particularly the ones that make us crack up laughing—are truly embodied, then deep thinking ought to make us sit up a little straighter and put our words more carefully in their place. The examined life requires alignment of spine as well as of thoughts.

Sorted garbage—the kind you can inspect and select at a safe distance—does not count as proper garbage. Processing body waste into chapters is a waste of time; much better to inventory the crotties as an index, if one insists on organizing them. Chapters carve the whole into reasonable joints, collating coherent parts with their like. This book has no formal chapters, not because it is some mystical whole irreducible to the sum of its parts, but because there is no initial totality to subdivide. Most particularly in "The Beginning," it boasts only crotties of thought, scatological episodes in medieval life: proverbs, education, riddles, marriage, death, privies, baptism, the devil, hell, exorcism, medicine, pneuma, air, wind, prayer, procreation, and alchemy and perfumery, which transform base substances into something precious, realizing the inner potential being of waste as an ontological and ethical mode rather than expendable product as such. This "introduction," itself just another crotty, fails miserably in the function of an introduction to "unite the fragments into something larger."[12]

Taking seriously the idea that the formless fart mirrors itself in a formless book requires that we bring content into a more meaningful connection with form. Both as writers and readers, we assume a book to be a whole, with its parts neatly interlocking; we label arguments (his, hers, mine), and place similarly colored ideas in the same drawer. But what happens when you take a scholarly argument and break it apart, scattering it across a book? What happens when, as with proverbs, the ideas are irremissibly embodied in the verbal bubbles in which they arrived? By breaking the argument thus into pieces, scattered as it were on the waste heap, readers are left to fish out what they want to claim in salvage as their own. What is on the waste heap is there for the taking. Breaking up the argument thus means stepping away from the strictly critical mode, in the direction of the creative, and no doubt falling between the two stools. Yet in the falling, we think more deeply about the rigorous distinction in scholarly writing—indeed in the history of Western thought—between argument and style, about the diminishment of the latter to a desirable but not required supplement, and about the professionalization of the former to a specialty. Moving away from the critical—and thus from the much specialized method of historical contextualization and close reading—implies moving toward the non-specialist reader, hence the translations and set pieces, as no prior knowledge of medieval thought is assumed. For the presentist reader, the medieval flatulent past may be less interesting for being medieval as it may be for simply being something other than the present. For this reason, the stretch of the medieval in this book expands and contracts across time, the period sometimes residing where it normally does (after the fall of the Roman empire and before the Renaissance) and sometimes as a moment of difference within the present. The medieval intervenes in the present as the occasion for defamiliarization. In the final section, the case study of Roland the Farter aims to give some historical balance, although it no more than sticks a toe into the water as far as inquiring into his significance for a history of court entertainment and feudal service. The general purpose is to pose questions about the medieval past in this curious respect of feudal farting. It would take a specialist historian to answer them. The hope is that a non-specialist would read the book and be delighted with the Middle Ages; that academics would think harder about how and for whom they write they way they do; that medievalists would do the same.

Nasty and brutish, rubbish has no predetermined shape, form, or definition; it is potentially endless, simply filling whatever space it is allowed. It enjoys no aesthetic unity. In mereological terms, rubbish is nothing but *disjecta membra*, pile up as much of it as you fancy, but it never adds up to a whole. So it is that this "drutle" lacks the causal sequence required of an Aristotelian beginning, middle, and end; it is both unfinished and endless; we never get past its beginning; it starts, and continues to start until it eventually stops starting. Logical arguments generally assume a characteristic pattern of beginning, middle, and end—a kind of ideal Aristotelian tragedy—but here the line of progress is bent back recursively upon itself in a ring, each of the three parts standing on its own but presupposing the others. One could feasibly start and end anywhere. A fart is a dismembered and disowned part, a wretched thing, a bum. Having no natural place in the cosmos, rubbish is found whereever it can go. Like Dante's neutrals and the peasants of Rutebeuf's *Le Pet au Vilain* [The Churl's Fart], whom hell as well as heaven rejects, waste is always unwanted.

The unwanted often end up in the academy. Roger Ascham remarks that, having spent "the most parte of my life in the Vniuersitie," he has long noted how the sons dispatched for schooling are "wretched, lame, and deformed."[13] In his ugliness, the scholar turns to books to sublimate desires unfulfilled by more immediate means; yet the unlovely bum owns no books. With no text to expound, no thesis to advance, and no one to listen, critique—the scholar's lingua franca of objective reason—degenerates into bomination. Ancient treatises on learned topics are characteristically in the ablative case, thereby indicating that they offer a commentary "upon" a topic worthy of comment, for example, Augustine's *De Doctrina Christiana* [On Christian Doctrine], or Aristotle's *De Partibus animalium* [On the Parts of Animals]; but *De Fartibus* [On Farting] denotes no actual text, extant or lost; and it is not a real Latin word anyway. Jacob Grimm, teller of children's stories, is better known among linguists for his philological research, in particular, for his observation that certain consonantal sounds in the original Indo-European, retained in Greek and Latin, transpose systematically into different sounds in the Germanic languages: German *der Fisch* [*fish*] is *piscis* in Latin; German *der Fuß* [*foot*] is *pes* in Latin and *pous* in Greek. From such systematic deviations, Grimm fashioned a law that maintained, among other things, that /p/ in Greek and Latin transposes into /f/ in the Germanic languages, which includes English. If so, then "*fart*" really is "*part*" [L. *pars*], and I could have stuck with *De Fartibus animalium* in the first place. With waste as the book's theme and sentence, its business is to ponder the resistance of the untidy past to the clean sweep of rationalized historical analysis. Even the scholarly research decomposed into rummaging, into snapping up unwanted trifles that fell out of books published years ago, like a bum that shakes a discarded packet for one remaining smoke. Rummaging for dross, as a logical method, is akin to the "full greyt dowtfull" question posed by the writer of the late-fifteenth-century parodic sermon, in which St. Peter asks Adam why he ate the apple unpeeled.[14] Adam's answer, that he did not have any fried pears, matches pointlessness with pointlessness. The business of butthole-scholarship, the "part" that finally stops this book, is to consider the historical case of Roland the Farter, and in doing so to pose the arsy-versy questions that deflate our pretended ability to become one flesh with the past, and to reinscribe laughter at the center of an epistemological relationship with the world that allows neither any safe distance between subject and object nor the collapse of difference between them. Only laughter, it would seem, "embraces the partial as partial."[15]

THE BEGINNING

Old Farts

My niece, Ruth, was once breakfasting on a balloon, and in order to stop her, her mother related a cautionary tale about another little girl on the news who had recently done the same thing and choked to death. Ruth listened closely, and then inquired after the color of the balloon. The ability to miss the point with such accuracy is a rare gift, arguably the object of historical inquiry.

> And in this yere, that is to seye the yere of our lord a mcclviij, there fel a Jewe into a pryve at Teukesbury upon a Satirday, the whiche wolde nought suffre hym selfe to be drawe out of the preve that day for reverence of his Sabot day: and Sr. Richard of Clare, thanne erle of Gloucestre, herynge therof, wolde nought suffre hym to be drawe out on the morwe after, that is to say the Soneday, for reverence of his holy day; and so the Jewe deyde in the preve.[1]
>
> [And in this year, that is to say the year of our Lord 1258, a certain Jew fell into a privy in Tewkesbury one Saturday, but he refused to be helped out in deference to his Sabbath. Hearing of this, Sir Richard of Clare, then Earl of Gloucester, refused to help him out the next day, Sunday, in deference to *his* Sabbath. And so the Jew died in the privy.]

Given that the Jews, their purses picked clean, were evicted from England not forty years later, this spiteful little story intimates why. "Well, isn't it obvious?" a Christian might say: "aren't Jews dogmatic literalists,[2] unable to recognize when the letter of the law should be waived in the interest of a greater good, such as the preservation of life? Aren't they a stiff-necked people,[3] clannish and stand-offish, spurning offers of help from honest Christian neighbors? And aren't they always sniffing around shit[4]—what was he doing anyway, that he toppled in?" There are other questions to ask, such as, "Is the story true?" Unlikely. The manuscripts of the *Chronicle of London* were compiled two centuries after the events described; the story is also a favorite urban legend appearing in appearing in many contexts from all over medieval Europe[5]; presumably, our chronicler found the story too tempting not to introduce into his humdrum entries about baronial skirmishes and the annual corn yield. And in a fifteenth-century sermon, the Jew symbolizes the man who would rather wallow in the "foule stynkynge pitte" of sin than repent.[6] The Jew's misfortune also comes suspiciously soon after the notorious case of Little St. Hugh of Lincoln, who died in 1255 after falling into a Jewish cesspit, creating accusations of Jewish ritual murder. If perchance the story were true, it is more likely that the privy was in disrepair and collapsed while the Jew was perched on his *siege perilous* than that he was peering in to see what he had done. In London alone, memoranda of damaged and dangerous common privies were a regular occurrence. In February 1377, the inhabitants living around London Bridge complained of the disrepair of the "necessary houses or wardrobes" annexed to the Bridge[7]; in the 1420s, the common privy at Ludgate was deemed "defective and perilous," and the "ordure rots the stone walls"[8]; and in the same decade—dangerous years for doing a pooh in London—a common privy by the churchyard in Fanchirche was left "broken and open, to the great danger of people and children at night."[9] At a time when testators regularly bequeathed money in their wills to the upkeep of public highways and bridges, charity appeared not to extend to the needs of the bottom, and the privies were allowed to go to pot.

Then there is the color of the balloon. Were privies common to men and women? Who used them—only the indigent or even a nobleman taken short? Did some wince with embarrassment at every explosion while others let rip with gusto?[10] Ælfric is known to have complained about women disgracing themselves at beer parties by eating and drinking together while sitting on the privy.[11] Were *arswyspes*[12] [arsewisps, asswipes] provided at the privy, or did one bring one's own supply, or just do without? Was a stick with a wet sponge provided there as in ancient Rome?[13] It was a critical enough issue, judging by contemporary jokes about wiping your ass with gorse or holly leaves.

> *Demaunde:* Which is the moost cleynlyest lefe amonge all other leues?
> It is holly leues / for noo body wyll not wype his arse with them.[14]
>
> [*Question:* Which is the cleanest leaf of all?
> The holly leaf, for no one is willing to wipe his butt with it.]

Everyone knows the importance of the material circumstances in which the act of nature occurs. The business of recent historicist inquiry has been to write "a history of silences"[15] surrounding the hodiernal trivia rarely thought worthy of the name of research (taking flatulence as cultural silence here, whatever the decibel count). One instance, admittedly well out of our period, illustrates how a fart can determine life choices in unexpected ways. In the late nineteenth century, a cad called Harshfield recounted at a gentlemen's dinner party in Bullitt County, Kentucky, that

> Cordie Hardin went to the store of Chris. Pauley's to buy some groceries, and while Chris. Pauley was waiting on her, she let a big fart that was heard all over the house; two or three young men being present, Chris. Pauley looked at them and laughed, and they walked out of doors. Chris. Pauley having fixed up the groceries, she took them, left the store and got on her horse, and forgot her glove. She got down and came back in to the store. He supposed she was demoralized by what she had done, the fart being impressed upon her mind so strongly she said, when she came back in to the store, "Mr. Pauley, did you see anything of that fart I let in here a while ago?" His reply was: "No; but I smelt it damned strong." Boys, ain't that a damned hard one on her?[16]

Cordie's fiancé got wind of the story and broke off the engagement, whereupon she filed suit for slander against Harshfield (January 23, 1890), claiming that the charge of the fart was false and slanderous. She lost; she appealed. Justice Bennett decided in her favor, entering his decision on March 1 of the same year. Justice Bennett's reasoning was that Harshfield's story, although not slanderous in itself, was capable of conveying the impression that Miss Hardin was an "immodest, indiscreet, coarse, vulgar young woman," and inasmuch as her engagement was procured in part on the basis of her reputation as a lady of impeccable breeding, Harshfield's story led to direct and material damage in the form of a broken engagement and loss of social regard. Justice Bennett's decision was printed privately as a publication entitled *Thundergust*. The ex-fiancé's name, by the way, was Charlie Bean.

Earlier instances of misplaced farts suggest the cultural constancy of its shame value. Edward de Vere, seventeenth Earl of Oxford (1550–1604), accidentally broke wind as he was bowing to Elizabeth I, the shame of which sent him abroad for seven years. On his return, the queen warmly greeted him with, "My lord, I had forgot the Fart."[17] Carsten Niebuhr, visiting Arabia in the eighteenth century, notes that a member of the Balúchís on the border of Persia had to leave his tribe for the shame of having farted; and in some tribes between Basra and Aleppo anyone who farts even once becomes a perpetual laughing-stock in the eyes of all.[18] The shame of the public fart is memorialized also in the sorry tale of "How Abu Hasan Brake Wind," told by Scheherazade on the four-hundred-and-tenth night. In this tale, Abu cuts such a "great and terrible" fart at his wedding banquet that—consummation now out of the question—he flees to India for ten years. Eventually returning in disguise, he overhears a young girl asking her mother when she, the daughter, was born, to which the mother replies: "Thou was born, oh my daughter, on the very night when Abu Hasan farted." Realizing that his fart had now entered the calendar, Abu Hasan returns to India and is never heard of again.[19] Editor Richard Burton finds the story fascinating in its taboos: "The Badawi who eructates as a civility has a mortal hatred to a *crepitus ventris*; and were a by-stander to laugh at its accidental occurrence, he would be cut down as a 'pundonor.' "[20]

There is evidence aplenty that one could be just as "squeamish of farting" in the Middle Ages as today (*CT*, 1.3337–8). It was a hygiene-conscious age when fines were regularly exacted for dumping dung in public streets,[21] although there is no dispute about the lower standards of sanitation. Yet consider also how the fart inhabits medieval culture publicly. "Fart" seems to have fairly common currency in the late Middle Ages, and not simply as a rude word. In 1477–1478, John Fenkill, a London draper, sued the mayor and sheriffs of London to recover "a cofyn fillid with fartes of Portyngale" and a barrel of marmalade, seized on Tower Wharf as uncustomed goods.[22] A basket of Portugese farts? A Portugese fart was a kind of pastry puff (*OED*, s.v. *fart*, n²); compare French *pets-de-nonnes* [nuns' farts], which refer to fritters made of choux pastry of a delicate lightness. Turning to local flora, try to avoid stepping on *une vesse de loup* [wolf-fart], which is a kind of puffball that farts as it explodes when stepped on ["elle pete en se crevant"], dispersing into a fine, dry, very smelly dust ["poussiere...d'une odeur fort puante"].[23] Late Middle English shares the terminology, recommending *wolues festes* for use on wounds (*MED*, s.v. *fist*, n²ᵇ).

Local geography also drew its inspiration from bodily wind. In Paris, 1451–1452, a large stone, probably a boundary marker, popularly known as "Le Pet-au-Deable" [The Devil's Fart], stood in front of the house of the virtuous Mademoiselle de Bruyère. The university students, notorious for mischief-making, stole it. It was retrieved and stored for safekeeping in the Palais Royal, but the students stole it again, along with the replacement stone from Mademoiselle's house, which they dubbed "*La Vesse*" [The Silent Fart].[24] François Villon is thought to have been involved in the incident. Certainly he knew enough about it to have written *Le Rommant du Pet au Deable* [The Story of the Devil's Fart], since lost, which he bequeathed to his adoptive father, Guillaume de Villon:

Je luy donne ma librairie,
Et le Rommant du Pet au Deable,
Lequel maistre Guy Tabarie
Grossa, qui est homs veritable.
Par cayers est soubz une table;
Combien qu'il soit rudement fait,

La matiere est si tres notable
Qu'elle amende tout le mesfait.
  (*Testament*, ll. 857–64)

[I bequeath to him my library,
And the *Romance of the Devil's Fart*,
Which master Guy Tabary,
An honest man, copied:
It's in notebooks under a table,
And although it's roughly written,
The subject matter is of such note
That it makes up for all shortcomings.]

Can we then support the belief that the word for "fart" was used with what Rosemary Woolf calls "innocent seriousness"?[25] She thinks not, dismissing the idea as a modern "romantic fantasy" of unalienated medieval corporeality, and argues against the occurrence of the verbal form "ferteth" as early as the thirteenth century.[26] It is true that the majority of occurrences of Middle English *fert* are fourteenth-century or later, but there may be a number of reasons for this: etiquette may have relaxed as scribal activity boomed and became secularized; and writing in the English vernacular was at its most restricted in the twelfth and early thirteenth centuries because of Norman supremacy. If *feorting* can exist as an Anglo-Saxon word in the eleventh century,[27] to reappear in the thirteenth, to flourish in the fourteenth and fifteenth centuries, then it seems likely that it was with us all along. Moreover, the evidence of the *Owl and the Nightingale*, written as early as the late twelfth century, suggests a high comfort level in Middle English poetry with scatology. The most recent readings of line 115 in the poem take *viste* as voiced *fiste* [wet fart], which certainly accords with references throughout the poem to the privy [*rumhus*], the toilet seat [*setle*], the bottom [*bihinde*], and the turd [*tort*].[28] The assumption that English bawdy verse was present but just not fairly represented in writing (whether by dint of clerical repression or the privilege of French) is no doubt right, but one that only takes us so far, and should not blind us to historical, cultural, and social differences internal to the Middle Ages. A tendency of many scribes to balk at writing indelicacies in the vernacular does suggest the perception that Latin sanitizes terms (usually sexual rather than scatological) by "hiding" them in a learned language, while in the native tongue, their full crudity is evident to all.[29] How and why that excremental bawdy was used is the inquiry of this book.

Past attitudes toward flatulence seem at once unremarkable and strange. It seems a bit steep to lose one's life for laughing at a fart, and it is hard to imagine a legal furor over a nonexistent fart, although we perhaps have enough historical empathy to appreciate the indignation of Cordie, left without a Bean. It requires perhaps the most difficult *saltus* [leap] of the imagination to envisage the circumstances in which a vassal could be required to fart before a king:

> Seriantia que quondam fuit Rollandi le Pettour in Hemingeston in comitatu Suff', pro qua debuit facere die natali Domini singulis annis coram domino rege unum saltum et siffletum et unum bumbulum, que alienata fuit per particulas subscriptas.[30]
>
> [The serjeanty, which formerly was held by Roland the Farter in Hemingston in the county of Suffolk, for which he was obliged to perform every year on the birthday of our Lord before his master the king, one jump, and a whistle, and one fart, was alienated in accordance with these specific requirements.]

The *Liber feodorum* or *Book of Fees*, from which the entry comes, records tenurial obligations. Feudal payments came in all shapes and sizes, from military service to food to labor to knick-knacks to money; but what stable economy could require an annual rental of a fart, paid up in person to the king himself, no less? Roland was quite likely an entertainer, but this only raises more questions as to the nature of court revelry, the relationship between monarch and subject, and an economic system that would formalize such a transaction.

Writing about Roland's tenure, William Camden in the sixteenth century observes, "Such was the plaine and jolly mirth of those times."[31] If Camden, living in the sixteenth century, seems to us to come from another age, Roland seemed equally remote to Camden. The sixteenth century saw active attempts to repress such revelries. However unsuccessful the prohibition may have been, it was a clear sign of the times when an order of the Visitors of Edward VI in 1549 forbade the appointment of a *dominus ludorum* [lord of the games] in any college at Cambridge.[32] The emergent Protestant sensibility was reshaping the relationship between the people and authority, trading different kinds of freedom for different kinds of conformity.

How then does the humble fart illuminate identity and social relation? If Roland's caper seems only to vindicate the common myth that medievals farted without regulation, we should keep in mind that the singularity of his tenure attests to an awareness of the unseemliness of farting in public, not to mention in front of your sovereign. Medieval farts bear the same burden of anxiety, low humor, and indifferent necessity that they do today, yet they also open up the gap of cultural consciousness that yawns across seven centuries and more.

For the Edification of Copious Shitters and Costive Maidens Whose Hours at Siege Should Be Profitably Employed

Dominique Laporte's *History of Shit* takes as its point of departure an edict of Francis I of France, published 1539, in which it was decreed that the good citizens of Paris henceforth must not dump their slops onto the streets, whose corruption and stench provoke "great horror and greater displeasure in all valiant persons of substance."[33] The burghers forthwith must retain their urine and dispose of it in the stream, giving it chase with a bucket of water. They also must collect all droppings, human and animal, keeping them inside their homes, from where the droppings must be taken outside the city. In other words, they have to keep their shit to themselves. Contrast the dishonor in the Icelandic sagas of inhabitants having to defecate indoors, having been barred by an enemy from using the outhouse.[34] The domesticization of waste and the birth of the modern subject are inextricably connected; as late as the eighteenth century, anxiety over the inhalation of noxious smells from the enclosed privy beset the bourgeois shitter.[35] Inasmuch as the anal stage is the site of the formation of personality, the anus, exclusively associated with shit, represents the domain of self, the individual, the private[36]; that is, it is characteristic of emergent capitalism.[37] Taking a page from Freud, for whom miserliness and constipation are conjoint symptoms of anal eroticism, Laporte regards the dejected space of the *domus* as the essential site of material accumulation of both money and poop.[38] The *privé* [private sector] is where one does one's business. Take a shit and wash your hands; count your money and rub your hands with glee. Only a bourgeois can be stinking rich. Capitalism is an economy that defines itself in terms of the accumulation of surplus. "[A] capitalist, under penalty of his own destruction, *must strive to accumulate wealth*."[39] Modernity—age of the bourgeoisie—defines itself around a split between public and private, which later becomes the domain of both shit and money. The aristocrat, on the other hand, belonging to an earlier era, regards such miserliness with disgust.[40] The nobility, splattering in reckless dispense, shat themselves into economic extinction. If domestic stockpiling of shit and money marks the emergence of the bourgeoisie, by implication, the medieval body shat where it stood, and the medieval civic body excreted its waste similarly in a reckless fashion. Copious shitters, the medievals lacked the continence, should we say costiveness, of a Lutheran bowel. This is the difference between an economy of abundance, in which wealth is circulated through munificence and accumulation is regarded with suspicion, and an economy of scarcity, which treats commodities not as rare in themselves but as objects of which one can never have enough—hence the desire to accumulate. Although not casting the medieval condition in economic terms, Rabelais nonetheless articulates the (early modern) perception of the medievals as uncontrolled shitters. Gargantua's hysterical pooping is the result of the bad (i.e., sophistic and scholastic) education he was ingesting. Only purgation and a strict regimen of humanist care for body and mind can produce a more rational poop, executed punctually and privately.[41]

In his study of Rabelais' works, Mikhail Bakhtin reaches similar conclusions. The Rabelaisian body, forever in the middle of some bodily function, offers a vision of connectedness and communality lost under a more modern Renaissance mentality, one that prefigured the privatization of capitalism. Where Rabelaisian interpenetrating bodies are perpetual-motion machines, always in transition, their cavernous orifices ever open and excessively productive, the capitalist body is punctual, closed, and set off from each other in a new ideal of community that incarnates a fundamental contradiction—a bundle of atomistic individuals.

> Contrary to modern canons, the grotesque body is not separated from the rest of the world. It is not a closed, completed unit; it is unfinished, outgrows itself, transgresses its own limits. The stress is laid on those parts of the body that are open to the outside world, that is, the parts through which the world enters the body or emerges from it, or through which the body itself goes out to meet the world.[42]
>
> As conceived by these [Renaissance] canons, the body was first of all a strictly completed, finished product. Furthermore, it was isolated, alone, fenced off from all other bodies...The ever unfinished nature of the body was hidden, kept secret; conception, pregnancy, childbirth, death throes, were almost never shown.[43]

From Hamlet's soliloquies to privatization of bodily functions, the early modern subject is marked by an interiority simply absent before or hitherto unrecognized as such. Despite clear signs in the Middle Ages of interest in psychic inner life, the cult of privacy is earmarked as the *differentia* of early modernity. Interiority, the space of the private, is a protected zone of authenticity where one can be one's true self, and gain respite from the incursions of societal demands. It takes its ultimate form as a Rousseauian, romantic model of subjectivity, which equates privacy with the individual and solitude.

Privacy, however, is in no way a synonym of either. A Latin term from the Roman era, *privatus* is opposed to *publicus*, the latter denoting something held in common, shared by society, the former denoting both what is exempted from or lacks the status of the common domain and what is particular to an individual. In this sense, chapter 33 of the Rule of Benedict of Nursia requires that no monk "own anything" [*aliquid habere proprium*] (*PL*, 66:551C). "Private" from the start bears the double sign of the *privilege* that comes from special exemption and the *deprivation* that comes from lack. The privy—and in monastic Latin *privatae* already denoted the latrines[44]—becomes the space both of sanctuary and of solitary confinement. The domain of the private can encompass both a community turned inward in retreat and the alienation of the outcast. The moral is modeled on that of Adam: it is not good for man to be alone; strength lies in the community. Solitude in Benedictine monastic life can be imposed as punishment for sin; the monk "a mensae participatione privetur" [is barred from sharing meals] (*PL*, 66:505A); yet for an anchorite, solitude can become a transcended form of community, a people of one.

Feudalism, that mode of production we identify with the Middle Ages, is often described as a "privatization of power."[45] The manor, essentially a gentleman's private home, is the "component cell" of medieval Europe, in which the estate became the state.[46] Its power lay in being both economic and political instrument; the manorial estate touched everybody's life in some way or another, whether as one's home, one's place of work, or a source of revenue. Public, civic life took its shape from the model of domestic management. "As society became feudal, the public sphere shrank steadily until ultimately everything was private, and private life was everywhere."[47] One may just as well say that everything privy went public. The private and the public are not intrinsically so, but domains that shift to preserve a manipulated relation of difference to each other.

Even if there was less privacy in the sense of secured solitude and space for a medieval to do his or her business, there nonetheless remains a psychic space around one in the act of nature. Solitude is possible within the public arena, an inner moment in an outer place, just as a medieval household can be the model of public life. While sanitation regulations may not have been all they are today, propriety was nonetheless observed. There was a time to void and a time not to void. Chapter 8 of the Benedictine Rule appoints a break before lauds for attending *ad necessaria naturae* [to the needs of nature] (*PL*, 66:410A), which, if there were any doubt about it, a later commentary clarifies as *ad purgandum ventrem* [to evacuating the bowel] (*PL*, 66:422C).[48] Bodily exigency must be served, but not just anytime. In contempt of such decorum, Greek philosopher Diogenes the Cynic, who has endeared himself to posterity by declaring Plato's lectures a waste of time, is said to have freely performed the "works of Demeter and of Aphrodite" in public, that is, he defecated and masturbated in front of others despite unanimous protest.[49]

Privacy was not simply the privilege of those late medievals who could afford an indoor toilet—it was an ethic of the body regulated by estate, gender, and material condition. The graphic account of Dominican Felix Faber of Ulm, who records the conditions of his travel to the Holy Land in 1480 and 1483 and offers some traveling tips for future pilgrims, registers the violent contrast between the quiet and solitude of his habitual monastic existence and the experience of a pilgrim ship.[50] Beginning his excursus with a poetic quote—"maturum stercus est importabile pondus" [a ripe turd is an intolerable burden]—Felix Faber describes how each pilgrim at night receives a vessel for urine and seasickness. The roll of the sea and careless feet result in frequent slops, creating an unbearable stench. The privies proper were on deck, which was littered with sleeping bodies, so a nocturnal visit became a *via dolorosa* in itself. A soaking was guaranteed in bad weather, to prevent which some stripped stark naked, much to the shame and arousal of other passengers. Others resorted to a dark corner below deck, or did it in their bedside potties, corrupting the air foully; the sick of course had no choice, not that that alleviated the stink.

The rude shock for Felix attests to the discrepant experiences of privacy among contemporaries. It is not that privacy was a luxury afforded only by the rich and noble but that the boundaries and spaces between bodies reflected the appropriateness of the activity, the requirements of modesty, the accessibility of the bodies in question. The body of monk or nun and of the female maiden were at particular risk when exposed, the bottom as much as the "shameful members." Medieval privacy is a zone of inaccessibility in which money plays only a small part; it is not a right, not necessarily desirable, often the mark of deprivation or disbarment from full social intercourse, and not always fitting. Modern privacy in contrast abstracts itself from local circumstance and individuated body to acquire the status of commodity; for the early modern subject, it is a luxury enabled by wealth. Privacy *in its abstract form* remains essentially a bourgeois state of being.

Certain faultlines run through the past, and the shift from the medieval into the early modern seems to be one of them. The emergence of a discourse and sensibility of "taste" gives disgust a new direction and "starts to make the private possible".[51] Yet viewed from another angle, the shift from medieval to early modern is itself destabilized by other shifts occurring within the Middle Ages, most notably around the twelfth to thirteenth centuries, which saw both the flowering of Gothic art and a marked intolerance of marginal groups whose members included sodomites, women, Jews, and heretics[52]; it is also marked by the burgeoning of scatological humor in the French fabliaux alongside courtly literature, and of various institutions of the self, such as confession or last wills and testaments. Fart humor can be explained as efficiently in terms of sexual repression and psychological interiority as it can in terms of (economic) privatization.

However, medieval regimens of chastity are not the same thing as the nineteenth-century prudery with which Freud contended, and we might do better to align medieval farts with a discourse of holiness and corruption rather than repression and rebellion. For Margery Kempe kissing female lepers and mopping up her husband's shit were occasions of devotion and penance,[53] and Catherine of Siena drank pus in the name of God[54]; bodily corruption preserves a connection with sanctity at one remove. When Innocent III writes "Formatus est homo...de spurcissimo spermate. Conceptus in pruritu carnis, in fervore libidinis, in fetore luxurie" (man is fashioned out of filthy sperm; conceived in the itch of the flesh, in the heat of desire, in the fetidness of lust),[55] his rhetoric reveals his fascination with the contemptible, which, were it really that miserable, would simply be passed over in silence. Medieval sanctity brings one close to the disgusting, and transforms body grot into prayer.

We need a different model of purity from that of hygiene, to rethink body waste as an aesthetic possibility. "Waste" is too general a term; its dominant sense in Middle English was a despoiling, or unreasonable abuse of proper resource, and it exists primarily as a verb or action rather than as a noun, as the product itself. The use of "waste" as a noun to denote refuse, particularly inorganic, industrial residue comes from the nineteenth century (*OED*, s.v. *waste*, n[11a]).[56] Illustrating the sense of waste as unnatural squandering, Dante's circle of the violent in *Inferno* delineates a taxonomy of acts as psychologically as it is ethically acute. In this surreal landscape of talking trees and snowing fire, we meet a bizarre classification of culpability where blasphemy is worse than murder, where the "exotic charm of another system of thought" marks the limitation of our thinking today, "the stark impossibility of thinking *that*."[57] Two sins in particular demonstrate the connection between violence and waste. Prodigality, a sin of violence against self (canto xiii), wilfully squanders one's substance, and is thus more abusive than merely spending too much, which is a straightforward sin of excess. Sodomy, a sin of violence against nature, also wilfully squanders one's substance.

It is not that no one threw anything out in the Middle Ages. Ordure—animal and human—was regularly collected by the *gongfermor* [privy cleaner], animal giblets posed an ongoing disposal problem, and the industrial side of medieval life—dyeing cloth, coal mining, iron mongering—polluted the water and air; but such circulation of product belonged to a mental and fiscal economy different from today where the stockpiling of surplus, reserved for no designated purpose, simultaneously generates the accumulation of refuse, also serving no purpose. The Middle Ages, with its lively sense of hell and bodily degradation, finds a proper place even for corruption.

"Sometimes I Sits and Thinks, Sometimes I Just Sits"

And in the afternoon [I] had a natural easily and dry Stoole, the first I have had these five days or six, for which God be praised; and so am likely to continue well, observing for the time to come, when any of this pain comes again:

1. To begin to keep myself warm as I can.
2. Strain as little as ever I can backwards. . .
3. Either by physic forward or by clyster backward, or both ways, to get an easy and plentiful going to stool and breaking of wind.
4. To being to suspect my health immediately when I begin to become costive and bound.[58]

Thus ended Samuel Pepys's bout of chronic constipation; he recorded his triumph and good resolutions in his diary on October 13, 1663. Maimonides, as we see, understood from the outset that the ethical life rested on good potty discipline, but Pepys learned the hard way. Mastering the fundamentals of the toilet brings wisdom, but only if one is willing to learn. Aristotle recounts the story about the philosopher Herakleitos, whose great repute brought people from afar to visit.[59] On arriving, they find him in unexpectedly humble circumstances, but Herakleitos, seeing their discomfiture, reminds them that even here the gods are present. The translations vary, but generally concur that Herakleitos was "in the kitchen, warming himself at the stove." "Kitchen" translates Greek *ipnos*, which primarily means "oven," hence by extension, "kitchen," but a secondary meaning of the word is "privy" or "dungheap."[60] Perhaps Herakleitos was toasting his buttocks at the stove, perhaps he was in the privy, but whatever it was, it was not dignified. Tending to bodily need, however, became an occasion for philosophy: tongues are in turds, books in burps, and so on. Herakleitos knew that the loftiest philosophical revelations could come, would come only with a warm ass. The Middle Ages are a rich stew of such cacatorial wisdom:

> Qui ne chiet ne puet joer
> (*PFA*, p. 73, §2016)

[He who doesn't shit can't enjoy himself]

claims an Old French proverb, in recognition that a sound mind comes only from a sound bowel. It may seem that farts do not have much to offer by way of instruction, and Middle English supplies instances enough of the worthlessness of flatulence: "Thy speach is not worth a farte" Balaack cries angrily to Balaham[61]; and catching a fart in a net is proverbial for doing nothing useful.[62] You can not catch hold of a fart; it is gone in an instant, useless, the meontological mark, sign of non-being itself. However, other medieval contexts amply demonstrate that there is moral substance to be learned when the bottom coughs.

The fart is a morsel of wisdom, microcosm of the larger moral occasion. English physician John of Arderne, discussing treatment of the anal fistula, notes the need for moral as well as bodily hygiene:

> Abstene he hym fro harlotrie als wele in wordes as in dedes in euery place, for ȝif he vse hym to harlotery in priue places som tyme in opene place ther may falle to hym vnworship of yuel vsage: aftir þat it is seyde, "pede super colles pedes vbi pedere nolles." "ffart vpon hilliȝ and thou shalt fart whar thou wolde noȝt agayn thi willeȝ."[63]

> [Abstain from harlotry in all places both in word and in deed. For if a man is wont to indulge in harlotry in secret then sooner or later he will expose his baseness in public; hence the Latin saying—"fart on the open hills and you're sure to fart somewhere you didn't mean to."]

What you do habitually in solitude will show up eventually in public. Farting habits are a surer index of the real you than any public gestures performed to display the self you want others to see. As you fart, so you are. If the truth of Arderne's claim is not already self-evident, saying it in Latin lends it *gravitas*.

French exults in these sapiential pearls, generally more so than English. The anemic saying "don't aspire above your station" is the equivalent of the more colorful French "il ne faut pas péter plus haut que le cul" [there's no need to fart higher than your asshole].[64] Only some of the thousands of Old French proverbs are scatological. For the most part, they are simple home truths, such as "de bon mangeor mauvés donoor" [big eater, bad lover] (*PFA*, p. 17, §472). Some are scatological versions of other homely sayings:

> Petite merde conchiee grans bra[i]es.
> (*PFA*, p. 59, §1620)

> [A little turd befouls a large pair of pants.]

Compare with this the English "one rotten apple spoils the whole cart."[65] The meaning in this instance is clear enough, but occasionally one has to grope deeper for insight:

> Asez demure de chier qui a (la) longaine vet peant.
> (*PFA*, p. 5, §135)

> [He who is overly slow to shit at the privy besmears himself (or besmears his cock).]

What exactly does this mean? That if you waste precious time on trivial things you achieve nothing? Or that if you enjoy contemptible things, they taint your entire life? Posed thus in abstraction, the moral stands obliquely and at many removes from the baldness of the original. Ultimately, the proverb is recursive; it means that he who is overly slow to shit at the privy besmears himself. The proverbs themselves are pithier, more compelling than any ponderous morals squeezed out of them. Delphic in their offbeat sagacity, crypticism, and the unforeseeable ways in which they may prove true, they refuse abstraction with their practical aptness. As with all proverbs, these Confucian utterances are untranslatable. They remain stubbornly in the shittery, arising from the singularity of one place and one moment, as occasional as a poem. Inextricable from the words, noise, and stink that brought them into being, the scatological proverb refuses to be waved away into moralization. To a medieval *mentalité* for which allegory stands in the highest regard, these crotties of wisdom resist transcendence.

Hard Lessons

The untranslatability of the proverb makes it an ideal translation brainteaser in the classroom, and it is in the classroom that many of the scatological proverbs were encountered. Here the schoolboy learned his Latin grammar by construing into and from the vernacular. In England, from at least the fourteenth through the sixteenth centuries, young scholars would construe into and from their native English. The method was to absorb the grammatical rules of Latin by means of the pitfalls of translation. If he got it wrong, there was the threat of the birch; and to register the point, the schoolboy was obliged to translate his pain into Latin:

> Socio meo vapulante cum virga lentiscina, ego sum vapulaturus cum scutica. My felow y-bete with a byrch 3erd, y ham to be bete with a whyppe.[66]
>
> [My schoolmate having been already beaten with a birch stick, I am to be beaten with a whip.]

For that reason Grammar, the most elementary of the seven liberal arts, was traditionally depicted with a whip—a sober warning to the tender-arsed scholar.[67] The workbooks are clustered with homely sayings and proverbs, often absurd, riddling, and sometimes scatological, for it spices up class time no end to learn rude words in Latin:

> bolkynge [belching]   *eructuacio*
> donge hylle   *sterquilinium*
> fart   *trulla* or *bombus*
> goo to pryvy, or to shytyn   *acello*[68]

and for the intermediate level:

wype thy nose	munge nasum
I am almost beshytten	
[I am about to shit myself]	sum in articulo purgandi viscera
tourde in thy tethe	merda dentibus inheret[69]

So widespread was this classroom experience that it appears satirized in the fifteenth-century play *Mankind*, in which Nowadays makes the following request to Mercy:

> I prey yow hertily, worschippfull clerke,
> To have this Englisch mad in Laten:
> "I have etun a disch-full of curdys,
> Ande I have schetun yowr mowth full of turdys:"—
> Now, opyn yowr sachell with Laten wordys
> Ande sey me this in clericall manere![70]
>
> [I beseech you, honorable scholar, turn this English sentence into Latin: "I have eaten a dishful of curd cheese, and I have filled your cake-hole with my turds." Now, open up your bag of words and say it in Latin!]

Latin is so noble that just to learn it brings deeper understanding. There is a workbook from the first half of the fifteenth century, compiled maybe by a schoolmaster somewhere around Lincoln for his pupils. An English sentence is given as the starting point, and the schoolboy is then required to translate it into Latin. This was not always easy, and the struggles of one young greenhorn are recorded elsewhere: "A hard latyn to make, my face waxyth blackke,"[71] which means something like, "This sentence is so impossible to put in Latin, I'm about to pop a blood vessel." In this Lincoln workbook, we find a proverb for translation into Latin, one that remains today in the bowdlerized form, "to fall between two stools:"

> Betwyx two stolys fals þe ars down.[72]
> [Between two stools the arse falls down.]

This proverb was highly popular in the premodern era, especially in France. Under the entry *Cul* [ass], Furetière interprets the phrase "il est demeuré entre deux selles le cul à terre" to refer to the failure to avail oneself of life's profitable opportunities. Rabelais, writing a hundred years after the Lincoln schoolbook, satirizes these mindless pedagogic rituals of recycling vernacular clichés into Latin clichés and back again by describing their results in young Gargantua, who "pissed in his shoes, shat in his shirt" and "sat between two stools with his arse on the ground" [se asseoyt entre deux selles le cul à terre].[73] But for the class of Lincoln, rebellion is still a century away, and even though some must have despaired, faces purple, the birch a certainty, one egghead got the right answer:

> Inter scanna duo concidit anus ruina.[74]
> [Between two stools the anus takes a tumble to its destruction.]

Egghead actually manages to elevate the miserable little English sentence to a new level of nuance. Latin *ruina* carries the double sense of physical falling and moral "ruination." English, with its conceptually thinner vocabulary (at least in the view of late medieval disparagers of the vernacular), can only embody one of the senses, the literal one of falling. In translation from English into Latin, meaning gains in depth, and shows the class that Latin has possibilities English lacks.

Old French, however, rich in its vocabulary of excrement, can create a Gallic version that rivals Latin in discrimination:

> Entre deus selles chiet dos a terre.
>   (*PFA*, p. 25, §692)
> [Between two stools, the back takes a pratfall to the ground.]

The verb *chier* means "to shit." Ever versatile, it captures both moral and literal senses of being on the skids. The compost of possibilities in *chier* creates a small vernacular triumph, rivalling the plasticity of the Latin tongue. Let Herakleitos bombinate about divinity in the quotidian; none will have learned better the lesson of the arse that fell between two stools than the ones whose own, by the end of class on that day, were too sore to sit on.

Scatological proverbs teach wisdom to the young. Score them on that soft skin early enough and they will stay for life, a guide during the later descent to the pachydermal when moral nature, like one's hide, is too tough to learn anything new. When you sit to shit, you take a stool in the school of life. "Stool," a word of Germanic origin meaning "seat," by a fine metonymy shifts from referring to the seated posture one assumes to do one's business, to the act of evacuation ("at stool"), to the name for the turd itself. "Siege," a word of French origin, also meaning "seat," follows a similar semantic trajectory and comes to refer to the fundament or anus (*OED*, s.v. *siege*, n.[4]). Whether we sit on the stool privately in close-stool, or publicly in the classroom, or before the congregation on the "stool of repentance," or before the village on the "cucking stool," we confess our lowliness, offense, and need. When "at stool," we humble ourselves before a greater authority.

Logic 101

Grammar mastered, but still "at stool," the schoolboy's curriculum next included logic, in which he learned the art of deductive reasoning. The ending of Chaucer's *Summoner's Tale* hinges on a question that would tax anyone's logical and mathematical abilities: how do you divide a fart equally among the Friar and his brothers? Much of the comic effect of the tale is the serious way in which the question is treated, as a scholastic poser. The quodlibet was a question, albeit on a more elevated subject of philosophy or theology, on which the medieval scholar would cut his teeth as an exercise in argument or disputation. The lord of the manor in the *Summoner's Tale* calls the question an *impossible*, a logical conundrum; we might call it an "insoluble." With po-faced humor, Chaucer treats the fart-division problem as a serious contribution to mereology, a branch of philosophy that takes us into the "deepest recesses" of metaphysics.[75]

Perhaps influenced by Chaucer's tale, a late–fifteenth-century text, *Les Adevineaux Amoureux* [Amorous Games or Puzzles], written probably for the amusement of the ladies of the court of Burgundy, offers a courtly version of the scholastic quodlibet, a miscellany of bon mots, riddles, and epigrams, set into a debate form between a lady and her lover, which both entertains and instructs the genteel. Not always so genteel, the questions, or *demandes joyous* include versions of Chaucer's poser, suggesting perhaps the existence of an entire medieval corpus of fart-division riddles and jokes:

> Comment partiroit on une vesse en douze parties?
> Faittes une vesse sur le moieul d'une roe, et douze personnes ayent chascun son nez aux xii trous, et par ainsi chascun en ara sa part.[76]
>
> [How do you divide a fart in twelve parts?
> Cut a fart on the hub of a wheel, with each of the twelve persons having his nose at the twelve spoke–divisions, and thus everyone will get his share.]
>
> Comment pourroit on partir une vesse en deux?
> Par bouter son nez ou cul d'une vielle. Et se bien l'estoupoit au vessir rechepvroit la moittié de la vesse en l'une narrine and l'autre moittié en l'autre narrine.[77]
>
> [How do you divide a fart in two? By shoving your nose in the asshole of an old woman. And if she bends over to fart, you will get half of the fart in one nostril and the other half in the other nostril.]

Ranging wildly in taste, the questions of *Les Adevineaux Amoureux* often wax philosophical or morally complex, posing situations in which the respondent must make a judgment. This judgment motif frequently occurs at the end of medieval tales, which is left inconclusive for the audience to decide. The end of Chaucer's *Franklin's Tale*, itself borrowed from Boccaccio, follows this pattern: who of the three men in the story, Aurelius, Arveragus, or the clerk, showed greater generosity and nobility? Fabliaux also end with a judgment between rival claimants,[78] as we see in the trilemma of *Les Trois Meschines*, in which three young girls, vanity their besetting sin, prepare for a village fair. Sueree knows of a cosmetic powder, which, when moistened, will make their cheeks bloom. They agree to pool resources for the product: Brunatin fronts the money, Sueree walks to Rouen and back for the rouge, and Agace volunteers to do the honors to make the paste, the diluting agent being urine. Brunatin holds the vessel of powder in critical position behind Agace, while Sueree, fatigued from her travels, sits to supervise. But Agace could not piddle a drop, so she squeezes hard:

> En ce que Agace s'esforce,
> Et un tres grant pet li eschape;
> Por neent deüst taillier chape:
> Pet fist du cul et poudre vole!
> "Qu'est ce, deable, pute fole?"
> Dist Brunatin, "que as tu fet?
> Certes, vez ci vilain mesfet!
> Toute as nostre poudre souflee:
> Ele m'est dusqu'es ieus volee,
> Si m'a enfumee trestoute."[79]

[In forcing so hard, an enormous fart escaped her; there was no avoiding soiling herself. The fart issued from her ass, and the powder blew to the winds. "What the devil was that, you stupid whore?" said Brunatin; "what have you done? That was a vile thing to do. All our powder has blown away; it's even flown into my eyes! I'm completely smothered in the stuff."]

Furious, befarted, and dust-bathed, Brunatin demands her money back. Agace refuses, blaming the fault on Brunatin for holding the pot at the wrong angle, underneath her ass [*cul*] instead of her cunt [*con*]. Brunatin counters, and they become embroiled in a tangle of contractual dispute. Sueree complicates the issue further by claiming a refund for her efforts in procurement, and the three agree to settle the matter at court. The narrator assures us that this is what they did, but withholds the outcome, calling on the reader to judge who should pay for the powder (ll. 124–8).

The ethical poser makes fun of weightier counterparts. We employ our practical reason to resolve the grossest absurdity. Yet such tales do more than blow raspberries at seriousness; they test the limits of that coveted faculty that supposedly sets humanity above the beasts—reason; they puncture the vanity of logic, and hint at ways in which experience can subvert a structure of rational order. Fart riddles are at the center of such a project. What, asks *Les Adevineaux Amoureux*, is half of a fart? What is half of nothing? What is one twelfth of nothing? What, poses the *Summoner's Tale*, is one thirteenth of nothing? The questions have something of the koan or Buddhist paradox to them, for they defy formal logic and open up a new consciousness of things. The OE *rædels* [riddle] is related to *rædan* [to advise], whence we get "to read"; much more than a joking witticism, the riddle opens up a moment of discernment and insight not ordinarily available in common language use. They are also jokes, and the laughter that they provoke convulses rational order in ways more complex than by inversion alone. Like a pun, the riddle brings together disparate phenomena—a fart, a cartwheel—and conjoins them in such a way as to subvert their natural place, identity, and telos as designated by a rationally ordered universe.

> Entre deux jambes le vis amble;
> Entre deux fesses le vif trepple,
> Et quant il vient a la porte,
> Son maistre hurte a l'anel.[80]
> [Between two legs the lively flesh ambles,
> Between two buttocks the lively flesh cavorts,
> And when it gets to the door,
> Its master bangs on the knocker / anus.]

And the answer is. . .a horse, whose rider knocks on a closed door. In the world of riddles, the obvious is taken by surprise, and logic gets a poke in the eye.

The ~~Music Album~~ Musical Bum

How do you get your hands on a fart to divide it into two? How do you eyeball one-twelfth of a fart? We measure farts by our ears and nose, in the currency of noise and smell. What is one-thirteenth of the boom or stink of a fart?

Exiting the realm of the eye, we find ourselves in places where the body is governed by different authority. French has the happy distinction of distinguishing linguistically between the fart noisy and silent.[81] Apart from the usual *le pet*, there is also *la vesse*:

> Vent que lâche le derriere sans éclat, & qui est d'ordinaire fort puant. On disoit autrefois vesne, dont Rabelais a formé le nom hume-vesne.[82]
> [A wind released from the backside without explosion, usually very smelly. Formerly known as *vesne*, from which Rabelais formed the name "Fart-Sucker."]

Old Icelandic also distinguishes between a sturdy farter [*fretr*] and making a weak fart [*físa*], the latter being more offensive by suggesting effeminacy.[83] Both *fert* and *fist* were in currency in Middle English, and the occurrence of them together in the phrase *fartes* and *fyestes in* Wynkyn de Worde's *demaundes ioyous* suggests a distinction possibly as systematic as that observed in French or Icelandic, although the silent variety is not attested widely in Middle English, the *MED* noting only one fifteenth-century instance of the verb *fesilen*.

Hippocrates recommends, "it is best to pass flatulence [*physan*] without noise [*psophos*] and breaking [*pradēsios*], though it is better for it to pass even with noise than to be intercepted and accumulated internally."[84] The silent fart may be medically more desirable, but in the musical sphere, the acoustic fart is the only one of value. Farting makes the bottom sing, to borrow Augustine's terminology in reference to certain men who have such control of their anal sphincter muscles "that they seem to make music" [*ut. . .cantare videantur*].[85]

The musical butt is ubiquitous in the Middle Ages, and presupposes a larger analogy between the human body and musical instruments. The fourteenth-century English Luttrell Psalter offers a bizarre conglomerate of man-instrument, part two-legged animal and part bagpipe, with a human face at the ends of the chanter and the drone (plate 1). The regally crowned head at the top plays a shawm-like pipe, of discrete size. At the other end is the cowled head of a peasant, who blows a huge shawm, cheeks bulging. The legs turn the bagpipe into an animal, with the chanter as the head and the drone as the butt. The shawm is the loudest of medieval wind instruments, and the large shawm altogether the loudest and deepest.[86] By functioning here as a drone, the large shawm produces continuous sound. We get the point: thunderous and incessant wind issues from the churlish backside of the biped bagpipe, threatening with its clamor to drown the finer voice of the chanter.

The large shawm also exhibits its connection with farting by a shared vocabulary. During the fourteenth century it acquired the name of *bombard* or *bumbard*,[87] a word related to Roland's *bombulum*, and sharing the root of Latin *bombinare* [to buzz]. *Bombulum* occurs in a letter by Jerome, referring to a toot or short burst of wind on a wind instrument (*PL*, 30:214A-B). Latin *flatus*, a word we now reserve exclusively for intestinal gas, occurs regularly in musical treatises as the term for air breathed into an instrument. And *fistula*, the term we use for an ulcerated butt, simply means "flute" or "pipe." It is difficult, in fact, not to encounter the butthole analogy.

The musical instrument serves as metaphor for the flatulent body. An ape points a trumpet at the backside of another ape (plate 2). Chaucer's churl John in the *Summoner's Tale* is carried to the fartwheel with his distended belly "stif and toght / As any tabour" [stiff and taught, like a tabor or small drum] (*CT*, 3.2267-8). In Rutebeuf's *Le Pet au Vilain*, the peasant's belly is "li tent con corde a citole" [stretched tight like a zither] (*NRCF* 5:369, l. 38). And in response to the raspberry that Malacoda blows at his cohort, Dante's devils make "del cul fatto trombetta" [trumpets of their butts] (*Inf.*, xxi.139). Butt-trumpets are as old as Aristophanes, whose character Strepsiades calls a gnat's rectum [*prōktos*] a bugle [*salpigks*].[88]

The musical bum figures most of all in Hieronomous Bosch's early-sixteenth–century triptych about fallen humanity, the *Garden of Earthly Delights*, where, in *Hell*, its nightmarish right panel, one poor sinner's upended butt on the far left serves as both music stand for and score of a part-song led by a croaking toad decked out as church precentor. The painting features an entire musical sequence of scrannel butt-noises, such as playing the fife through the fundament.

Bosch's evocative panel continues the larger analogy between instrument and body,[89] with a human face peeping out of a huge drum (center), which is beaten by a whiskered beastie. Some sinners on the right hold their hands over their ears in an effort to block out the cacophony of hell's tortures. Instruments and bodies interpenetrate: across the back of the sinner who plays the fife with his butt a bombardon rests contiguous with his spine. All the bodies are distorted in some way, and anal noise is a powerful image of moral and spiritual disharmony, doubly ironic in that the harp, lute, hurdy-gurdy, and bombardon were all church instruments.[90] On the far left edge of the picture, a spotted toad has been spitted onto a stick, maybe a conductor's baton, and set alight; the smoke ascending conjoins the aural and the olfactory, reminding us that hell's music stinks.

Apart from these scatological and demonic images, there stands an ancient religious analogy between body and musical instrument. Hilary of Poitiers finds the shape of the lute-like *psalterium* [psaltery] reminiscent of Christ's body (*PL*, 9:237B). For Gregory of Nyssa, the proper acts of the human tongue are speech and song, for which reason our hands do chores that other animals perform with their tongues.[91] The human tongue is like the plectrum of a cithara; with words, we pick out notes of praise just as our fingers pluck out tunes on instruments.

In the music treatises themselves, the analogy unfolds in more detail. The human body is an orchestra in microcosm: the throat, like a pipe, represents the wind instrument; the chest, like a harp, represents the stringed instrument; and the pulse a percussion instrument.[92] *Vox* [voice] refers to a single note of an instrument as well as to human sound. Predecessors of the keyboard, the sliders on the medieval organ were called *linguae* [tongues].[93] Musical terminology plunders that of grammar, aligning the verbally correct and the musically pleasing phrase, as if to imagine an instrument speaking or playing an homunculus. Carved heads frequently adorn the top of late medieval stringed instruments, and the bagpipe-turned-human such as in the Luttrell Psalter is ubiquitous in marginal illumination (plate 1).

Metaphor aside, (animal) bodies and instruments overlap literally, with strings made of dried gut; in his letter, Jerome mentions the use of elephant hides in the construction of the organ (*PL*, 30:213B). Where animal bowels are plucked and played, human guts sympathetically gurgle out the notes of intense emotion such as fear and grief. "My bowels shall sound like an harp for Moab and mine inward parts for Kir-haresh" (Isaiah 16.11), write the translators of the King James version of the Bible, while the Wyclif Bible offers: "Vp on this my wombe [*venter*] to Moab as an harpe shal sounen, and my boweles [*viscera*] to the wal of the anelid tyl [baked tile]."

Even into the sixteenth century (and after), the analogy between the body and the musical instrument held sway. In 1535, Italian music theorist Sylvestro Ganassi sums up the centuries-long tradition:

> Be it known that all musical instruments, in comparison to the human voice, are inferior to it. For this reason, we should endeavour to learn from it and to imitate it. . . .just as a gifted painter can reproduce all the creations of nature by varying his colours, you can imitate the expression of the human voice on a wind or stringed instrument. . . .only the form of the human body is absent, just as in a fine picture only the breath is lacking.[94]

Butts and Instruments: Nature versus Art

Ganassi's claim that the instrument imitates the body reproduces the time-honored axiom that art imitates nature, for the instrument "artificially" recreates the "naturally" occurring music of the human body. The distinction between artificial and natural music has roots in the very origins of music theory. Drawing from this long tradition, a thirteenth-century treatise explains that musical theory distinguishes between natural music [*musica naturalis*] and instrumental music [*musica instrumentalis*].[95] Natural music then subdivides into human music [*musica humana*] and the music of the cosmos [*musica mundana*], while instrumental music subdivides into strings, wind (or "instruments with apertures"), and percussion (or "instruments with vessels") (figure 1).

This primary division in the *Summa musice* between the natural and the artificial parallels divisions in other domains, such as rhetoric, in which the treatises identify "two kinds of memory, one natural [*natural*], the other the product of art [*artificial*]."[96] Poetics also recognize the same distinction; Geoffrey of Vinsauf advises poets to relate events in an artful sequence rather than a "natural," chronological sequence of narration.[97] If human music is intrinsically natural, then the characterization of the body as

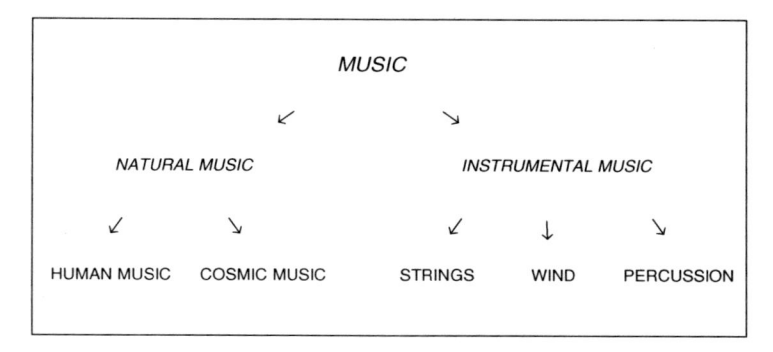

```
                          MUSIC
                    ↙            ↘
           NATURAL MUSIC      INSTRUMENTAL MUSIC
           ↙         ↘         ↙      ↓      ↘
    HUMAN MUSIC  COSMIC MUSIC  STRINGS  WIND  PERCUSSION
```

Figure 1   The division of music according to *Summa musice*

instrument and of an instrument as body in the ways we have seen deliberately blurs the boundary between natural and artificial, organic and inanimate.

What exactly is an instrument? One of the common words for it in Greek is *organon* (L. *organum*), yet it is from this word that we get "organic" and speak of the "organs" of the body, further undermining any strict separation between living entity and implement. Vitruvius distinguishes between a machine [*machina*] and an instrument [*organum*]; by the former is meant a large device operable by many men; the latter, however, requires the "careful application" [*operae prudenti*] of one skilled person.[98] His distinction perhaps recalls that of Plato, who differentiates between mere knack learned through habituation [*tribē*] and skill requiring rational judgment [*technē*].[99] The skilled use of an instrument requires practical if not speculative reason.

At least at the level of theory if not necessarily of practice, the musical treatises value cerebral over manual such that it is thought nobler to be a theorist rather than a performer of music, no matter how skilled, for ears and instruments are empirical and unreliable. Boethius says, "Physical skill serves as a slave, while reason rules like a mistress."[100] Theory frees one from preoccupations with bodily facility such as fingering or breathing to let the mind dwell on mystical ratios and harmonious proportions of the universe. It is theoretical appreciation of the "artificial" instrument that enhances our "natural" gift of reason, and it is "natural" for us to make "artificial" music with instruments. The principles of nature and art nest within and inhabit one another rather than stand opposed as contraries. "Nature," that is, is neither static and inviolable nor independent of nurture and the incursions of art, for art is necessary to realize nature's potential.

The analogy between musical instrument and body represents every part and function of the body as an aesthetic event. If creating art is our nature then our natural body is also our art. Bodily comportment and the satisfaction of bodily need provide the occasion of virtuous or vicious acts and constitute an art of living. Song is rational in design; its utterance enacts our self-fashioning. Where animals use tongues for practical tasks, the human hand performs such jobs, leaving the tongue to the preserve of reason in singing and speech. Indeed, since music is a discipline founded upon mathematical reason, only humans can properly be said to "sing." Animals "sing" by analogy because they are compelled by nature rather than by choice to make music.[101] To fart as if singing, to make a trumpet of the butt, to beat out the syncopated rhythms of a jump, a whistle, and a *bombulum*—this is to facilitate reason. We may not be able to think with our butts, but a musical butt may help us think.

Farts certainly seem to have a mind of their own. In mystical theology, music often possesses a kind of external imperative that chooses us, rather than our choosing it. Worshipful song descends involuntarily like grace, such that one mystic speaks of how song "broke forth" from him.[102] If words signify reason, music signifies grace, because of its sweetness and intensity. The lyrics of the psalms capture this intensity. Take Psalm 44.2, "eructavit cor meum verbum bonum." The Wyclif Bible translates, "Myn herte hath teld out a good word;" but *eructare* also means "to belch," and "I have belched out my praise" is as fair if less decorous a translation. The Christian hymn, invented by Ambrose, pictures itself as an incarnation of world harmony, as liturgical *responsio* rather than as an originary utterance;[103] it is summoned imperiously out of us. Our bodily wind thus worshipfully "repeats" its last supper. In this way, our music-making bodies are by "nature" "instruments" of grace. In a colorful sermon on the Song of Songs, Bernard of Clairvaux comments at length upon the uncontrollable belch of worship:

> Why should you look to find connected prayers or solemn declarations in a belch [*ructus*]? What rules or regulations do you impose upon yours? They do not admit of your control, or wait for you to compose them, nor do they consult your leisure or convenience. They burst forth [*erumpere*] from within, without your will or knowledge, torn [*evellere*] from you rather than uttered. . . . "My heart has belched a goodly theme."[104] They were all filled with the Holy Ghost,[105] and their belchings filled all things with goodness.[106] Do you ask for Jeremiah's belch? I have not forgotten; I was building up to it. . . .Breathe it in [*admovete naribus*].[107]

Whether singing, farting, or belching, the body in the throes of a pneumatic seizure can be conceived either as an instrument played by some force higher than choice, or as a mechanical wind box squeezed into action by digestive necessity. Bodily wind puts free will on the line. The bowels play a singular role in the complex relationship between voluntary and involuntary. Digestion, for example, is involuntary and thus entirely "natural," but excretion, "the rejection of excrement from the bladder [*la vessie*] and the bowels [*les boyaus*]," is "mixed [*melé*]."[108] For Augustine, this "mixed" quality of the fart carries profound theological implication. Before the fall, all bodily acts and functions were performed by choice; neither bowels nor genitals operated without the sanction of reason; there was no distinction between mind and body.

> Hence man himself too may once have commanded even from his lower members [*membra inferiora*] an obedience that by his own disobedience he has lost. . . .Certain human beings. . .can at will do with their bodies some things that others find utterly impossible to imitate and scarcely credible to hear. For some people can actually move their ears, either one at a time or both together. . . .Some people produce at will without any stench [*sine paedore ullo*] such rhythmical sounds from "down there" [*ab imo*] that they appear to be making music [*ut. . .cantare videantur*] even from that quarter.[109]

Roland's fart show, ironically enough, can remind us of bodies once perfect in integrity and control. Farts are the occasion for self-examination, for questioning the extent of our freedom and the nature of self-mastery.

The Musical Universe

Human and instrumental music are only two of the three kinds discussed in the Middle Ages; *musica humana*, and *musica instrumentalis* are joined by the music of the spheres, *musica mundana* [earthly music].[110] *Musica mundana* has various senses. In one, the phrase refers to what we call the "music of the spheres," a doctrine that stretches back to Plato and Pythagoras. In the geocentric Ptolemaic universe, the motionless earth is surrounded by successively large concentric spheres, all of which move at varying speeds, from the smallest and most sluggish (the Moon), to the largest (the *stellatum*), which whirls at a velocity beyond imagination. Motion is the cause of sound—no movement, no noise—so it follows that these globes send out differently pitched tones. "It is unquestionably right to assume that harmonious sounds come forth from the rotation of the heavenly spheres, for sound has to come from motion, and Reason, which is present in the divine, is responsible for the sound being melodious."[111]

Although the motionless earth itself makes no sound in this singing cosmos, it is full of virtual harmonies that develop other senses of the idea of *musica mundana*, such as the dance of the four elements and the diversity between the four seasons.[112] The elements—earth, fire, air, water—together form the stuff that is matter, and their qualities—hot, cold, moist, and dry—exist as contraries to each other. Matter itself is a well-proportioned mixture of opposites, and *musica mundana* holds these warring elements and opposing contraries together in a rightly proportioned ratio: they combine in harmonious counterpoint, none losing its individual identity. By the sheer act of existing, we make music, for just as *musica mundana* holds the elements together in due proportion, so *musica humana* unites immortal soul with mortal body.[113] *Musica humana* is an ontological condition, our very being a kind of music.

Since the earliest times, music and noise have been one of the profoundest expressions of right and wrong relations within the universe, and the intensity of its power is driven by the belief in a symphonic cosmos. The vision of music coming out of the backside catalyzes these primal associations. If for Bosch, anal music records the godawful noise of hell and sin, for Augustine, it is a residual mark of a body at once both wholly innocent and all powerful. Whether an image of paradisal harmony or infernal noise, the musical bum defamiliarizes the ordinary—ordinary assholes, ordinary music—altering their state of being and our consciousness of their being. In rearranging sound and matter in this way, the musical bum provides the occasion to mediate awhile on the mystical alignment between body, soul, and cosmos.

So crucial was music for classical Greece that, along with gymnastics, it formed the foundation of all education; so broad was it that it included singing, storytelling, and dancing. Where gymnastics trains the body to excellence, music perfects the soul.[114] The "choric art" [*choros*] entails both song and dance,[115] establishing a totality of sound and motion of which a vestige remains in a "chorus line." "Carols," understood as Christmas songs, in medieval times meant festive singing and dancing, secular or religious. Voice and movement go together; music is something we see as well as hear. It operates on many levels: as a practical performance art; as the science of ratios and proportions; as worship or ecstasy; and ultimately as the healthful alignment of one's whole being, body and soul, with the mystical rhythms of the universe.

Mousikē has particular importance for youth (hence its significance in early education), because young children habitually bounce around and make noise, requiring a regime to harness and regulate excessive energy. Just as song is peculiarly human and birds sing only by analogy, so the same distinction holds for movement: "whereas all other creatures are devoid of any perception of the various kinds of order and disorder in movement (which we term rhythm and harmony) to us men the very gods. . .have granted the pleasurable perception of rhythm and harmony."[116] Although beauty and grace belong to all of God's creatures, only humans have an active consciousness of grace, a theoretical awareness of coordination.

Nature's tendency toward violent excess in the young and energetic must be curbed and purged in such as way as to restore the organism to its homeostatic golden mean. Dance provides such a purgation, a controlled, rhythmic release that acts out with the limbs the operations of reason. Shaking a leg is the discipline of right expenditure of excess energy. Because of its purgative properties, dancing expels excess wind, as Tibbe, heroine of the "Feast of Tottenham," discovers at some cost to her dignity. Perkin the bumpkin has jousted and won her hand, and at her wedding banquet, she arises to swish around in front of the guests, but to her horror "As sche dawnsid she late a fart."[117] In similar vein, Scots poet William Dunbar writes of the sour-faced dame Dounteboir who was dancing in the queen's chamber, when "an blast of wind son fra hir slippis" [a blast of wind soon slips from her].[118]

Any energetic motion can bring on a fart: exercise, notes the writer of the *Secretum Secretorum* in a "full profitable epistle" for the conservation of health, "breketh all ventositees."[119] In the cases of Tibbe and dame Dounteboir, the fart pops out unexpectedly and unintentionally; but Roland the Farter demonstrates that there are occasions when the fart is intentionally induced and publicly theatrical, for the pleasure of the assembled. In such circumstances, the fart *is* the dance. Alongside story narration, acrobatics, stand-up comedy, and playing an instrument, performance farting takes its place as legitimate entertainment, as music in its broadest and original sense, although it is doubtful whether it would ever have made it onto Plato's ideal syllabus.

Canticus Canticorum [Song of Songs]

Dancing is one of the ways to dispel trapped wind. Another is to take a remedy; carminative foods—such as ginger, nutmeg, cardamom, anise, or caraway seeds—disperse intestinal gas. Garlic "desoluyth grose wyndes"[120]; so does thyme, and fennel seed helps one to "breke wynde."[121] Peas and beans, on the other hand, are what make you flatulent in the first place and require an antidote, for they "doth replete a man with ventosyte [windiness]."[122] That antidote is a "carminative." *Carminatif* is a Middle English word that entered the language via French. The *OED* claims its derivation from Latin *carminare* [to comb or card wool]. In his *Dictionary of English Eymology*, Hensleigh Wedgwood explains that the term derives from the theory of humors, according to which carminatives "dilute and relax the gross humours from whence the wind arises, combing them out like the knots in wool" (s.v. *carminative*). However, why should "carminative" not derive from Latin *carmen* [song, charm]? Why should not a carminative make your bottom sing? It makes as much sense as wool combing.[123]

Carmen means "spell, charm" as well as "song"; where modern English distinguishes between all-purpose "singing" and mystical "incanting" or "chanting," the one verb *cantare* [to sing] originally served both senses. "Carminative" is also connected to *charme*—a charminative. Although Middle English *carminacioun* [the dispersion of flatulence] occurs generally as a prosaic medical term, it echoes the ancient bonds between physic, magic, and music, suggesting that one chants one's flatulence away. "The ancients were able to cure fever and wounds by incantation,"[124] and according to Macrobius, "gifted men sing out remedies for the ailing."[125] Medieval charms were very common, and implicitly musical, whether sung or not, for they are highly rhythmic. Note the rhythmic and repetitive patterning of the following charm for staunching blood, one of the commonest conditions needing treatment:

> Aliud carmen: Primo inquire nomen et dic quinquies Pater Noster et Ave et tunc dic: "For þe woundes þat God sofrid on þe crois for to by us out of al þe world, stanch, blod; in the worship of five blodi teres þat Our Lady lete for Cristes love, stanch, blod;. . .for the blode þat Crist bled on the crois in þe worship of þat blode, stanch, blode." Et tunc dicat quinquies Pater et Ave Maria.[126]
>
> [Another charm. First find out the person's name and say the Our Father and the Ave Maria five times, then say: "For the wounds that God suffered on the cross for to buy us out of all the world, staunch, blood; in the worship of five bloody tears that our Lady let [fall] for Christ's love, staunch, blood;. . .for the blood that Christ bled on the cross in worship of that blood, staunch, blood." And then say the Our Father and Ave Maria five times.]

Sound, in medieval physics, is nothing other than air that is "beaten," and music, as a subspecies of sound, is air beaten or percussed in pleasingly rhythmic ways.[127] Incantations "beat" the air in rhythmic motions, which in turn evokes a sympathetically rhythmic motion within the soul of the patient, just as strings plucked resonate within the body of a guitar or violin. Incantation massages a knotted intestine without palpation, "carding" it into a therapeutic fart.

Central to the connection between physic and music is the doctrine of sympathy, according to which the strains of music temper the soul's turbulent motion. Alex's joy in Beethoven's Choral Symphony in Anthony Burgess's *Clockwork Orange* offers a faint modern parallel to the ancient awareness of the ethical virtue of music. By his psalmody, David was able to appease the conniption fits of King Saul. No one disputes the power of music to put us in the mood, but the ancients extend the power of harmony to actual manipulation of the flesh. The aulos, associated both with the cult of Dionysius and with healing, had properties that directly affected body parts. Its "sweet tones" [*moduli lenes*] were guaranteed to cure a gouty hip[128]; the aulos could also affect the loins in a different way. It so aroused one drunken youth into a rage over a woman that Pythagoras had to stop him dead in his tracks with a timely spondee.[129] Likewise, Plutarch, in his "Advice to the Bride and Groom," mentions a certain tune designed for the aulos called the "Rampant Stallion," which, when played before a stallion and a mare, resulted in foals.[130]

Closing in on afflictions "down below," the Anglo-Saxon makers of charms had a number of incantations for diarrhoea [*utsiht*]. One incantation for *utsiht* is "to be sung on a soft-boiled egg nine times for three days."[131] For *wambewaerce* [colic, bowel pain], keep this in mind:

> When you see a dung beetle on the ground throwing up earth, seize him and the heap [it has made] with both hands, wave him vigorously with your hands and say three times, "remedium facio ad ventris dolorem" [I concoct this cure for pain in the abdomen]. Then throw away the beetle over your back; take care not to look after it.[132]

One practical joker in the Middle Ages came up with nostrums to cause fart attacks. Perhaps they originated as an incanted curse, perhaps just as friendly horseplay, but whatever the reason, the following home recipes from the hugely popular *Book of Secrets* promised to inflict galloping flatulence on the chosen victim:

> If the hairs of an Ass be taken, which are nigh his privy member, and be given to any man broken in with any kind of wine in a drink, he beginneth anon to fart. Likewise if any man taketh the eggs of Pismires [ants] and breaketh them, and casteth them into water, and give them to any man in a drink, he ceaseth not anon to fart. They do likewise with wine.
>
> Take the blood of a snail, dry it up in a linen cloth, and make of it a wick, and lighten it in a lamp, give it to any man thou wilt, and say "lighten this," he shall not cease to fart, until he let it depart, and it is a marvelous thing.[133]

These prescriptions have by this point lost their incantatory virtue and descended to superstitious maledicta. Yet they carry a memory of language of such force that it enacted its own intentions; such language incants, revealing the rhythms of both music and grammar. Language in its most powerful and persuasive form is *carmen* [song, spell, charm] demonstrating that the first and most powerful utterance of all, *fiat lux* [let there be light], charmed creation into being.

Broken Air

In this *musica mundana* where the four elements—earth, air, fire, water—coexist in symphonic tension, the air we breathe is not a pure single element but a compound of the four. Common earth, fire, and water, such as we see and use every day, are not pure substances but an admixture of all. We thus move within and inhale a medium that itself replicates the euphonic ratios of the universe. There is a "symphysis" between our inner being and the elements, and between the lower *aer* of the earth and the upper *aether* of which the heavens are composed.[134]

The air is impregnated with sound, and a well-tempered air is intrinsically harmonious, because it is "mixed" in good proportions. Bad-tempered air is already a kind of noise even though it may not register on the ear. Harmony is *concordia discors*, a careful proportion of sounds different but compatible. "Consonance is the concord of mutually dissimilar pitches brought together into one."[135] Dissonance occurs not only when incompatible pitches sound together but also when two sounds, each trying to dominate the other, percuss and intermingle unpleasantly in the ear.[136] A sixteenth-century tract notes how a man, unable to gain the attention of a group while music was being played, "let goe a rouncing poupe, which base was hearde above the counter-tenor."[137] The offense lies not only in the rouncing poop's sheer volume but also in the insubordinacy of a lesser tone, of the one that should remain muted. Noise possesses a moral force lost on modern ears; it is a kind of audible violence; corruption is something one can hear. Within the acoustical cosmos, noise inhabits sound less as *audibilia* of some precise pitch or decibel count than relationally, as a principle of violence.

In a cosmos of singing spheres, silence itself represents sound that earthly ears cannot register. Because our mortal ears are so dull, we cannot hear the harmonies perpetually sounding above us and beneath our feet: "The ears of mortals are filled with this sound, but they are unable to hear it."[138] Whatever moves makes sound naturally, and apparent absence of sound is no more than a hidden presence. If silence is a kind of utterance, noise prevents one from hearing the sound of silence; it disallows stillness. It is not silence that is the other of sound, but noise. The decorous "silence" of women and peasants is justified ideologically not as muzzled absence of *vox* but as musical undertone that tacitly assents to and sustains the clear voice of authority.

Noise in the sense of sheer volume also violates harmony. Any sound, no matter how pleasing, will displease and damage if increased sufficiently in volume. When the cannon first assumed its place in European armies in the fourteenth century, its arresting quality was less the danger posed by its projectile possibilities than its sheer loudness.

> Also to make them within afrayd, they made a marveylous great bombard of l. fote of lengthe, shotyng stone of a marveylous weyght; and whan this bombarde shot, it might well be harde by day tyme fyve myle of, and by nyght ten, and it made suche a noyse in the goynge, as though all the dyvels of hell had bene in the way.[139]

We have already seen how the musical "bombard" is related to Roland's *bombulum*; here we have the same word applied to battlefield artillery[140]; it conjures up the image of the new weapon as an iron butt that farts out cannonballs. Noise is itself a weapon, accosting a body with external force, reducing totalities to shattered parts, bursting eardrums, and breaking asunder. Noise spells danger to physical integrity.

There is a dense nexus of ideas that connects the highly disparate ideas of "air" that we inhale, that we sever when we break wind, that is violently sundred in noise; of a musical "air," as in Bach's "Air on a G String," an "aria" of a soloist, the "air" of a person (as in their manner or disposition), and an "aura." All these denote different ideas, yet the same word connects their roots—Latin *aer*, which itself derives from Greek *aēr* [mist, air]. The air of ancient cosmology supports the earth with its density, hugging the *terra* like a corset to prevent it bursting from its stationary position in the cosmos.[141]

Air affects our moods with its weight and character just as music does. In another fifteenth-century grammar book, the word *aura* (a synonym of L. *aer*) appears translated in English as "weather."

> "Y am sclepy for þe weder ys sleepy."
> "Ego sum somnolentus quia aura est somnefera."[142]

Where the more precise Latin distinguishes between sleepy [*somnolentus*] and sleep-inducing [*somnefera*], the English uses the same word, bestowing, as it were, human properties on the air surrounding us. *Aer* is spoken of almost as a living, embodied thing: "the air [*aer*] itself sees and hears and makes sounds alongside us, for none of these operations can be executed without the air; why it even moves with us."[143] So encompassing an animate presence has air that we find ourselves never alone, even though no one else is around. In a world where we guard jealously our personal space from invasions by other bodies, pongs, and sneezed microbes, this companionable air attends us continually, sustains us in breath, and makes a community of one. Creaturely in itself, the air rearranges subject/object relations as a continuum, and causes our selfhood to expand and contract with the elements.

Air is both various and changeable in its temperament. Latin *temperare* means "to combine" (as in "tempered steel"), "to regulate," and "to restrain" (as in "temperance"), and all these meanings lie within the notion of a well-tempered air, or, in the case of Bach's *Das wolhtemperierte Clavier*, of an equal-tempered tuning of the keyboard. Well-tempered air is mixed in good or equal proportions; it is sweetly dispositioned, and creates a like mood within one who moves and breathes within it. A musical "air" simply makes aurally explicit the implicitly harmonious character of the air we inhabit. Because percussed air produces sound, the sweet sound of an "ayre" represents air that percusses and mixes in a rhythmically pleasing way.

We emanate air, most evidently when we speak, breathe, belch, or fart, and also when we withhold breath. Medieval iconography regularly depicts holiness as an aura around the head or a mandorla or a *vesica* [L. literally, "bladder"] around the body; most usually the aura surrounds the head as a halo because the highest part of the body, the head, as worthier part of the body [*dignior pars corporis*],[144] was considered the most divine part, ruling over the rest of the body.[145] The upper part of the body is the holiest. It was the head, breast, shoulders, and brachial joints of the Holy Roman Emperor that were anointed with holy oil, the lower body representing his mundane aspect, just as Christ's head represents his godhead, and his feet, his manhood.[146] Likewise, it is the openings of the head alone that are anointed in baptism. As a pagan and imperial symbol, the halo denotes perpetuity and dignity, and can adorn not only humans but also holy cities, such as Rome.[147] Christianized, the symbol comes to represent sanctity. Pagan or Christian, the halo denotes a different physics of space and time within its sweep; it marks out a line of separation between two modes of being, perpetual and mundane, sacred and profane. The monarch's crown enacts in noble metal the idea of the halo, while stained glass, manufactured in huge quantities in the Middle Ages, casts an aura of colored light around the various representations of saints and worthies in church windows. Latin *halos* ultimately derives from Greek *halōs*, a (disc-shaped) threshing-floor. The circular threshing-floor becomes the holy space where actors, performing in the name of Dionysus, assumed the aura of divinity by incantation and the wearing of masks. Yet to a medieval Latin clerisy with minimal knowledge of Greek, *halos* has more immediate and obvious connection with Latin *halare* [to breathe]; a halo is a divine exhalation.

The halo, or "nimbus" or "aureole," does not simply emanate light but also impregnates the air. A nimbus literally means "storm-cloud," and can be understood as a protective sheath that descends upon a divine presence, to veiling its radiance from profane onlookers; such clouds, (denoted in the Latin by *nubes*) appear in the Christian story of the transfiguration (Luke 9.34–5), in the Hebrew story of the giving of the Ten Commandments

(Exodus 19.16), and in Greek myth when the gods come to earth in disguise.[148] The Christian halo represents the force or virtue of the saint's presence, which overpowers the surrounding air, imbuing it with sanctity. These emanations or auras can be sensed variously: visually, as light or the *nubes* of smoky darkness; aurally, as music; and olfactorily, as perfume. The fragrance of "roses, lilies, and many other flowers"[149] routinely surrounds the corpses of saints, such as St. Guthlac; while in ancient Egyptian tomb paintings, cones of solid perfume, depicting the dead person's blessedness, performs the symbolic work of a halo.[150]

Secular haloes also exist. For Petrarch and other Italian and Provençal love poets, the beloved is surrounded with an aura that is both radiant and musical. The heroine of Petrarch's *canzoniere*, Laura, is, quite literally, inhaled by the poet, for her name itself—*l'aura*—constitutes his living breath,[151] while her heavenly singing and voice form a gentle breeze or aura (*l'aura*) around her.[152] The air around her is permeated with music, and her fleeting moods form the surrounding "climate."[153] Even pages emanate an aura. When in *Purgatorio* Dante salutes the painter, Oderisi of Gubbio, and praises his illumination, Oderisi modestly defers to the greater art of Franco of Bologna, whose pages, he claims, "smile" more than his own (xi.79–83). Dante's metaphor draws from the tradition that the rich adornment of manuscripts made the letters shine with joy, as if "illuminated."[154]

Finally, consider the anti-halo. The illuminator of the *Romance of Alexander* creates a number of butts in the margins, but one in particular shows the tainted air of a fart (plate 3.)[155] The farter's head twists around to get a look at the effect he creates. Look closely at the buttocks, which the man holds apart. Issuing from the butthole, three squiggles can only mean one thing. It is rare enough for a fart to be drawn in this way in medieval illumination; usually it is more indirectly figured; but here, in this antihalo of stink, noise, decay, and carnality, we come face to butt with an undivine exhalation, the grotesque inversion of sanctity.

Bad-tempered air, *mal-aria*, is no joke. Henry of Huntingdon relates that, in 1135, the stench [*foetor*] from the corpse of Henry I of England was so vile that it killed the bystanders.[156] Sharp noises we all know to avoid, but Boorde is more anxious about noxious odors, the dangers of "all thynges the whiche is vaporous or dothe fume," such as: "caryn [carrion], synkes, wyddrawghtes [drains], pisse-bolles [piss-bowls], snoffe of candellys, dunghylles, stynkynge canellys [channels], and stynkynge standyng waters, & stynkynge marshes with suche contagyous eyres [airs]."[157] All these hurt the head, brain, and memory. Worse, bad air infects the blood, and engenders corrupt humors, such that nothing except poison can so damage us as contagious air.[158] Where all other sensory data must pass through the thalamus before reaching the cerebral cortex, smell is first processed in the limbic lobe, which triggers our most basic instincts.[159] Even before we consciously register a smell, and put a name on it, we have reacted to it with our bodies. In his own contemporary frame of reference, Galen also attests to the immediacy of smell, claiming that it is the brain rather than the nose that smells, the nasal passages being mere conduits.[160] What we inhale at once becomes a part of ourselves, even before we consciously register the fact.

The Nose Knows

Humans are not good smellers, almost anosmatic in comparison to our canine friends. Sight is invariably the aristocrat of the five senses, while for Aristotle smell ranks last, so inferior is it in the human organism.[161] Plato's explanation for the lowliness of the sense is that our nostrils are too narrow for the two elements of earth and water to enter and too wide for those of fire and air; since smell fumes are more rarefied than earth or water, but coarser than fire or air, our nostrils are both too wide and not wide enough. Where the other senses employ a complex taxonomy of percepts, the human nose really possesses only two categories into which all pongs must fall, namely, pleasant and unpleasant.[162] A donkey sitting in front of a musical instrument is a medieval emblem of the inability to interpret aright,[163] and something similar would be fitting with humans and smells. Just as we remain deaf to cosmic music, so we never smell the infinite smell secrets carried in the air. Imagine the sensory overload of smelling everything: what a burden of omniscience, what simultaneous loneliness and involvement in the intimacies of all. Süskind's Grenouille, protagonist of *Perfume*, possesses the god-like yet tragic power such olfactory knowing brings. Moreover, smell is the most powerful catalyst of all to memory. Proust's "vast structure of recollection" is captured in a drop of essence.[164]

It is no casual figure of speech that intuition is olfactory, when, for example, we talk about something smelling fishy. The biographer of Cola di Rienzo offers a curious commentary on Aristotle's *On Prophesy in Sleep*, in which he argues that revelatory dreams are in part composed of the smells of other people's thoughts about us. For Aristotle, dreams are the operation of the inner sense called the imagination,[165] which is capable of retaining and replaying sense images long after the initial object of sense perception has been removed. During the waking hours, these imagined sensory impressions are held in check by the actual impressions of the external senses and by our conscious reason; but at night, with no external stimuli to distract, with reason napping, the imagination is at liberty to hyperbolize. A faint ringing in the ears becomes a thunderstorm in the dreamer's imagination, a drop of spit honey, and mild warmth a burning fire.[166] In all this exaggeration may lie a scintilla of truth, which in the waking hours is indiscernible, but when vindicated by subsequent events in waking life, appears in retrospect prophetic.

Imaginative life is intensified during sleep because bodily forces withdraw inwards: "sleep is a sort of concentration, or natural recoil, of the hot matter inwards."[167] When awake, our spirits are naturally dispersed and outwardly focused, but at nighttime "all the spirits are brought together within the fantasy and the imagination, and thus they are more sensitive."[168] Already in a heightened state of potency and receptivity, the imagination is doubly strengthened at night, for in the quiet hours, the air is a more perfect medium for the transmission of sense impressions from without, which would, in the daytime, be quickly dispersed.[169] Our Italian commentator then elaborates on Aristotle's text to explain how the dreamer may discern the thoughts of another:

> Now Aristotle maintains that the air is changed not only by physical action, but also by the will. Let us now imagine a man who wishes to kill another; the spirits within him are inflamed; the inflamed spirits change the air according to the quality of that kindled choler; the changed air reaches the intended victim. He is asleep, and therefore his spirits are attuned and sensitive; he senses the anger of his enemy, either in his own appearance or in something similar.[170]

We inhale another's hatred, and "smell" it only in our sleep, so subtle is the whiff of heated choler. The intentions of another are fumous, smellable, and can be discerned by those "temperate persons who have not clouded their minds with debauchery and strange foods, and especially at the time of night called aurora, when. . .the brain is purified, and the spirits temperate."[171] Night is the time for mystery, for quietude, when noise is not permitted, when curfew is imposed. It is the "natural" time for sleep and restoration of the body. The sleeping person, breathing rhythmically at the top end and farting in time at the other, exhibits the body in repose, its north and south ends aligned with the stars, inspiring and expiring. In this state where reason is quieted and the dominion of the eye ended, the nose reigns.

Expounding Aristotle further, the writer notes how air, the medium through and in which we move and breathe, is permeable and receptive to all motion. Chaucer uses the same image as does the biographer of Cola di Rienzo, namely, widening concentric circles when a stone is thrown into water.[172] We have already considered the definition of sound as broken air; the point here is that the air is "cut" by anything that changes its composition, such as movement of a physical body, or smell. Air also touches us, for it is a kind of body, says Aristotle: one should think of the touch of the air as a sort of rubbing, like a wiping or a washing.[173] Stinks hit the air and then the stinking air hits our noses. Hatred, inflaming the spirits within, heats the choler and sends out hate fumes; the angry person emits an aura of malicious intention. In waking hours, one would not usually sniff out another's hostile thoughts, but at night, when the spirits are at their most powerful, we smell out another's intentions and apprehend them as a dream. The commentator gives a physiological reason for the dream's significance, and the argument that the stimulus is choler fumes from the person thinking about you is remarkably molecular in conception.

Does hatred have a distinctive odor? We think of substances as unchanging substrates that acquire different smells as their external circumstances change; the noun remains constant and the adjectival qualifier changes. Yet there are cultures where the passage of time itself is marked out in terms of smell changes.[174] The biographer of Cola di Rienzo seems to have understood that at least in the quiet of the night our olfactory powers have a similar potency, that knowledge itself smells. The nose can discern truths not translatable into words or *visibilia*. In Apuleius' story, in which he was metamorphosed into an ass, the witch Pamphilë summons good-looking men to her to take them as lovers by the "stench" [*nidor*] of their own hair burning in her enchanted fire.[175] As powerful as an incantation, smell wordlessly moves us by its paralinguistic authority.

With air as porous and receptive as it is, *aeromancy*, divination by the air, was a recognized art,[176] though often tainted by an association with witchcraft. By the early modern period, it had weakened to mean little more than canny weather forecasting (*OED*, s.v. *aeromancy*, n.), but its earlier sense bears witness to the mysteries of the pregnant air. As late as the eighteenth century, the art of reading the air occasionally resurfaced. Bottineau, a Frenchman working in the Isle of France (now Mauritius), claimed the art of "nauscopie,"[177] of being able accurately to predict the arrival of ships days before they were visible by means of watching the horizon and "anticipating by means of smell."[178]

The captured and distilled "essence" of a plant smells intensely, and, Lucretius observes, it comes from deep within us, emanating when that inmost being is broken open, for "everything seems to smell more strongly when broken or ground up or disintegrated by fire."[179] Smell's dispersal throughout the body becomes a way of imagining our very life force, the vital spirit: "As easily could the scent be torn out of lumps of incense without destroying their nature as mind and spirit could be abstracted from the whole body without total dissolution."[180] As a materialist and atomist, Lucretius is perplexed by the question of how a body can give off smell (atoms) and not diminish in size; his conclusion is that odor particles are both too minute and too evenly dispersed throughout the body for their emanation to diminish bodily mass appreciably:

> Therefore the vital spirit as a whole must consist of very tiny atoms, linked together throughout veins, flesh and sinews—atoms so small that, when all

the spirit has escaped from the whole body, the outer contour of the limbs appears intact and there is no loss of weight. The same thing happens when the bouquet has evaporated from the wine, or the sweet perfume of an ointment has escaped into the air, or some substance has lost its savor.[181]

Smell expresses our innermost being, invisible to the eye. It plays a central role in sacrifice because it occurs when the body is broken open. It is as if the act of breaking open or of violation of a body makes it more present than when it is whole. This assumption also lies behind the idea of desecration that informs medieval carnivalistic humor. In debasing the image, its reality intensifies. The literalization of the lamb of God as a real lamb in the Towneley *Second Shepherds' Play*, and of the Holy Spirit as a fart in Chaucer's *Summoner's Tale* are not just examples of a perverse pleasure in profaning the sacred, but express the belief that in descrecation we encounter the holy. Defacement makes the transcendent immanent. The tired contrariety between sacredness and profanity we call the hallmark of medieval art is understood better as a higher order of synthesis in which profanity becomes a kind of devotion. "Desecration is more than the inverse of the sacred or sacrifice. Something more complicated than inversion is going on. . . . Unmasking is a device for making, rather than dissolving, mystery."[182]

Smells, says Plato, occur when substances are in the process of "liquefaction, decomposition, dissolution, or evaporation."[183] The smellable is in transition, in an intermediate state of becoming rather than being; its identity uncertain. The fart existentially belongs to such a mode of transition, for not only is it the result of organic decomposition, it also comes into being only when the body is "broken open," and strikes the air. As the intestines disown the fart, the question of propriety, in its twofold sense, arises: "who owns that fart?" and "how fitting was it?" Continuous and without boundary, odor throws into disarray the lines of space and decorum between selfhood and otherness, lines that seem self-evident and indisputable to eyes that can see only two separate bodies.

I / Thou

Disciples of wise men are accustomed to behave with great modesty. . . . . Even after entering the toilet, one must be modest and not uncover his garments until he sits down. He shall not wipe with the right hand. He shall move away from everyone and [for example] enter the innermost room of a cave and relieve himself there. If he relieves himself behind a fence, he shall go far away so that his fellow man will not hear a sound if he breaks wind.[184]

Thus prescribed Maimonides, twelfth-century Jewish philosopher-physician. His rule of toilet etiquette occurs in a work, *Hilkhot De'ot* [*Laws*

Concerning Character Traits], which concerns itself with wisdom, the care of the self and right social relations. Sounding more like Aristotle in his definition of virtue as the mean between extremes than an exegete of the Torah, Maimonides spends his first chapters elaborating how the wise man controls his individual character and passions to follow the "middle way"; his last chapters provide guidance for such moderation in society as a whole; his fifth chapter, from which this quote is taken, mediates between care for the self and for society, and concerns itself more with actions than with character tendencies, suggesting that it is by an individual's actions that the one and the many unite as a social whole. By breaking wind and wiping yourself, even on the quiet, you perfect the duty of a social being. To be a good neighbor, one has to learn to fart right.

The ritual of the privy, as its name suggests, usually stakes out the moment of the self in solitude, when the body is set off from society, tending to its needs in private. Farting and defecation are deemed solitary acts, ostensibly from modesty, but also from an intuitive sense of hygiene, and an ancient fear of vulnerability to attack when assuming the squatting position.

Although solitude is deemed the proper circumstance for evacuation, body functions are inherently sympathetic acts, inspiring others by natural accord to participate. Laurent Joubert observes the mimetic aspect of body functions, by which a "natural accord" excites us to laugh when another laughs, or yawn when another yawns, and sometimes even "we piss out of fellowship" ["on pisse par conpagnie"].[185] In its necessary acts the body not only takes care of itself, it also invites the world to join the party.

A farts occurs in a space small enough for smellability and audibility. Recipients are not far enough away not to smell it, yet never so united with it that they mistake it for their own. Lucretius explains how the olfactory sense requires a shorter firing range than hearing, for smell is composed of larger atoms than is sound, and cannot pass through dense thicknesses (such as stone walls) where sound atoms can.[186]

Not only is smell a more physically intimate experience than hearing, but certain kinds of smell, rotten ones to be precise, are more intimate again.

> Al swete smyllyng thing hath more purite,
> And is more spiritual then stynkyng may be;
> wherfore it is in Ayre more pentratife,
> And more extendible, & is also to lyfe
> More acceptable, as frende to nature.[187]
>
> [All sweet smelling things are purer and more airy than stinky things. Thus they penetrate and disperse in the air more efficiently, and are more wholesome, an aid to nature.]

Sweet smells diffuse more easily because their purity makes them lighter. In contrast, stinking smells are heavy, having more matter in them, or, in modern chemical terms, the stink molecules are less prone to become airborne because they are large and stable. It is particularly gross then to inhale another's fart, because of the solid matter it contains. An intimacy one hesitates to share with just anyone, the fart brings the other near at hand, into a state of "intimate exteriority or 'extimacy' " in which one is neither fully subject nor fully object, neither pure identity nor pure difference.[188] Occurring on the extimate threshold between self-identity and otherness, the fart both sets apart subject from object and confuses them. The one-who-is-not-you, the body of the other, the corpus of the Middle Ages is only a *bombulum* away.

Ambiguity between fart perpetrator and victim resides also at the level of language. Middle English *smell*, like the Modern English verb, describes the states of either perceiving a smell or emanating one. An apocryphal anecdote about lexicographer Samuel Johnson relates that once, when a woman rebuked him with, "You smell, sir," he corrected her: "No, you smell me, and I stink." The "full greyt dowtfull" uncertainty of the subject is also evident in an entry from the diary of Samuel Pepys, June 7, 1665:

> This day, much against my Will, I did in Drury-lane see two or three houses marked with a red cross upon the doors, and "Lord have mercy upon us" writ there—which was a sad sight to me, being the first of the kind that to my remembrance I ever saw. It put me into an ill conception of myself and my smell, so that I was forced to buy some roll=tobacco [*sic*] to smell and to chaw, which took away the apprehension."[189]

Given the general belief that plague could be caught by inhalation, we understand Pepys's "ill conception of himself and his smell" as his anxiety that disease had penetrated his system via his nose, an unease only dispelled by overriding the inhalation with the stronger smell and taste of a quid of tobacco. However, in grammatical terms, it is not clear whether "smell" here denotes the pong he exuded or the one he sniffed.

Pepys seems intently aware of himself as an active subject doing the inhaling, yet he is in fact the object or patient or sufferer of the noxious whiff of plague. In medieval faculty psychology, *passio* refers to the motion of the senses; sense, says Aquinas, is essentially a passive power (*ST*, 1a.78.3). It comes from the Latin verb *pati* [to suffer], from which "passion," "passive," and "patient" variously derive. We have in Modern English lost the connection between passivity and passion, although "affect" in its nominal and verbal form does retain some link between emotion and the state of being acted upon. The lesson from the vocabulary of medieval faculty psychology, now erased by Modern English, is that the "I" who senses, the subject of the act of inhaling, is in that moment also the object of the act. To sense is to suffer, to undergo. Smelling another person constructs simultaneously an active olfactory knowledge and passive sufferance of him or her. Smell undoes the grammar of difference between subject and object, self and the world.

> Belche thou neare to no mans face
> With a corrupt fumosytye.
> But turne from such occasyon, friend
> Hate such ventositye.[190]
> [Don't do a smelly burp in someone's face; avert your head, for such belches are stinking wind.]

The precept comes from a sixteenth-century book of social etiquette for the young. It may take us aback that the rule should be spelled out thus, yet it registers the delicacy of the extimate space between self and other. What is today ineptly called "personal space" is more accurately a smell exchange where subject/object relations are put to the test and sorted; some may enter, others definitely may not. The extimate belch is not so different from the fart, for the belly's food is already decomposing, and is simply a fart *in potentia* and upwardly mobile. Our respiratory and digestive pipelines are conduits that give entrance and exit to the same gases and substances. For Galen, attraction and discharge occur in the same channel[191]; hence vomiting is described as diarrhea from the upper part of the stomach.[192] He also refers to the distressing condition of *ileus* or *volvulus* in which the anal exit is blocked so that turds must exit through the only available orifice left to them, viz. the mouth.[193] Galen's description of bodily waste as an "alien load"[194] demonstrates how even before one's shit and farts put into question the relation between self and one's neighbor, they have already rendered one's own bodily product a stranger, already changed identity into difference and made an object out of a subject. Poop is baby's first gift to the world, the first medium of a circulation and exchange that would culminate in money.[195] Our earliest labor was lovingly to recreate ourselves by making a turd in our own image. Here in the contents of our diapers, in our stomach's remains, we saw ourselves as objects beaming back at us. In our mortal leftovers, we attained a first moment of self- reflection, exclaiming with excitement and disgust, "That's me! Look at me!" Just so did the fart extend our puny bodies into space, creating a stinking aura of a presence impossible to ignore.

In modern evolutionary terms, we chart the progress of the senses as a development from the lower faculties of taste and touch to the higher ones of sight and hearing. The most rudimentary life forms only apprehended that with which they made direct contact; knowledge was a process of bumping into something and gobbling it down, as they experienced the world "one taste at a time."[196] Smell, the next evolutionary development, facilitated sensation via the mediation of the air; still blind and deaf but now with a snout, animate beings snuffled their way into knowledge of a world out there. After that develop the powers of hearing and finally of sight, but smell marks the great evolutionary advance into a higher being that can control one's environment, that can project one's influence into the space around. Smell extends the self beyond the perimeter of flesh.

Long before modern biology, ancient faculty psychology plotted the hierarchy of the senses in similar fashion. Lowest on the ladder of sensate being, notes Aristotle, are the "inner" senses of touch and taste, so called because they require unmediated contact with their object. Taste, smell, and touch are "sluggish" [*tardus*] alluding no doubt to their need for direct proximity with the sense object.[197] The outer senses of hearing and sight, on the other hand, apprehend through a medium, and render the extended world knowable, nameable, and controllable. Spank in the middle comes smell, somewhere between needing direct contact with its object and being able to know it from afar. The lowest common denominators among all animate creatures are touch and taste, because these are necessary to nutrition.[198] Without taste, they would gulp in poison not knowing until too late the difference between it and food. Only to locomotive animals are given the higher senses of smell, hearing, and sight, for they operate by means of external media. Lowly smell has more in common with taste, the sense that lies below it, than it has with hearing, the sense above it.[199]

With touch and taste, one knows only by touch and taste. Forget about Platonic ideas or abstract reasoning, for the only things worth knowing about are what touches the skin or enters the mouth. Suck it and see. To apprehend only haptic realia means that the object to some degree has to become the subject in order to be known. We draw the world toward us, literally incorporating it, making it part of our own bodies. In this engagement, there is no fixed sense of object, no real "Other," for in order to know it, one has made the object "self" if only for a moment until one spits it out or moves away. Self and the Other are to that extent largely undifferentiated. Conversely, we have no fixed sense of subject. "Of all the senses, that of smell—which is attracted without objectifying—bears closest witness to the urge to lose oneself in and become the 'other.' "[200] With hearing and sight, most egregiously with sight, we make objects of things; creating critical spaces between self and the rest of the world, even as we touch things we watch ourselves doing so. With eyes trained to identify things at a distance, we cannot but make objects of things. Smell, somewhere in between the aloofness of vision and the immediacy of touch, throws into question the ontological and epistemological relation between ipseity and alterity.

It is generally Plato rather than Aristotle who regards smell as a fumous substance, and if for Plato's fumes we understand molecules, then our modern explanation for olfaction is reasonably consistent with that of Plato.[201] Aristotle in contrast emphasizes the immaterial nature of the sense percept, and this emphasis becomes the ground of scholastic faculty psychology. What the senses receive is not an actual piece of the object sensed however tiny but information, or in scholastic terms, the form or species or intention of the object. The argument works for sight and hearing, but is obviously problematic for taste and touch. Belonging to the median sense of smell, the olfactory "intention" seems to be both information and the object itself in minuscule quantity. Inasmuch as smell is one of the contact senses (taste and touch), it functions by immediate inhalation of actual matter. However, existing between the contact senses and the virtual senses (hearing and sight), it also functions by virtual apprehension. Thus Norton speaks of the fume as "the liknes of the same thinge / From whome that fume had his bigynnyng," speaking about the pong as some kind of imago or idolon.[202] To this extent, smell apprehends its object indirectly by means of likeness as well as through immediate contact; it reflects even as it senses. It objectifies in the same moment as it subjectifies, and distances itself from the thing smelled even as it draws near.

Defining knowledge as immaterial species or intention applies best to the aristocrat of senses, sight. After all, when we see a stone we do not have a piece of the stone in our eye. In Chapter 4 of his *Poetics*, Aristotle betrays this bias toward the visual in knowledge:

> We enjoy contemplating the most precise images [*eikonas*] of things whose actual sight is painful to us, such as the forms of the vilest animals and of corpses. The explanation of this too is that understanding gives great pleasure not only to philosophers but likewise to others too, though the latter have a smaller share in it. This is why people enjoy looking at images, because through contemplating them it comes about that they understand and infer what each element means, for instance that "this person is so-and-so."[203]

Most reflective of the sense-organs, the eyes hold the world at a distance and know from afar. The space between sensing subject and object of sensation enables games of representation, simulation, seeming, imitation, and thus the play of recognition. The spectacle that drama is affords this pleasure of recognition, even when the scene is painful. A simulated taste of something horrible, on the other hand, is just as vile as the real thing.

Direct sensation—pleasant or unpleasant—cannot reflect, cannot distinguish between the authentic and the imitated, and can neither seem nor play games. The object touched and the feel of it on the skin are indistinguishable; in contrast, it is not the object seen or heard but the sight or hearing of the object that moves us. Participating in both reflection and direct experience, the nose alone responds directly to the thing-in-itself and mediately to the smelled apprehension of it.

In what sense do we know another when we smell them? Sight is the sense most closely identified with knowing, but smelling is believing too. In 1584, Chaucer was congratulated because he "smelt out the absurdities of poperie."[204] "Do you smell a fault?" asks Shakespeare's Gloucester.[205] The sixteenth century offers a wealth of phrases that demonstrate the wide purchase of the olfactory as a kind of intuitive knowing (*OED*, s.v. *smell*, v.[2a,2b,3]), and the phrase "to smell a rat" also comes from this period.

In contrast, Middle English is comparatively impoverished in smell–figures of speech. Why should this be? It is not that smell is not mentioned in medieval writing. Sin is routinely described by homilists in terms of stench, usually excremental. It is a crying shame, says John Mirk, that the Holy Spirit has to hold his nose on smelling our sins while physical pongs are the only things that offend our nostrils.[206] The clustering of olfactory metaphors in the early modern period is significant precisely because they are metaphors. That is, as smell is increasingly recognized as an organ of empirical knowledge—and not a very important one at that—it increasingly becomes a metaphor for (animalistic) intuitive perception; hence, the blinded Gloucester is thrown out to "smell his way to Dover."[207]

Earlier medieval use of the olfactory, on the other hand, is no metaphor. It has its empirical uses, medieval treatises regularly recommending to smell urine for signs of distemper; medieval smell can be disparaged as an animalistic sense; but it is also associated with divinatory powers and with sanctity. It represents a way of knowing beyond language and commonplace powers of perception; it outs identities that are otherwise imperceptible. St. Anthony, once in a boat, complained about a devilish pong [odor pessimus et amarus]. The boatmen dismissively attributed it to the fish and pickled meat on board, but St. Anthony was not to be deterred, whereupon a young man possessed by an evil spirit declared himself.[208] The olfactory is both animalistic and mystical, which is a reason for its being invoked so often in devotional writing to convey both the stench of sin and the fragrance of holiness. For St. Augustine, influenced by Neoplatonic idealism, smell smacks of the sensual and has little to offer by way of epistemological insight: "as for the seduction of sweet smells, I am not too interested in it" ["de inlecebra odorum non satago nimis"][209]; Nietzsche, however, sick of the stink of metaphysics, saw in smell the possibility of knowledge marginalized, from Augustine to

Hegel, to the raptures of mystics, the thunderings of po-faced preachers and the snufflings of dogs.[210]

Like ears, nostrils never shut voluntarily. Permanently open for business, they are how we receive the world. Ears may be stopped for an indefinite period, but without inhalation, we die within minutes. The very act of drawing breath is one with smelling: "man only smells during inhalation. . . .To perceive no smell without inhaling seems to be peculiar to man."[211] For as long as we are alive, we sniff the world around us, including ourselves. To be is to smell. The fact that "essence," as in essential oil, comes from *essentia*, "being," reminds us that smell sums up our ontological identity. To be is to stink. An essential oil is a substance's self in a bottle. The association between essence and refined fragrant fluid develops, we believe, out of the alchemical search for the fifth essence, or quintessence. Smell, after all, is one of the primary means for ascertaining that an alchemical transmutation has taken place, so it follows that the quintessence sums up the odorous being of a thing. As alchemy dwindles through the early modern period into mere perfumery, the links between smell and ontology loosen; to be is no longer to be a stinkard. The meaning of "essence" as purest fragrance seems to gain currency in English around the seventeenth century. Once more, the early modern period marks an epistemological shift when essence qua smell forgets that its roots lie in being. Ben Jonson, however, does not forget, and reminds us that the essence of a fart is a metaphysical *mysterium*.

> *Nath:* They write from Leipzig (reverence to your ears)
> The art of drawing farts of dead bodies,
> Is by the brotherhood of the Rosy Cross
> Produc'd unto perfection, in so sweet
> And rich a tincture—
> *Fit.* As there is no princess
> But may perfume her chamber with th'extraction.
>
> *P. jun.* There's for you, princess!
> *P. Can.* What, a fart for her?
> *P. jun.* I mean the spirit.[212]

It is our warmbloodedness that makes us exude so many smells. Through every pore and orifice we wrap ourselves in smell, signing the air. As dogs well know, urine offers the most exact signature, shit and saliva close runners up.[213] To smell the intestinal by-product of others brings one into extimate relation with them; more profound than psychoanalysis, it entails a knowledge of them more intimate than sight or hearing, more detached than touching or licking, a knowledge of others where their very being participates in yours. The stink of a fart belongs to a different mode of being and knowing that does not sort the world in terms of self and other.

One Flesh

Extimacy—not a bad word to describe that sweet torture we call marriage, but what do farts have to do with mating?

Freud's Rat Man was a noted *renifleur* or osphresiolagniac, which is to say that, like a dog, he both recognized everyone by their smell and derived pleasure from it (*SE*, 10:295). Freud had observed similar phenomena in other neurotics, and it was observance of such olfactory obsessions that led him to theorize the equation between civilization and the repression of smell; the more we advanced, the more we repressed the olfactory. Our advance beyond primitivism is tracked by the proportionately inverse relation between disgust at body smells and interest in hygiene (*SE*, 21:93). For the primate, smell becomes less important and the visual more necessary; bodily verticality requires the domination of the eye. This point is as ancient as Plato, who, in mapping the body, finds symbolic significance in the head's position as the body's farthest point from the earth. Eyes look through air, but noses sniff the ground, and there's the difference between humans and quadrupeds.

That most animals would mate only when the female is menstruating or in heat reveals the close connection between the olfactory and the sex urge. Yet religions have systematically prohibited coition during menstruation, inverting animal wisdom in the name of purity. The human sex urge, now stimulated perpetually by the eye, becomes constant and containable rather than seasonal and imperative. Inasmuch as the suppression of smell is required in order to civilize, and female menstrual odor represents nature's key mating signal, then both smell and female animality must be suppressed in the name of progress. Shit, associated with animal sensitivity to smell, also becomes repugnant, and coprophilia—the erotic possibilities of shit—must be denied or, if indulged, sidelined as perversion. Pleasure also is repressed and such repression brings language in its wake. As man evolved slowly into *homo erectus*, the olfactory sense atrophied, and sex became increasingly a subject for taboo and anxiety, and thus for discussion. Sex is inextricably linked to the pungent smells of body fluids and waste, the very smells we wash away and object to in others. It has become our fate as a species to be aroused and disgusted in the same breath.

We spend a lot of money on perfume. Middle English *fume* is a hunting term meaning "deer turd." The word entered English from French, *le fumier* [manure]. So, *pare-fumier*, though named from the process of saturation by smoke, can also be thought of as an antidote to dung.[214] It is not only that the word for shit nestles inside perfume; perfume—or rather, countermanure—contains by the law of similars trace elements of that which it seeks to banish. Any perfumer knows that the most heavenly of scents contains small quantities of substances that, if inhaled singly and in concentrated form, would be repellent. In the historical fantasy *Perfume*, Frog [*Grenouille*], the unlikeable protagonist possesses the best nose in the world, "analytical and visionary,"[215] but was himself cursed with no odor and was therefore liked by no one; so in a desperate bid to connect with humanity, he douses himself with his own concoction. His first step is to create a basic essence of "human-being-who-gives-off-a-scent," and it proves most successful, being composed of a subtle blend of rose, geranium, lavender, peppermint, lime, old cheese, singed pork rind, sardines, rotten egg, ammonia, and cat shit.[216] Latin *fumus* [smoke] and Greek *thymos* [mind, spirit] are cognate (*OLD*, s.v. *fumus*), reminding us that essential being and stinking are the same thing.

The heavy floral essences, which number amongst the most desired of fragrances, have an almost narcotic aroma, inducing a sense of "receptivity and surrender."[217] What they have, in fact, is a fecal undertone, naturally carrying the chemical ingredient indole, which is also present in large quantities in human pooh.[218] The sultriness of such fragrances comes precisely from the smell of rot and decay that lies within its sweetness. The line between desire and disgust is fine indeed. Dogs know that smelling another dog's bottom reveals much more than does looking at a hairy face; humans always did get things the wrong way round.

The base notes of a perfume are the most ancient and precious of all perfume ingredients: sandalwood, civet, musk, amber, and so on.[219] On their own, they tend to be dark, sticky, viscous, and so gamey they seem to stink. Their virtue lies in the ability of the base notes to blend with other lighter notes. Over time, the overpowering strength of the base notes lessens and grows gentler. One needs patience with such dark sticky substances, for their being emerges only over time; their meaning evolves. The great strength of manure lies in its ability to mix itself. Shit, announces the author of *Geoponica*, requires three to four years to break down and lose its stench.[220] Haste is of the devil, assert the alchemical treatises.[221] Compost is a metaphor for marriage itself.

In covert recognition of this, a number of medieval comic tales center upon spousal waste. In the following two French texts, one narrative poem and one drama, the husband finds himself subjected to the bodily waste of his woman, in one case porridge mistaken for feces, in another a fart. Gautier le Leu recounts the story of two peasants who stay overnight with a married couple; one of them falls ill during the night and the other, Rogier, rises to get him a ladleful of gruel. He returns to the wrong bed, where the wife's bare rump sticks out from under the coverlet, and he mistakes it for the head of his companion. Rogier puts his finger to the "hole" [*le trau*] to feel if it is hairy, because his friend is bearded. It is. Rogier now sticks his nose there, thinking the man has fainted, and seeking to revive him with a kiss:

> Entrués qu'il baise le crenel,
> Li saut uns vens fors de l'anel,
> Qui rendi grant noise et grans pous,
> Il cuida qu'il soflast le pous.²²²
>
> [While he kisses the opening, a strong wind blasts forth from her fundament, gusting so noisily that he thought the companion was blowing (on the gruel).]

Rogier complains about his partner's halitosis and uncooperativeness, but the wife farts away in oblivion until, exasperated, he empties the ladle of gruel on her bottom. At this, her husband awakes, chastises her for fouling their bed, and bringing disgrace on her family name. The wife is mortified, and remorse makes her subsequently as submissive and docile as a wife can be.

The other narrative, the late-fifteenth-century *Le Pet* [The Fart],²²³ is a dramatized burlesque lawsuit fought over a wife's untimely fart. Beginning from the egg, as Horace says, the story runs as follows. It's dinnertime, and Hubert is agitating for food. Flustered, Jehannette, his wife, bends down too low and cuts an audible fart, at which her husband exclaims, "Sus donc! O que ay-je ouy sonner?" [Woah! What did I just hear?].²²⁴ Jehannette plays dumb, but in the interval of their short exchange, the stink has spread and Hubert is able to answer his own question. "Par le sang de bieu, c'est ung pet" [God's blood, it's a fart].

Jehannette is now committed to denial, and so she argues on all fronts that (1) whoever smelt it dealt it; (2) that it is impossible for her to have committed the act unknowingly; (3) that anyway she is too nobly born to have done such an unladylike thing. It is a textbook example of the kettle logic of which Freud speaks in *Jokes and Their Relation to the Unconscious*, where a man, accused of putting a hole in a borrowed kettle, offers successive and mutually exclusive defenses: "I returned it intact" and "it already had a hole in it when I borrowed it" (*SE*, 8:62). Not exactly a joke, notes Freud, it is, however, an egregious "piece of sophistry," which is exactly the kind of abuse of logic that legal argument should eschew—remember, this is a play performed for Parisian lawyers.

An eavesdropping Procureur, smelling profit, intervenes to get to the bottom of the mystery. Playing counsel to both sides (another sideswipe at avaricious attorneys), he worms a private confession from Jehannette, who fears public humiliation; her self-defense is that she farted from exertion because Hubert would not help her with moving a bundle in order to lay the table for dinner. She and the Procureur agree that this is cruel and unusual punishment [*peine extraordinaire*] on the part of Hubert, but the Procureur represents Hubert also and so, in a turn of events reminiscent of *Les Trois Meschines*, the dispute continues at court.

Hubert has been subjected to both the noise and the stink of the fart, which, we know, contains excremental matter, and this too-intimate knowledge constitutes the trauma he has suffered:

> Ung pet [. . .]
> dont j'eus si peur
> Que encores le cul me hallette.
> Et moy, qui veulx ma maison nette,
> Sans y souffrir aucune ordure,
> Je vueil qu'el[l]e répare l'injure,
> Qu'e[lle] m'a faict en ma maison.²²⁵
>
> [A fart. . .at which I took such a fright that my ass is still quivering. And I, who likes my house clean, who allows no filth, want she who cut it in my house to make good the damage.]

In the Procurer's presentation, this becomes formal grounds for complaint. The fart was so sneaky that it made Hubert quake from terror ["il en tressaillit de grand peur"] and befouled his home.²²⁶ But the judge's final decision is not what Hubert wanted to hear. Since husband and wife are one flesh and substance [*une mesme chose*], "il fault que l'ayez faict" [it follows that you cut it]. "Ce qu'il brasse, il le vous fault boire" [what one brews one must drink], announces the judge unsympathetically.²²⁷ The *obiter dictum* has a more colorful and apt counterpart in Old French, which would no doubt have sprung to contemporary minds:

> Ki merde brace merde beive
>   (*PFA*, p. 72, §1989)
>
> [He who brews shit drinks shit].

Hubert has no case against his wife, since he married her asshole [*cul*] as much as he married the rest of her; farts go with the territory of holy matrimony. Hubert appeals the decision on the grounds that he did not marry that part of her, but Jehannette claims he most certainly did, and on her wedding night at that, when he mistook her asshole for the conjugal orifice. To Hubert, this is a low blow; he cries foul, reminding her of the darkness of that particular night. But he has lost his case; he and his wife are one flesh, *cul* and all. The argument appeals to a famous judicial concept, namely, that it is impossible for a man to act unjustly toward himself: "a man cannot commit adultery with his own wife, or burglary on his own premise, or theft of his own property."[228] In our story, here comes the downside of the argument, for the converse is also true, and a wife, as part of her husband, may do him no injustice by farting in front of him. She is his own flesh and bottom; Hubert cannot sue his own ass. Whether Jehannette farted noisily or silently ["a peté ou vecy"],[229] Hubert must endure it patiently. Within the marital space, air is common, and the distinction between noise and stink, hearing and smelling evaporates.

There are a couple of points to note in these stories. First, both women's involuntary farts represent the female body as incontinent. While there are occasions when women in medieval comic tales fart deliberately,[230] they more often do it by accident. Peasants, male and female alike, are ubiquitously associated with excrement, but it is the wives' inability to control their bodily functions that is so noxious to their husbands, reminding us and them that women need a master to keep them in line. The stigma of serfdom is ultimately a "humiliating productivity"[231]—productivity of labor, bodily substance, and words—and a peasant woman is doubly sentenced by both estate and sex. Where Jehannette's bottom loses control in the kitchen, her mouth proves unruly in the courtroom, obliging the Procurer to silence her repeatedly: "Merde!/Taisez vous" [Shit! Shut up].[232] She inherits her runaway mouth from Eve, for, as one fabliau attests, after God created her, the devil added some finishing touches, including an auditory-turned-tactile flourish of a fart on her tongue, "which is why women are always yapping" ["por ce a fame tant de jangle"].[233] Second, the fact that Hubert has to take shit in the form of wifely wind obliquely recognizes, through inversion, the prerogative of Adamic authority. These stories enact both the curse of Eve and her revenge. If she must be ruled by virtue of being the weaker vessel, let her vessel be a bladder (Fr. *la vessie*, "bladder"), let her moral slackness be a question of loose bowels, let the old man get a good noseful of that frailty whose name is woman.

Many women in medieval comic literature fart by accident, such as Jehanette, the wife in Gautier's story, Tibbe, heroine of the "Feast of Tottenham," Dunbar's dame Dounteboir, and Agace in the French fabliau *Les Trois Meschines*. Accidentally farting women are figures of incontinence rather than impertinence, soiling themselves shamefully. As a parodic strain in troubadour poetry attests, even courtly ladies fart.[234] The containment of the female body, *sine qua non* of chastity, domestic governance, heredity, and patriarchal right, is undone with flatulence. Excessive in wind, moisture,[235] and words, women along with their bottoms are forever assuming an autonomy to which they are not entitled, much to their own and their husbands' mortification. The female ass acts out the legacy of the fall, for, as far as Augustine is concerned, the mark of original sin is the self-rule of that which should be ruled. His discussion of the singing bottom takes place in the larger context of his analysis of original sin. When our first parents sinned, will and the flesh separated. Before the fall, farting, erections, and all other spontaneous motions of the body occurred at the behest of the will, but after sinning, the fleshly members moved on their own, without the sanction of reason. This assumption of self-rule by that which should remain subservient is a shameful thing, and that is why we name the genitals *pudenda*, from *pudor* [shame].

> It is reasonable then that we should feel very much ashamed of such lust, and reasonable too that those members it moves or does not move by its own right, so to speak, and not in full subjection to our will [*arbitrium nostrum*], should be called "shameful parts" [*pudenda*], as they were not before man sinned.[236]

If disobedience marks the movements of our genitals and bowels, how much more so does it mark the behavior of woman, and how much more again a flatulent wife?

The husband in Gautier le Leu's story, on waking to the mess in the bed, is angered at the shame she has brought on himself and her family [*lignie*]; this is a note struck by Jehannette also, when she defends herself, claiming that "I come from a better and more unsullied family than you assert" [je suis de meilleur lignaige / Et plus nette que vous ne dictes].[237] We are back to Freud's link between civilization and hygiene: rationality entails cleanliness; well-bred people do not fart; the Rat Man's mother called his father a "common fellow" precisely because he farted at will in public (*SE*, 10:292). Hubert's grievance focuses upon the issue of hygiene. His bodily integrity has been violated and his home befouled.

The judge obliges Hubert to "have his part" [*avoir part à*] of her fart,[238] a phrase that implies sexual intimacy. Likewise, in his initial description, Hubert calls it "ung peu de vend / Que j'ay sentu, dont m'en desplaist" [a bit of wind that I smelt and which displeased me].[239] The Old French verb *sentir* means not only to smell, but also to feel in the palpable sense, to touch, and hence to embrace and to make love to. In smelling the fart, he embraced it with pleasure, yet it "displeased" him. The conflict between desire and disgust emerges explicitly as logical contradiction and explains the otherwise rather gratuitous reference to Hubert's wedding night, on which his efforts at lovemaking culminated in anal sex, or *sodomia perfecta* as the confessor-priests preferred to call it. Poor Hubert has had carnal knowledge of Jehannette's backside, by wind and by buggery. In desire, he fucked his wife, and gained excrement for gratification; then he breathed her in, and found excrement again. If Freud is right in asserting that disgust is but the repression of desire, then Hubert's petulant tirret is the measure of a desire that can express itself only by denial.

"Accordez les nez et les culz / Ensemble à tous sentemens" [let noses and assholes be of one accord in all their perceptions of things], concludes the judge in his *obiter dicta*.[240] Husband and wife are finally reconciled, but the stuff of the play is Hubert's rage, comically treated though it may be. Compare it with the angry rebellion of the sexually overworked husband of *Porcelet* against his wife's insatiable demands. The story acquires its title from the names bestowed on their genitals. The wife's genitals are called "Piglet" or "Piggy" because they are never clean and the husband's semen is called "Wheat" [*Fromant*]: their private joke is that Piggy is always hungry. One day, the sexually exhausted husband plants a single fart [*Un pet*] in the wife's lap, claiming that there is only bran left in the barn and the wheat is all gone (*NRCF*, 6:185–91, 1.38). His wind constitutes his uprising against the vincula of matrimony, against not owning his own body outright, against continually having to repay the never-ending marriage debt. The distinctively male form of his rage relies on the fantasy of the voraginous vulva as the black hole of appetite into which the man's member disappears. Rabelais, as ever, sums it up in the story of the lion who thinks an old lady's "what-d'ye-call-it" [*comment a nom*] is a mortal wound and brings eighteen bales of moss to pack it. Sixteen and a half bales later, the lion is still stuffing, and exclaims in amazement "Que diable ceste playe est parfonde" [This wound is devilish deep].[241] It is a fantasy also present in medieval medicine, when the treatises speak of the womb as if it were a magnet, attracting sperm so forcefully that "sucks in the penis,"[242] and is capable of vacuuming up male ejaculate out of tepid bathwater.

We laugh at Rabelais's story because one bale would be more than enough thank you; and at *Porcelet* because we well know that in reality the shoe is on the other foot, that more often it is the woman who receives the man's unwanted sexual demands. Against the fabliaux grotesques of voracious women such as Chaucer's Wife of Bath stands the real-life story of, for example, Margery Kempe, and her attempts to win back her body from the marriage debt so that she may take holy vows. In a world where a woman's body is hedged around with restriction, the fabliaux provide a fantasy space where it is allowed free play, where her body functions are splendidly, supercalifragilistically excessive.

The clustering of wind and excrement within the intimate space of marriage offers a commentary on that hallowed institution that declares two creatures from different families and communities to be one flesh. With low cunning, these stories fix on the one reminder guaranteed never to lose potency that the other person is most definitely not you: their intestinal waste. Most personal and prolific of bodily products, its daily presence acts as a constant reminder that spouse is not self, that one flesh consists of two, that the singleness of marriage constitutes within itself the inescapable and perpetual presence of the other.[243]

The extimate fart zone of the spousal fart also designates the privacy of the pair, establishing intimacy and excluding the outside. In the animal world, stink marks a territorial boundary that acts both as apotropaic sign to potential intruders and as the embracing of the inner community of all within the stink perimeter.[244] If your beloved's fart provides a choking reminder of the threatening otherness of this "one flesh," it also affirms that difference begins and ends with your spouse's body, that here within your arms is all the otherness there is in the world, here your horizon of being. The spousal zephyr seals off the possibility of other intruding smells. It constitutes the limit of desire and disgust. Marriage, although an exclusive relationship set apart from all other societal relationships, is a microcosm of community, an encounter that sets the constitutive limit on the encounter with the other. The spousal fart creates the first social boundary.

These ribald meditations on the intimacy and aggressions of marriage uncover the violence surrounding the daily invasions by the spouse of one's personal space. Fabliaux generally feature either lesser gentry or peasants, in other words, people who live at close quarters. While they are frequently cited for their sexist and ultimately conservative validation of every misogynist calumny in the book, they nonetheless depict scenarios where women get to shit on their husbands for a change.

Despite the fact that there was no word in Old French or Middle English for a married "couple" in the sense we know it, the nameless pair stood at the very heart of the feudal relation and of the clan.[245] The cultivation of the self has long been harbored in what is known as courtly love; it has traditionally been in medieval romance, with its cult of affect and passionate love, that an emergent subjectivity can be found. One finds one's reason to be in *fin'amor*, when wooing and in love, whether that love is adulterous or premarital. Romance ends with the wedding. Once they become a "couple per se," they vanish linguistically resuming reentry only into narrative, whether romance or fabliau, when adultery is in the air. In medieval storytelling, only the raucous fabliaux and farces show interest in the married couple, and give an airing to the petty aggravations of domesticity. Fabliau narratives usually center around trickery of some sort, so many of them deal with adultery; but in the scatological fabliaux the marriage is more frequently secure from outside incursion, and no adulterers jeopardize the holy marital estate, which by the thirteenth century had been generally recognized as sacramental. Spousal excrement, ingested like a wafer, attests to the exclusivity and permanence of the marital relation.

Yet in this apparently stable domesticity, farts and shit place personal space, dignity, and acceptable behavior on the block. The estate of marriage has little mysterious interiority; in contrast, adultery or the wooing build-up to marriage trades in unspoken desire, vows of secrecy, a world of inner self-hood and affective self-discovery. The fart, so private it is unsmellable unless you are up close, questions an institution so public and practical; it renders the external interior, brings desire into necessity and the aesthetic into the utilitarian.

The question of privacy is played out in the ménage à trois of Chaucer's *Merchant's Tale*. January the old knight has married the young wench May. In love with May, Damian the squire has *prively* written his feelings for her, and then retired to bed, lovelorn and sorry for himself. January sends May to wish him good health, for Damien is as reliable and *secree* [discreet] as you can get in a manservant these days. As she sits by his bed, Damien presses the billet-doux, written *in secree wise* [in secret] into her hand. May hides it in her bosom and goes to the bedchamber where January "kisseth hire ful ofte" and then falls asleep. The old codger having nodded off, the coast is clear:

> She feyned hire as that she moste gon
> Ther as ye woot that every wight moot neede;
> And whan she of this bille hath taken heede,
> She rente it al to cloutes atte laste,
> And in the pryvee softely it caste.
> Who studieth now but faire fresshe May?
> Adoun by olde Januarie she lay,
> That sleep til that the coughe hath hym awaked.
> Anon he preyde hire strepen hire al naked;
> He wolde of hire, he seyde, han som plesaunce;
> He seyde hir clothes dide hym encombraunce,
> And she obeyeth, be hire lief or looth.
> (*CT*, 4.1950–61)

[She pretended she had to go where one answers the call of nature. And after she had taken in the contents of the billet-doux she tore it into shreds and quietly threw them in the toilet. Who is in a dither now but pretty young May? She lay down beside January, whose cough awoke him, upon which he asked her to strip off naked as he wanted to take pleasure of her and her clothes got in the way. She did what he asked, like it or not.]

It is a remarkable portrayal of interiority. May's bosom, which she uses as a pocket for the letter, is both literal and metaphorical, for "bosom," apart from denoting the breasts, also refers to the space between them and her dress, her dress itself, and by extension to a pocket or receptacle. Metaphorically it means a repository of secret thoughts, and one other medieval meaning, now obsolete, is of the womb (*OED*, s.v. *bosom*, n.¹ᵈ), which, in view of subsequent events, is highly apt. The "feyned hire" points to the split between apparent and real intention. Likewise, the phlegm-ridden January's lovemaking is framed by May's private thoughts: she "studieth . . . be hire lief or looth."

At the center of all this self-examination and plotting stands the toilet, which contributes to the plot not only of this but also of Chaucer's *Miller's* and *Reeve's Tales*. Even then, it offered sanctuary, a place where you could get some peace and quiet. The scene caricatures the secret and adulterous love so glamorized in medieval romance. It also doffs a cap in the architectural direction of the slow development of the internal domestic soloseater. Much more, it offers the privy as the place where one confronts one's most vicious thoughts, where self is set against self, where the sacrosanct relation between self and spouse is betrayed in mind if not in deed. The lavatorial is political. Behind closed doors, sedition begins with a plop.

Pneuma

Direct inhalation of another's fart, especially done at the close quarters of marriage, offends and injures. Toxins in farts—methane, hydrogen, carbon dioxide—if inhaled continuously, would poison the system, although asphyxia would strike first because there is too little oxygen in a fart to allow the subject to breathe. If the author of the *Life of Cola* was right, if we really can inhale the fumous intentions of another even as we sleep, what did January breathe while May plotted? What expressive pongs aside from farts emanated from that privy? As the tale subsequently demonstrates, January is both figuratively and literally blind to the truth about May, but had he been wiser he might have perceived which way the wind blew. Silent witness to everything, the air has much to impart to those who know how to read it.

Take a nice shiny new (bronze) mirror, says Aristotle, place a menstruating woman before it, and the glance she casts at it will produce a near-indelible bloodshot cloud on its surface.[246] The reason for this is that gaseous menstrual discharges emanate from the entire body, in particular, from the eyes, which are heavily veined and therefore wet and porous. The proximate air is moved by this bloody issue and in its turn taints the surface of the mirror. Not only mirrors are at risk. *De Secretis mulierum* warns that the fumes of a woman's menses, being hot and toxic, rise to the eyes, from which evil humors emanate, corrupting the air, infecting [*intoxicare*] young children, and making men hoarse.[247] An old woman, whether menstruating or not, is particularly laden with noxious humors. Woman, generally soggier and cooler in temperament than her male counterpart, is prone to giving off these potentially dangerous vapors.

How did Aristotle and the medieval monks understand the physical composition of this eye-fart? A ray of light? A burst of heat? A corrosive gas? We come up against a nexus of words for which there exists no proper translation, for the differing vocabularies point to a larger conflict between modern and premodern taxonomies of physics and chemistry. The Greek word *pneuma*, whose common denotation is "wind," lies at the center of a dense cluster of meanings and associated ideas, gaining new inflections over the centuries and from translation and retranslation. The terms for "air" (one of the four elements out of which all material entities were made) were various—Greek *pneuma*, Latin *spiritus* or *aer*—and they possess too broad a range of reference to translate accurately into a single English word. In different contexts, we might translate *pneuma* as "oxygen," "breath," "air," "gas," "wind," "spirit," or "soul." Latin *spiritus* and *anima* [soul] both bear these pneumatic associations. The *spiritus Dei* [Spirit of God] was operative at creation (Genesis, 1.1), and is the very means by which our souls are animated.[248] The climatic moment of creation is described as a kind of inflation:

> Inspiravit in faciem eius spiraculum vitae et factus est homo in animam viventem.
>
> (Genesis, 2.7)
>
> [The Lord God] brethide in to his face the brething of lijf; and man was maad in to a lyuynge soule.
>
> (Wyclif Bible)

Pneuma and *spiritus* inhabit both medical and theological vocabularies in ways that frustrate modern equivalence. As a medical term, pneuma means both wind and air, that is, both the element of air and its blowing force when displaced. It also often substitutes for *thermē* [heat], because wind is the result of heat and movement.[249] *Pneuma* is at once the substance of hot, refined, purified air, and a force that carries life and sensation to all parts of the living organism. Long before oxygen theory emerged in the late eighteenth century, and, consequently, the oxygenation of blood, the necessity of breathing was recognized as a regulator of body temperature. Indrawn breaths cool the heart, the hottest part of the body.

The many meanings of *pneuma* emerge through the layered associations of *spiritus*. By "spirit" we usually refer to some immaterial principle, as when we say that the spirit is willing but the flesh is weak. Note the slightness of morphological distinction between Latin *anima* [soul] and *animus* [mind, spirit], suggesting a certain ambiguity in Western Christian vocabulary between the eternal soul and the body's invisible but material gases. In Middle English, "spirit" tends to occur with reference to the bodily spirits: natural, animal, and vital, which *treble spirytt* knots man's soul to his body.[250] *Spiritus* is a kind of power or virtue, yet it can function as heat, liquid, or gas. In understanding *spiritus* as a power, we see more clearly how it becomes associated with the soul. *Anima* is essentially a Christian theological term, and denotes a wholly immaterial principle, while *spiritus* animates the physical body; yet a certain materialism is evident in the cooperative work between *anima* and *spiritus*, for when *spiritus* departs from the body, when the last breath is gone, soul goes forth in that exhalation. This implicit materialism held understandable dangers for medieval theology. Tertullian saw a close association between human *pneuma* and *Pneuma*, the Holy Spirit[251]; but Augustine, in a characteristic attempt to separate material from immaterial, distinguishes linguistically between physical breath and eternal spirit, *pnoē* and *pneuma*, *flatus* and *spiritus*.[252]

Beyond its connection with chemical gases, "spirit" denotes a refined fluid or essence; it is in this sense that we refer to alcoholic spirits or hard liquor, a word that in Middle English carries alchemical and transformative association.[253] *Spiritus* of the body is a refined distillate of one's life force. The concept of a distilled bodily fluid underlies another, equally slippery, medical term: "humor." By it Galen means a "juice" [*chymos*] proper to the organ or body,[254] and its association is with bodily fluids in general; the cardinal humors are blood, phlegm, black bile (melancholy), and yellow or red bile (choler). An entire theory of personality or "temperament" emerges from the way in which these humors combine within the individual; by the late Middle Ages, *humour* has begun to shed its literal connection with body fluid and acquire a more figurative meaning of "mood" or "disposition" (*OED*, s.v. *humour*, n.⁴). Now largely free of it moorings in physiology, a "humor" no longer has any evident reason for its existence, and hence acquires by the late sixteenth and early seventeenth centuries the sense of "mere whim" or "fancy"; by this association with caprice, the word assumed its present jocular meaning. Humor, the condition under which laughter operates, preserves an originary connection to the spirit of life. Our moods and humors are exhalations of the vital juices that both keep us alive and sum us up.

The soul lives in the breath; *dum spiro spero*, while I breathe I hope. *Vento vivere. Homo bulla.* Dead donkeys do not fart.[255] This strange substance—air, wind, essential fluid, and soul—cannot be fixed in modern medical parlance yet represents the life force itself. It is not only a medical and theological concept; it is also a meteorological principle. "For everything between earth and heaven is full of wind [*pneumatos*]. Wind is the cause of both winter and summer . . . Nay, the progress of sun, moon, and stars is because of wind."[256] "Three things are necessary for the nourishment of the humans and animals: food, drink, and wind [*pneuma*]."[257]

The conceptual flexibility of *pneuma* does not, however, allow us to collapse all difference. Hippocrates specifies his terms of reference by using two other words: *pneuma* outside the body is called *aēr*, inside the body is called *physa*.[258] It is the word *physa* that gives us the ancient Greek word for flatulence [*physōdis*], and the treatise, entitled *Peri Physōn*, is concerned with bodily rather than atmospheric wind. *On Breaths* is the more dignified way to translate his title, but it might equally be called *On Farting*. Hippocrates finds all diseases, however various they may at first appear, to have one common essence and etiology.[259] Air is the cause of life in the well and of disease in the sick,[260] and the writer's assertion that all diseases evolve from the air[261] provokes Rabelais the physician to make a bold claim:

> Aussi toute maladie naist et procede de ventosité, comme deduyt Hippocrates lib. de Flatibus.[262]
>
> [Every malady is born of and develops from flatulence, as Hippocrates demonstrates in his book *On Wind*.]

Looking closer at this ancient word for bodily wind, *physa*, we note its connection to *physis*, from which we get "physical" and "physics"; but *physis*, coming gradually to describe everything that is, also gets translated into Latin as *natura* [nature].[263] Traditionally conceived, nature presents *physis* as a fixed principle of objective being; for example, Aristotle distinguishes between things that on the one hand subsist by themselves, that contain within themselves their own principle of growth and decay, and, on the other, things that are created or fabricated, that are caused by a principle external to them.[264] Martin Heidegger, in an attempt to get away from this prevailing conception of nature as static and to convey something of its dynamism, likens *physis* to the blossoming forth of a rose [*das Aufgehen einer Rose*].[265] *Physis* denotes a bursting forth of an inner reality. It is dehiscence, a word that comes from Latin *dehiscere* [to gape open]; the prefix *de-* suggests "top to toe," which, added to *hiscere*, gives us the sense of an opening all the way down. *Physis* thus carries the force of a sudden coming-to-presence out of hiddenness and concealment. It has a certain something that, if one cannot quite call it a surprise, might be thought of as a revelation or epiphany. *Physis* is less a formally definitive concept that fixes the "nature" of a thing than it is a sudden appearance of destined being. Tertullian suggests a more gradual emergence of being: "fructus omnis iam in semine est" [the fruit is already present in the seed].[266] Coming from Gr. *phyō* [I grow], *physis* implies that its appearance comes as a promise from within, just as a bud grows into a blooming flower. *Physis* bursts forth on the scene of being just as flatulence [*physōdis*] does from the intestines, sometimes explosively, sometimes gradually. We might even say, pace Descartes, *crepito, ergo sum*; I fart, therefore I am.[267] In my wind is my being. Like Proteus, the medieval fart shape shifts continuously between smell and sound, air and vapor, always on the move between earthly elements, bodily senses, people, and buttocks.

A Short Excursus on Wind

If *pneuma* reveals bodily wind to be the microcosm of terrestrial wind, if it is the source of all health and disease, if it represents Being itself, the meterological winds around us also carry life and death in their breath. Wind frequently plays a key role in creation. Hebrew *ruaḥ*, translated in Christian scripture as the "spirit of God" in Genesis 1.2, is more accurately understood as "breath-wind-spirit."[268] For atomist thinker Lucretius, in the beginning of creation there was just a *nova tempestas* [strange tempest].[269]

Wind is also an equally powerful sign of destruction, occurring often as an ubi sunt theme and image of desolation, hence the elegiac refrain, "Autant en emporte ly vens" [Even so must the wind take all].[270] In the creation mythology that opens Ovid's *Metamorphoses*, the winds must be captured and restrained at the four corners, as if to save the earth from sure destruction[271]; and in Book 6 of the *Odyssey*, Aeolus captures all the winds in a leather sack but one, the west wind, in order that Odysseus may reach home directly. Wind has a natural force to create or destroy, before which mortals do not count. Although wind is a constant mundane companion—enabling breath, speech, burps, farts—it also represents presence of the divine.

Each wind possesses its own temperament, and affects our constitutions directly; one even positions a city to benefit from the most healthful of the winds.[272] A sudden change in the wind can provoke an attack of epilepsy; the north wind has a wholesome drying and rarefying effect, but the warm south wind turns everything soggy.[273] Since epilepsy is induced by the blockage of air in the veins by moist phlegm from the head, the ill effects of a sudden south wind will be evident. Nevertheless, it is not all bad news. A chilly wind restrains lust, for which reason, satirically notes Walter Map, the Cistercians go permanently bare-assed.[274]

The north and south winds are the strongest and the main contrary forces, all other winds being subject to their rule.[275] *Septentrio* (Gr. *Aparctias*) is the name of the cold and dry north wind, which brings cold and snow; its contrary is the warm and moist south wind, *Auster* (Gr. *Notus*). The "sweet breath" of the west wind, named *Zephyr* in Greek (L. *Favonius*) features in many descriptions of spring (*CT*, 1.5–7), and is perhaps the most famous of all winds, certainly more than its easterly counterpart, *Subsolanus* (Gr. *Apeliotes*). The naming of the twelve winds is a traditional motif of natural histories; the list often develops beyond the twelve, and does so in Pliny and Lucretius.[276] Pliny's description of the winds occurs during his discussion of the element of air, the element that links earth to heaven. The space between earth and moon constitutes a blend of celestial air, which pours forth the breath of life [*vitalis spiritus*] and terresterial vapor [*terreni halitus*].[277] The earth is envisaged as a kind of sling, which swings back and forth and generates discord by the velocity of its motion. This is the realm of the winds [*regnum ventorum*].

Pliny's description of natural phenomena—thunder, lightning, storms, earthquakes, and rain—sounds exactly like the symptoms of an upset stomach.[278] Earthquakes [*tremores*] result from trapped wind [*ventus*].[279] Earthquakes will stop once the trapped wind has found an outlet, so for this reason, it is better to construct buildings with windholes.[280] The earth itself exhales noxious vapors [*spiritus letales*] through special ventholes [*spiracula*].[281] When, on occasion, the earth swallows landmasses on account of trapped air, it burps them back up elsewhere as new islands.[282] Two islands in Italy change their shape regularly because of the force of the wind.[283] The bog of the angry in Dante's *Inferno*, with its low-lying, rank odor, it thought to breathe out [*spirare*] its fumes (*Inf.*, ix.31). The Hippocratic assertion that all health and disease share their origin in wind holds equally for the constitution of the terrestrial body. Whether Pliny is speaking about the regular blowings of *ventus* [wind] or occasional blasts of *flatus* [air],[284] the pneumatic disposition of the earth is central to its well-being.

It is a medieval medical fact that the male erection is caused by wind. Modern medicine has it all wrong, for it is not blood that rectifies the *verpa* but air, and with this balloon of desire, babies are conceived (medieval medicine gives most of the procreative credit to the male). As late as the sixteenth century, the hard-on was considered pneumatic, popular medical treatises referring to the hole in the *yard* [penis] through which "passeth incensible polissions and wynde, that causeth the yard to ryse" [wind and the emissions of seed pass without sensation, and the wind causes the penis to rise].[285] From discussions such as Constantine the African's *Liber de coitu*, it is clear that heat and wind are essential to sustain an erection, for heat is the beginning of motion.[286] The rank wind that blows through hell's bottom made by the flapping of Satan's wings paradoxically symbolizes the absence of all motion, heat and love. Medieval physics also asserts that all motion is a caused by desire or its opposite, repulsion. Desire is first an eager movement of the soul toward the object of desire; the body follows consequently. Beans, not diamonds, turn out to be a girl's best friend, for they "doth replete a man with ventosyte" and "doth prouoke veneryous actes [veneral acts]."[287]

The fruitfulness of the fart is entirely literal. Far from being a deterrent to passion, farts are a sign of potent virility, and would-be fathers could do a lot worse than to eat plenty of chickpeas, recommends Constantine the African, for they nourish semen, generate wind [*ventositas*], and possess both warmth and moisture.[288] Rabelais illustrates the fecundity of flatulence in relating how, from one huge *pet* [loud fart] that made the earth tremble, Pantagruel engenders 53,000 misshapen male dwarves, and from one huge *vesne* [silent fart], the same number of bowed women. The bent dwarves all marry each other, and this is how pygmies came into being.[289] An Italian poem claims that it was the noxious wind [*malvaxio vento*] of a donkey's fart that brought the first "stinking peasant" [*vilan puzolento*] into existence.[290]

A vigorous fart is the promise of potent coitus, an association that explains a thirteenth-century lyric that celebrates springtime with deer farts:

> Sumer is icomen in—
> Lhude sing! cuccu.
> Groweth sed and bloweth med
> And springth the wude nu—
> Sing! cuccu.
>
> Awe bleteth after lomb,
> Lhouth after calve cu,
> Bulluc sterteth, bucke verteth,
> Murie sing! cuccu.[291]
>
> [Summer has come in—sing loudly. Cuckoo. Seed grows and meadow blooms and the wood is in leaf. Sing. Cuckoo. The ewe bleats for her lamb, the cow lows for her calf, the bullock leaps and the buck farts. Sing merrily! Cuckoo.]

A promise of the anal wind that jetpropels the act of love can be found even in terrestrial gusts. Certain mares in Spain are impregnated by the wind; and when the right breeze blows up their asses, hens can be induced to lay that miracle of nature, *hypenemia* [wind-eggs].[292]

Till Death Us Do Part

If wind brings life, it follows that death occurs when pneuma separates permanently from the body. Materialist thinker Lucretius envisages death as a

THE BEGINNING

sort of windy exhalation of atoms: "The particles of spirit diffuse through the openings of the entire body."[293] Christian theology, however, insists on the incorporeality of the departing *anima* [soul], and thus death is that event in which material and immaterial part company, "qua separantur anima et corpus" [by which soul and body are sundered].[294]

How do body and soul actually separate? Popular tradition has it that the soul exits through the dying person's mouth. To breathe one's last is more than a figure of speech; the egress of the soul is made audible in the death rattle, *crepitus mortis*, or, as Rabelais calls it, the "le ped de la mort" [death-fart],[295] thereby suggesting that mouth and nostrils are not the only available exits for the departing soul. He recounts how intestinal wind, which is just a gross kind of pneuma, governs the entire life of everybody on the island of Ruach, and marks the death of each one. "They all fart as they die, the men loudly, the women soundlessly, and in this way their souls depart by the back passage."[296] Rabelais again genders the fart, in this case at death, when the loud *pet* befits the man and the soundless *vesse* the woman.

The soul's egress through the bottom is a marker of low social estate. Rutebeuf recounts the story of how a devil mistakes a peasant's fart for his soul. The peasant, bent double with pain, retires to bed:

> Tant ot mangié bon buef aux aux
> Et dou graz humei qui fu chauz,
> Que sa pance n'estoit pas mole,
> Ainz li tent con corde a citole.
> N'a mais doute qu'il soit periz
> S'or puet porre il ert garis.
> A cest effort forment s'efforce,
> A cest effort mest il sa force;
> Tant s'esforce, tant s'esvertue,
> Tant se torne, tant se remue,
> C'uns pes en saut qui se desroie.[297]

[He had eaten so much hearty beef with garlic and swallowed so much rich stock that his belly isn't soft, but stretched as tight as the string of a zither. Without doubt he is a goner. If only he could cut a fart now he would be cured. To that end he forces himself, so mightily does he strain, he gives it everything he's got, so much does he squirm, so much does he wriggle that at last a fart leaps out, which throws everything into disarray.]

A passing devil thinks the peasant to be in extremis and so he bags the fart and takes it off to hell. No one can tell the difference between a churl's soul and his fart, so debased is peasant nature.

The possible anal egress of the soul appears, at least in some cultures, to have provoked real anxiety. In his study of middle eastern sexual life, Allen Edwardes attests to the case of a Brahmin having been found by another in the act of sodomy with one of a lower caste: "having been tainted below the waist, the dishonored Brahmin desired to be suspended by his feet so that his soul would not pass out of his anus, a foul route, into the purgatory of eternal reincarnation in the basest forms of life."[298] Hanging also appears to have been considered to block the passage of the soul through the mouth,[299] which may contribute to its perceived ignominy as a way of dying. Despite insistence from the theologians that the soul is immaterial, there is a pervading sense that it inhabits the body in concrete ways, and needs a real physical orifice to exit. Medieval legend has it that one of the reasons Judas's bowels spilled out was that the soul was unable to exit from his mouth because he had kissed Christ only days before.

> And for þe fiend might not draw his soule out by þe moþe þat had kyssed þe
> mouþe of Goddys sonne so late befor, þerfor he barst his wombe, and
> outsched hys guttys, and drew out his soule þat way, and bar hyt to helle.[300]

Touched by sanctity, Judas's mouth blocked the passage of his corrupted soul, "for it would have been incongruous that a mouth which had touched the lips of Christ should be so foully soiled."[301] Thus, his soul sought the nearest way out.

Death—the expulsion of the soul from the body—and the expulsion of bodily product from the anus are intimately linked, and not only in comic satire. The grimace of the human face in the act of eliminating the bowel grotesquely mimics the face in death. Dying stamps itself most intimately on the face. Emperor Claudius particularly enjoyed watching the netfighters (*retiarii*) dying, as they wore no masks on their helmets, rendering their faces visible.[302] While the blessed "lagh and make mery" in heaven, the damned sit in the other place, gnawed by hell-worms and "grennyng with hor teþe."[303] Guibert of Nogent mentions a certain monk, who had wrongly accepted a small sum of money and was shortly thereafter "seized with dysentery" [*dysenteria comprehensus*] (*PL*, 156:884B). Fearing the death of the monk, the abbot came to shrive him, but found him sitting on the can.

> His abbot saw him sitting, and the terribly contorted lines on the monk's face
> incited terror. After they had stared at each other, the abbot was ashamed to
> be meeting with him in a place such as this, so the wretched fellow had nei-
> ther the opportunity nor the will to confess his sin and be absolved. The
> abbot withdrew, and the monk made his way from the pail to the bed to rest,
> but he had hardly laid himself down when the Devil suffocated him . . . And

so he died unconfessed and unanointed, having done nothing about that cursed money.[304]

It is a highly visual moment. The contortions of the man's face induce terror in the abbot. The pain of evacuation wrenches the face into a rictus of what looks like death. Speaking of Sylla's "exquisite tortures" of his victims, Augustine notes how one, whose eyes were gouged out and limbs hacked off incrementally, "was forced to live a long while, or rather to die a long while, in such torments."[305] Intense pain mixes death and life in the same moment in the same body; it is a purely liminal, transitional experience. The fart that seems to wrench one's very being out of one's bowels microcosmically enacts the final separation that is death. In that exhalation, one is truly in extremis, at the boundary between two states of being. Pain is precisely the experience of that double existence, the suffering of two absolute contraries—life and death—within the same body.

It is noteworthy how in Guibert's story the needs of nature vie with the needs of the soul. The dysentery-afflicted monk had no choice but to relieve his bowel, while the abbot, quite understandably, felt unable to shrive him while he sat there shitting; it would be a shameful thing to administer the last rites to such accompaniment. Concentration divided, the monk was unable to *wipe*[306] his soul and his ass at the same time. There is comic potential in such diametric opposition of spiritual and bodily need, as is attested in *Mankind*, in which Mankind has to interrupt his prayers to take a dump.

> For drede of the colike, and eke of the stone,
> I will go do that nedys must be done.[307]
> [For fear of colic and kidney stones, I'll go do what a man has to do.]

Or as Nought bluntly puts it, "I am doinge of my nedingys."[308] In recognition of the absolute authority of the bowel, a frequent Latin euphemism for the toilet was the *necessarium*. The bowels follow their own clock and have scant regard for social propriety let alone eternity. More than the appetites of lust or hunger, which can be disciplined and tamed, the clamor of the bowels cannot be silenced. On account of the dangers of colic arising from squelching farts, counsels Lydgate, "Spare not to blowe!"[309] The practice of fasting in early Christian and medieval mysticism, carried to such an extreme in the case of Catherine of Siena that she could not hold down any food at all, is driven by a desire for self-mastery that mortifies not only the appetite but also the sphincter itself. Do I fart or pray? To shit or confess, that is the question, one fraught with theological repercussion. Ancient prohibitions against simultaneous farting and praying attest to the incompatibility of the two. This is evident in a directive from the *Shulḥan Arukh*, the sixteenth-century codification of Jewish laws and practices that had been in place for centuries prior. This Code makes provision for those moments when one farts while at prayer:

> If a worshiper feels that a bad odor is about to come out of him, and cannot restrain himself, then if he prays privately at his own house, he should walk four cubits (about seven or eight feet) either backwards or forwards or to his side, let off wind, wait until the odor vanishes, and then return to his place and say: "Master of the Worlds! Thou hast created us full of orifices and vessels. Our shame and disgrace are revealed and known unto Thee. We are a shame and a disgrace while we are alive, and worms when we are dead." After that he may conclude his prayer. If a person lets off wind accidentally at the place where he prays, or when he prays with a congregation and he would be embarrassed to walk backward, then he need not walk away from his place, nor need he say "master," etc., but he should wait until the odor vanishes and conclude his prayer.[310]

Mankind's inability to take care of soul and body at the same time is an artificial opposition borne of religious prohibition. In contrast to the Semitic and Christian religions, a distinctive trait of nondualist thought is the symbiosis of mental and fleshly activity, for thought originally emerges from bodily function. Waiting for his hemlock to arrive, Socrates reassures his grieving companions that death is not the cessation but the great climax of philosophical work: "oi orthōs philosophountes apothnēskein meletōsi" [real philosophers practice dying].[311] Socrates has just defined death as the release [*lysis*] and separation of the soul from the body,[312] and only philosophy can teach one so to disengage from fleshly preoccupation. The privacy of the "privy" offers the occasion for introspection, for a detachment that is both literal and figurative. The act of sphinctral dilation performs in the guts and with the butt-muscles what the soul must do every day, namely, let go of trivial concerns and possessions that are no more than stinking wind.

Commenting on Socrates's words, Cicero translates the "practice" of dying with *commentatio*, which means more a slowly planned process of "mental preparation" for death.[313] To Montaigne, however, this "practice" sounds more like a philosophical seizure:

> C'est d'autant que l'estude et la contemplation retirent aucunement nostre ame hors de nous, et l'embesongnent à part du corps, qui est quelque aprentissage et resemblance de la mort.[314]
>
> [It is because study and contemplation draw our souls somewhat outside ourselves, keeping them distracted from the body, forming a sort of apprenticeship for and resemblance to death.]

Philosophizing is a double action, being both a fleeting moment of intellectual ecstasy and a daily habit of detachment. Anticipating his own demise, Montaigne conveys the twofold sense of death as sudden and violent *raptus*— "How many ways are there for death to catch us unawares?"[315] and as a long-awaited and prepared-for visit—"I am untying all the knots. . . .No one has let go of everything more totally than I am trying to do."[316] Montaigne's choice of the verb *desnouer*, "to untie," is felicitous, for untying is exactly what Greek *analysis*, the basic method of philosophy, means. Secondary meanings of *lysis* include evacuation and ejaculation, which return cerebration to the basic bodily action that it is. Analysis is a kind of evacuation or ejaculation; theorizing a kind of seeing [Gr. *theōreō*, "I look at"]; and testifying in court so called perhaps because of vouching on the testicles.[317] The dilemma between praying and farting is not a given, and has more to do with a sense of divinity that has no use for a body.

There is a further shade of meaning in Montaigne's *desnouer*. The untying image parallels the metaphor in the word "carminative," which comes, as we know, from Latin *carminare*, "to card." Wool-carding is a process in which unspun wool is brushed in opposite directions between two stiff brushes or combs, thereby cleaning and straightening out the fibers and enabling them to be spun. Carding the wool unties knots and combs out tangles; by extension, it applies to curing flatulence, whereby a carminative was thought to "comb" out the humoral knots that bung up the guts. When Montaigne "unties" all the knots, he is carding or combing out the snarls of daily passions and pettiness that obstruct the airy motion of the soul. Philosophizing has an abstersive function; it acts as a carminative for the soul, purging us of corruption; it is both the daily grunt work of grooming the spiritual intestines and the rapturous spasm of the soul's sphincter.

To philosophize is to let go of life's petty concerns, and what else does one do when one farts or defecates than let go? At the moment of death, everything relaxes. The last thing released is not the hand of our loved one but the sphincter muscle that clenches greedily onto life. As it releases, we exit this world and go to meet our maker in a mess of shit, piss, and wind, come to think of it, just as we entered it, being born, as the phrase goes, *inter urinas et faeces*. The fart frames the gamut of our days in this world.

"The holding of the breath produces strength,"[318] and exhalation expends it. The process of respiration involves the counter-motions of inhalation and exhalation, or rather, keeping true to the root word *spirare*, of inspiration and expiration. To breathe out is to expire. Every exhalation represents a loss of vitality, every fart a small leakage of vital spirit. Each fart is *un petit mort* [a little death], a pungent prolepsis of the exhalation of air that will be our last; it is a death rattle [*crepitus mortis*] in the waiting. The first thing we do when we are born is to inhale, the last to exhale. Breath frames our being, and the fart marks our ontological exit offstage. Dammit, Maimonides was right about finding a quiet spot to do your business. With all this to think about, who wants anyone else around?

Dying involves a practical letting go of one's earthly possessions as well as sphincter muscles, and farts make an appearance in late medieval last wills and testaments, at least in the literary or poetic wills if not the actual historical ones. Most of the Middle English literary wills are edifying rather than satiric[319]; the charters of Christ, in which he gifts his body and blood to make the parchment for a charter with mankind, represents one strain of the tradition,[320] but there are also nonreligious wills, such as Henryson's *Testament of Cresseid*. A recognizable feature of the tradition of medieval satiric wills is to have a generalized heir[321]; hence, the fictional testator of the late-fifteenth-century *Le Grand Testament de Taste Vin, Roy de pions* bequeathes a knobbly walking stick [*baston*] to any man cursed with a nagging wife [*femme noyseuse*].[322] And Copland's heroine, Gill of "Iyl of Braintford's Testament," leaves most things to these generalized heirs. To him who is angry with his friend, to him who sells all he has and has to live as a servant, she bequeaths a fart. She leaves a fart to everyone who wastes their life, who squanders God's gifts to them; and those men who withhold sexual attention from their "faire wench" at night "shall haue a fart to clense his eye sight."[323]

The last will and testament represents much more than the dispersion of material possessions; it signifies a kind of confession, a retrospective upon the ultimate value of one's life, on the larger legacy one leaves. Such official instruments did not become habitual in the Middle Ages until the thirteenth century, the period that saw other formalizations of a discourse of subjectivity, such as confession. The documents observe a general pattern, commonly beginning with the bequeathal of the dying person's soul to God, and continuing with distribution of alms, and with burial specifics, along with the saying of masses for the testator.

A will also offers a chance to get the final word, and by what better means than to bequeathe a fart? The anonymous satiric will, *Le Testament de Vert Janet*, written in the sixteenth century as *hommage* to Villon's poem, plays on the fact that the "Vert Janet" is a kind of pear, and Old French *poire* means both "pear" and "to fart."[324] Bequeathing a fart pithily sums up one's estimation of the inheritor, and plays into the tradition, especially popular in animal testaments, of bequeathing parts of one's body[325]: in the human testament, God gets the best part, the soul; the heart goes to the beloved; one's body goes to the earth; sins go to the devil. In Copland's poem, Gill, a hostiller, throws a party and includes the curate to write down her will or testament. Her guests and neighbors are both witnesses and inheritors. On the curate, a sponger who demands payment for his clerical duties,[326] Gill generously bestows one and a half farts, much to his chagrin. Villon also makes a gift of his bodily wind. To his jailers at the prison of Meung-sur-Loire, those "vile sons of bitches," he gifts "farts and belches" [*petz et rotes*], at least, he would if he could but he cannot because he is seated as he writes the poem.[327] Copland also briefly captures this image of the physical difficulty of farting when sitting down, when he depicts Gill lifting up a cheek to force one out.

> With that she groned as panged with pain
> Griping her bely with her hands twain
> And lift vp her buttok somwhat a wry
> And like a handgun, she let a fart fly.[328]

Getting the last word not only involves being the last in sequence, but also shuts down the conversation by offering a witticism to which there is no answer. Demonstrating ingenuity similar to that of Thomas in Chaucer's *Summoner's Tale*, Gill's gift of one and a half farts to her curate poses significant logistic problems for any executor of her will, problems that direct us to the question of the division of the fart. Villon's *Testament* shows its wit in its puns and equivocations. The *branc* [cutlass] that he leaves to his lawyer also means "excrement," and the *reau*, a gold coin, which he bequeaths to the man, is a homonym of *rot* [belch].[329] The bequeathal of a fart to rapacious survivors says as much about the worth of the testator's legacy as it does about the inheritors. The fart-inheritance reminds us of the vanity of earthly possessions, which, viewed from the perspective of eternity, are no more than wind.

Farts represent payback; they settle differences, and equalize the relation between things, levelling distinctions between lender and borrower, giver and taker, active and passive, subject and object, and by analogy, between superior and inferior, man and woman, master and servant, lord and vassal, head and foot, and inhalation and exhalation. Rabelais's Panurge is about to get out of debt, but he is far from pleased at the prospect, for cancellation of debt, he argues, signals death. *Capital circulant* represents motion and motion is the sign of life. "For every farter in the whole world says as he farts: 'Now we're quits!' My life will soon be over, I can foresee that. . . .I shall die pickled in farts [*confict en pedz*]."[330] Farts set the record straight, wipe the ledger clean, and erase all signs of activity. They are the sign of the end of all things, all inequity, and the end of life itself. With our last fart, the *crepitus mortis*, we call it quits, pay back Death what we owe, and bequeathe our windy remains to posterity.

Inspiration

If the fart can in some grotesque way signify the holiest part of our being and be present at the most momentous events of all—birth and death—it comes as little surprise that it also figures as divine presence. Chaucer's *Summoner's Tale* recounts the story of how John, a greedy friar, is farted on by a bedridden peasant, Thomas, who has had enough of the ecclesiastic's hypocritical greed. Before Thomas makes the donation, however, he makes the friar promise to divide the gift into equal parts with the twelve brothers of his convent. The tale turns into a logical poser of how to divide a fart into thirteen equal parts. The solution offered by the lord's squire is to get a cartwheel and to lay a brother at each of the twelve spokes' end, while Brother John, deserving of the finder's fee, is to assume the best seat at the hub of the wheel. The peasant is then to position himself above the hub and let rip:

"My lord," quod he, "whan that the weder is fair,
Withouten wynd or perturbynge of air,
Lat brynge a cartwheel heere into this halle;
But looke that it have his spokes alle—
Twelve spokes hath a cartwheel comunly.
And bryng me thanne twelve freres. Woot ye why?
For thrittene is a covent, as I gesse.
Youre confessour heere, for his worthynesse,
Shal parfourne up the nombre of his covent.
Thanne shal they knele doun, by oon assent,
And to every spokes ende, in this manere,
Ful sadly leye his nose shal a frere.
Youre noble confessour—there God hym save!—
Shal holde his nose upright under the nave.
Thanne shal this cherl, with bely stif and toght
As any tabour, hyder been ybroght;
And sette hym on the wheel right of this cart,
Upon the nave, and make hym lete a fart.
And ye shul seen, up peril of my lyf,
By preeve which that is demonstratif,
That equally the soun of it wol wende,
And eke the stynk, unto the spokes ende,
Save that this worthy man, youre confessour,
By cause he is a man of greet honour,
Shal have the firste fruyt, as resoun is."
The noble usage of freres yet is this,
The worthy men of hem shul first be served;
And certeinly he hath it weel disserved.
He hath to-day taught us so muche good

With prechyng in the pulpit ther he stood,
That I may vouche sauf, I sey for me,
He hadde the firste smel of fartes three;
And so wolde al his covent hardily,
He bereth hym so faire and hoolily."
(*CT*, 3.2253–86)

["My lord," he said, "when the weather is fair, without wind or disturbance of air, have a cartwheel brought here into the hall; ensure that it has all its spokes—twelve is the usual number—and then bring in twelve friars. Do you know why? Because thirteen makes up a convent, as I see it.[331] Your confessor here, because of his worthiness, will make up the number of his convent. Then they will kneel down at the same time and each will solemnly lay his nose at the end of a spoke. Your noble confessor, God bless him, will hold his nose under the hub. Then have the peasant brought here, with his belly as stiff and tight as a drum, and set him on the wheel of this cart, right over the hub, and have him cut a fart. And I lay my life on it, you will see as demonstrated proof that the sound and stink will disperse to the end of the spoke; except that this worthy man, your confessor, seeing that he is a man of such great honor, is to have the first fruits of the fart—it's only reasonable. The esteemed practice of friars is that the worthiest of them should be served first, and he is certainly deserving. He has this very day so edified us by preaching in the pulpit that I would promise, at least as far as I see it, that he have the first fruits of the smell of [not one but] *three* farts. I think his convent would agree, so well and devoutly does he conduct himself.]

Think about it. Thirteen friars, spiritual scions of the holy apostles, assemble in one place. Above them breaks forth a mighty wind that the friars inhale and savor. It should sound familiar. Chapters 1 and 2 of the Acts of the Apostles recount the story of how the disciples—sans Judas but restored to twelve by the addition of St. Mattias—assemble in Jerusalem to await the baptism of the Holy Spirit, which descends upon them like a "greet wynde," translating the Vulgate's *spiritus* (Acts, 2.2).[332] It is the story of Pentecost, of which many medieval depictions include the Virgin Mary with the disciples, bringing the assembled number from twelve to thirteen. Where the apostles were genuinely filled with the Holy Spirit, this hypocritical friar is inspired only with gas. The fart also represents a fitting punishment to the friar. He has been metaphorically farting through his mouth by reason of his hypocritical sermon, and his gluttony is the further cause of literal gas[333]; thus the Dantesque *contrapasso* of his sins is to be farted on. A "testament" signifies, as in the biblical sense, a confession of faith. Much of Christ's language near the close of his ministry foreshadows that of medieval testaments, in which individuals take final leave of those left behind and bestow gifts.³³⁴ Where Christ's biblical bequest was the Holy Spirit, this false friar's "gift" assumes the form of an almighty, inspirational fart.

Inspiration, from Latin *inspirare*, literally means "to blow upon," and the literal inhalation of fumes is central to prophetic powers. The use of incense in Christian worship faintly echoes sniffings that in older cultures were entirely literal. Pneumatic convulsions of the body—sneezing, farting, and even yawning—hold a special role, for they take violent possession of the body, and open it up to the beyond. Such momentary seizures mimic the kind of *mania* Socrates identifies as the mark of divine prophecy.³³⁵ Not only the prophetic human body but also the body of the earth is inspired. The earth can exhale lethal breaths [*spiritus letales*] variously called the "jaws of hell" or "breathing holes."³³⁶ In the legend of Cupid and Psyche, Psyche must climb through a ventilation hole [*spiraculum*] of the underworld in order to reach Pluto's palace in Tartarus (the hole being at Taenarus, near Lacedaemon).³³⁷ The fumes from these holes were considered deadly to all except a priest, who becomes intoxicated by them and utters prophecy; Apollo's oracle at Delphi was just such an exhalation. Emanating from the dark hole like a telluric fart, the wind's fumes put one in touch with chthonic forces from below. Allowing only the pneumatic blast of the Holy Spirit as inspiration, Tertullian regards such prophecy as mere digestive wind, and shows scant regard for "those persons who are supposed to be god-possessed, who by sniffing at altars inhale a divine power in the smell, who cure themselves by belching [*ructando*], who declaim panting."³³⁸

The fart ultimately has hermeneutic force, and its originary myth is recounted by Homer. Hermes, the precocious son of Zeus, was born to the nymph Maia in the morning; by afternoon he had killed a turtle and learned to play the lyre; by evening he had stolen the favored cattle of Apollo, older half brother by Zeus, and god of divination and reason, the oracle at Delphi being sacred to him. Apollo confronts baby Hermes, who plays dumb; when he grabs the infant, Hermes "intentionally released an omen, an insolent servant of his stomach, a reckless little messenger," and followed up the fart with a sneeze.³³⁹ Undaunted, Apollo interprets these pneumatic signs and finds his cattle. In the end, the two cut a deal: Hermes tends the cattle and is crowned master of thieves, Apollo gets Hermes's lyre, and remains master of divination. Apollo met his match in Hermes, for divination and reason were matched in the young god's fart-omen by the non-linguistic, nonrational sign. Thus was born the *herm*eneutic of the fart, as a type of arsy-versy divination. The Greek word "messenger," as a euphemism for a fart, is aptly chosen, for Hermes's subsequent function in the Olympic pantheon is to be the messenger from Zeus to humanity, to mediate between mortal and immortal. Hermes's first message is gas; the *soun and savour* of a fart is the original divine summons. Commuting and communicating between earth and the heavens, as does wind, Hermes is thus "the father of eloquence, patron of orators, musician, master of words, noise, and wind," "precursor of information theory."[340]

Wind frequently signifies divinity's intervention in human affairs. Though disparaging of the real power of the pagan gods, Augustine alludes to Book 1 of Virgil's *Aeneid*, in which Juno stirs up Aeolus, the king of the winds, against Aeneas and the fleeing Trojans.[341] "Kamikaze," which means "the wind of the gods," refers to the attempted invasion of Japan in 1281 by Kubla Khan, the Mongol Emperor of China, whose huge fleet was decimated by a massive storm. And in Irish medieval lore, the divine wind in question is an actual fart. Old Irish mythology tells of an unusual bitch, Fer Mac, who stuns Donn and Dubán, thus causing them to be slain: "At that the bitch raised her tail and a magical wind of druidry rushed from her, that caused the shields of the two sons of the King of Ulster to fall from their shoulders, their spears from their hands, and their swords from their sides."[342] Later, as an encore, she causes enemies of Finn mac Cumaill to kill each other when "she raised her tail and put a foul wind beneath them."[343]

Invisible yet all powerful in its effects, and wreaking havoc against the enemies of the Lord's chosen, wind is a fitting sign of the presence of the almighty. Wind fills the space between and connects heaven and earth, just as breath links soul to body. Breath also moves freely between the interior and exterior of our bodies, making short shrift of the boundaries of flesh that divide us into individual bodies. Crucial for mental concentration, regulated breathing is itself a kind of yogic prayer. Although there is substantial difference between the Eastern religions, which emphasize the centrality of breathing in prayer, and Western Christianity, for which praying is a kind of speaking (as in "orisons" and "oration"), the saying of the rosary, which involves multiple repetitions of the *Paternoster* or *Ave Maria* counted out on a string of beads, conveys a sense of the importance of rhythmic breathing and incantation in medieval mystical devotion.[344] Inasmuch as praying is identified with inspiration, it is quite literally a breathing.

The connection between divine presence and the backside does not rest on wind alone. Exodus 33.18–23 recounts the story of how Moses asks God that he may see his glory. God agrees, but refuses to reveal his face, for were he to do so, Moses would not survive. Instead, God promises to hide Moses in the opening of a rock [*in foramine petrae*], and, as he passes by, to screen Moses's face from seeing his own. On withdrawing His hand, Moses will be able to get a look at God's arse [*posteriora*]. *Foramina*, the Latin word used for the opening of the rock, denotes any kind of opening, and is used elsewhere to refer to the body's orifices.[345] Thus Moses, already wedged in a crack, has a look at God's crack. "Posteriora ejus quae sunt?" [What do his buttocks mean?] asks Augustine in his *Enarrationes super Psalmos* (Psalm 120), concluding that God's face represents His divinity, and His arse signifies the word made flesh (*PL*, 37:1610); Christ's body is God's backside. If this be so, then the unveiling of an arse is a revelation. In the buttock unmasked, haloed by wind, is divine presence.

Stuck in the Lavatory

These singular revelations of divine presence are essentially private moments, experienced either alone, as in the case of Moses, or by a select few, as in the case of Pentecost. The "privy" moment, however, has been seen to carry semantic doubleness, suggesting that in it one might equally encounter the Devil as one might God. Dark things happen in the toilet, where ominous fumes are literally inspired. Gilles de Rais, notorious pederast and serial killer, having on one occasion raped and decapitated a nine-year-old boy, had the headless corpse stuffed down the latrines of a house in Vannes.[346] Amid the stinks of the latrine, one more, that of a rotting corpse, will hardly be spotted. Poitou, Rais's servant, has to descend into the pit to cover the corpse; he also has to be helped out of the privy by two others, for we already know from the unfortunate Jew of Tewkesbury that the privy is easy to get into but hard to exit.

The appointed place to let go, the privy is the most appropriate of locations for death, that last act when we let go of the works.[347] King Edmund, nicknamed Ironside, came thus to an undignified end in 1016:

> When the king, terrible and most fearsome to his enemies, was at the height of his reign, he went one particular night to the house of ease ["in domum evacuationis ad requisita naturae"], where the son of ealdorman Edric, lurking at his father's advice in the pit of the privy, struck the king twice with a sharp dagger right in the privates [*inter celanda*]; and thrusting the point into the king's bowels [*inter viscera*] he left it in there, fleeing.[348]

The privy remained as appropriate a location for murder in the fifteenth century, when James I of Scotland (1394–1437), ambushed at night while visiting the queen in her apartments, hid in the privy (whence he would have been able to escape through the drainage hole "for the cleansing of the ordure," only he had had it plugged up days before, because he kept shooting balls into it). Successfully eluding a first search, the king yelled for help to a lady-in-waiting, who promptly fell in. The traitors, on returning, found Elizabeth Douglas and him in "privy" embrace. Highly amused, the assassins killed him anyway.[349]

Place of refuge and danger, the toilet is double in nature, and its doubleness neatly captured in its recent, twentieth-century pet name, the "throne." The posture of being seated can denote both power and vulnerability. In the privy, one's privates are exposed. Itself a place of sanctuary, the privy nonetheless offers no further escape. If you can hide there, you can also be cornered there; its virtue is also its weakness. Maybe it is owing to the privy's double aspect of santuary and prison that hell, residence of the greatest plotter of them all, is regularly identified with the scatological. In one fourteenth-century Icelandic tale, *þorsteins þáttr skelks*, a demon appears to the hero through the inner hole of a twenty-two seater privy.[350] Late medieval art lovingly and copiously embroiders the demonic with shit. The dramatic representation of the fall of Lucifer, popularly the stuff of late medieval mystery plays, in which local guilds performed biblical events, was frequently accompanied by the tune of crepitation. In the drama of the "Fall of Lucifer," as Lucifer thuds to his stinking sty, he wails, "for fere of fyre a fart I crake" [for fear of fire I crack a fart].[351] Diabolus, posing as a serpent, similarly cries out in the "Fall of Man" as he is cursed:

> For þis falle I ginne to qweke.
> With a fart my brech I breke![352]
>
> [On account of this fall I'm starting to quake. With a fart my britches I brake.]

Dante gives us the full story of Satan's fall. The velocity with which he fell from heaven was such that it actually created the pit of hell, so ponderous was his sin. He who was once the most ethereal of creatures dropped like a lead weight into the internal core of earth's globe, which, in Dante's Ptolemaic universe, represents that point of the universe furthest from God's presence in the Empyrean. The very earth shrank in fear from the contamination of Satan's approaching body, and this created a void filled by hell, while the displaced landmass formed the island-mountain of Purgatory (*Inf.* xxxiv.121–6). Like the flakes of fire that descend on the sterile planes of the seventh circle, the gravity of Satan's fall exemplifies the physics of unnatural acts. Light things should rise, but here fire, in the form of the Light-Bearer Lucifer, plummets in a downward motion that is *contra naturam*. If, in the popular theatrical imagination, Satan's descent to bottomless perdition is punctuated by flatulence, it is a natural consequence to picture him as the load that heaven discharges into hell, the shithole of the cosmos.

Dante's hell, although highly derivative and by no means the first to be so scatologically peppered, offers perhaps the most profound meditation on excremental theology. The shape of hell itself, an inverted cone lined with narrow defiles, is reminiscent of a coiled intestine that tapers to the cul-de-sac of the universe, the internal center of the earth's globe. It is in the penultimate circle, the eighth, where reside the worst category of sinners, the fraudulent, that the scatological schema, symphonic in symbolic complexity, is at its grandest. The ten rounds of the eighth circle collectively constitute the Malabolge, literally "evil pouches," and these pouches are reminiscent of intestinal sacs containing all of the moral filth of the universe. In the second bolgia, beneath the panders and seducers, Dante and Virgil find sinners "puffing with their snouts." Small wonder. The sinners are plunged in a monster privy, its walls plastered "by the exhalation from below," implying that the rising fart fumes, laden with fecal sediment, leave their crusty deposit on the *bolge* above.

> Quivi venimmo; e quindi giù nel fosso
> vidi gente attuffata in uno sterco
> che da li uman privadi parea mosso.
> E mentre ch'io là giù con l'occhio cerco,
> vidi un col capo sì di merda lordo,
> che non parëa s'era laico o cherco.
> (*Inf.* xviii.112–17)
>
> [We went there, and thence in the moat below I saw people plunged in excrement (*sterco*) that seemed to have come from human privies, and searching down there with my eyes I saw one with his head so befouled with ordure that it did not appear whether he was layman or cleric.]

There they sit in shit, inhale shit, and even wear shit for hats, all because "down here my flatteries have sunk me with which my tongue was never cloyed" (*Inf.* xviii.25–6). Having produced bullshit all through life, these flatterers are stuck in it for eternity.

In canto xxi, Dante and Virgil encounter the head devil Malacoda [Evil-Tail], and his subordinates, a motley crew, collectively named Malebranche [Evil-Claws], who exchange the infamous salutations that arrest Dante with their strangeness.

> Per l'argine sinistro volta dienno;
> ma prima avea ciascun la lingua stretta
> coi denti verso lor duca, per cenno;
> ed elli avea del cul fatto trombetta.
> (*Inf.* xxi.136–9)

[They (the devils) wheeled round by the dike on the left; but first each pressed his tongue between his teeth toward their leader for a signal and he made a trumpet of his ass.]

Dante does not specify what kind of noise or signal the demons make. It is likely, given the upended nature of these lines—where simonists in the third bolgia are stuck upside down in holes with their feet waving around (canto xix), and where fortune-tellers in the fourth bolgia have their heads twisted backward so that their tears drop onto their buttocks (canto xx)— that the devils blow a farting noise with their tongues; certainly what comes out of their mouths is nonverbal and modern translations interpret the raspberry as a fart-noise. Considering that Malacoda "replies" to them with a real fart, it seems to fit that they should engage in topsy-turvy dialogue, where Malacoda makes his butt behave like a mouth, and the Malebranche make their mouths behave like butts.

These same demons are also employed in dunking down with their pronged spears any sinners who rise to the surface of "a thick tar" [*una pegola spessa*] that bubbles in the fissure of the fifth *bolgia*, where corrupt politicians and businessmen dwell. The imagery in this and the succeeding cantos is profuse, but the sight of these sinners, who ease their pain by breaking the surface only to be prodded back by the Malebranche, makes Dante thinks of one analogy in particular:

> Non altrimenti i cuoci a' lor vassalli
> fanno attuffare in mezzo la caldaia
> la carne con li uncin, perchè non galli.
> (*Inf.* xxi.55–7)
> [Just so cooks make their scullions plunge the meat down into the cauldrons with their forks that it may not float.]

Dante then ends his cooking class of a canto with Malacoda's fart. The bubbling filth in which the sinners are cooked is also reminiscent of an open sewer; these *bolge* remind Dante explicitly of the moats of a castle (*Inf.* xviii.10–13), and the moat was the place into which the contents of castle privies directly dropped, since the "garderobes" of medieval castles were set into the external wall.[353]

Cooking, privvies, and farting? Dante is not mixing his metaphors here, for medieval medicine continuously draws a parallel between digestion and cooking. The stomach is one of the two main retentive organs of the body (the other being the uterus); it is a cauldron in which food gets "cooked" just as babies, buns in the oven of the womb, bake to a turn.[354] The inevitable result of cooking is excess hot air, and pneuma, which is necessary for blowing the food along the intestinal pipes, "is of great service in digestion."[355] The guts of hell are monster digestive and excretory systems, consuming, belching, farting, and excreting in an endless recycle. Thus, in the *Vision of Tondal*, a work of the mid-twelfth century and an important inspiration for Dante's *Inferno*, we find in the valley of the homicides sinners simmering in exactly the same kind of cooking pot, placed over coals. The souls fall on top of the sieve-like top, which then liquefies them so they plop into the stew below.[356] Another beast in hell sits on top of a pool of ice fishing for the souls of unchaste priests and nuns. As soon as he catches one, he eats it and then defecates it on the ice as a turd-soul, where the soul, regardless of sex, is impregnated and gives birth to serpents, which burn and gnaw the genitals of the same turd-beings that give them birth.[357]

Farts and excrement abound throughout Dante's final cantos. In parody of the Holy Spirit, whose vital breath creates and inspires, the foul wind made by Satan's flapping wings blows like a fart through Judecca, the floor of hell, and reverses the divine spiration of creation. Where wind in this world is a sign of heat and heat of life and desire, the stagnant gusts that eddy through Judecca from Satan's wings represent the absence of all motion, desire, and life. *Inferno* at its epicenter resolves into a stinking fart that encapsulates the essence of antiessence, pure privation and non-being, which for orthodox Christian theology defines the nature of evil. It is no accident that Dante comments increasingly on his inability to describe hell's bottom as *Inferno* moves to its finale, for we are at a place of existential absence, where language, the mark of reason, breaks down in the face of reason's complete non-being. As Satan's stench blasts around him, the wind Dante requires to make speech departs from him. The narrative describes how Virgil, carrying Dante on his back, climbs precariously down Satan's body; but on reaching the level of Satan's ass, Virgil, suddenly and with intense strain, turns himself round and starts to climb upward whence he had been descending. Dante is alarmed for he thinks they are returning to hell, but Virgil explains that they have reached the center of the earth, and that every step they now take is a step upward toward the daylight on the antipodes, where stands the mountain of Purgatory. The allegory is heavily freighted. Reason is pushed to its absolute extremity as Virgil (personification of reason), with his face (that part of the body that most represents reason) on a level with Satan's ass (the part that least represents reason), and at the farthermost point from heaven, has literally to turn upside down and start climbing up the ascent to purgatory. At the worst possible place in the universe, Satan's butthole, reason is inverted, strained to snapping point, turned inside out and upside down. And the measure of this inverted relation between rational language and demonic meaning is the fart, this little tucket from the butthole of Nasty-Ass Malacoda.

No doubt with Dante's *Inferno* somewhere in mind, many fifteenth-century illuminations of hell represent the devils very much as in the fifth bolgia, cooking sinners in big pots, dunking them back into the stew with sticks and tridents.[358] Sinners' bodies are arranged higgedly-piggledy, suggesting the topsy-turvy nature of sin; and there are multitudes of them. "I' non averei creduto / che morte tanta n'avesse disfatta" [I should never have believed death had undone so many] (*Inf.* iii.56–7), muses Dante as he gazes on the despised neutrals, before even having come to hell proper. Endemic to the experience of hell is the claustrophobic sense of crowding and jostling, essentially an urban moment, with Florence never far from Dante's mind. Sinners pack into tight spaces like tinned sardines, Satan himself is locked in ice, personal space is violated, and freedom of movement taken away. Stench is the other sign of hell's lack of community, for stinks are contrary to each other.

> This olde opinion ye may tech your brodire
> How no good odour is contrarye to a nothire;
> But it is not so of stinking smyllis,
> For stynch of garleke voidiþ stynch of dong hillis."[359]

[Teach this old adage to your brother: that no pleasant odor is contrary to another. But this is not the case with vile smells, for the stink of garlic gets rid of the stink of dunghills.]

Stinks arise in overpacked spaces, but cannot harmonize. The nightmare of crowding seems a peculiarly late medieval phenomenon; consider Dieric Bouts's Hell, where sinners squash and jostle.[360] In contrast, his paradise depicts bodies close but not squashed, with limbs rightly aligned; it preserves the idea of community, but with plenty of room, suggesting a proximity borne of choice rather than necessity.[361] This anxiety over personal space is a peculiarly late medieval touch, in synchrony with the development of perspective, in which the self is conceived spatially as much as it is psychologically. Extimacy, the zone in which subject/object relations are put to the question, in hell is violated to a degree that threatens the subject fatally. Aquinas asserts that *animam esse hominem* [the soul is the man] (*ST*, 1a.75.4.corp), and thus the soul sums up our selfhood. That selfhood, as the mark of being, is painfully eradicated in hell, yet paradoxically continues to subsist at some infernal level. At the very worst point of hell, and confronted by Satan himself, Dante attests to the loss of subjective awareness that grimly foreshadows the permanent experience of the place:

> Com' io divenni allor gelato e fioco,
> nol dimandar, lettor, ch' i' non lo scrivo,

però ch'ogne parlar sarebbe poco.
Io non mori'e non rimasi vivo:
pensa oggimai per te, s'hai fior d'ingegno,
qual io divenni, d'uno e d'altro privo.
           (*Inf.* xxxiv.22–7)

[How chilled and faint I turned then, do not ask, reader, for I do not write it, since all words would fail. I did not die and I did not remain alive; think now for thyself, if thou hast any wit, what I became, deprived of both death and life.]

Here at the worst point of hell, contorted bodies are trapped motionless in glassy ice, just as Satan is transfixed. If God at the opposite end of the universe represents the motionlessness of pure *ens realissimum*, of a perfected being that wants for nothing, Satan's immobility represents the lack of all freedom, realized concretely as locomotive immobility. That is the difference between not moving because you have everything and not moving because you cannot even though you want to. The invasions of one's space and overcrowding, so pervasive throughout hell, represent an obliteration of selfhood, a death that is spiritual rather than merely corporeal. If Satan's foul flapping betokens the stench of flatulence, his punishment includes not being able to escape from it. As the experience of prostitute-turned-saint Thaïs illustrates in the *Golden Legend*, there is nothing like sitting for years in your own waste as grand penance for gratified lust.[362] Margery Kempe also found that cleaning up her husband's shit, after he became incontinent in his old age, was a fitting *contrapassso* to the pleasure she once took in his body. It is not simply that bodily waste is unpleasant to the nose; "having to go" represents necessity at its most fundamental, and being unable to dissociate from one's own detritus spells total servitude and ultimately death itself. Babies, crying as they sit in a mush of poop, register not only discomfort but also the angry frustration of powerlessness, recognizing that the reach of a fist is always shorter than the extent of the need, an early intuition of the human condition.

Noise, another characterizing feature of hell, also enacts the principle of violated space. The ear enjoys a relatively privileged position in the hierarchy of the senses. Like sight and second only to it, hearing belongs to locomotive animals and requires distance between sensing subject and sense object. By sight and hearing, we know the world from a distance, and extend the self into the domain of the beyond, in contrast to tactile and gustatory sensation, which needs direct contact with its object, thus doing away with the critical space between self and other. Noise violates the ideal distance between the hearing subject and object, forcing sound too close, to deleterious and "noyous" effect on the ear, and demoting hearing to the level of the haptic. This is what happens in *Porcelet*, when the sexually overworked husband plants a fart in his wife's lap, that is, he farts *on* her, turning auditory sensation into tactile.

The "volume" of noise injuriously diminishes the "volume" of air that separates self from other, and compromises the interval between bodies required for an ideal community. In its own way, the marital hell of violated space played out around the husband's bran-fart and Jehannette's butt-boom anticipate the eradication of self that the real hell promises.

As the directives of the Jewish code demonstrate, the fart violates holy space and air; to preserve holiness, one must move away from it. Western Christianity is generally less scrupulous in establishing systematic provisions for such occasions, but the sense of contamination remains. One must not overeat when watching and praying, for "belching and hiccoughing is not only personally unpleasant, but it makes us unworthy of the grace of the Spirit"[363]; and "belchings with undigested food turns away the favors of the Holy Spirit just as smoke puts the bees to flight."[364] Baptismal water, infused with the presence of the Holy Spirit, must be discarded if baby shits in the bowl while his soul is being cleansed.[365] The stink of excrement, whether wind or matter, sours the fragrance of worship.

Enforced immobility takes one's humanity away; this is the grounding assumption of imprisonment. Hell represents something like being locked in the lavatory for eternity, subjected to the enforced inhalation of farts, the final symbol of non-being.

"There was an old lady who swallowed a fly. . ."

If overcrowding is one of the myriad glum prospects awaiting one destined for hell, life up here carries a reminder of down below by the terrifying number of demons watching one's every move. God represents the sacredness of unity, so when it comes to the devil, numbers run riot. Babel, with its cacophonous noise of tongues, stands as the nightmarish counterpart to the singleness of the Adamic language. Not for nothing did a demon claim that "Legion is my name, for we are many" [Legio mihi nomen est, quia multi sumus] (Mark, 5.9); according to one sermon, a legion numbers 6,666.[366] The number of demons was of singular interest to the medieval theologian, a question counterpointed by the apocryphal question of how many angels could stand on the point of a pin. A needle dropped from heaven to earth is bound to strike a demon; one writer reckons the demons at more than 30,000, another more than the grains of sand in the sea.[367] St. Anthony reckons it pointless to count them:

> Multa est itaque eorum turba in aere qui est circa nos, et non sunt longe a nobis. Et multa quidem sunt, in ipsis differentia, et de proprietate ipsorum et differentia magnus sermo, et nobis non competit.[368]

[A huge throng of them inhabit the air that surrounds us, and they are not far from us. Indeed they are many, and there are no words that can account for their diversity, properties, or specific nature].

The best image of all to the medieval imagination seems to be swarming insects. For Bonaventure, the demons move "ad modum muscorum in maximo numero" [like a big swarm of flies].[369] Emperor Vespasian apparently had such a horrible disease of the face that "out of hys naseþurles [nostrils] droppyd wormys [worms] out lyke wasps."[370] And in Chaucer's *Prologue* to the *Summoner's Tale*, he speaks of a friar who visits hell, and, finding no friars there, assumes them all to be in heavenly bliss. His guide corrects him: "many a millioun" reside in hell, but they are all in the hospitality suite:

"And now hath Sathanas," seith he, "a tayl
Brodder than of a carryk is the sayl.
Hold up thy tayl, though Sathanas!" quod he;
"Shewe forth thyn ers, and lat the frere se
Where is the nest of freres in this place!"
Right so as bees out swarmen from an hyve,
Out of the develes ers ther gone dryve
Twenty thousand freres on a route,
And thurghout helle swarmed al aboute.
                    (*CT*, 3.1687–96)

["Now Satan," he says, "has a tail broader than the sail of a carrack. Lift up your tail, Satan!" he said. "Give us a look at that arse of yours, and let the friar see where the nest of friars is down here." Just as bees swarm out of a hive, so from the devil's butt tumbled out twenty thousand friars in a group, and hither and thither throughout hell they swarmed.]

Just as fleas like to inhabit the anus of quadrupeds, because it is cosy and far from the reach of claws, so the most prevalent parasite of late medieval society, mendicant friars,[371] take sanctuary in their natural galactic habitat, Satan's asshole. Ecclesiastical satire aside, it is the awareness of sheer number that arrests us here. Satan, avatar of shit and farts, is also maestro of mind-boggling multiplicity, and he is everywhere, not simply in hell. "Space," paradoxically, is full of malevolent presence.

It is bad enough that the Lord's preachers should be imaged as a swarm of butt-fleas, but the analogy is even more damning when one reflects that insects were themselves occasionally regarded as instruments of Satan. A singular feature of Europe's late medieval legal system was that animals and insects could be brought to trial both in the secular and the ecclesiastical courts; a general distinction can be drawn between capital crimes committed by domestic animals and tried before secular tribunals; and vermin, insects or rodents, which were subject to summons, exorcism, and anathema.[372]

Insect trials reached their peak in the sixteenth century, and are possibly connected to the ubiquitous witch trials of the period,[373] though they were not unknown in the Middle Ages.[374] Such insects were an institutional *periculum* to a community whose livelihood so depended on agriculture; they also posed a personal, bodily danger. In the case of the young maiden near Joachimsthal in 1559, who swallowed a demon-possessed fly while drinking beer, it took two years to exorcise her, the final crisis lasting twelve hours.[375] How easy to be possessed by a demon, as easy as drinking beer.

There are, notes Hugh of St. Victor, nine openings [*foramina*] in the human body by which everything flows in and out [*influit et effluit*].[376] These are the apertures by which health is regulated, but they are also the doors by which sin sneaks in. Two eyes, two ears, two nostrils, one mouth, one anus, one urethra. Ladies, note, one is missing! Hugh is wedded to the mystical number nine for it both is the square of the divine number three, and mirrors the number of heavens in the Ptomolaic universe; the man's body, orifically speaking, is a perfect microcosm of cosmic totality and harmony. Woman, that manifold of corruption, has a placket too many. Super-perforated, she offers the devil one entrance extra by which he may enter. For this reason, the treatises on virginity celebrate the intactness of the virgin, whose womanhood remains unbreached. The virgin is the next best thing to a man: strong, warrior-like, "a brilliant militia waging war for the kingdom of heaven."[377] She keeps the vessel of her body closed, locked with "the key of integrity."[378]

Body functions, which regulate health, require the dilation of its apertures. In so opening, the body attends its necessaries yet also is at its most vulnerable to the entrance of invisible and unwelcome elements, such as demons, that can gain access through any opening, especially through the mouth during yawning and the nose during sneezing, for which reason we give the benediction of "God bless you" or *Gesundheit*.[379] A fit of hiccoughs could, for example, be a sign of elf-possession.[380]

One little body open to a mighty host of invisible, lurking demons— behold the medieval body convulsed in its daily functions. For all the scholastic emphasis upon *ratio* as the mark of humanity, active, rationally motivated choice plays little part in such depictions of interaction between mortals and the beyond. One might occasionally squelch a yawn, sneeze, belch, or fart, but they have a violent exigency. In such throes, the body is permeable and available to visitations from something as minuscule as a fly. That something so ordinary should become the occasion of the encounter with the beyond suggests the instability of the line between normal and paranormal. In this dangerously porous moment when the body is open to external influence, anxiety—or anticipation—attends the simplest of its functions.

When the young maiden near Joachimsthal gulps down the devil that lurked in the fly that swam in the beer that sat in the tankard, she interpenetrates with both another material body and spiritual forces. If the devil can be in that fly you just snapped up, if a menstruating woman may infect you by her glance by contaminating the air, then maybe also God is in the breath of a holy person or in the touching of a relic. Whether for good or ill, the fart conveys immanent being, presence. How ironic that a *mentalité* imbued with abstract metaphysics should find physical space and concrete matter so ready to be hallowed, so apt to incarnate the invisible.

Farting at the Devil

The multitudinousness of the demons means that you are never entirely alone. The air itself is full of their presence; the air even consists of them. St. Gregory notes how the fallen angels both constitute and inhabit the heavy air that is closer to the earth.[381] God's cherubs live further up, and their presence tends to be less immediate than that of the evil spirits. Like a noxious pong gravid with rotting matter, demons are weightier than their heavenly counterparts, and thus naturally gravitate downward in our direction, laden with wickedness. The distribution of demons in the air is not homogeneous; they scarper from anything holy, but have a majestic nose for moments when the soul is in jeopardy. In a motion of natural sympathy, demons are drawn like a magnet to sinners *in flagrante delicto*. Even an animal, guilty, for example, of homicide or of unnatural congress with a human, left unpunished, is a sitting duck for demonic occupation. Short of access to living flesh, demons might even inhabit the scene of unexpiated crimes, creating an *aura corrumpens* that malingers where the evil deed was done.[382]

Even the pleasures of taking occupancy of a crime scene or a shameless donkey cannot match that of the biggest catch of all, namely, a human soul. The immanent death of a mortal offers no more authoritative summons to a demon, and the stink of a dying man's wind assembles Satan's crew as imperiously as the stench of Pamphilë's enchanted fire in Apuleius' *Metamorphoses*. Guibert of Nogent relates how a monk, dying from a fatal chill brought on by a nocturnal visit to the toilet in scanty clothing, is attended by a clattering swarm of demons who "entered the church, went past the sacristans's bed, hurried between the choir and the altar toward the dormitory where the ailing monk was lying.. . .Death alone was the reason for such a gathering of demons."[383] Despite their airiness, demons are rendered more frightening by having apparent mass, weight, and noise.[384] Although they are not technically supposed to be able to attack or harm the human body,[385] they often break the rules—they are devils, after all—and are to be found forcing the breath out of their victims. The same dysentery-afflicted monk of whom Guibert of Nogent speaks, whose diarrhea prevented him from being shrived, was hastened to his death by the devil, who sat on his chest and killed him: "you could see his chin and his neck being violently crushed against his chest as if under some violent pressure."[386] Devils are rarely happier than when striking mortals with bowel disorders. Fourth-century Evagrius of Pontus warns how demons tickle our noses, scratch our ears, tighten our stomachs, and bloat us with flatulence to distract us from religious observation.[387] Hence, Titivillus, a mischief-making devil, interrupts Mankind, who is kneeling and saying his *Pater noster*.

> *Titivillus:* I am here ageyn to make this felow irke.
> Qw[h]ist! Pesse! I shall go to his ere and tityll therin.
> A schorte preyere thirlith hevyn. Of thy preyere blin.
> Thou art holier then ever was ony of thy kin.
> Arise and avent the[e]! Nature compellys.
> *Mankind:* I will into thi[s] yerde, soverns, and cum ageyn son[e].
> For drede of the colike, and eke of the ston[e],
> I will go do that nedys must be done[e].
> My bedys shall be here for whosummever will ellys.[388]
>
> [*Titivillus:* Here I am again to plague this fellow. Whisht! Ssssh! I'll go and whisper into his ear. "A short prayer pierces heaven. Stop your praying. You're holier than anyone else in your family. Get up and evacuate your bowels. When Nature calls, you jump."
> *Mankind:* I'll just nip into this little spot, Lord, and will be back soon. I don't want to get colic or kidney stones, so I'd better go and do what I have to do. I'll leave my prayer-beads here for anyone else who wants to use them.]

In Rutebeuf's fabliau, *Le Pet au Vilain*, a colic-striken peasant lies abed trying to pass wind, and a devil thinks the man is in extremis. Like Guibert's demons, he uses the man's taut belly as a trampoline to express the soul more hastily, and expectantly holds a leather sack up to the peasant's ass to bag the loot ["un sac de cuir au cul li pent"]. Booty indeed. Sack bulging, the devil returns to hell and opens his bag in jubilation. So unlovely is the fragrance of this "soul" that the devils are discountenanced and, at an emergency general meeting [*chapitre*] held the next day, they ban all peasants from hell thenceforth, on account of the stink. The story has a number of points: peasants are always farting and their preoccupations never rise above bodily functions; like Dante's neutrals, peasants are rejected by heaven and hell alike, so their souls, says Rutebeuf, must go and sing with the frogs; finally, devils are so stupid they cannot tell the difference between a fart and a soul.

At the surface level, this is yet one more story that displays revulsion for the laboring estate as repulsive in their physicality, a common theme of fabliaux. *Le Vilain asnier* tells of how a peasant is overcome by the sweet smells of the Montpellier spice market, but instantly revives with the odor of dung ["du fiens la flairor"].[389] At a deeper level, Rutebeuf's story demonstrates the power of flatulence in excremental theology, and displays an ancient, apotropaic wisdom, where the stink of a fart repels the evil one.[390] The stage devils of medieval theater are notorious farters, frequently punctuating their exits offstage with a rasping fart. One demon took possession of a worthless fellow who mocked a sacred shrine.

Primoque nudato inguine incestavit aera, tum deinde crepitu ventris emisso turbavit auras.[391]

[And first with his privates exposed he befouled the atmosphere, then next having emitted a loud fart he disturbed the air.]

In Rutebeuf's story, however, it is the peasant's sulphurous fumes that make hell's imps run for cover. Fart at the devil and he will flee. Conventional Christian protections against the tempter include actions such as praying, crossing oneself, saying "bless you," reciting one's Pater Noster or Creed, holy water, and so on. They invoke a power greater than that of the devil. More ancient, pagan prophylactics function differently by turning the very things associated with the devil against him: hissing and spitting, bronze, iron, fire, garlic, onions, pigs, salt, and smoke from incense or a yule log or from asafoetida, whose "fetidness" [L. *foeditas*] gave rise to its name in German, *Teufelsdreck* [Devil's turd].[392] Magic would generally be too strong a word for these pagan protections, and many of them were syncretized comfortably enough with orthodox observance; hence salt was used in Christian exorcisms and incense remains an integral part of Christian worship. In similar fashion, the gargoyles that ornament the exterior walls of gothic cathedrals warn the unclean to stay away; functioning as drains from the gutters, their mouths spew out the very filth against which they caution. Medieval iconography revels in these apotroapic devices and gestures such as mooning or flashing, sticking out the tongue, and raised fingers.[393] These are the very things that devils do to us.

Such devices provoke laughter, and thus a sharp exhalation, a bodily action that closely resembles ancient exorcistic practice. The devils hissed [*sibilare*] and pranced [*saltare*] at the long-suffering St. Anthony,[394] perhaps in mimicry of Eden's serpent, since snake language is commonly acknowledged as hissing.[395] St. Anthony tells of how "I exhaled sharply [*exsibilare*] at him," at which the devil promptly fled.[396] The saint answers the devil in his own language, but the word also carries theological resonance. Violent exhalation was formalized in early Christian rites of baptism and exorcism. The two rites used to be connected owing to early doctrines of original sin, according to which the devil was thought to possess all humans until actively expelled through conversion and baptism.[397] Exorcism used to apply to all. This colorful expulsion exists in vestige only in modern baptismal rites in abrenunciation, in which the catechumen renounces the devil and all his works. The Protestants, unsurprisingly, took much of the fun out of such rites; Luther increasingly pares down baptism to its essentials, eliminating exsufflation and retaining only the formulaic dismissal of Satan.[398]

The act of hissing or blowing sharply is referred to as *exsufflatio*. In the "scrutinies"—Latin masses dating from as early as the third century, during which exorcisms were performed on those preparing for baptism—"exsufflation" occurred when the priest blew into the catechumen's face.[399] Exorcism remained part of the baptismal rite in the Middle Ages; Aquinas explains the symbolism of the actions. The portals of the body are anointed in baptism, at least the cephalic ones.

> Quam quidem expulsionem significat exsufflatio. Benedictio autem, cum manus impositione, praecludit expulso viam ne redire possit. Sal autem in os missum, et narium et aurium sputo linitio, significat receptionem doctrinae fidei quantum ad aures, et approbationem quantum ad nares, et confessionem quantum ad os.
>
> (*ST*, 3a.71.2, corp)
>
> [This exsufflation itself signifies expulsion. The benediction, along with the laying on of hands, bars against the expelled demon from being able to find a way back in. Salt placed in the mouth and the anointing of nostrils and ears with spittle signifies the receiving of the doctrine of the faith by the ears, and the approval (of its fragrant odor) by the nostrils, and confession of it by the mouth.]

The ignoring of the nether orifice did not go unnoticed. A sixteenth-century joke recounts how a woman holding a baby at baptism farts accidentally, and the priest announces that the sound was the Devil leaving her body. As God's minister blows on the face, the devil gets blown out of the catechumen's bottom.[400] And a French riddle poses the following question:

> Pourquoy par coustume put le cul et non la bouche?
> Pour tant que au baptesme on met du sel a la bouche et non au cul.
> [Why does the asshole habitually stink, but not the mouth?
> Because salt is placed on the mouth at baptism, but not on the asshole.][401]

Along with hissing and snickering, the devils of old liked to "dance, whistle, caper, fart, and prance" in front of the church fathers.[402] The description anticipates to the letter the antics of stage demons in medieval theater. At such pranks and at pictures of bared bums what do we do? We exsufflate, we hiss, we expell gross humors from our bodies by means of belly laughter and, if the laugh is hard enough, a fart. Laughing and farting both exorcize the spirit of gloom and toxic vapors and repel the greater forces of evil that lurk within and about us.

Filthy Lucre

Rutebeuf's story of a peasant's soul that turns out to be nothing other than wind neatly turns the tables on the usual exchange, in which it is the devil's gift that is illusory. Devils' gold turns out to be shit, but here in *Le Pet Au Vilain*, the demon gets a taste of his own medicine, gaining nothing but a stinking fart for all his efforts. St. Anthony finds a silver plate in the desert, which, once commanded to go to hell, disappears like smoke [*quasi fumus*].[403] Once the devil appeared clad in gold and purple to St. Martin of Tours, claiming to be Christ. Smelling a rat, St. Martin asked to see his stigmata, and "at these words, the other instantly vanished like smoke, filling the cell with such a stench as to leave no doubt that it was the Devil."[404]

"Smoke" for us today has a fairly precise meaning of visible volatile products from burning that are suspended in the air, but the term in medieval Latin and vernaculars is broader in meaning, and points to a different understanding of the element of air. Middle English *smoke* comprises any kind of tainted or affected air. The context in which John Trevisa speaks of "smoke [*smoke*]. . .that comes from the thing that is then smelled" indicates the broadness of the term.[405] While *smoke* need not signal a rotten smell, it does not generally refer to pleasant odors, precisely because sweet smells are light while smoke is heavy and inert. Trevisa also refers to *fume* in the same sense as smoke, meaning generic smell, and *fume*, as we know, means "deer turd," implying that the infernal fumes left behind the apparition of gold smell of the bowels.

Just as perfume and manure spring from the same origins, so do gold and poop, an association of which Freud made much. In Oude Kerk St. Nicolas, in Amsterdam, a late-fifteenth-century misericord depicts a squatting man who poops gold coins.[406] Carved from wood, misericords—literally "mercies" from the Latin—supported weary church cantors as butt rests when they felt weak in the hams. Frequently comic, sometimes rude, the figures mocked from underneath: wives beating husbands, wolves preaching, men sniffing the bottom of the monk sitting above.[407] The ducat man on an Amsterdam choir stall offers a seriocomic meditation on earthly riches for the monk or canon to sit on.

Freud attests to the association between shit, money, and the devil. Possibly, he remarks, in "filthy lucre," one makes an ironic connection between that which is the most precious substance (gold) and utter waste (shit) (*SE*, 9:174). By this logic, the substitution of shit for gold represents the characteristic displacement of the unconscious, which represents the one by its opposite; in Freudian theory, "no" simply means a "yes" in denial, and terms of opposition, even at the level of philology, ultimately resolve into sameness. In *Cratylus*, Socrates tells us that Pluto, god of the underworld, is named "giver of wealth [*ploutos*], since wealth comes up from below out of the earth."[408] The desire for gold at bottom represents a sublimated desire for shit, for sticky pleasures of babyhood indulged without let or hindrance. Those whose childhood development stuck in the anal stage, observes Freud, are thus often characterized as tightfisted, tightlipped, and tightassed; hanging onto money, morals, and shit amount to much the same thing (*SE*, 21:96–7).

The love of gold represents also the misdirected desire for immortality and lack of bodily corruption; the cautionary story of Midas relates how, once his desire to possess the golden touch was granted, he found himself unable to eat, drink, or touch a loved one. Considered psychoanalytically, the love of gold represents the denial of finitude and death, themselves represented by shit. Shit and gold stand as repressed metaphors for each other. To a Christian moralist, their close relation offers a salutary reminder of *vanitas* and the need to lay up treasure in heaven. Yet any farmer knows just how valuable *stercus* can be, and urine (lant) was used widely for its detergent and bleaching properties. Like chocolate, shit is full of nutrients and dark promise. It must, of course, be refined and preserved; but shit to the farmer is as lead to the alchemist: gold *in potentia*. The alchemical transmutations by which base metal becomes gold conduct at a higher level of abstraction and artisanship the organic process by which compost is made. The precious metal of gold is, as Ovid says, hidden away *in viscera terrae* [the earth's bowels].[409]

This primordial kinship between gold and shit enables some nuances to emerge in Chaucer's *Summoner's Tale*. The Summoner has begun his story with a *Prologue* asserting that friars as a species are destined for Satan's asshole. He continues to recount the story of how John the friar preaches both in church and in peoples' homes with greedy passion, exhorting his victims to pay their church dues and make donations for the betterment of their souls. On his itinerary through the village, he visits the house of his favorite stooges, a couple whose son has recently died, the implication being that they had already paid through the nose for John's bootless prayers. Making himself at home, John pushes the cat off the bench, orders every delicacy in the pantry, casts a glad eye at the wife, and then preaches an interminable sermon against the vice of anger to the husband, Thomas, who is sick and bedridden, and growing angrier at every word issuing from this hypocrite's mouth. Cautioning Thomas against spreading out the donation too thinly among the various good causes, and implying that all the monies should go to him, Friar John asks, "What is a ferthing [farthing] worth parted in twelve?" (*CT*, 3.1967). Furious, Thomas promises a donation on the strict condition that the friar apportion it equally among his brothers and himself. John agrees. Thomas now invites the friar to retrieve the gift by sticking his hand down his back too "grope wel bihynde," in recognition of the ancient truth that possessions are so named from that upon which we sit (L. *possidere*).[410]

> "Bynethe my buttok there shaltow fynde
> A thing that I have hyd in pryvetee."
> "A!" thoghte this frere, "That shal go with me!"
> And doun his hand he launcheth to the clifte
> In hope for to fynde there a yifte.
> And whan this sike man felte this frere
> Aboute his tuwel grope there and heere,
> Amydde his hand he leet the frere a fart;
> Ther nys no capul, drawying in a cart,
> That myghte have lete a fart of swich a soun.
> (*CT*, 3.2141–50)

["You'll find a little 'private' something underneath my buttock that I've been saving up." "Jolly good," thought the friar; "that 'something' is coming home with me." He scoops his hand down to Thomas's asscrack in hopes of finding a donation. As soon as the invalid felt this friar foraging around his asshole, he let rip a fart in the middle of the friar's hand. There isn't a workhorse pulling a cart that could have cut one that blattered so.]

Sputtering with the very rage against which he was preaching only minutes earlier, John rushes to tell the lord of the village of the great insult done to himself by "This false blasphemour that charged me / To parte that wol nat departed be/To every man yliche" [this false blasphemer who made me promise to divide that which cannot be divided] (*CT*, 3.2213–15). But the lord misses the point entirely, for instead of taking offense on the friar's behalf, he is intrigued by Thomas's ingenuity, and the narrative deflects from vengeance for insult done to the logistics of dividing a fart into thirteen.

There are many ways to interpret the tale. The gift of a fart from a sickly man to a greedy friar is reminiscent of the flatulent theme we have already detected in satiric wills, and which has a close analogue in the sixteenth-century *Till Eulenspiegel* stories, in which a priest, searching for the testator's gold, finds it in the bottom of a full chamber-pot.[411] Viewing the tale in terms of societal and economic conflict, Thomas is an enraged peasant exploited by the church. This butt-flea of society, this mendicant friar is himself a kind of demon terrorizing the Lord's people, and Thomas's "donation" becomes an apotropaic fart that exorcises the evil spirit of ecclesiastical hypocrisy from their house in much the same way as the peasant in *Le Pet Au Villain* blows away the devil with his beef and garlic fart. The peasant who twits the Devil has popular appeal, and continues in a sixteenth-century joke about a farmer who promises the Devil his soul on condition that the Devil catch hold of his fart and sew a button on it. The Devil leaves in dismay.[412]

There are just as many indicators in the narrative, however, that point to Thomas as emblematic of the devil. The lord's comments about Thomas's ingenuity are revealing: "I trowe the devel putte it in his mynde. . . . I holde hym certeyn a demonyak!. . .Lat hym go honge himself a devel weye!" [I think the devil must have put it in his mind.. . .I reckon he's demon-possessed!. . .Let him go to the devil!] (*CT*, 3.2221, 2240, 2242). Thomas the churl, "certeyn a demonyak," has exhibited a wicked cunning in his poser put to friar John. It is only appropriate that the friar should have been groping around the devil's arse because that is, as the Summoner has already informed us in his prologue, exactly where he will be spending eternity. The friar's avarice has driven him to accept a gift from the devil, whose promised donation of gold turns out to be a fart in the hand. In the preceding tale, told by the pilgrim Friar, a devil in disguise befriends a wicked summoner only to claim his soul for eternity. The Summoner's fabliau trumps the Friar's by rendering not just this friar but also all friars to the Evil One's nether eye. Fabliaux have a way of making sweeping and damning pronouncements: all husbands are cuckolds; all women whores and liars; all peasants stink; all summoners go to hell, announces the Friar, and all friars go to hell's hell, Satan's asshole, replies the Summoner. Thomas's "donation" represents the mirage that avarice offers. In quest of gold, he got a fart in the hand. The devil offers only illusion, false appearance, deception, and the fart, summing up the worthlessness of such empty promises, is the just price of avarice.

Shitting Ducats

The Dutch ducat man is one of many medieval images that portray a world turned upside down. Comic details and marginalia depict many such images: wives beating husbands, a baboon writing, a wolf dressed as a friar and preaching to a flock of sheep. The comic images make the satiric point that values have become upended and order should be restored. Defecating gold coins, however, verges on a different kind of reality, a world of *impossibilia*.

Too easily dismissed as mere fancy, the art of the impossible requires creative imagining that one day becomes scientific possibility. Charlatanism aside, medieval alchemy—the study of the transmutation of base metals into noble—was a serious scientific dreaming that in its way helped bring us to the point where we can "grow" diamonds in a laboratory. It also has symbolic force: alchemy for Jung was about the transformation of the human soul through conflict and crisis.[413] The main aim of alchemy is the creation of the "philosophres stoon, Elixir clept" (*CT*, 8.862–3), by which base metals are transmuted into noble.

Alchemy in the Middle Ages was big business: treatises were written about it, and laborious experiments conducted in its name, though it also had a darker side of con-artistry; Chaucer's *Canon Yeoman's Tale* and Ben Jonson's *The Alchemist* offer excoriating attacks on how learning can be debased in the interest of fraud.

At its most visionary level, alchemy is about revelation, for the transmutation brought about is not simply that wrought by human hands but has stirred up the deepest creative processes of nature; it is a semi-divine event, an epiphany. Alchemist Nicholas Flamel (1330–1417), knew decisively when the moment of transmutation had occurred (Monday January 17, 1382): " 'Finally I found what I had longed for, and I recognized it at once by its strong smell; and when I had it, I accomplished the work.' "[414] The smell should not surprise us, for saturated air marks revelation. At the giving of the Ten Commandments, the thunder roared and a dense cloud [*nubes densissima*] surrounded Mount Sinai (Exodus, 19.16). The entire mountain *fumabat*, which translates equally as "was smoking," "was steaming," and "was reeking" (Exodus, 19.18). A mighty wind accompanies the revelation of Pentecost, when the Holy Spirit came upon the assembled apostles. The feast of the epiphany, as celebrated by the Western church, recollects the presentation by the three kings to the child Jesus of gold, myrrh, and frankincense, the last two of which are both strongly fragrant spices. The noblest of metals marks its own purity by the accompaniment of odor. Saturated air shrouds those within its cloud from the prying sight of others; it inspires the initiated with power by its fragrant fumes.

Alchemia is thought to derive from Arabic *al-kimiya*, one possible meaning of which is "[Egyptian] black earth" (where alchemy flourished); it may have been a symbol for *material prima*.[415] Quite apart from a symbolic relation between gold and dung, the black earth carries an implied relation to shit, for alchemists refer to the grosser part of the alchemical mixtures as "feces,"[416] and to the "*Mineral Bowels* of the *Earth*."[417] Like "excrement," feces by the time of this translation refers to both ordure and sediment, each a kind of ejected matter. Alchemical tests make use not only of metals but also of every conceivable substance, including *merdis, & vryne*,[418] that is, the *donge* and *pisse* used by Chaucer's Canon's Yeoman in his bogus experiments (*CT*, 8.807). Arguably, there is a close association between the revived interest in the early modern period in both alchemy and the fertilizing possibilities of ordure.[419]

Alchemy relies on a dynamic and perfective notion of identity. Base metals are "sick," and gold represents the ultimate "health" and goal of the metallic nature. " 'Copper is restless till it becomes gold,' "[420] and lead is but gold *in potentia*, as Ben Jonson's alchemical con-artists explain:

> *Subtle.* No egg but differs from a chicken more
> Than metals in themselves.
> *Surly.* That cannot be.
> The egg's ordained by nature to that end,
> And is a chicken in potentia.
> *Subtle.* The same we say of lead and other metals,
> Which would be gold, if they had time.[421]

When the alchemist views a lump of dross metal, he sees not the worthless lump in his hand but the possibility of perfection and promise of gold. The alchemist brings to the object of perception eyes that, like those of Tiresias, are blind to the obvious and see only hidden and future possible things. In contrast, the "sovereign power of the empirical gaze" looks no further than the object in view; it turns darkness to light,[422] and hones itself into "an acute perception of the individual,"[423] free of abstract typologies of metallic natures and scholastic twaddle about species. Gazed thus upon, a lump of base metal can be nothing other than a lump of base metal; what you see is what you get.

Empiricism, which bases its authority on the individual instance and which characterizes modern science, is neither the first nor the sole objector to alchemy's seemingly cavalier disregard for the difference between the natures of things. To the medieval naysayers of alchemy, natures are discrete and fixed; pigs are pigs, gold gold, serfs serfs, and that is that. These "distinct Species and Diversities of Things" enact among metals the difference in nature that we see all around us in the social order.[424] At the alchemical endeavor, they sneer: "We see no *Oxe* transformed into a *Goat*, nor any one *Species* transmuted into another...Therefore, seeing *Metals* differ in themselves, can you transform one into another?"[425] The answer is that of course alchemists cannot play God and transform species into species, yet in the individual case, that is exactly what they achieve. Drawing their authority from observation of putrefying flesh, alchemists argue that if a dead dog can spontaneously transmute into worms, then why should not this particular lump of lead turn into gold?[426] The alchemist works with this and only this particular piece of unworthy metal, seeking to realize some hidden inner possibility of being greater than it currently is. If this piece of lead might one day be gold, then that fart, transmuted into another form, might possibly be a soul or a prayer or a glorious fragrance. The worse the stink, the greater the possibility of transformation.

Teleology, that thoroughly Aristotelian doctrine that identifies things in terms of a fixed, innate, purposive principle of being, seems at odds with the dynamic becoming of alchemy, which allows things to become different from what they are. Yet teleology also embodies this principle of becoming. The *telos* of a thing is a perfecting, progressive process, and if, as Jonson insists, copper is gold *in potentia*, then alchemy is none other than natural growth in rarefied, accelerated, contrived and idealized conditions. "What *Nature* cannot perfect in a very long space of time, that we compleat in a short space by our *Artifice*: For *Art* can in many *Things* supply the *Defect* of *Nature*."[427] Both alchemical becoming and teleology share the urge to perfection. The fixed natures of medieval teleology contain within them both remembrance of a sometime perfect flesh and a radical striving to betterment.

Teleology also works in reverse. All things reduce to their prime substrate: dust to dust, ashes to ashes. Shit inhabits perfume and a fart the soul. Before rendering gold, the work of alchemy must decompose the four elements, out of which all things are made, into their underlying sub-stance, literally, that which "stands under" the outer form of earth, fire, air, and water. The four elements are ultimately reducible to each other.[428] Just as water can mutate from solid to liquid to vapor, so any other material can transform its outer aspect. Fire is hot and dry; air hot and wet; earth cold and dry; water cold and wet. This means that there is no element whose parts are not contained in other elements, and hence none that cannot be reduced to others. That which stands beneath these outer aspects is what the medievals called *prima materia*, "prime matter."

Metals were understood in the Middle Ages to be compounds, composed of three elements that subsist in differing proportions, and in gold, in perfect proportions: mercury, sulphur, and salt or arsenic. Neither any of the four elements nor the metallic ingredients of mercury, sulphur, and salt should be confused with their everyday manifestations as common fire, air, chemical mercury, and so on. These pure elements are present only residually in our everyday instances of them; they are already mixed and conglomerate. True to scholastic ontology, the essential nature of the metal and its physical existence are never quite the same thing. In the process of transmutation, metals must first reduce to their common components, namely, mercury, sulphur, and salt, and from there into the underlying substrate, prime matter.

Prime matter must be understood in relation to Aristotelian hylomorphism, from *hyle* [matter] and *morphe* [form], which dictates that everything that exists exists by virtue of a coincidence of passive or receptive matter and active form. The famous example is a wax seal: the wax gives the thing its corporeal features and solidity, and can be thought of as the material principle; the stamp of the seal represents form, for it exists only in the wax, yet without it the wax would remain a shapeless blob and not be the seal that it is, stamped and designated for a specific purpose. Thought of in these terms, anything that exists can notionally separate into its components of form and matter. Matter is the passive principle, the capacity of receiving from the active principle of form its shape and specific identity. Behind the solidity of a lump of wax, behind any physical body, prime matter is paradoxically and ultimately a metaphysical notion for it denotes matter in an entirely immaterial state. Prime matter cannot exist in the way any other body does, for if it did it would already have form; it represents pure responsiveness and potentiality, the capacity to become something, the readiness to acquire distinction; it has no active or resistant aspect to it, which might obstruct the master design of form as it impresses itself in the matter. Imaginative renditions of prime matter describe it as dark and "down there."[429] Pure form likewise cannot exist as such in the physical world, for as soon as it physically exists, it possesses the limitation of matter. Pure form represents the will to being and identity; prime matter, as endless capacity to become, the ability for primordial change, the ground of difference and otherness.

Alchemy's reduction of metal to prime matter represents the ultimate degradation of a substance, for it must lose even its humble specific form of lead to become virtually nothing. Without initial degradation, without the return to the "noise" of *prima materia*, there is no attainment of the noble nature of a higher metal. Inchoateness is a necessary preliminary before assuming the fixity of new identity: hence, alchemy's dictum is *solve et coagula* [dissolve and solidify].[430] By means of another metaphor, the base metal must "die" before it may resurrect in renewed and perfected form. Alchemy's work invites religious interpretation, and was frequently syncretized with Christian theology. The Old Testament transmutes into the New, just as *Eva* transmutes into *Ave*.[431]

From Augustine we learn that musical farts could yet figure as antitype of a remembered bodily and spiritual perfection; and thus as promise of perfection to come. A worthless party trick prefigures a future integrity. The fart is a gust of hope, a wind that augurs change for the better. The obligatory degradation of a metal to prime matter brings a substance to a moment before form, before completion, determinate shape, and circumscribed identity; degradation represents nature in transition and on the way to betterment.

Alchemy is all about discovering the fifth essence [*quintessentia*] within a material body. The other four essences, or elements (*viz.*, earth, fire, air, and water) combined provide corporeal aspect to a body. The fifth essence represents the life spirit or soul of that body, the imperishable essence, which, through various alchemical treatments, may be extracted from the material entity. The most obvious example is the distillation process by which essential oils are extracted from herbs and flowers. Quintessence expresses the inner "being" [*esse*] of a thing in its purest form, separated from ancillary extrinsics of corporeality. While it is in a sense imperishable, it is also volatile and evanescent. It is pure spirit, and thus may all too easily vanish into the air, which it most resembles. That said, the fifth essence is often described as an elixir, suggesting a liquid state. The boundary between the elements of air and fluid is particularly unstable, and more so when the fluid is this refined liquor.

> Liquour is a thing moveable,
> Of fletinge substance and vnstable;
> Alle such thingis folowyn the moone
> More than stondinge kyndes doone.[432]
>
> [Liquor is a mutable thing, of transient and unstable nature; all such substances change like the moon, not like stationary things.]

The alchemical work is also described in terms of cooking and digestion. According to ancient physic, digestion is the "cooking" of food in the belly. The alchemists' oven, or athenor, is a womb-like enclosure, hermetically sealed, in which the substances are "cooked" to their perfected nature. Alchemical work also employs the metaphor of marriage, echoing the more general description of physical motion and cosmic balance in terms of love (*Inf.*, i.37–40). The four contrary elements are "knytt with a knott" of love that holds them together in harmonious balance.[433] Alchemical "copulation" occurs when a white woman, denoting quicksilver, and a red man, denoting sulphur, marry and conceive together to bring forth noble metal.[434]

The metaphor of metals reproducing treads dangerously close to usury, which represents a violence committed against industry. Where nature ordains living creatures to reproduce themselves, metal coins are not so ordained, for they are the inanimate product of human industry. Usurers, through their extortionate lending rates, make coins copulate and have babies. Usury also cheats the honest rewards of time-consuming labor with its quick profits, and for this reason is the thief of time.[435] Although alchemy causes metals to reproduce under artificial conditions, it does not cheat time in the way that usury does. Alchemy speeds up the process of nature to achieve by artifice "what *Nature* cannot perfect in a very long space of time."[436] Alchemists enhance and accelerate the work of nature rather than parody her procedures.[437] But even acceleration requires patience; "festination," repeats Geber, "is from the devil's part."[438]

The only way something can multiply is by putrefaction or sexual reproduction.[439] The belief in multiplication by putrefaction arises from such phenomena as worms hatching in decomposing bodies. Since "metallis do not multiplye" and make babies,[440] the only way they can reproduce is is by putrefaction. If, as Geber argues, a dead dog may transmute its species into that of worms, then putrefaction is the process whereby a metal may also change species. The alchemical crucible recreates the environment of the earth's bowels, where metallic fodder gets putrefied into shit, en route to becoming gold.

Putrefaction requires heat, since "donge hillis in somyr stynk more then winter seson."[441] The action of heat is like the action of digestion: "Digestion in this werk hath grete lyknys / To digestion in thingis of quyknys" [Digestion in this experiment is very much like digestion in living things].[442] Indeed, the alchemical generation is most like the creation of man.[443] Hence, only man and the alchemical stone can be called "Microcosmos,"[444] because the entire universe is contained in them. Just as the alchemical alembic is a womb where the marvellous transmutation occurs, so in the athenor of the stomach, an equally marvellous transmutation takes place every day. The stool is the end product of the digestive process, and the fart its perfumy essence. All things are in them. Revealing everything about the health of the creature, they are a microcosm of self.

As Flamel's experience attests, smell seems to be the ultimate sign that transmutation has occurred. The moment of mutation may occur at any time, but the nose knows when it happens. Sensory experience intensifies in alchemy; reality becomes more real. Norton says that where physicians can identify only nineteen different colors in diagnosing urine, alchemy opens the eyes to a hundred different colors or more.[445] A substance smells because it is in the act of becoming something else, in the state of "liquefaction, decomposition, dissolution, or evaporation."[446] The body in chemical transition, with no fixed identity to wear as a badge, announces its being with stink. Smell is what stands between itself and nonexistence. Alchemy requires a good nose, for it gives access to a realm of truths not evident to the eye. Given its importance, smell is anatomized in detail by Norton.[447] Stench is stronger than sweet smells and overpowers them, although some were more optimistic that the fragrant would prevail[448]; as the saying goes, a teaspoon of sewage will spoil a barrel of wine, but a teaspoon of wine will do nothing to sweeten a barrel of sewage.[449] Smell, although a kind of air, is close to liquid, a kind of "invisible sweat."[450]

As one smells, so one is. A gentle heat applied to a pure substance results in a temperate odor, but the same heat applied to an impure substance results in an unpleasant odor. The chain of causation easily lends itself to moralization of smell. Peasants, for example, smell because of their degraded nature. Stench is a fumosity "resolved" or loosened from things of evil complexion that putrefy and produce a horrible odor. If the quality of something is accordant and sympathetic to one's own substance, it will smell appealing; but if the substance is contrary to one's nature, then the smell will be offensive. For this reason, devils flee the odor of sanctity.

As any perfumer knows, the extraction of the pure essence from a plant is difficult. The simplest way is by pressing and then distillation. Many plants, however, are so delicate that strong heat or pressure may destroy their essence. The spirits of the rarest substances must thus be enticed from them, by the most cunning methods of artwork, such as distillation, or enfleurage, in which the volatile perfume molecules are captured in fat. "The souls of these noblest of blossoms [jasmine and tuberose] could not be simply ripped from them, they had to be methodically coaxed away."[451] Perfumer and alchemist alike know how the capture of the soul of a substance requires skill and patience, how one success represents a thousand failed attempts. In the alembic of the intestines, occasionally one's whole soul is in a fart. Farts are not all equal. Most are ho-hum, run-of-the-mill farts that are just a question of necessity. Some, however, are great and noble farts. They have resonance, volume, stink, they bring relief, express one's mood, extend the self outward; they are one's very soul expressed, squeezed, enfleured, captured, and displayed as an offering of the self, available just for a moment, then gone on the wind. In erupting from the body, the fart splits the body open, rendering it no longer single and hermetically sealed. Its orifice apert, the body has become double within itself; difference and otherness are within. This is the Fart Absolute, the distillate of distillate of one's being.

One of the derogatory names for an alchemist was a puffer, or souffleur in respect of the job of supervising the bellows, which continuously fan the fire beneath the oven or athenor, in which the philosophic egg is heated. In 1317, Pope John XXII issued a bull condemning the "souffleurs" for their potentially disruptive financial activity, for coinage must remain the prerogative of kings.[452] They were also called blowers, and the Middle English verb "to blow" referred to farting as well as to puffing through the mouth. Chaucer's Canon's Yeoman has a face empurpled from blowing the fire continuously (*CT*, 8.666–7), and everyone can identify him by his smell:

> Men may hem knowe by smel of brymstoon.
> For al the world they stynken as a goot;
> Hir savour is so rammyssh and so hoot
> That though a man from hem a mile be,
> The savour wole infecte hym, trusteth me.
> Lo, thus by smellyng. . .this folk they knowe may.
> (*CT*, 8.887–91)

[He is recognized by the smell of brimstone. They (the alchemists) stink like goats. Their pong is so ram-like and strong that even though someone is a mile away, the stink gets to him, believe me. Thus by smelling can you identify these people.]

Savour, which today refers only to the taste of things, in Middle English denotes taste and smell equally. The fullness of the double sense is apparent in Chaucer's *Summoner's Tale*, in which the friar is fated to inhale and ingest churl Thomas's fart (*CT*, 3.2226, 2196).

There are too many correspondences between Chaucer's *Summoner's* and *Canon Yeoman's Tales* for coincidence: when the alchemist Canon urges his latest victim, a "covetous" priest, to examine the results of the experiment, he tells him to "put in thyn hand and grope" (*CT*, 8.1236), a phrase that mirrors exactly churl Thomas's exhortation to the rapacious friar to "put in thyn hand...and grope" for the gift under his butt (*CT*, 3.2140–1). Both tales get even with a church already too rich and greedy for more. Just as Thomas's rage against the friar's hypocrisy mounts until it explodes in a fart, so does the Canon's alchemical project blow up (*CT*, 8.906–21).

Scatology runs by implication throughout the *Canon Yeoman's Tale*. While the Canon busies himself with his mumbo-jumbo, the priest does the Canon Yeoman's job by playing *souffleur*, bending over the coals and blowing on them even as he is duped. So well does he blow that in the "pannes botme," "the water rombled to and fro" (*CT*, 8.1321–2), and while the priest thus blows, the Canon places the "alchemical" silver "wonder pryvely" (*CT*, 8.1323). This ritual in a hidden place where one bends over in exertion, sweats, puffs, waits to produce in the end a lump of precious substance and an explosive stink, what is this but the experience of the privy?

The alchemical *souffleur* is reminiscent of a mechanical invention of the Middle Ages called the *sufflator*, a kind of bellows shaped in the likeness of a human form.[453] The *sufflator* was usually shaped in the form of a human head, and the pressured steam escaping out of the mouth clearly mimicks the linguistic act. The Summoner himself is "a study in the dynamics of heat and expanding gases,"[454] with all his "whelkes white" [pimples with heads on them]. Friar John anticipates the duped *souffleur*-priest of the *Canon Yeoman's Tale* as, by means of the hot air of his sermonizing and begging, he fans the flames of the churl's rage until Thomas finally comes to the boil and explodes in a steam-pressured fart. Friar John, who quotes Psalm 44.2, "*cor meum eructavit*" [my heart has uttered or belched out praise] (*CT*, 3.1933–4), is himself like a *sufflator*, hissing out the stinking wind of idle words.

There is something of the violent in the alchemical transmutation, for volatile forces more powerful than human art awake.[455] It is explosive work, as the denouement of Jonson's *The Alchemist* demonstrates. Even when the experiment does not collapse in a big bang, alchemical transmutation operates as dehiscence, as the coming-to-presence of that which was potential within the basic substance, just as *physis* blooms forth into the nature of a thing. "Alchemical cosmology is essentially a doctrine of being, an ontology."[456] Just so the dehiscent fart can "be" only when it bursts forth from the hermetically sealed athenor of the guts. Though alchemy draws its metaphors from the mundane processes of digestion and nature's action, it is essentially a work of mystery, a "transubstantiation,"[457] in which a miracle reveals itself to the initiated few who stand close enough to smell it.

Duck-Rabbit, Face-Bottom

A nineteenth-century postcard of the Angel and Royal in Grantham shows its front almost entirely covered in ivy. Possibly, when it was stripped, not only ivy came off, for only a few miles away, in St. Helen's Church of Brant Broughton, an ornament on the south face of a man exposing his anus shows him blessed with unfeasibly large genitals (plate 4).

The gargoyle at the Angel may have had similar decoration, may have been quite explicitly lewd in the endearing way medieval public decoration can be. The main point of the gargoyle is that from a distance its first appearance is of a face with its mouth rudely pulled open (plate 5). By looking up at it from beneath, however, it shows itself to be a pair of splayed legs and bottom, the anus serving as the gutter's waterspout (plate 6).

Playing with perspective in such ways was a popular visual device in late medieval and early modern art. Holbein's painting *The Ambassadors* (1533) is a famous example of anamorphosis, in which a cryptic visual device, unrecognizable when viewed from any conventional position, emerges as a skull when viewed from a certain oblique angle. Anamorphosis makes a certain truth emerge when "one has lost one's bearings or, strictly speaking [is] nowhere."[458] Not quite an anamorphosis, the Angel's gargoyle does make sense from a conventional position, for it appears as a face. Yet from an intermediate distance, it could be either, an intersection of possibilities where seeming and being inhabit each other. The closer one approaches, the more its appearance changes into a butt. By the time full recognition dawns, one is standing under its spout and on the threshold of the entrance, already committed, already wet. It is not that the appearance of the face is unmasked for the reality of the butt. Not just a face, not just a bottom, the Angel's gargoyle is a face-bottom. Our knowledge of the gargoyle as bottom involves a recursion to the knowledge that it is also a face; and our initial knowledge of the gargoyle as a face involves the deferred recognition that it is also a bottom; yet despite this, we can "see" it at any one time only as face or bottom. The reality apprehended is not single. This perception cannot frame itself in empirical terms.

Thresholds are of considerable symbolic and psychological importance in medieval art. On the door of hell, Dante is arrested by the chilling warning depicted across it (*Inf.* iii.1–12). Chaucer's narrator of the *Parliament of Fowls* is paralyzed by the doubleness of the inscription over the gate of the garden (*PF*, ll. 120–54). The heavy ornamentation of church and cathedral doorways registers the different sense of space and presence into which one is about to enter. The gargoyles perched outside question our right to enter, warn of the consequences, and shit on us anyway as we go in. The Angel's gargoyle is only a face from a safe distance. Butt-recognition requires the intention of movement, and possesses a belatedness that leaves it too late to do anything about it once we are aware. It demands that we move too close for comfort, into the painful zone of extimacy; it makes us wet, and it makes us laugh.

Plate 1 Luttrell Psalter, f. 185b. English, first half, Circa Fourteenth Century (Hand sketch of detail by Gary Zaragovitch).

Plate 2 Beinecke MS 229, f. 147r Old French Prose Lancelot, Circa Thirteenth Century (Beinecke MS 229, f. 147r, courtesy of Beinecke Rare Book and Manuscript Library, Yale University).

Plate 3 Romance of Alexander, MS. Bodley 264, f. 90v. French and English, Circa Fourteenth–Fifteenth Century (Hand sketch of detail by Gary Zaragovitch).

Plate 4 St. Helen's Church, Brant Broughton, Lincolnshire. Circa Thirteenth Century– Fourteenth Century (Photographed by Valerie Allen).

Plate 5 Gargoyle (from front), Angel and Royal Hotel, Grantham, England. Possibly Circa Fifteenth Century (Photographed by Valerie Allen).

Plate 6 Gargoyle (from beneath), Angel and Royal Hotel, Grantham, England. Circa Fourteenth Century, possibly Circa Fifteenth Century (Photographed by Valerie Allen).

IN BETWEEN

In the Beginning was the Word

My sister, she told me, was recently walking down the footpath when she farted and all the streetlights went out. A butt speaks, "Let there be darkness" and there was darkness. For Enlightenment philosopher David Hume, all events, however regularly they may coincide, are merely contiguous, and have no necessary relation between them. Causation is not a sense-impression, which for Hume is the origin of the only real knowledge, namely, empirical knowledge. Even in the case of apparently "necessary" physical laws, "All events seem entirely loose and separate. One event follows another, but we never can observe any tie between them. They seem conjoined, but never connected."[1] A carminative and a fart; a severed nerve and loss of feeling; a fart and darkened streetlights; for Hume, all such are mere crotties of fact drutled along the path of time, without intrinsic relation, however consistently some may coincide, however "necessary" physical "laws" of causation may seem. By naming one event "cause" and another "effect," we are not describing objective reality so much as articulating the rules of a game called truth, with which we manage the world. A "cause" is not a thing, but a convention of language, a tacit agreement to arrange events in a particular way.

Yet according to medieval theology, Christian and Semitic, the world began with a blast of divine wind. Adam's first labor of naming the animals brought "being" and "being named" into close relation. Babel brought babble, noise; the languages we speak are fractured and many. Medieval etymology reconnects a word with its origins, its first cause. Such views of language may be metaphysical, yet they conjoin directly with the noises that come out of the mouth. "Homo bulla," goes the proverb.[2] Man is a bubble, full of air and gone in a puff. The proverb reminds us against *vanitas*, but the medievals also took their bubbles quite literally. A schoolboy's earliest years were spent learning how to puff air correctly by studying grammar, logic, and rhetoric, the three verbal arts of the trivium. These gave him the structures of thought that gave him the words with which he would later assign names to *realia*.

Farts figure regularly in medieval thought as antilanguage, yet their significance is confined not by being just symbolic or grotesque alone. On the pneumatic continuum, air upwardly mobile is a word, downwardly so a fart. The glottal block between the respiratory and digestive systems as defined by Western biomedicine diminishes in importance in the broader pneumatic view of the porous body, where farts and words commute. Between the beginning of intention and the end of action resides the hot air of imperatives, declaratives, and conditionals. Wind, assert the cosmologists, is the source and medium of all movement.

The Silver-Tongued Butt

Promised gold that turns out into a fart is a perfect *contrapasso* to John the friar's sin, which is something more complex than avarice. He violates the inspired language of prayers and preaches bullshit. One of Augustine's abiding themes is that true eloquence comes from speaking the truth in love rather than from the mannered tropes of rhetoric. St. John Chrysostom's name means "golden mouth," and he traditionally appears in iconography with a beehive, suggesting sweetness. Gold as an image of language alludes both to truth spoken in love and to the musical sound of words as they strike the ear. Chaucer's slimy pilgrim Friar seeks "to make his Englissh sweete upon his tonge" (*CT*, 1.265) in order to winkle money out of old women and sex from young ones. No matter how poor a widow was, he "wolde he have a ferthyng, er he went" (*CT*, 1.255). The procurement of the farthing comically foreshadows Thomas's donation to the friar in the *Summoner's Tale*. For his own eloquent lines, Chaucer is celebrated by his successors as the father of "aureate" language, "golde dewe, dropes, of speche and eloquence."[3] Dante complains about the horrible dialect of the Aquileans, who "belch forth" [*eructare*] their words in crude accents.[4] Of the guttural Germanic dialect, Rabelais's character Eusthenes remarks that "if God wished us to speak through our backsides we should speak like that too."[5] Burp- and fart-words signify both moral corruption and the grating phonetics of dialects other than one's own.

Gold ducats of wisdom issue from the mouth of Crysostom, but deceitful or idle language makes turds of words. For that reason, the flatterers in Dante's hell sit in excrement. It is a medieval commonplace that sin stinks, and stinks variously: hypocritical prayers smell worse than a decomposed dog,[6] and flattery is notoriously excremental.

> The fikeleres meoster is to hulie the gong-thurl. Thet he deth as ofte as he with his fikelunge ant with his preisunge writh mon his sunne, thet stinketh na thing fulre. Ant he hit huleth ant lideth, swa thet he hit nawt stinketh. The bac-bitere unlideth hit ant openeth swa thet fulthe, thet hit stinketh wide.[7]

[The flatterer's work is to cover the [devil's] privy-hole; he does this as many times as he conceals with his flattering and praising someone's sin, which stinks more foully than anything else. And he hides and covers it over, so that it does not reek. The backbiter takes the lid off and uncovers the filth, so that it stinks far and wide.]

Flattery violates the most basic law between speech and truth, and further violates the communal bonds that forge together society. Adam's first social contribution, his naming of the animals, brought Edenic language into reality. Flattery, by which the serpent supposedly prevailed on Eve, works to undo the connection between thing and its name, *res* and *verbum*; it destroys the fruits of Adam's first productive act. Flatterers separate "the word from the soul, tongue from the mind, speech from thought" [ab animo verbum, a mente linguam, ab intellectu loquelam]; they belch out honeycombs [*favos eructare*] of praise.[8] In lying, the *telos* of language is disturbed, for the word arrives at a meaning different from its destined intention. More than metaphor, the fart as antilanguage literally deviates wind from its upward direction downward to the butthole. In *Inferno*, flatterers reside in the circle of fraud, where language is robbed of its proper meaning, and meaning is misdirected toward the object of financial gain rather than truth. These sinners turn their "no" into "yes" for cash (*Inf.*, xxi.41–2) in recollection of Christ's exhortation that "yes" should mean "yes" [3*he*, 3*he*] and "no" "no" [*nay, nay*] (Matt. 5.37). Language itself in these cantos enacts at the level of grammar the moral and philosophical confusions between appearance and reality, word and intention.

In *Inferno*, the talking butt opposes the talking face as lies oppose truth. Yet in a nondemonic context, it may stand to the face as innocence does to duplicity. *Le Chevalier qui fist parler les cons* [The Knight Who Made Cunts Talk] tells the story of a countess who challenges a knight, reputed to have the power to make cunts talk. Beforehand, she plugs her orifice so that it remains gagged when the knight tries to exercise his powers. The resourceful knight, who had secondary gifts in reserve, calls upon her bottom, which trumpets the deception, and the countess loses her wager; her veriloquous ass speaks more truth than her mouth.[9] The face is rational and hence capable of deception, but the butt has a plain speaking that the will cannot control. Butt-speak possesses an organic real presence where *vox* trades in seeming and absence. The butt is the other of the face as window of reason, for neither can be contained fully together in the same sweep of the eye across the same body. The butt erases sexual differentiation in generic similitude. In the face resides modesty—dropped gaze, blushing cheeks—but the butt is shameless, big, and brutish. The bit we cannot shield properly with our hands or stop people looking at when we walk away, it attests to the fragility of our dignity and to a certain bestial innocence. It does not wink or look shifty; it just wobbles and clenches. If expressionless, it is blessedly free of double-speak.

Double-speak and malice, however, prevail in *Inferno*'s circles of fraud. The last creature Dante meets as he descends to the ninth and final circle is Nimrod, alleged designer of the Tower of Babel, a figure of violated language, whose untranslatable gibberish rings in Dante's ears as he enters the next circle. Nimrod may as well have been blowing signs out of his ass, as Malacoda does. "For me," muses Cynic Demetrius of Sunium, "the talk of ignoramuses [*imperiti*] is like the rumblings [*crepitus*] which issue from the belly [*ventrus*]. For what difference does it make to me whether they resound from upstairs [*susum*] or downstairs [*deosum*]?"[10] When reason is upended, the linguistic sign undergoes similar torsions and farts become words. Canto xxi ends with Malacoda's echoing fart: "he made himself into a butt-trumpet" is the very last line. In the stunned silence between this and the following canto lies a dismay to which philosophy can offer no consolation. Dante opens canto xxii with a simile of Miltonesque amplitude (*Inf.* xxii.1–9), building to his climax of perplexity: "I've seen a lot of command signals given in my time, but never have I seen one as strange as that" (*Inf.* xxii.10–12). For the fart to be a meaningful sign is, in Dante's book, the most outlandish thing he has yet encountered. How the devil can a fart signify? How can anyone talk out of their asshole?

The Grammar of Farts

Nothing is free from the burden of (mis)signification in *Inferno*, and farts do their allegorical bit along with everything else. Dante routinely invites the reader to ponder over the hidden meaning of his lines, as if foreseeing the wealth of glosses and commentaries that would expound the lines of the *Commedia* throughout the subsequent two centuries.

We should remember that school grammar was closer to literary criticism than to the formalism of diagrammed sentences. The medieval schoolboy learned Latin through reading Latin poetry, rendering grammar a highly literary process and the appreciation of poetry highly grammatical. Consider Geoffrey of Vinsauf's recommendation for the following stylistic embellishment:

...Ego rem sceleratam
Consilio feci...
Consilium stimulus faciendi...
...Suggestio pravi
Consilii sceleri causam se praebuit.[11]

[I have done the evil deed on purpose...My purpose was the spur to action...The prompting of a crooked and vicious purpose offered itself.]

The English translation makes it look as if Vinsauf could not think of any other word to use instead of "purpose," but check the Latin: "purpose" has been declined through various cases—ablative, nominative, genitive—creating elegant variations on the one word. Modern English, which lacks such formal declensions, cannot recreate this. The ambitious Dante, aligning himself with Virgil, invites similar close reading of lines written now in the sweet tones of his native Tuscan. At this time in Italy and Western Europe, to learn grammar was to learn Latin grammar; formal grammars of vernacular languages were two centuries away; yet the *Commedia* reveals at every turn a brimming confidence in its own verbal craft and ability to sustain linguistic scrutiny. How the hell then does one scan for the metrical arsis and thesis of Nimrod's balderdash "Raphèl maì amècche zabì almi" (*Inf.* xxxi.67)? What part of speech is Malacoda's fart? How can we diagram the raspberries that the Malebranche blow? Is it possible to parse an arse?

Medieval treatises on grammar offer some answers. Priscian the grammarian, himself in *Inferno* for sodomy, authored the widely read and influential *Institutiones grammaticae* [Grammatical Principles]. Early in his first book of the treatise, he considers in depth the fundamental category of *vox* [voice, vocal utterance]. *Vox* generally has a broad semantic range; one may speak of the harmonious *vox* of a flute, but in this grammatical context, the word best translates as "vocal utterance or sound," that is, any patterned sound that comes out of the mouth, for "speech," as we will see, seems too narrow a translation. The question put to Socrates of whether a gnat hums through its mouth or its butt now assumes some grammatical importance.[12] The answer—that the air issues violently out of the asshole, which is a bugle— prefigures Malacoda's butt-trumpet imagery. Priscian's category of *vox* must exclude the fart proper because it does not issue from the mouth, but in Dante's upended landscape, grammatical law is suspended, heads and butts change places, and a fart attains the status of *verbum*.

Priscian first subdivides *vox* into four aspects: articulate [*articulata*], inarticulate [*inarticulata*], scriptable, or capable of being written down [*literata*], and nonscriptable [*illiterata*].[13] The terms need some explaining. Meaning literally "jointed," and referring to limbs and knuckles, *articulata* is joined, says Priscian, "cum aliquo sensu mentis" [with some mental understanding], suggesting that by the term he refers to distinct meanings. *Articulata* thus best translates as "intelligible," meaning an intelligible unit of sound, such as a syllable or phoneme.

Literata connects both the writable and phonological aspect of utterance. If there is an acceptable combination of vowels and consonants capable of capturing the sound made by the mouth then the sound is *literata*; if not, *illiterata*. Take, for example, *grust, blomby, ngust,* and *glbombr*.[14] None of them means anything in English and thus all are "unintelligible vocal utterances" [*voces inarticulatae*]. *Grust* and *blomby*, however, could feasibly become words, since they satisfy all the phonological criteria by which syllables group together in English. They are "writable vocal utterances" [*voces literatae*] because their sounds can be transcribed onto the page. But *ngust* and *glbombr* do not conform to that pattern of English phonemes from which we form syllables. There are restrictions on the combinations in which English phonemes can occur. The /ŋ/ phoneme (as in *ngust*) does not begin a word although it can end one (as in *sing*)[15]; and the consonant cluster *glb-* simply does not occur in the English language though it may in some other. Deep sound laws, varying between languages, make only some sounds intuitively acceptable: in English, *ngust* and *glbombr* are not acceptable; they are both *inarticulatae* and *illiteratae*, most unintelligible of voice-noises.

From these four aspects of speech, Priscian composes four categories. The first, *vox articulata literata* [intelligible, writable speech], refers to voice-noises that are grammatically meaningful, noises that can be parsed into formal structures such as the eight parts of speech, the sounds that make up words and sentences. *Vox articulata literata* creates rational discourse, the gift of humanity. Hence the example Priscian offers comes from what was arguably the greatest poem of his culture, the *Aeneid*, written by Virgil, Dante's personal tour guide: *Arma virumque cano* [Arms I sing and the man]. The rules of grammar emerge from reading not any old thing but from the work of the masters, ideally the strict metrical arrangement of poetry, which presents language in a perfected form, because it both speaks and counts, joining *numerus* with *verbum*. Metrical control is implied in the art of grammar, which builds up muscle memory so that the correct placing and coordination of vocal organs become instinctive. Buccal organs that are flaccid only make noise, but in *vox articulata literata* we see stomatic movements licked into the shape of *sentence*.

The second category, *vox articulata illiterata* [intelligible, nonwritable speech] refers to voice-noises that are semantically distinct [*articulata*] but not capable of being written down [*illiterata*]. Priscian does not supply specific examples here, instead illustrating by the general descriptors of hisses [*sibili*] and moaning [*gemitus*]. We all know how to convey a world of meaning in a well-placed sigh or click of the tongue, and to that extent "intelligible non-writable speech" signifies just like any other word; but its sounds are confused and can only be approximated in writing—"mmmmm," "tsk," "hrrumph," "pshaw." Lacking vowels, or using unacceptable consonant clusters, these are not proper "words" or parts of grammatical speech. Although today we do write them down, and I just have, they are to Priscian, unscriptable, *illiteratae*, and he would not dignify them by making "literature" of them. These *voces* are the hisses [*sibili*] and moans [*gemitus*] that come out of our mouths in place of expletives proper. In contrast, interjections, such as "damn," "hooray," or Latin *heu* [alas], are bonafide grammatical emphases, one of the parts of speech proper.

This category demonstrates the interdependence between writing and formal grammatical rule. Hissing and moaning augur an access of emotion prior to and beyond rational expression. In *vox articulata illiterata*, affective experience breaks through the limits of formal concept, perhaps because of its intensity, which is why such signifying but unscriptable plosions litter the *Inferno*, where the bepooped flatterers "moan" [*nicchiare*] continuously (*Inf.*, xviii.103), and the suicides-turned-trees, who can only speak when their "articles" are broken apart, "moan" [*gemere*] words in pain through the wounds in the bark (*Inf.*, xiii.41). *Gemitus*, Priscian's example of *vox articulata illiterata* and repeated here in Dante's Italian by *geme*, applies also to animal noises, just as Priscian's hisses [*sibili*] can apply to snakes. The sounds on the one hand are sublinguistic, on a par with beast noises, and on the other, metalinguistic, transcending language. "Gemitus quoque et lacrime necessaria penitentibus sunt" [Both moaning and tears are necessary in penitents].[16] For this reason, the desert fathers hiss at the devil foreshadowing the formal *exsufflationes* of exorcism, as if in search of a language beyond all languages, all parts of speech and linguistic rule.

Priscian's third category is a sound that you can write down but that has no meaning: *vox literata inarticulata* [writable, unintelligible speech]. These are sounds that have the appearance of words but lack meaning: we have already considered *grust* and *blomby*. Priscian offers only animals noises as examples—the frog's *coax* [ribbit, ribbit] and the crow's *cra* [caw, caw]—but it would seem that it is here we may place the voice-noises of Nimrod: "Raphèl maì amècche zabì almi." You can write it, you can pronounce it; this makes it *vox literata*; the only problem is that it is gobbledegook, *vox inarticulata*. Nimrod stands for an abuse of rational discourse that pulls language down to and below the base level of blood-stupid animality.

The fourth and last category is "unintelligible, unwritable speech" [*vox illiterata inarticulata*]. Priscian's examples are "rattling" [*crepitus*] and "roaring" [*mugitus*]. As with the second category of *vox illiterata articulata*, he offers only generic descriptions because the specific instance is properly unwritable. What kind of sound is Priscian's *crepitus*? *Crepitus* is certainly a common Latin term for "fart," although a fart cannot be meant here because Priscian deals only with vocal sounds [*voces*]. He seems to refer to silly noises here, and crying, which has neither phonetic nor semantic valence. Perhaps belches can be included in this category (although *ructus* is the correct term for burp, not *crepitus*). In this category reside the nonwords—the voice-fart or raspberry—that the Malebranche make to Malacoda. Neither belches nor raspberries can be measured in vowels and consonants; nor does either mean anything. Dante's hell resounds with *voces illiteratae inarticulatae*. Here, in the outer darkness of the eighth and ninth circles of hell, the description of hell from the Sermon on the Mount assumes literal incarnation: "ibi erit fletus, et stridor dentium" [there will be weeping and gnashing of teeth] (Matt. 8.12). *Fletus* [weeping]—a word temptingly similar to *flatus* [farting, blowing] and belonging in the same grammatical declension—represents the ultimate breakdown of language.

If it is by the stately strains of the *Aeneid* that Priscian teaches the lessons of speaking aright, it is from Dante, who places his feet, metrical and corporeal, wherever Virgil steps (*Inf.*, xxiii.148), we learn the grammar of the soul. Just as Donatus includes examples of the abuses of language—the solecism [*solecismus*] of a phrase, the barbarism [*barbarismus*] of a single word, and other such vices [*vitia*]—so in *Inferno* we learn to discipline our tongue by witnessing the horrors of verbicide: language put on the rack, garotted, strappadoed, and quartered, words that break into sobs [*fletus*] and farts [*flatus*], words that once stood proud, tall and *erect*, like the *recte loquendi* [right speaking] that defines the art of grammar. Canto xxvii, where sowers of discord experience death by a thousand cuts, best illustrates the mangling of flesh, body politic, and stems of words. The principle of *lex talionis* is for Dante most perfectly come to pass in the figure of Bertran de Born. In parody of Diogenes the Cynic, de Born carries around his head like a talking lantern, decapitated for having set Prince Henry of England against his father, Henry II, head of both family and realm. Having severed the symbolic head from its trunk in life, de Born's crime is reenacted sempiternally and fitly upon his body in hell. "Because I parted those so joined I carry my brain, alas, parted from its root in this truck; thus is observed in me the retribution [*contrapasso*]" (*Inf.*, xxviii.139–41). More than anywhere else in hell, this ninth bolgia celebrates the grisly festival of retribution associated with medieval public punishment of high treason. Here Mohammed, guilty of rupturing the Christian faith with the heretical doctrine of Islam, is horribly disemboweled [*storpiare*]. Digestive ducts turn into the plumbing reminiscent of classical Rome's great feat of civil engineering, the Cloaca Maxima, finest sewer of the imperial world.

> He was ripped from the chin to the part that breaks wind [*trullare*]; between the legs hung the entrails [*minugia*]; the vitals [*corata*] appeared, with the foul sack [*tristo sacco*] that makes excrement [*merda*] of what is swallowed.
> (*Inf.*, xxviii.24–7)

Here Piero da Medicina prepares to speak by clearing a windpipe that gapes red and raw for all to see. By this spectacle of bloody innards, human discourse deteriorates into peristaltic swallowings and wind blowing through arterial pipes connecting mouth to fundament. *Homo bulla.* Man is a bubble. The rational animal has become the billycan of wind implied by *trulla* [fart], which in Latin, literally means "little ladle." In the body, broken for eternity, words literally break wind.

Potent Words

The world itself came into being at the call of *vox*. The command *fiat lux* brooks no rupture between intention or action; the very utterance of "light" is itself the cause of light; potency lies in the enunciation itself, in the funneled breath that shaped the sound that produced the effect. Medievals took their oaths and their grammar seriously, though none thought their logos powerful enough to create with just a word. Nevertheless, a deep sense of the word as effective cause remains in the prevalence of spells and curses, and shows in the concern Aquinas expresses about the sacramental "incantation" of the Divine Liturgy. If the priest flubs his words, will the sacramental work still be efficacious?

> Verbum operatur in sacramentis, *non quia dicitur*, idest non secundum exteriorem sonum vocis, *sed quia creditur*, secundum sensum verborum qui fide tenetur. . . .Ille qui corrupte profert verba sacramentalia. . .si sit tanta corruptio quae omnino auferat sensum locutionis, non videtur perfici sacramentum. . . puta si, loco ejus quod est In *nomine Patris*, dicat, *In nomine matris*.
> (*ST* 3a.60.7.ad 1, ad.3)

> [The word is effective in the sacraments, *not because it is spoken*, that is, not because of the extrinsic sound of the voice, *but because it is believed*, in accordance with the meaning of the words, which we hold by faith. . . . In the case of one who distorts the sacramental words. . .if the distortion be so great that it obliterates the meaning of the phrase, then it would appear that the work of the accomplished sacrament would not be effected. . .for instance, if instead of "In the name of the Father (*patris*)," he says, "In the name of the mother (*matris*)]."

The analysis treats of two issues: the phonetics of the phrasing (*patris* must not be confused with *matris*), and the intention of the utterance, that is, the consciously directed nature of the relationship between *verbum* and *res*. Heart and lips must be aligned.

One thing above all differentiates modern and medieval theories of language: the relationship between semantics and phonetics, between the content or meaning of words and their grammatical or phonetic form. Medieval grammar holds a word to be essentially a sign of a thing, thus never losing its umbilical connection to the referent; a grammatical sentence must actually mean something. Modern linguistics, in contrast, separates sign from referent, linguistic form from meaningful content, avoiding any confusion of morphology with semantics. "A linguistic sign is not a link between a thing and a name, but between a concept and a sound pattern."[17] This establishment of language as self-referential culminates in the formalist parsing of Chomsky, who claims that "colorless green ideas sleep furiously" is an acceptable grammatical sentence even though it is semantically void.[18]

Medieval grammarians had their own version of colorless green ideas: *equus patronymicus* [patronymic horse] and *hypothetici sæculares* [hypothetical shoes][19]—but they regarded such howlers as gas rather than language, a version of Priscian's *voces inarticulatae*. Salisbury describes these joining of words as unions barren of the fruit of meaning, and his terms, inherited not invented, are explicitly sexual: such words "couple" with each other [*copulare*] fruitlessly [*dictionum junctura inutilis*] (PL, 199:843A). Although sexual metaphors have largely disappeared from modern grammar, they are ubiquitous in Latin grammar. There is, for example, much mileage in a deponent verb, which is (femininely) passive in form but (virilely) active in meaning. *Caelum* [heaven] or *ostrea* [oyster] takes one gender in the singular form and then switches to another for the plural; other words denote a masculine referent but belong to a feminine declension—*nauta* [sailor]. Even grammatical "declension" and "case" mask lewd allusion. "Case" [*casus*] denotes a "falling" away from the uprightness of the *nomen* [noun] in subject position into an oblique relation; "nominative" is not, strictly speaking, a "case" at all, for *casus rectus*, literally meaning "the upright obliqueness" or "upright falling" is a contradiction. The declining of a noun is then the measurement of a word's angle of declivity from its nominative, upright position through vocative, genitive, dative, and so on. There is much mileage to be had from the pun of a student obediently de-clining—that is, bending over—for his grammar master. For medieval Christian Latinists, the symbolic possibilities in theorizing the "Fall" of a word are too good to ignore: moral *lapsus* [fall, lapse] and grammatical *casus* [fall, declining] interchange felicitously.

The sexual pun affects also the basic categories of grammatical and logical predication. "Subject" [*subiectum*] comes from Latin *subicere* [to place beneath], and was applied in the most basic of senses, as in placing a mare beneath a stallion. "Adjective" [*adiectum*] in its turn comes from Latin *adicere* [to insert, to hurl (oneself) on top of], and if we follow the analogy, subjects are women and adjectives men. Grammatical etiquette demands that subject and adjective must agree in case, number, and gender, but sexual etiquette dictates that man and woman be different in function and position. Playing up the discrepancy between grammatical and sexual propriety, Alan of Lille castigates the practise of nouns and adjectives enjoying same-sex union.[20]

How ironic then the fate of Priscian in *Inferno* xv. This most famous of grammarians, who taught us how to generate meanings properly, is damned eternally for violating the proper generation of the body—sodomy—a kind of solecism of the butthole. Words are semantic semen, and they must direct themselves into the correct hole for them to breed meaning. Dante places Priscian in the seventh circle, the circle of the violent, where are sinners whose sin is worse than those caused by moral weakness, but better than those caused by malice or fraud. Priscian's unnatural sex (*contra naturam*) is not mere lust—that would be a sin of weakness—but violence done to nature, establishing an opposition between what is "natural" and what is "violent," as in the difference between a natural and a violent death.[21] Violence here means less a barbaric act or excessive force (although that is implied) as a literal deviation, a swerving offtrack of a thing from its original destination or telos. Dante's representation of duplicitous speech as misdirected breath that does a U-turn and comes out as a fart both exhibits fraud and subsumes violence within it. Just as there is a proper way to make words and meanings, so there is a "proper manner" of sexual congress in accordance with its proper objective.

For the record, here is how love in the right hole should occur. Vituals having been taken, digested and excreted, the man should make his move just before daybreak, when the humors are best disposed. "He should speak to her in a jesting manner, kiss and embrace her, and rub her lower parts with his fingers" to activate her eggs. The critical moment of entry comes "when the woman begins to speak as if she were babbling," but she should not wriggle lest "the seed be divided and a monster generated." Try not to let too much air in during the act, and afterward, the man should remain atop the woman (missionary position being taken for granted), keeping the cork in to ensure the semen's arrival at the target. An hour later, the husband may get up and go about his business, but the flattened wife should remain lying. For a son, turn to the right, left for a daughter.[22] The sealing and guarding of orifaces, the observation of proper time and circumstance, the careful positioning of bodily members, the strict maintainance of active and passive roles, the teleological purposiveness of it all: such are the appurtenances of right speaking just as they are of right coupling.

The task of medieval grammar is to guard the tongue, that shameless member, from promiscuity by teaching it linguistic decorum. Propriety is all. "Propriety" and "property" both share the same Latin origin: *proprius* [one's own]. A word that is used properly [*proprie*] is a word used in its "own" or literal sense as opposed to its figurative sense: "nam per voces significatur aliquid proprie et aliquid figurative" [for by words something is signified either properly or figuratively] (*ST*, 1a.1.10 ad 3). There is something "improper" about a metaphor, for a name that belongs to one meaning transfers to the ownership of another meaning. Metaphors and other such tropes use language improperly, temporarily ousting the "proper" owner, but by the special powers of poetic license, they get away with it.

A "proper name" [*nomen proprium*], grammatically speaking, is a name exclusive to self (John, Margery) as opposed to a "common name" [*nomen appellativum*] by which we designate generic identities (man, women, tables, pig). Priscian takes a moment to deal with the problem of the same proper name being bestowed on more than one individual, finding it an accident of sound [*fortuitu et sola voce*] rather than any irregularity of definition.[23] The proper/common distinction appears to invite a primary division between the one and the many, but the category of *nomen proprium* includes group identities, revealing that the line between specific and generic identity is relative rather than fixed. The Roman-born male received three names: *praenomen*, a first name, the purpose of which is simply to distinguish between siblings, and in the case of the firstborn, might even be the same as the *nomen*; *nomen*, always ending in *–ius*, denoting the common ancestor, hence the *gens* or clan to which the male belongs; and *cognomen*, a later development and a mark of distinction, denoting the family or branch within the clan, and often referring to some personal or physical trait; in the case of Caius (*praenomen*) Julius (*nomen*) Caesar (*cognomen*), the *cognomen* refers to the caesarian manner of the ancestor's birth. The concept central to the *nomen proprium* is less individuality than exclusivity, of being entitled to the distinction of a name disallowed to others. A Roman woman did not even have a *praenomen*, and thus the two daughters of Marcus Antonius were Antonia Maior and Antonia Minor.

Propriety and legitimacy are in this context synonymous. It is not enough for a birth—whether word or person—to have occurred. The child must have been born on the right side of the blanket to receive a name, and a sound must be the properly conceived child of a referent—that is, it must be meaningful—in order for it to be a word. Just as deviant sex [*coitus inordinatus*] in an unnatural position creates a monster [*monstrum*],[24] so a grammatical solecism makes a freak of speech. Explicitly employing the terms of genealogy, the fourteenth-century Provençal *Leys D'Amors* differentiates between words connected by sound alone, which are bastards [*bortz*], words connected by meaning alone, which are adopted sons [*filhs adoptius*], and words connected by meaning and sound, which are legitimate heirs by blood and law ["filhs leyals e naturals"].[25]

Propre in Old French means "clean" as well as "own"; and today it also means being able to use the toilet. Proper words are potty-trained. Priscian's treatise begins not with grammatical categories but with phonetics. Consonants, vowels, dipthongs, the correct shaping and elongation or shortening of a vowel, rhythmic utterance, and the placing of tongue and teeth are critical in the formation of first syllables, then words, then sentences. Grammar, like dancing, puts its metrical feet in the right places; it "makes," in the original sense of *poesis*, and it keeps the beat. Just as writing is all about digital control, about how to hold the pen, form letters deftly, and not blot the parchment, so grammar trains the buccal organs how to shape and clip off the passage of air with teeth, tongue, and lips in such a way that various and meaningful sounds emerge. Grammar, the *scientia recte loquendi* [science of right speaking] (*Etym.*, 1.5.1), is matched by the science of the *rect*um, *disciplina* of the backside. There is a time to fart, and a time to clench. The fundament must observe the correct rhythm of occasion, and keep silent at times: an *ars tacendi* [art of keeping silence] of the butthole.

Legitimate Etymology

For the medieval grammarian, it is a matter of kinship. Disown them or even have a blood transfusion, but parents remain parents; just so do words bond to the thing that gave them semantic being no matter how much they may change in morphological appearance. Tracking the etymology of a word in medieval linguistics is the same thing as constructing its family tree. Isidore of Seville held the study of the parents of words to be so important that he wrote a large treatise on the subject; for Isidore, semen [L. *semen*] is, quite simply, semantic [L. *semanticus*].[26] In absolute terms, genealogical origin is always located in Adam and Eve, from whose sons all races descended. Etymology puts the question to *verba*, searching their souls that they may confess their parentage, groping after the gold of their origins.

That origin governs everything that succeeds it. Greek *arche* means both "ruling power" and "beginning" or "coming first"; it names both commandment and commencement, observing an order that is both jussive and sequential.[27] Modern English retains the sense of governance in "monarchy" and of primacy in "arch-enemy" or "archbishop"; "archaic," meaning "ancient," derives from the sense of coming first and therefore being oldest. Latin *princeps* [first, chief] similarly gives us "principal" and "principle" or *principium*. A "first principle" is a tautology. The origin of a word combines the two principles of being foremost in meaning and first in succession, from which it follows that subsequent linguistic change is a diminution of the charisma of the etymon, a straying away from the originary center. The task of etymology is to realign a word's axle, to reconnect it to the source of its power, to its *fons et origo*. The search for the origin of a word is less a quest for fixed nomenclature than an ongoing striving against wandering away from proper meaning.

Having made the rupture with semantics, modern linguistics accords etymology a different heuristic method, which proceeds by means of sound laws. According to Grimm's law, modern "foot" and "pedal," which look entirely unrelated in form, are actually cognate, the /f/ deriving from an earlier /p/, retained in Latin *pes* (genitive *pedis*) [foot]. By the same logic,

Germanic /t/ derives from an earlier /d/, retained in Latin *dens*, making "dental" and "tooth" also cognate.

The ancients observed no such sound laws, or rather, made them up as they went along. They "made no serious effort to determine what was the stem and what was the inflectional ending.... Therefore a Roman could imagine that *vulpes* (fox), genitive *vulpis*, really was fly-foot, compounded of *volo* I fly and *pes*, foot, genitive *pedis*."[28] *Lepus* [hare], genitive *lepor-is*, was similarly deemed to derive from "light-foot," a combination of *levis* [light] and *pes* [foot]. Latin inherited such etymologizing from the Greeks, and Plato's dialogue *Cratylus* gives us perhaps the best example of morphological analysis that, by the standards of present-day sound laws, approaches the deranged. "Hera," for example, comes from "air" [*aēr*], but disguises its derivation by putting the *a* at the end of the word; all becomes clear if you repeat her name very fast.[29] Inserting or dropping letters, changing accents from grave to acute, and changing vowels are all fair game in forcing similitude between unlike words in the interests of ingenious semantic connection: the more ingenious the connection, the more arresting the etymology. For Plato, this was no derangement, but the imitation by the word of the inner essence of the thing that the word denotes. Precisely because the word is only an imitation and not the thing itself, the accidental externals of letters dropped, added, or rearranged will inevitably be different.[30] However fanciful, such breaking of words enables new understanding, enabling us to define a fox by his swift-footedness. Just as one person comes from two parents, so "hare" breaks down into "light" and "foot." There is *in fine* nothing to distinguish medieval etymology from exegesis or interpretation. By means of etymology, the exegetes could authorize the meaning of a text. The original meaning of a word governs its subsequent wayward semantic identity, which, when etymologized, returns to the heel of origin.

What then is the *fons et origo* of "fart"? How may we break this verbal bit of wind to release the fragrance of its inner *spiritus*? In Chaucer's *Summoner's Tale* the friar asks, "What is a ferthing [farthing] worth parted in twelve?" (*CT*, 3.1967), which, in view of subsequent events, also and proleptically means "farting." Benjamin Franklin subsequently makes the same verbal connection, no doubt with Chaucer in mind: The "Science of the Philosophers," he concludes, is "scarcely worth a FARThing."[31] Could "farting" and "farthing" be etymologically related? The lexicographers say no. *Ferthing* is a pun, nothing more; quarter of a penny, a farthing means a "fourthing" (OE *fēorthing*). "Fart," the *Concise OED* tells us, derives from Old English **feortan*,[32] a verbal form that does not actually occur in any extant document (although the nominal form does),[33] but is inferred from the Old High German *ferzan* and Old Norse *freta*, which in its turn came from Germanic **fertan*, another reconstructed form. The long vowel in *feorth-* would also have sounded different from *feort-*. For the same reason, the Latin suffix *–ānus*, *anūs* [old woman] and *anus* [asshole], which are all homographs, using the same letters, are not homophones, being pronounced three different ways. Finally, the *t* in "farting" is phonologically distinct from the *th* in "farthing." Together, these factors indicate a distinct linguistic lineage.

Back to the drawing board. "Fart" is a Germanic word, so Grimm's law gives us a clue to the word's kinship. By the same logic that *"foot"* can be related to Latin p*ed*-, so can *"fart"* be shown to be cognate to Latin *pēdere* [to fart] and the noun, *pēditum*. English *f--t* corresponds to Latin *p-d*. The "intrusive *r*" in "fart" occurs frequently enough in other contexts[34]; certainly Greek seems to have acquired a medial *r* in *perdomai* [to fart] from the reconstructed Indo-European root **pezd-*.

The Norman Conquest introduced many things to England, including the fart Gallic, *le pet*. With its Latin roots, *pet* began its coexistence with Old English *feorting* and later Middle English *ferte*; apparently different words, they in fact shared a common Indo-European ancestor, although it is doubtful whether anyone saw a connection in the twelfth and thirteenth centuries, when French loan words entered English at their greatest rate. In trilingual medieval England, English, Insular French, and Latin could all appear in the one sentence in the form of mixed inflections or loan words. Hence in the Latin records of the *Calendar of the Close Rolls*, Walter the Farter appears in 1234 with a first name in Latin and the last in English: *Walterus Fartere* (*MED*, s.v. *ferter[e]*, n.). Friend Roland appears with the French article in the Latin manuscripts as "Rollandus, le Pettus"; or with French suffix *–our* as "le Pettour"; or in a mixture of French suffix *–our* and Anglicized suffix *–er* in "le Pettur."[35] Finally, one Johannes le Fartere appears in full macaronic glory with Latin *Johannes*, French *le* and English *Fartere*.[36]

The mixing of languages strongly suggests that *ferte* and *pet* coexisted successfully as many other French and Anglo-Saxon words did, although in accordance with clerical bias toward Latin and Insular French, no written records of "fart" exist earlier than the thirteenth century. "*Pet*" seems largely to have evaporated once English reinstated itself as the language of official record, although it did remain in occasional use as late as the sixteenth century and is now obsolete.[37] What *pet*- words in English remain? Only one is uniformly acknowledged: the petard. The earliest recording of the word is by Shakespeare in *Hamlet* (III.4.206), in which he speaks of "the enginer/ Hoist with his own petar." The petard was an early bomb used to blow in a defensive structure such as a wall or door.[38] Made of iron or bronze, and shaped like a short cannon, it was packed with about seven pounds of gunpowder, wadded, and attached to a wooden board, which itself was attached to the surface to be blown in. Then light the fuse and run. Petard descends directly from OF *pet*, and ultimately from L. *pēditum*. The *–ard* ending denotes "one who does to excess" (*OED*, s.v. *–ard*, a.). Of great popularity in the sixteenth century, the suffix was just the ticket to describe this noisy explosive. Pet-ard meant something like "Old Fart Butt," and carried the same derogatory innuendo as did "dotard," "drunkard," "coward," "laggard," "saggard" [?boaster, ?sagging person], "stinkard" "wizard," and, worst of all, "Spaniard." "Being hoist with one's own petard" means all or any of the following: being blown up by your own bomb; being destroyed by your own devices against others; being stunk out by your own fart. No etymological relationship with farting is claimed for the following *pet-* words, but why not?

To be in a pet. The OED claims its first use from the sixteenth century and its origin uncertain, possibly from "pet" as an animal or spoiled child. Suspicious.

Petulant, petition, impetus. These three words seem unrelated, but are not. "Petulant" derives from Old French *peter* [to seek], at once establishing a connection between "petulant" and "petition." *Peter* itself derives from Latin *petere*, which means not only "to seek" but also "to move in the direction toward," "to hurl a missile at," and "to attack"; and by this, "impetus" completes the triangle of relation.

However, we speak of a "petulant" wine, meaning not that it is ill-tempered or unpleasant but that it possesses a slight effervescence. A wine described in French as *pétillant* is "bubbling" or "crackling," etymologically drawing not from *peter* [to seek] but from *pet* [fart]. Groping for the derivation of "petulance" by means of Latin *petere*, philologists have ignored the possible association that sits under their noses—trapped wind. Remembering Hippocrates' claim that all diseases have their provenance in bodily wind, we might entertain the possibility that being petulant, bad-tempered, in a pet, and ill-humored all belong to the family of colic and refer to emotions arising from the discomfort of trapped wind.[39]

The OED derives "petulant" from Latin *petulāre*, diminutive of *petere* [to seek, assault, aim at]. *Petere* supposedly derives from the reconstructed Indo-European root *pet-*, meaning "fly" or "fall." *Pet-* words are then an extension of the original concrete action of hurling something through the air, or one body toward another. We throw ourselves on the mercy of another when we make a petition; we throw ourselves at another when we assault or seek them. This etymology only brings farts, *petition, petulance* and *impetus* conceptually closer, giving us a punning connection between letting fly a dart [*petere*] (*OLD*, s.v. *peto*[3]) and letting fly a fart [*pēdere*]. Nicholas of the *Miller's Tale* "leet fle a fart" in Absolom's face (*CT*, 1.3806), and as we have seen, the vocabulary of medieval and early modern artillery derives directly from flatulence.

The connection between farting and flying suggests itself by another route. "Partridge" (ME *partrich*) derives from OF *perdriz*, which derives from

L. *perdix*, which is transferred from Greek *perdix*. The *perdix* supposedly made an explosive sound when suddenly flushed out of the bushes (*OED*, s.v. *partridge*, n.).[40] Did *perdix* originate from the Indo-European root for flying, *pet-, or from the Indo-European root for farting, *pezd-, into which the Greeks inserted a medial *r* to produce *perdomai* [to fart]? Whether so named for its prowess at flying or at farting or both, the partridge could well have ended up as a "fartridge." While on the subject, note that OF *poirre* [to fart] is often spelled without its digraph—*poire*—and *poire* means "pear." Figuratively, *poire* can mean an object of little value: "ne prisier deus poires" [to not give two pears] means the same thing as "ne prisier un pet" [to not give a fart]. This sheds some new light on the old Yuletide carol. Although folklore holds the partridge and pear tree as fertility symbols for male and female, like the holly and the ivy, maybe the gift of a partridge in a pear tree from the beloved was not such a treasure after all. Why stop here? Did Old French *impetuosité* [turbulence] in some instance mean "enfarted"? And was Latin *impetus* [violent onslaught] ever used to mean a fart attack? If we play this game of comparative philology for long enough, it would seem that all words, like all diseases, take their origin in bodily wind.

Rebuilding Babel

In this search for origins, the medievals naturally wondered what word fell from the lips of Adam first. Dante speculates that it must have been *El*, the Hebrew word for God, for no worthier name could spring to our first parents' lips.[41] He also attempts to parse the word; *El* cannot have been an imperative, for no creature commands his maker; *El* must have been a *responsio*, for the creature should respond, not initiate. The first sound that came out of Adam's mouth was thus antiphonal. The first liturgy, a word that means "public duty," was to echo and magnify the name of the Lord. Even before bestowing *nomina* upon the animals, Adam's first work was to repeat, to burp up God's name, to "belch" out a "goodly theme."

El is neither question nor answer, but something beyond all parts of speech. Here is *vox articulata illiterata*, an utterance that transcends formal language. In his Belch Sermon on the Song of Songs, Bernard describes the sounds of love the Bride makes:

> So a strong and burning love, particularly the love of God, does not stop to consider the order, the grammar, the flow, or the number of the words it employs, when it cannot contain itself, providing it senses that it suffers no loss thereby. Sometimes it needs no words [*verba*], no expression [*voces*] at all, being content with aspirations [*suspiria*] alone. Thus it is that the Bride,

aflame with holy love, doubtless seeking to quench a little the fire of the love she endures, gives no thought to her words or the manner of her speech, but impelled by love she does not speak clearly, but bursts out [*eructare*] with whatever comes into her mouth.[42]

Language in its purest state is aspiration, breathing, the wind [*physa*] of the body, which is why the Eastern art of meditation is essentially a regulation of breath and a transcendence of language. The fixed and degenerate taxonomies of grammatical categorization we use in common parlance remain as the small boxes in which we preserve the fragments left from that first resonant sound, collecting them up where after Babel they scattered uncontrollably, with a thought to restore them one day. Until then, we keep those boxes as remembered fracture and hope of wholeness.

Medieval etymology has a centripetal force that pulls all words toward the very beginning of language. Language behaves in accordance with Aristotelian laws of physics, by which all things move toward their natural elemental place, impelled by desire to unite with it. This "natural love" makes the world go round, fire rise, earthy things fall, draws a man to a woman, and a word to its origin. Ultimately, the whole universe strives in love to come to rest in God, its prime mover, its etymon, that first divine breath. Medieval *verba* desire an Oedipal return to the place whence they sprang, to unity with *res*, "where language comes to a standstill, where meaning becomes intrinsic," "where arguments end, where sound gives way to silence, motion to rest, and where words begin to border on meaning and meaning on things."[43]

Modern linguistics rejects this myth of origin. Take, for example, the sound law of ablaut or gradation,[44] which illustrates the potential endlessness of linguistic excavation. Ablaut charts vocalic alternations within different classes of verbs and ultimately explains the difference between formations of the past tense in verbs: between "weak" verbs that tack on a suffix ("I fart, I fart*ed*") and "strong" verbs that require an internal change in the stem vowel ("I shit in my pants, I sh*at* in my pants"). On realizing that ablaut is a feature of the earliest known languages, Jacob Grimm, who despite his contributions to modern philology still thought in some respects like a medieval etymologist, decided that ablaut was a given of the very first languages, and that he had tracked the evolution of words "back to the very beginnings of language."[45] Grimm argued that the nucleus of the verb lay in the consonant sequence alone, without the medial vowels, which mutated according to need. In other words, semantic criteria dictated the original vowel mutation in strong verbs, for a change of tense is a change of meaning. The implication of Grimm's conclusions was that the laws of sound, hunted down through time to the very first languages, finally give way to semantic first principles, that meaning ultimately governs (vocalic) sound change.

Modern linguists, however, explain ablaut vowel mutation as the result of phonetic, not semantic, criteria. Vowels change because the change feels right in the mouth, not because it denotes a change in meaning, thereby rendering semantic exigency secondary to phonetic. The causes of ablaut were thus of greater antiquity than Grimm thought, in the original accents of Indo-European. Grimm was being "unscientific" in attempting to track language back to its *terminus a quo*, to the moment before which language did not exist. "For us today ablaut is a result of phonetic laws: it is no longer a sign that our spade has reached the bottom in linguistic excavation, but on the contrary it is an indication that, however deep we may have penetrated, there are many strata below."[46] Sound laws govern linguistic change, but even they do not purport to account for how language first came into being, just as evolutionary biology does not account for the moment of creation. No special privilege attaches itself then to the earliest known instance of a word or reconstructed protoform, for although it is the first (until we know more) it is not the foremost. Without *arche* or *principium*, linguistic science is anarchic and unprincipled inquiry that pays no heed to the authority of that first breath.

For Isidore, letters are the *signa verborum*, "the signs of words" (*Etym.*, 1.3.1), yet to the "father" of the *OED*, "words are combinations of *sounds*, not strings of *letters*."[47] Admirably democratic in proclaiming all words equal in rank, modern linguistics nonetheless observes its own aristocracy of descent by the rule of sound law. What exactly are these deep laws that can pronounce Germanic /f/ to be really an ancient /p/? What invisible authority declares that "fart" is related to "partridge," denies that "farting" is related to "farthing," and sneers at the idea of *vulpes* deriving from *volo* and *pes*? Parentage is no longer a matter of meaning, but sound. A false etymology is false because it does not conform to established sound laws.

Words do not have the liberty to opt out of these sound laws, which "admit no exceptions,"[48] and the task of linguists is to explain apparent exceptions in various ways: by identifying definitive temporal periods during which the sound laws are only operative; by isolating the irregular word as an imported borrowing from a different language; or by introducing a secondary law that nonetheless proves the rule by creating a new one.[49]

No native horse sense could figure out that Latin *dens* is cognate to our modern *tooth* without recourse to Grimm's law. Sound laws are all the more in total control for being both hidden and counterintuitive, and there are plenty of them: Saussure's, Brugmann's, Grassman's Hartmann's, Lachmann's, Sievers' (1 and 2), Pedersen's (1 and 2), and even Notker's law (Notker III, not to be confused with Notker the Stammerer).[50]

The sound law of umlaut, which occurred in English as early as the seventh century,[51] illustrates how comparative philology understands one language in terms of another, just as the coccyx in homo sapiens can only be explained as an evolutionary change from other (tailed) species. Umlaut also goes by the name of *i*-mutation, for it indicates the change of a vowel under the influence of a vowel in a following syllable, in particular *i* or *j*, *u* or *w*, and it explains why, for example, the plural of mouse [OE *mūs*] is mice [OE *mȳs*] and not mouses. "*I*-mutation" denotes a change brought about by the presence of *i* or one of its comparable sounds. Take OE *sellan* [to sell, give], which descends from the older Gothic *saljan* [to offer, sacrifice]. Umlaut explains how that older medial *a* in *saljan* turned into an *e* in Old English *sellan*. Like *i*, the *j* sound in *saljan* is formed high up and in the front of the mouth while in contrast the *a* of *sal-* is formed low and at the back of the mouth.⁵² Having just gone to the effort of forming *sal-* at the back and bottom of the mouth, the tongue got ready prematurely for the upcoming *j* sound, gradually dragging the *a* further up and to the front of the mouth; the *a* became fronted and raised, turned into an *e*, and *saljan* became *sellan*. By expending less mouth muscle, *sellan* survived *saljan* as the fitter of the two. Umlaut also explains why the plurals of "tooth" and "foot" should be "teeth" and "feet." Old English *tōþ* and *fōt* must once have formed their plurals as *tōþi and *fōti.⁵³ Under the influence of the *i*-suffix, the root vowels became fronted and raised into *tēþi and *fēti. With singular *tōþ* and *fōt* already now differentiated from the plural by the change of stem vowel, the *i* suffix becomes redundant, drops off, and we are left with the attested forms of *tēþ* and *fēt*. In the instance of OE *sellan* and Gothic *seljan*, native wit alone tells us that they are related words. The law of umlaut, however, relates the languages historically, fixing *seljan* as the earlier word, and thereby a chronology of sound changes. In the instance of OE *tōþ / tēþ* and *fōt / fēt*, we should never have hypothesized the lost, intermediate forms of *tēþi and *fēti without the paradigm provided by umlaut. With sound changes thus rationalized as a diachronic phenomenon, comparative philology allows us to fix the parentage of words, enabling us in the same moment to declare other explanations as false etymologies. The very idea of a word's etymology being "false" is a new one, coming into being as philology constructed itself as science. Evolution of sound originates in the body. *Fōti turned into *fēt* because it more efficiently used the mouth's economic resources. It is said that the receded larynx made homo sapiens conquerors of the world, not because it enabled us to choke but because it facilitated more articulated sounds and hence a more evolved language.⁵⁴ Language no longer is the sign of reason, differentia of humanity, but a function of biology.

I-umlaut demonstrates the comparative and historical nature of modern philology. We may only fully explain the vowel structure of *sellan* in relation to an earlier and different verb, *saljan*. We explain the present in contrast to the past, and identity in contrast to alterity. The etymological "truth" of a word (Gr. *etymos* meaning "true") is hidden unto itself, and we can only gain access to it by understanding what it is not; *sellan* is spelled (and thus pronounced) *sellan* because it is not spelled (and thus pronounced) *saljan*. Philology is now a matter of "the elucidation of one language by reference to a related language, explaining the forms of one by appeal to the forms of the other."[55] *Sellan* is explicable only when *saljan* is identified as the older of the two languages. Comparative philology *is* historical philology. The past itself is now measured in terms of difference from the present; language study becomes an archeological enterprise, a science of excavation.

The possibilities of this subterranean digging for truths unavailable at the conscious level of a single language were not lost on Freud, for whom, in his essay, "The Antithetical Meaning of Primal Words," language is seen to behave exactly like the unconscious (*SE*, 11:153–61). Archeological excavation persists as a profound metaphor in his work for his own methods of analysis. Historical semantics—shifts of meaning over time—tends to disregard contradiction, often making antonyms mean the same thing; the process is called enantiosemy.[56] The logic of the unconscious exhibits a similar liking "for combining contraries into a unity or for representing them as one and the same thing" (*SE*, 11:155). As Freud remarked elsewhere in response to Dora, "No other kind of 'Yes' can be extracted from the unconscious; there is no such thing at all as an unconscious 'No' " (*SE*, 7:57). He would have raised no eyebrow at the sinners from the circle of shit who turn their "no" into "yes" (*Inf.*, xxi.42).

Freud's point of departure is an essay by linguist Karl Abel, which shows how the ancient Egyptian language sustained a substantial number of words that could also mean their opposite, as if "strong" also meant "weak." Over the passage of time, the original word that sustained antithetical meaning underwent a process of splitting or phonetic reduction whereby the one word became two, the differentiation occurring by means of a vowel change or some other minimal modification. Hence, Freud explains, Egyptian *ken* means "strong" while *kan* means "weak." Egyptian also contains compound words composed of opposite meanings, yet the compound word only denotes one of those elements, as if there were a word "strong-weak" that nonetheless only meant "strong" and would have meant the same thing had the word stood independently.

We explain such phenomena by the assumption that identity is established only in relation to difference. If there were no darkness, there would be no word for light, for we only know a thing once we apprehend that it is capable of not being or of being its contrary. Structural linguistics proceeds precisely around such oppositions. Phonetic and semantic value are determined by negation or difference: "*f*art" is phonemically different from "*st*art," "*c*art," "*chart*," etc. Noise is the conceptual contrary of silence. Only later did words split off and develop independently as positive values: "strong," "weak," "smelly," "fragrant." Such independent phonetic and semantic values are only apparent, however, for they repress an implied contrary.

The older the language, word, or concept, argued Freud, the greater its ability to contain contradiction. At its origin, it is as if every word possesses a double meaning and every meaning possesses at least two words for it. Words are the tools of psychoanalysis, the talking cure, which aims at a reconstruction of psychic wholeness effected only by first uncovering the foundations of the unconscious where words and concepts are forged, or, in alchemical terms, by returning the element to prime matter. Part of the work of analysis is to rebuild Babel. At this primal site, formal logic, which can only proceed by means of conceptual oppositions between identity and difference, affirmation and negation, has no purchase.

Looking at languages closer to our own, Freud notes the double meanings of L. *altus*, which means both "high" and "deep," of *sacer* [sacred, accursed], and German *Boden* [garret, ground]. He also notes the slightness of difference, whether orthographic or phonological, between words of opposite meaning: L. *clamare* [to cry], *clam* [softly, secretly] and L. *siccus* [dry], *succus* [juice]. Alongside these conceptual reversals, we find phonetic reversals. Ancient Egyptian apparently sustained the ability to reverse sounds, usually the initial and final consonants, yet retain the same meaning; as if German *gut* [good] could also be pronounced and spelled *tug*. In English, we might think of "*boat*" and "*tub*," or "*care*" and "*reck*," which are similar in meaning but have their initial and final consonants reversed. The official etymology, however, of "care" traces it to Latin *cura*, and "reck" derives from a Norse or Scandinavian word that shows no evidence of reversal; in other words, there is no etymological connection between "care" and "reck" whatever Freud says.

Reversal or metathesis also operates across languages: *p* and *t* in German *Topf* and English "*pot*;" *t* and *w* in German *täuwen* [tarry] and English "*wait*." The *OED* however derives "pot" from popular Latin *pottus* rather than from *Topf*. Likewise, "wait" derives from Old French *guaitier* or Germanic *wahtan. The preference is always to trace back a linear descent of heritage than to allow any sideways leap of metathesized sound reversal. The derivation of Old English *leaf* from the reconstructed Germanic *laubhaz-* retains the purity of the (Germanic) family relation and ignores any possible metathesization of Latin *folium* [leaf].

Metathesis happens everywhere: "butter-fly" (OE *buttor-fleoge*), underwent its own transmogrification from "flutter-by"; and "dirt," which carries the specific sense of "ordure," exists in Middle English as both "dirt" and "drit" (*OED*, *s.v. dirt*, n.[1,2a,2b]), from which we get Scots "drutle." Yet were we to rewrite the *OED* entry to say that butterfly is a flutterby, which hides its derivation by reversing its initial consonants, we should begin to sound like Socrates in *Cratylus*. The sciences of lexicography and philology go to some length to keep distance from whimsy, yet scientific grammar and occult *gramarye* have an ancient kinship. Grammar, synonymous with the mastery of Latin, was the key to learned secrets, and eventually to occult sciences such as astrology and alchemy, whence came its other name, "glamor" (*MED*, s.v. *gramari[e]*, n.[1b]). Linguistic science makes claims that, to at least one infantile mind, seem like legerdemain: to a pupil of James Murray, editor-to-be of the *OED*, "Such was his skill and knowledge that many of us firmly believed that by Grimm's law he could prove that BLACK really was the same word as WHITE; at least that was how it seemed to our poor intelligences."[57]

Linguistics does recognize metathesis, but it is not a sound law, is not considered any kind of systemic change, and has closer relationship to the mistake; for this reason, it often appears under the name of spoonerism, so called after Reverend W.A. Spooner (1844–1930), warden of New College, Oxford, whose vaguely dyslexic tendencies produced howlers like "Kinquering congs their titles take." From unintended spoonerism, it is easier still to relegate metathesis to horsing around with puns, where it is allowed to flourish unconstrained as word play, examples of which are endless. Rabelais remarks that a woman who is *folle à la messe* [foolish in mass] amounts to the same thing as her being *molle à la fesse* [moist in the ass].[58] And the difference between a preacher and a lady bathing is that one of them has hope in his soul. . . . This kind of mischief has no standing in philology, which recognizes only the mixing of *verba* between sheets that are clean and "proper," only the word that is "the legitimate heir to the succession."[59] Words that rub their bacon in the corners of the minds of the ignorant and the frivolous produce exactly the kind of improper copulations of which John of Salisbury warned.

The final surety of legitimacy for a word is entry into a dictionary, but what counts as a word? "The quotations were the evidence that a word had been used at a particular date in a particular way or sense, but was it sufficient if only one example had been found? What about words invented 'for the nonce,' or as a joke, or mis-spellings?"[60] In 1938, P.G. Wodehouse refers to a man who, "if not actually disgruntled, was far from being gruntled."[61] It is a grammatical joke that analogizes from formations such as discovered/covered to disgruntled/gruntled, but Wodehouse's coined *bon mot* became fashionable, and entered the annals of the *OED*. If enough people use it, a joke-word can become offical English, but in order to do so, it becomes ordinary language, loses its surprise, and hence its status as a joke.

If metatheses are happening all the time in language, so also are grammatical analogies such as "gruntled." Saussure's main example of the latter is L. *honos* [honor], whose *s* became rhoticized (turned into *r*), creating an accusative case *honorem*.[62] Over time, a new nominative form evolved—*honor*—on the analogy of third declension words such as *orator, oratorem*. Honor, which eventually replaced *honos*, may originally have come about through ignorance, wit, poetic licence, or an intention to rationalize irregularity. For Saussure, analogizing is a "creative principle," a psychological phenomenon[63]; unlike sound changes, which obliterate the sound that went before, analogy rejoices in surplus and can coexist with the original, *honos* and *honor* being for a time interchangeable,[64] which is to say that analogy is promiscuous.

When Panurge refers to "his beggarly befarted body" [mon paillard et empeté corps],[65] he analogizes from past participles used as passive adjectives. *Empeté* [befarted] did not become common parlance, remaining a Rabelaisian nonce word. On the other hand, *décrépit* [decrepit] is a legitimate French word, descending from Latin *decrepitus* [worn out by age]. *Decrepitus* itself derives from *crepitus*, which means both "rattle" and "fart," so *décrépit* does mean "befarted" even though it applies in a different sense. Why is not "befarted" a proper word, whether in English or French? The logic by which one meaning prevails and another vanishes is largely unavailable to analysis. Usage is capricious yet definitive. Language forever invents new words, most often based on analogies, and forever plays around with sounds, reversing some, adding others, dropping others, yet the word play rarely if ever features as a category of linguistic change because it follows no perceivable system.

Freud's interest in contrasting words that collapse upon each other continues in his interest in puns. In his essay, "Character and Anal Eroticism" (*SE*, 9:171–2), he footnotes an encounter he had with a patient, who told him that a friend, on reading Freud's work, laughed uproariously at the thought of a baby on the potty deliberating whether to obey nurse and shit now, or to disobey her and defer the pleasure. The patient subsequently and (for Freud) revealingly reminisced about how as a child he used to think himself to be the cocoa manufacturer Van Houten. To this Freud the punster quipped, "Wann haut'n die Mutter?" [When does Mummy spank?], *Van Houten* and *Wann haut'n* being similar in pronunciation.

Only later did Freud fill in the logical blanks that underlay the apparently disconnected exchanges. Mummy spanks [*haut'n/Houten*] when [*Wann/Van*] you've soiled yourself with caca [*Kaka/Kakao*]. Multiple displacements and reversals disguise the patient's emotive recollections of defecation and spanking. The central connection rests on the pun between "caca" and "cocoa." The patient disavowed the prospect of infantile delay of anal pleasure by laughing derisively at it via a friend, but then obliquely testified to being a caca manufacturer himself by the memory of cocoa man Van Houten. "Shit" and "spank" disguise themselves in puns, the act of expelling caca hides under the inverse act of ingesting cocoa, and the patient's own denial is displaced onto the scepticism of the friend. There is no linguist anywhere who would agree that "caca" and "cocoa" are cognate. Apart from similarity of sound (and color), there is no connection, their verbal alliance purely playful. Where metathesis disguises identifications within entire languages, puns unravel similar repressions within the individual unconscious. Word play, which falls outside the proper scope of linguistic analysis, performs both the concealment and disclosure of psychic drives as powerful as any sound law.

In its treatment of the etymon as paradise lost, in its attempt to converge in centripetal motion upon its own hidden center, medieval etymology shows itself conservative and backward looking. By claiming Adam and Eve as the first parents of all languages, it finds a way to map all languages and dialects into a hierarchy of nobility and commonness. The pedigree languages of Hebrew, Greek, and Latin take pride of place as noblest and most ancient, while the half-breed vernaculars wax and wane, as fleeting as lust. In this way, the medieval etymon reduces multiplicity to fixed difference of estate, just as from Noah's three sons sprang all social groups: from Shem freemen [*liberi*], from Japhet, knights [*milites*], and from Ham serfs [*servi*].[66]

Yet common ancestry just as easily may level all difference. As English rebels marched in protest in 1381, they challenged the origin of hereditary aristocracy and serfdom by chanting, "When Adam delved and Eve span, who was then the gentleman?" If medieval etymology is conservative and authoritarian, it also disseminates wildly, like rabbits, making many words out of one. Already offspring of other meaningful words, words cultivate the potency of their wind in order to generate more words, to make meaning-babies. Jet-propelled from the windpipe, words spawn a multitude of little *verba*. *Vulpes* supposedly derives from *volo* and *pes*, because the fox's feet fly. *Volo* means both "I wish" and "I fly" (*velle* [to wish]; *volare*, [to fly]).[67] *Velle* and *volare* married and sired *volo*, who in turn married *pes*, from whose loins sprang *vulpes*. Genealogies also conflict. Translating Bartholomeus, John Trevisa alleges that *vulpes* comes from gimp-footed, referring to the sidling shiftiness of the fox's cunning: "The fox hatte *vulpes* and haþ þatte name as it were 'walowynge feet asyde' and goþ neuere forþright but alway aslont and wiþ fraude."[68] Some say that *musica* derives from *Moys*, flowing water whose gurgling sounds sound harmonious; and some say it derives from *musa*, shepherd's pipes[69]; yet Socrates asserts that *mousikē* [music] and *Mousas* [Muses] derive from *mōsthai* [philosophical searching].[70]

Far from undermining the singleness of linguistic authority, the alternative interpretations of medieval etymology enhance the inexhaustible possibilities of a word's origins. In this theological landscape of language, the etymon is the Logos, and its mystical fulness cannot contract into one word; it is a whole always greater than the sum of its verbal derivatives. Multiplicity is testament to the unceasing abundance of the origin. To modern philologists, on the other hand, conflicting etymologies pose a problem.[71] The discrepant etymologies of "carminative" signal a lack of evidence that disables consensus. For some, the word derives from Latin *carminare* [to comb or card wool]; for others, from Latin *carmen* [song, charm]. Some leave the door open on both possibilities,[72] but both cannot be correct.

> It is remarkable that the latest edition of Ogilvie's Dict. derives carminative from the Low Lat. *carminare*, supposed to mean "to charm," because such a remedy acts suddenly, as a *charm*. This is not a good guess, because it gives no good sense; and this *carminare* properly means "to compose verses." It is not meant that *carminatives* compose verses, or that they charm the patient; the sense intended is that of ridding or expelling which is merely a figurative use of the verb *carminare* that was first mentioned.[73]

How is it possible to clinch the parentage of a word? Much of the time, etymology is little more than informed guesswork. Even if we were lucky enough to locate some medieval discussion of the meaning and derivation of *carminatif*, what makes it right for simply being contemporaneous? Given that ancient and medieval etymologies are almost always wrong by modern standards, does an early user's belief in a certain derivation have any authority at all? Yet the entry of a word into language "must be an act of an individual, despite the fact that in language, anonymous tradition reigns supreme."[74] The intentionality of the first user appears, when known, to be decisive: "Snark is certainly, not probably, a blend of snake and shark, because Lewis Carroll explained his coinage."[75] Inasmuch as anyone thought about it, some must have assumed *carminative* to be so called because it combed out knots of flatulence, while some attributed it to the music of a well-tempered gut. What linguists call false or popular etymologies nonetheless often become the basis of use and thereby the means at least in part by which a word takes hold in a language. They are the surrogate rather than biological fathers of words, yet who is the real sire? Most of all, what has the mother been doing when no one was looking? Fatherhood is a problematic metaphor to use, for it is an inexact term, fudging the roles of "pater" and "genitor," legal and biological parent. Paternity is an agreement, not a bodily fact, and as the Captain in Strindberg's *The Father* knows, it could not be proved (at least at the time).

Genealogy has no place for promiscuous mothers, or etymology for promiscuous words. *Promiscuum*, a Latin word, is a grammatical term, meaning "common," as in a "common noun." Our ancient theorists of language, with their crackpot etymologies, recognized that words are always at it, and have multiple parents. The overdetermination of ancient etymology undoes the difference between true and false origins, native words and borrowed. The origin turns out to be itself multiple and full of noise[76]; the "first" cause proves to be many, for mother language is a harlot, unsure of the paternity of any of her offspring. Words are always whoring around because it is fun; why else would it be called word play? Retracing genealogical and etymological steps takes us on a path that, if it ever does converge on a single Edenic origin, must first pass through the impossible labyrinth of Babel. If the medieval etymon sucks all words up its asshole, eradicating linguistic difference, it also farts them all back out in centrifugal motion, proliferating into bewildering purposeless babble, into punned, punctured, punctuated words, it makes sounds for their own sake rather than for meaning, it poops copulatives wildly. While the genitals produce word-genealogies, around on the other side of the linguistic body is the fruitful farting of word play.

Isidore traces the parentage of *ars* [art] from Greek *arete* [excellence] (*Etym.*, 1.1.2). But as the word converges on Babel, another kinship emerges. In Chaucer's *Summoner's Tale*, the lord of the manor marvels at the difficult problem of *ars-metrike* that churl Thomas has put to the friar: how does one divide a fart equally in twelve, let alone thirteen?

> How hadde this cherl ymaginacioun
> To shewe swich a probleme to the frere?
> Nevere erst er now herde I of swich mateere.
> I trowe the devel putte it in his mynde.
> In ars-metrike shal ther no man fynde,
> Biforn this day, of swich a question.
> Who sholde make a demonstracion
> That every man sholde have yliche his part
> As of the soun or savour of a fart?
> (*CT* 3.2218–26)

[How did this peasant have the gumption to put such a quodlibet to the friar? I've never heard anything like it. The devil must have put him up to it. Not in the entire discipline of arithmetic will you find a problem like this—not until now that is. Who is able to give the solution to the question whether the noise and savour[77] of a fart may be divided equally, to every man his part?]

Ars-metrike clearly puns on "arithmetic" and "arse-metrics," as does *ferthing* on farthing and farting, yet the *MED* never mentions that, at least once in the English language, *ars-metricke* means "measurement of the butt," or that *ferthing* can mean *ferting*. Why not?

The difference of vowel length between *fēorthing* and *feorting* holds the two words apart, and means that they would have been pronounced differently. Neither ancient nor medieval manuscripts, however, tend to indicate the length or shortness of vowels; this is certainly the case in manuscripts of the *Canterbury Tales*. (The twelfth-century *Ormulum*, with its unique phonetic spelling, is a well known exception.) Vowel lengths can be disregarded when the occasion requires. John Mirk maintains that "gospel" means "goodys spelle, þat ys, Goddys word" [good news, that is, God's word].[78] Old English *gōdspel* [gospel] is a calque of Latin *evangelium*, which literally means "good message," and by the early fifteenth century, the long vowel had already been registered orthographically by the digraph *oo*. "God," with a short *o*, is a different word. Mirk no doubt recognized the phonological distinction, but took the pun to reveal linguistic connection at a higher level, showing "God" as true origin of the "good." With respect to the difference between medial *t* and *th* in *feorthing/feorting*, one can be a dialectal and orthographic variant of the other, and there is frequent interchange between medial *th* and *d* and between *d* and *t*. A common variant spelling of "farthing" is "farding" (*OED*, s.v. *farthing*, n.), and a certain measurement of land recorded in the Domesday Book was called a *ferting* or *ferding*.[79] If *ferting* as a term of land measurement was familiar to Chaucer, his readers, or his scribes, then the friar's question "What is a ferthing worth parted in twelve?" scores a triple pun.

Farthing/farting, arse/art, and good/God are all, to the modern linguist, word play, falling outside the category of strictly communicative language. Play-words are bastards, born on the wrong side of the semantic blanket. By so distinguishing between legitimate semantics and word play, the pun is excluded from serious grammar and relegated to literary device, at best.

But literary device is not entirely extrinsic to meaning. For Augustine, its point is not eloquence for its own sake but to reveal "that which lay hidden" [*quod latebat*].[80] Word play is, however, always subservient to message or content, *verbum* subservient to *res*. Augustine prefers grammatical correctness at all times, but he allows a coined analogy such as the plural form *sanguinibus* from *sanguis* [blood], a word that exists only in the singular, as long as it has some instructive point. Certainly incorrect Latin that instructs is preferable to correct Latin that does not.[81] In the instance of *os* [bone], plural *ossa*, Augustine prefers the incorrect nominative singular form of *ossum*, which analogizes *ossum: ossa* after *bellum: bella* [war]. He does so in order to prevent any ambivalence in distinguishing *os* [bone] from *ōs* [mouth], because "African ears make no distinction between short and long vowels."[82] Maybe there were a few jokes after all going around Africa about the old woman [*anūs*] and the asshole [*anus*]; there certainly were in fifteenth-century England, as one scribe writes, "Dum dormitat anus, velud ancer sibulat anus" [While the old woman naps, her arsehole hisses like a goose].[83]

Vowel length is a key criterion in distinguishing between etymological relation and word play: even in classical Rome the word pair *avium/āvium* [of birds (possessive case, plural)/pathless place] is considered a clear case of punning.[84] Suppression of dialectical variation of those "African ears" that violate vocalic precision, maintains the purity of Roman Latin. In the dictionary, it facilitates a manipulated standardization of pronunciation and keeps puns and "true" etymologies far apart.

By comparison, medieval Latin grammar is more inclusive of ornament that smacks of the ludic. As for medieval vernaculars, the notion of grammatical correctness is too latent to support sustained discussion of tropes. So entwined are the medieval disciplines of grammar and of rhetoric that Augustine can speak of tropes [*tropi*] as belonging to the art of grammar.[85] Verbal ornament is not an optional extra, but a part of the fulness of rational speech, for even food consumed for survival alone needs a bit of salt and pepper.[86] Grammar disassembles and reassembles *verba* in ways both endlessly playful and seriously exegetical.

Just as sound laws validate the procedures of modern etymology, so do grammar and rhetoric validate medieval etymology. The medieval *nomen* [noun] subdivides into many classes, of which one group is so large that Priscian devotes an entire book of his *Institutiones* to it: *nomina denominativa* [denominative nouns]. Denominative nouns are nouns that in some way derive from other words. Examples include: *Cicero*, derived from *cicer* [chickpea]; *Caesar*, derived from *caedo* [I cut], and from which we get "caesarian"; *tentorium* [tent] derived from *tendo* [I stretch]; *regina* [queen] from *rex* [king]. Sorting through Priscian's examples, we might be tempted to categorize them grammatically: thus *Caesar* and *tentorium* are formed from the supine of the verbs "cut" (*caesum*) and "stretch" (*tentum*); and *regina* is formed from the possessive of "king" (*regis*). But Prician sorts them by sound clusters, so that *regina* appears along with other *–ina* suffixes, such as *medicus, medicina; doctrix, doctrina*.[87] In another group, ending in *–(m)en*, Priscian includes *flumen* [river] from *fluo* [I flow] and *lumen* [light] from *luo* [I get rid of].[88] It makes a whole lot more sense to connect *lumen* with *lux* [light], but maintaining the phonetic analogy with *flumen* and *fluo* obliges Priscian to assert that *lumen* derives from *luo* because light "gets rid of" darkness. Despite that umbilical connection between word and referent, medieval grammar here produces its own kind of sound laws to determine connection. "Denominativum appellatur a voce primitivi sic nominatum, non ab aliqua speciali significatione" [The denominative noun is called thus first and foremost by its sound, not by any special meaning].[89]

By this process of sticking *–men* or *–ina* or *–bundus* or somesuch onto a word, we make a new word and at the same time demonstrate its parentage.

Yet this is exactly what eymology also does, and Isidore makes his point with the same example that Priscian uses: *flumen*. Etymology, he says, explains the names and words we use to describe things, "inasmuch as *flumen* [river], because it came into being from *fluendo* [flowing], is named from *fluendo*" (*Etym.*, 1.29.1).

Medieval rhetoric corroborates etymology just as soundly. Deriving one thing from another is not only a grammatical phenomenon, *nomen denominativum*, but also a stylistic device, *denominatio*, commonly known by its Greek name, "metonymy." Metonomy or *denominatio* names a thing in terms of some aspect of that thing. Thus, for example, we name a cause in terms of its effect or an effect in terms of its cause: Mars is the cause of war, war the effect of Mars, numbness the effect of cold, cold the cause of numbness.[90] The four kinds of metonomy correspond to the Aristotelian four causes[91]: material, formal, efficient, and final. The efficient cause, explains Aristotle, is the initiating source of change; thus, the father is the (efficient) cause of his child, which explains how metonomy works in the *Iliad*, when Agamemnon is so often called by his father's name, Atrides. By denoting a thing in terms of its cause, metonomy expounds meaning even as it embellishes sound. Medieval etymology wields its etiological authority by means of linguistic strategms that are essentially grammatical and rhetorical. Etymology and etiology are the same. In Aquinas's discussion of the fourfold meaning of scripture—whose terms are usually called the literal, allegorical, moral, and anagogical—he discusses St. Augustine's preference for the term "etiological" over "moral" (*ST*, 1a.1.10). As do the categories of metonomy, the four levels of scriptural meaning derive from the Aristotelian four causes: the literal corresponds to the material cause, the allegorical to the formal, the moral (or etiological) to the efficient, and the anagogical to the final. In an attempt to standardize terminology, modern Thomist editors have emended manuscript witnesses of *secundum ethymologiam* [according to the etymological sense] to read "according to the *etiological* sense." But by reinstating the variant reading, we see more clearly how the etymon explains the etiology of a word; it is the efficient cause of a word, the parent who spawned it.

Because ancient etymology relies on phonological resemblance as much as it does on semantics, it is capable of wholly ironic connections between a word and its derivative, as in Priscian's derivation of *lumen* from *luo* because light "gets rid of" darkness. *Bellum* [war] may be said to derive from *bellus* [beautiful], on the grounds that war is *not* beautiful[92]; Varro claims that the unclean *latrina* [latrine] derives from *lavare* [to wash]—*Ex quo apparent latrinam a lavando dictam esse*[93]; Augustine claims that *lucus* [grove] derives from *lux*, because minimal light shines there [*quod minime luceat*].[94] Such etymologies proceed by taking two unlike things—grove/light; light/banishment—and surprising us by their hidden connection. So ironic are these "contrary origins" that Augustine names this "trope" *antiphrasis*. Yet could we not equally call this a pun, paronomasia? How do we catch hold of the tail of these wriggling words? Are they *nomina denominativa*, or antiphrases, or metonomies, or puns? Where does grammar end and etymology begin?

A pun para-names a thing, as the word "paronomasia," from the Greek, or the Latin *adnominatio* suggests. By means of a modification of sound or change of letters, a close resemblance to a different word emerges, so that similar words express dissimilar things.[95] The figure is a figure of speech rather than of thought, that is, one of the "easy" ornaments, which adorn the face of a word without touching its mind. Etymology works in the same way. *Lux* as contrary origin of *lucus* proceeds by means of the principle of dissimilar things conjoined by similar sounds. Yet even when the etymology is not ironic, it brings to presence some hidden aspect of the thing that has been lost from the surface meaning. "For when you see from what place a name originates, you understand its meaning more quickly" (*Etym.*, 1.29.2). The same principle informs Priscian's *nomina denominativa*, in which *tentorium* [tent] can be understood in terms of its parent *tendere* [to stretch]: tents are stretched, rivers flow, and Cicero takes his name from a chickpea.

If two words can be brought into punning relationship, then there is some feasible relation of derivation or etymology, feasible at least to a medieval philologist. So then, does "ass-metrics" derive from "arithmetic?" It is not likely that Chaucer's audience would have laughed because he was trivializing or falsifying the rules of etymology. The intended humor more likely emerges from the demystification of an elevated concept, from the exposure of its base origins: arithmetic, the art of number, one of the seven liberal arts is all about dividing farts. Rabelaisian etymologies desecrate in similar fashion with their inglorious origins. On visiting the area north of Orléans, Gargantua remarks that he likes it fine ["je trouve beau ce"], and hence the area is subsequently called La "Beauce"[96]; and the capital of France, when Gargantua urinated on it for a joke [*par ris*] and flooded it, was henceforth dubbed "Paris."[97] This degraded provenance unseats the exalted belief that the city derives its name from Paris, son of Priam, king of Troy, from whom the French kings are supposed to have descended.[98] The Roman *cognomen*, brought about in order to re*cog*nize patrician distinction, similarly exposes its base origins. The high-born Brutus is stupid, Verrucosus warty, Strabo crosseyed, Varus bow-legged, and Capito a fathead.[99] Cicero's association with a chickpea might refer to his penis or the squashed end of his nose, or to his status as a grower of garbanzo beans—in other words, he is a country bumpkin.[100]

Etymology, like genealogy, undoubtedly privileges patriarchal origins as the source of a word's power or a family's blood. Yet it also has the capacity to level exclusivity, to reduce legitimacy to promiscuity, and signification to uncontrolled punning. The reduction to or exposure of disreputable etiology is a consequence of the very act of verbal breaking that is etymological analysis. Even within orthodox etymology, there exists the recognition of the difference between aristocratic and plebian genealogies.[101] Just as a fart betrays the truth of one's insides—what one ate, the health of the stomach—so the breaking of verbal wind yields knowledge of a word's parentage. Buried within the idea of farting is breaking or cutting, as in the expressions "to break wind" and "to cut a fart." The modern Greek word for fart, *klania*, derives from ancient Greek *klaō* [I cut] and its noun *klasis* [cutting, breaking]. "To cut a fart" has something of the tautological to it, and the phrase returns us to the sense of air as a body severed by the force and noise of a fart. The most sacred moment of the Eucharist when the priest announces, "This is my body, broken for you" has provoked many a snigger among Greek schoolchildren. Breaking suggests on the one hand desecration and destruction yet on the other the releasing of inner goodness; hence one speaks in hunting of the breaking of the deer or in religion of the breaking of bread. It is as if the violence done to something brings its inner being to presence more forcibly than when it is intact. It is in desecration that we encounter the holy. Etymology involves poking around in the "paternal dungheaps" [*paterneus fumiers*] of words.[102] Take a deep whiff as a word breaks wind, for its meaning assumes a resonance that ears cannot register and a presence that eyes cannot see.

Bastard Laughter

The pun brings us back to before Babel, to a common place where all topics connect. Its topsy-turviness is captured in poems such as the playfully utopic fantasy *Land of Cockaigne*, in details such as the Dutch misericord of ducat-poop, in mad marginalia that adorn Gothic manuscripts. In a pun, sacred and profane are obliged to couple; queen and peasant rub their bacon together. The dissimilarities of meanings in puns take one by surprise, tripping us up by an unexpected homograph or by a homophone that had been sitting in the ears all along.

One of the most famous surprises in literature occurs when Oedipus in Sophocles's play, *Oedipus the King*, learns that the couple he thought his biological parents were only adoptive parents, that the stranger he killed earlier was his blood father Laios (and hence that he is the murderer for whom he has been searching), and that Jocasta, the woman to whom he is married, is his own mother. Aristotle, a deep admirer of the play, discusses that moment of revelation, *anagnorisis*, when everything falls into place.

Recognition [*anagnorisis*], as the very name indicates, is a change from ignorance to knowledge, leading to friendship or to enmity, and involving matters which bear on prosperity or adversity. The finest recognition is that which occurs simultaneously with reversal [*peripeteia*], as with the one in the *Oedipus*... Such a joint recognition and reversal will yield either pity [*eleos*] or fear [*phobos*], just the type of actions of which tragedy is taken to be a mimesis; besides, both adversity and prosperity will hinge upon such circumstances.[103]

Anagnorisis frequently translates as "discovery" or "recognition." *Gnorimon* denotes what is logically evident.[104] *Ana-* as a prefix means "again," "back," or "up," and is best approximated in English by the prefix re-, from Latin. So, "re-cognition" translates *anagnorisis* well enough. Recognition suggests that somewhere inside you knew what you now see clearly, but had not put a name on it, that the initial misrecognition was not entirely innocent but a repression now returned or a dissociation now connected. This is surely the case for Oedipus who had had warning enough in the form of early slanders about his parentage and Delphic oracular prediction. On this last day of being king of Thebes, Oedipus finally recognizes who he is.

For Heidegger, *Oedipus Tyrannus* embodies the interplay between seeming, Being and not-Being. In his effort to dig, by means of etymology, underneath the apparently stable foundations upon which metaphysics stands, Heidegger traces three senses of the German word *Schein*.[105] *Schein* means to "shine" or "glow"; it also means to "show," or "make an appearance," to "be manifest," or to "come out"; finally, it means to "merely seem," to "be that which is not actual." In the first two senses, *Schein* means the same thing as Being, for in shining or lighting up, something makes an appearance; but to make an appearance means to be apparent, to seem so. Here Heidegger establishes connection between Being and the third, apparently contradictory sense, that of mere seeming, and in doing so throws down the gauntlet to Western metaphysics, which since Plato, has systematically enforced the opposition between the real and the apparent. Mere seeming partially distorts its own Being, and thus introduces the possibility into Being of not-Being. At the beginning of the play, Oedipus appears in all the shining light of his seeming; but then, in seeking out the murderer of the former king, Laios, he sets out on a course of self-unconcealment, until his true Being—namely, murderer of his father, husband of his mother, and brother of his own children—finally unfolds in all its horror. Confronted by his own Being, Oedipus responds by blinding and exiling himself, proclaiming by this his desire for not-Being. At the first fateful crossroads of his life, where three roads met, he fulfilled the oracle's prophecy by killing

Laios; at the second juncture, where seeming, Being, and not-Being intersect, Oedipus dares everything at the crossroads of existence to find out who he is. Oedipus possesses an "eye too many"[106] that fuels his passion for unveiling, yet it is this that makes him a great and tragic hero, and the play a profound meditation upon Being [*physis*]. *Physis* is not an abstract idea, not a rational principle, nor is it a practical action, executed with intention. It occurs as the mode in which an inner reality emerges. As Jocasta runs offstage in despairing recognition of the truth, a tense silence ensues, at which the leader of the Chorus says: "I am afraid evil [*kaka*] may burst forth [*anarrēksei*] after this silence."[107] *Kaka*, the word for both ugliness and evil, gives us modern "caca" and ancient *kakkē* [shit]. But Oedipus welcomes the release: "Let it burst."[108] *Anarrēksei* refers to any act of violent outbreak, from the breaking of an animal's carcass to the eruption of boils and volcanoes. Self-realization comes upon Oedipus as a bodily eruption. From flatulence we model our ontological terms. We might even say that Oedipus is a great farter.

The horrible moment of recognition is the stuff of thrillers, when the hero realizes that he is actually dead or that a trusted intimate is the murderer. A "thriller" is not named amiss, for in that shock of discovery lies epistemophilic pleasure. A larger discussion of the role of similitude and imitation in knowledge prefaces Aristotle's discussion of dramatic art.[109] Knowledge is nothing less than the perception of similitudes. Similitude is the basis of all cognition, all consciousness, and in similitude, in knowledge, lies pleasure, a word that rightly names the climatic moment when Oedipus recognizes the similitude between himself, the stranger who killed Laios where three roads meet, and the baby whom the Theban royal servant gave to a Corinthian shepherd. *Anagnoresis* is exclusively human. Animals may recognize, but do not, according to scholastic faculty psychology, recognize that they recognize; mental reflection belongs only to the rational animal. So despite the fact that by anybody's standards Oedipus was having a bummer of a day, there is pleasure somewhere in that awful recognition, which ironically shows him at his most human. Deep down inside, when we commit the act of knowing we smile with pleasure. Even bad news sounds good. Smiles are the sign of *anagnorisis*. As Joubert notes in his dedicatory epistle, laughter, which registers most in the face, is the most fitting mark of humanity [propre indice de l'humanité]. Risible material first registers in the brain, then instantaneously informs the heart, whence comes the passion of laughter.[110] The *contemptus mundi* motif—the recognition of the triviality of earthly existence—comes as a revelatory smile to Dante, as he gazes down from Paradise on the heavens below (*Paradiso*, xxii.133–5); and Chaucer's Troilus looking down from the heavens laughs at those who mourn him (*TC*, 5.1821–2).

Natura...hominem tantum nudum et in nuda humo natali die abicit ad vagitus statim et ploratum, nullumque tot animalium aliud pronius ad lacrimas, et has protinus vitae principio.[111]

[Only man does great Nature cast naked on the naked ground the day he is born, to burst immediately into wailing and crying, and of all the animals there is none more prone to tears, which come immediately from the beginning of life.]

If sorrow is our lot, so is laughter. Tears are the garb of both; both mark our passage into knowledge. The human is the only animal that can be tickled and can laugh.[112] For Isidore of Seville, "man is a rational, mortal, biped animal that moves on land, and is capable of laughter" [homo est animal rationale, mortale, terrenum, bipes, risu capax] (*Etym.*, 2.25.2). Despite laughter's distinction, many medieval theologians identified it as the mark of original sin, claiming that Christ himself never laughed, or if he did, it was at the harrowing of hell, when he liberated the souls of virtuous heathen who lived before him[113]; but this registers triumph rather than amusement. Laughter and sorrow are siblings, even identical twins, yet it is nobler to be accounted a man of sorrows rather than a clown.

In his discussion of jokes, Freud tells a rather excellent one about a man who is curiously like Oedipus. Serenissimus, a Latin name that means something like "Fairest of Men," learns his true, or rather untrue, parentage:

> Serenissimus was making a tour through his provinces and noticed a man in the crowd who bore a striking resemblance to his own exalted person. He beckoned to him and asked: "Was your mother at one time in service in the Palace?"—"No, your Highness," was the reply, "but my father was."
>
> (*SE*, 8:68–9)

On seeing his double, Serenissimus assumes the man to be a bastard half brother, sired by his own father, the king, on some palace wench. His question is based on this assumption. The man's answer, namely, that it was his father not mother who worked at the palace, now puts Serenissimus's own parentage in question, for if some palace servant sired Serenissimus on the queen, Serenissimus's claim to the throne by right of patrilineal heredity is nullified. It is a "your mother" exchange of ingenious indirection and rudeness: Serenissimus covertly and insultingly asks the man whether his mother was a slut; to which the man, under guise of respectfully answering the king's question, replies, "no, *yours* was the whore." Safehouse of the seed of the king, the queen apparently lets the servant deposit his also. Just as Oedipus unwittingly initiates his own self-discovery, so does Serenissimus. The *anagnoresis* of the joke reverses the expected answer, thereby observing Aristotle's requirement that *anagnoresis* should follow on the heels of a reversal just as it does in *Oedipus the King*. *Anagnoresis* thrills because it surprises by coming up from the blind spot where we think not to look, which is, as we all know, from behind. The butt may mirror the face but it has no eyes. *Anagnoresis* gooses us in the ass.

Re-cognition, as its name suggests, is a knowing again, and presupposes a preceding period of unknowing in which the truth was possessed but unregistered. In the joke, *anagnoresis* catches the hearer offguard, and they laugh at the sudden reappearance of what they had forgotten. This element of surprise, not usually attributed to medieval theories of laughter, is intuitively exploited in the humor of Chaucer's *Miller's Tale*, where the funniest moment comes right at the end, after we think the joke has already been told. With the distraction of the subplot of Absolom—his humiliation at having kissed Alison's butt, and the humorous revenge he exacts by scalding Nicholas in the ass—we had quite forgotten about the theme of the flood and husband John, who is still fast asleep in a boat suspended from the ceiling. But with Nicholas's cry for water, John reenters the story, and we recognize with laughter the connection we had temporarily forgotten. "Duh" marks the moment of *anagnoresis*.

We take the "plot" of Serenissimus as a joke, but elaborated differently, it might have been a tragedy. Conversely, the plot of *Oedipus the King* has, when you think about it, a certain black humor.[114] That gut-wrench of tragic *anagnoresis* and the dropping of a joke's penny are not so different. Aristotle explicitly mentions that the effects of *anagnoresis* may be love, good fortune, and a happy ending just as easily as their contraries; and *anagnoresis* becomes a recognized characteristic of Greek New Comedy, which hinges on the mixed identities and disguises of farce.[115] The contrivances of *anagnoresis* slip readily into the parodic, as farcical as a handbag left at Victoria Station. Aristotle also notes that *anagnoresis* works best if it arises straight out of the events of the plot itself, just as it happens in Oedipus.[116] The less we individualize character—whether Oedipus was handsome or ugly, or preferred grapes to olives—the more the narrative sequence stands out in its pure form as joke. Likewise, we need know nothing about the personality or individual habits of the characters in the *Miller's Tale*—except perhaps that John is old, Alison young, and Absolom did not like farting. This is why Aristotle says, "without action there could be no tragedy, but without character there could be."[117] The mere narration of the plotline should be enough to produce the requisite feelings of pity and fear that constitute the proper tragic response. "For the plot should be so structured that, even without seeing it performed, the person who hears the events that occur experiences horror and pity at what comes about (as one would feel when hearing the plot of the *Oedipus*)."[118] Yet this is exactly what a joke does. Because we do not know or identify with Serenissimus, we are able to laugh rather than feel pity or fear. The ironic dovetailing of events makes us laugh at Chaucer's story, and feel horror at Sophocles's. Tragic and comic *anagnoresis* prove to be "identical twins."[119]

On this fateful day when *anagnoresis* dawns fully upon Oedipus, appearance breaks down as the inner truth of his origins erupts. Recognition, says Varro, involves naming, for *nomen* derives from *noscere* [to know, recognize].[120] For this reason, Aristotle spends considerable time on the felicitious use of names or nouns.[121] Names must denote clearly to enable proper recognition, but apt use of metaphor is necessary to discern similarity in dissimilarity.[122] What Oedipus discovers is a massive pun that collapses difference into identity. In him, the genealogical line bends back recursively upon itself. His wife is his mother, his sons are his brothers, and sisters daughters.[123] Worse, in ploughing the very furrow whence he sprang, Oedipus is become his own father, and in springing from the very place he inseminated, Oedipus is become his own son. "Oedipus" is its own etymon; he is his own point of origin. On that day, Oedipus discovers that he himself is the punch line. Recognition of Being causes us to break out in bastard laughter.

In the Middle Ages, the story of Oedipus was little known in its own right, but by an interesting conflation, the main events of Oedipus's life—killing his father and lying with his mother—were transferred onto Judas Iscariot.[124] The story circulated widely, for example, in the legend of St. Mattias, the disciple who replaced Judas after his suicide,[125] where we read of his abandonment as a baby by his parents because of a prophecy, growing up as another woman's child, killing his blood father, and marrying his blood mother. On discovering his identity, he seeks repentance from Christ, but is unable to overcome his despair, so he finally hangs himself, and in doing so, "to-brast the myddil, and alle hise entrailes weren sched abroad" [et diffusa sunt omnia veriscera ejus] (Acts 1.18). Hanging is a messy business, and the victim inevitably loses control of all bodily functions—shit, piss, semen, and air emit freely in the last throes.

> Rebecquez vous la montjoye
> Qui desvoye
> Votre proye
> Et vous fera du tout brouer.[126]

[Avoid the gallows, that will loosen your asshole and make your guts burst out.]

Laughter produces similar results.

> It is then likely that when these [epigastric] muscles press a long time and with much violence, soliciting the bowels [*les boyaus*] and the bladder

[*la vessie*] to surrender all their contents (as it happens in laughter), if there is a quantity of liquid matter, all escapes us indecorously [*vilainement*]. For the agitation and jouncing [*secousse*] is so strong that the sphincters are unable to resist.[127]

An early medieval tradition maintains that Judas was repulsively bloated, and popped like a balloon. Papias of the first century records that Judas was wider than a wagon and his eyelids so puffed that his eyes disappeared:

> His private part was larger and presented a more loathsome sight than has ever been witnessed; and through it there oozed from every part of the body a stream of pus and worms to his shame, even as he relieved nature. After suffering an agony of pain and punishment, he finally went, as they express it, to his own place; and owing to the stench the ground has been deserted and uninhabited till now; in fact even to the present day nobody can pass that place without holding his nose. So abundant was the discharge from his body and so far over the ground did it spread.[128]

Whether Judas popped or pooped, the dawning of *anagnoresis*, of self-knowledge as the betrayer of Christ brings a massive expenditure of bodily product. The sorrow of what is known mixes with the pleasure of knowing, and these emotions register in the contorted rictus of a hanged face.

> When one pushes a little while moving the bowels [*aller à selle*], or if one has a bellyache [*douleur de vantre*]. . .one plies the mouth [*rechigner*] just as when laughing. Why is that? Because of the diaphragmatic contraction [*le retirement diaphragmique*], for when it draws into itself in order better to push against the bowels and to force out [*vuider*] of them what is harmful and unpleasant [*ce qui nuit & deplait*]. . .there comes about a grinding of the teeth, with a stretching of the lips, as if one were laughing.. . .Consider two men in a painting, one of which is laughing so hard that he becomes completely undone, the other flails about horribly, complains and weeps large tears; even if the work is finely done you will not know to which to assign pleasure and to which sadness, so much are the faces alike in these two passions.[129]

The face contorted in pain, in dying, evacuating, or creased with pleasure, in laughing, in orgasm assumes the same muscular pose. In the critically detached space in which the eye observes, the face in ecstasy and agony looks the same.

Better Out Than In

In Chapter 6 of his *Poetics* Aristotle claims that tragedy "by means of pity [*eleos*] and fear [*phobos*] brings about the purgation [*kartharsis*] of such emotions."[130] Although interpretations of the term can conflict, one long-standing interpretation is that *katharsis* is essentially a medical term, referring to the cleansing of the system after a vomit, crap, fart, burp, or other such emission. Tragedy acts then like a laxative [L. *laxare*, "to loosen"] or an aperient [L. *aperire*, "to open"] to douche our systems of humors and emotions that unbalance the soul, so that we may return to the virtuous golden mean, to homeostatic equilibrium.

Aristotle's phrasing also indicates the homeopathic nature of tragedy's therapy, that emotions are purged by means of such emotions. Tragedy arouses the passions only to expel them, much as we take an effervescent drink to get rid of other trapped gas; the natural attraction between the incoming gas and the trapped gas overcomes the blockage and empties the system. According to such homeopathic principles, this is how some carminatives work, curing flatulence by inducing it, *similia similibus curantura* [like being cured by like] as does the hair of the dog that bites.

The second book of *Poetics*, on comedy, is lost, but Aristotle must have been aware of the cathartic properties of laughter as well as of tragedy. Laughter's expulsive properties are evident. Laughter is the opposite of pity [*compassion*],[131] and comedy of tragedy. The "passion of laughter" [*la passion risoliere*][132] registers its motions in the heart, the seat of passion. It is a mixture of joy and sadness—sadness because we laugh at what is ugly and painful to behold. In experiencing the joy that gives rise to laughter, the heart "expands thirstily, as if wanting to receive and embrace the object presented, whence it sends forth joyfully its blood and its humors [*ses espris*]."[133] For this reason, we redden, cry, and even piss or fart from laughing. At the same time, the sadness we experience from regarding ugliness causes a contrary motion, and the humors [*les espris*] retreat to the heart.[134] This counterbalance of joy with sadness prevents laughter from being dangerous to the point of death and turns it into the occasion of virtue; laughter strikes a golden mean between the contraries of intense joy and intense sadness. It lives in the middle, for laughter originates in the diaphragm, which divides the nobler upper parts of the body from the lower.[135] "Laughter is born of two contraries, one of which hinders the other from being excessive, and this is the reason that one does not easily die of laughter."[136] Sadness tempers the evacuation, or kenosis, that accompanies laughter, and this prevents one from cackling oneself to death, from the prodigal spending of bodily humors into self-extinction. This much at least for decorous laughter, which possesses a rhetorical sensibility in keeping its proper time and place. Aristotle calls good spirits, of which laughter is surely the sign, a virtue. *Eutrapelia* is the virtue between buffoonery [*bōmolochia*] and boorishness [*agroikia*], between the excess of laughing and its defect, grumpiness.[137]

The expulsion of bodily product involved when "one pisses, shits, and sweats by virtue of laughing" [on pisse, fiante, & suë a force de rire][138] is a therapeutic release of surplus, but if excessive, is a dangerously extravagant outlay of vitality. Excessive laughter is physically dangerous and morally undesirable. The Emperor Claudius, known for his unseemly [*indecens*] laughter,[139] once composed an autobiography and gave a public reading, but the reading was abandoned because, a very fat man having broken a number of benches, Claudius could not stop laughing even after the commotion died down.[140] Chrysippus the philosopher was supposed to have died from laughing at his own joke. After an ass ate his figs, he called out to an old woman to give the ass some wine to wash it down. This struck him as so amusing that he laughed to death.[141] Joubert also relates Chrysippus's joke, and considers the phenomenon of being tickled to death, as well as the curious case of Zeuxis, whose portrait of a scowling old woman made him die laughing.[142]

The expulsive properties of tragedy are less obvious. Aristotle mentions pity [*eleos*] and fear [*phobos*] as the chief emotions aroused by tragedy. Pity is provoked when the misfortune is undeserved, but not so undeserved or so close to us that it would outrage us.[143] For this reason, the tragic protagonist is neither extremely good nor extremely bad.[144] Pity itself occurs somewhere between indignation and satisfaction, so it must not be excited too far either way. For this reason, all grisly events in Greek tragedy occur offstage: Antigone's and Jocasta's hanging; Haemon's stabbing; Oedipus's blinding; and Medea's murder of her children. To perform these acts onstage would be "obscene."[145]

To illustrate the distinction between pity and indignation, Aristotle cites Amasis, who watched dry-eyed as his son was led to execution (indignation), but wept to see his friend begging (pity).[146] The physiological effects of pity are tears, excess of moisture, but they also involve the bowel. I John 3.17, for example, describes the emotion in a curious way:

> Qui habuerit substantiam mundi, et viderit fratrem suum necesse habere, et clauserit viscera sua ab eo: quomodo caritas Dei manet in eo?
>
> He that hath the catel [chattels] of this world, and seeth that his brother hath nede, and closith his entrailis fro hym, hou dwellith the charite of God in hym?
>
> (Wyclif Bible)

The opening of the bowels registers the soul's motion of sympathy, its "imitation" of the scene of sorrow before it. Our most primal feelings express themselves in the place where, having ingested food, we process foreign substance to make it part of ourselves and dispel what is alien. We may know concepts with our heads, but "gut-feelings" are the source of intuitions that do not have to syllogize about anything; the guts mirror the outside world, measuring the distance and determining the relations between self and other.

Fear as well as pity registers in the intestines. We already know that Satan farted from fear in his descent from heaven to hell. Even donkeys fart from fright.[147] The combination of sudden movement and deep emotion is registered when, as Rabelais recounts, "Thaumaste got up in great alarm, but as he did so let a great baker's fart [un gros pet de boulangier]—for the bran followed."[148]

> And fear [*la peur*], what force it is seen to possess at times!. . .The hair stands on end, and the voice sticks in the throat: one bepisses [*se compisser*] and beshits [*se conchier*] oneself, and sometimes one dies from it or falls into a long and grievous illness.[149]

We can fear only what is near at hand, what is close enough, as it were, to smell.[150] "Anything causes us to feel fear that when it happens to, or threatens, others causes us to feel pity."[151] Fearing for another really means pitying another; what we fear we fear for ourselves both directly and insofar as we regard another as part of ourselves. Through mimesis, we identify with Oedipus however confident we may feel that our spouse is not our parent. Even though we already know what is coming, and know that it is not happening to us, we nonetheless await the *anagnoresis* in fear. Recognition, when it comes, is both terrible and a great relief. Directly linked to *katharsis*, it hurts so good. Extreme access of emotion—fear, pity, joy, laughter—marks the passage into knowledge or recognition. Mind and bowel, dilating and contracting, together register the bursting forth of knowledge.

Spend A Penny, Save a Penny

Despite the riotous disbursement of bodily product and strength involved in laughter, we speak of the economy of the joke, which, at least in certain forms, shortens, attenuates, and chops up words in various and unexpected ways: "The technique of the jokes lies in the fact that one and the same word. . .appears in it used in two ways, once as a whole, and again cut up into its separate syllables like a charade" (*SE*, 8:31). The joke compresses meanings and sounds, creating the famous brevity that is the soul of wit. Freud's example is the one about the doctor who asks his young male patient how often he masturbates, to which the patient replies emphatically,

"O na, nie!" [Oh, no, never!]. Run the words together and we get a pun on onanism [*die Onanie*]. Jokes bring dissimilar things into similitude (*SE*, 8:11), the pun being perhaps the most efficient way of doing so, and thus it is the recognition of the similitude between "oh, no, never" and "masturbation" that delights us, the denial that unintentionally affirms. A condensation has occurred (*SE*, 8:24), and condensation is a kind of labor saving, by which one word or sentence does the work of two or more. The joke's brevity is a kind of thriftiness (*SE*, 8:43). Puns bring us back to a noisy primal language where words possess at least two meanings and each meaning is denoted by at least two words. Directly analogous to dream work, the work of the joke defamiliarizes its truth by means of compression, and then waits smirkingly for the penny to drop, for the moment of *anagnoresis*. Like dream analysis, joke analysis reverses the condensation in a time-consuming, plodding process of logical reconstruction, much as Aristotle describes when identifying the various kinds of *anagnoresis*. Recognition by reasoning occurs, for example in Aeschylus's *Choephori* [Libation Bearers] when Electra reasons, "someone like her has come, no one is like her except Orestes, therefore *he* has come."[152] We fill out the enthymeme-like suppressions of the joke with the dilations of syllogistic reasoning.

The energy consumption of laughter raises the question of motive. Like vomiting, laughing works a lot of muscles, burns energy, and empties us out—why on earth would we ever do it? In the passion of joy that lies at the center of laughter, notes Joubert, the heart's diastolic motion sends out its sanguine vapors and humors to the external limbs leaving itself bereft— hence "such waste and spending of humors [tel gast et depanse d'espris] normally suffered by those who die of joy."[153] Agreeing that the joke economizes by getting at least twice the linguistic labor out of one word or expression, Freud nonetheless questions the true saving. Quite apart from the effort of laughing, there is the effort of wit to seek out the one word that conveys two thoughts rather than simply opting for the plain utterance (*SE*, 8:44). He likens the cathectic investment to a housewife who makes a long detour just to save a couple of *pfennig* on her food bill. He has a point. There is an air of redundancy to a joke because one always has to go well out of one's way to bring about the *mot juste*; there was really no need for it in the first place; the joke may be penny-wise but it is pound-foolish.

The hearer of the joke wastes equally. Had we been paying full attention in the first place to the *Miller's Tale*, we would not have forgotten about the carpenter hanging from the roof so we would not have been caught unawares when the narrative triangle of Nicholas, Alison, and Absolom collided with the prior one of Nicholas, Alison, and John. Had Oedipus kept the oracle properly in mind, he would have given elder people a wide berth, and we could have all gone home early from the play or not gone at all. *Anagnoresis* rubs our nose in the fact that we already knew what we have just known again.

Why all this effort to find one word for the work of two? Why the trouble of forgetting in order to explode with laughter once you remember it? Why not pay more attention at the beginning of the mystery to avoid the anxiety of the denouement? Ironically this hide and seek of forgetting and remembering, of repression and recognition, of ignoring and noticing, the hard work of finding the *mot juste* is a kind of "play." Word play is hard work. Heath Robinson's cartoons of elaborate "laborsaving" machines to perform tasks such as lifting a pea to the mouth sum up well the redundancy of the joke. Jokes delight in their own ingenuity, practicing their art for art's sake, and as such, are quite useless and quite innocent (*SE*, 8:90–5). The more "innocent" and trivial the joke, the more purely it connects pleasure with its form. Just as the dream is at its most revealing in its irrational aspects, so is the joke in its triviality and lack of purpose [*Tendenz*].

Yet Freud later opines that there really is no such thing as a purely innocent joke, that they all ultimately serve a purpose, all are intentional, all tendentious (*SE*, 8:132). As we know from Freud's observation of a child's game of Fort/Da, in which he throws his reel away from him, shouting *Fort* [gone] only to retrieve it with a triumphant *Da* [there], the infantile "play" masks a displaced anger at the mother who has the irritating habit of being "gone" when he wants her "there" (*SE*, 18:14–17). In ludic repetition, he "works" out his anger to achieve powers of repulsion and retrieval not possessed in real life. Junior is learning the lesson of civilization: that hostility, along with lots of other highly enjoyable impulses, must be repressed in the name of social progress. " 'Where we now say "Excuse me!" we used to give a box on the ears' " (*SE*, 8:102). A rattle or a witty joke sublimates anger that a good smack on the head would better satisfy. Desire works in the same way, and obscene jokes enact the self-exposure that etiquette forbids. Freud speaks of the pleasure and relief of being able "to throw off the burden of pretence" (*SE*, 8:106) when we laugh at a joke. A blocked, forbidden impulse is allowed out with the escort of humor. The redundancy or "false" economy of the joke ultimately serves a cathartic purpose. If jokes seem to be penny-wise and pound-foolish, it is equally the case that they spend a penny to save a pound.

Simultaneously intentional and without purpose, the joke can at one and the same time be useful for nothing and everything, just as the dream can be both insignificant and burdened with meaning. The playfulness of Charlie Chaplin in *Modern Times* lies in his ability to find a use for everything. He turns a chicken carcass into a funnel; he uses a bore to make holes in a block of cheddar to masquerade as Swiss cheese. He sees connections between all things, and lifts the divisions and restrictions set upon designated purpose.

He turns things into puns; his films belong in Babel, even if they are silent. More soberly, Seneca mentions a German gladiator due to fight in the morning exhibit. Excusing himself to perform the one thing he was allowed to do in private [*ad exonerandum corpus*], he grabbed the wet sponge [*spongia*] stuck on top of a stick of wood [*lignum*] that was used as an asswipe, "for the vilest purposes" [quod ad emundanda obscena], stuck it down his throat and choked himself to death. Bereft of freedom and dignity, the gladiator regained them when, grabbing whatever was around, "by sheer strength [he] turned objects that were by nature harmless [*non erant noxia*] into weapons of their own."[154] Rules of designated teleology are suspended in play or death, rendering all things and words new.

Puns make words take on multiple uses. Lambert of Ardres recounts the story of a lager lout who, at the nuptials of Arnold the Old, bragged that he could drink up a keg of beer. Arnold took up the bet: the beer-drinking spectacle for a horse. The rogue kept his word; he drained the keg and his bladder at the same time, pissing as he drank. He then called triumphantly for his horse, and in answer Arnold the Old, with mordant wit, hanged him. This killer of a pun works equally in the actual vernacular exchange and in Lambert's language of record, Latin: Fr. *le cheval* [horse]/*le chevalet* [rack]; L. *equus* [horse]/*equuleus* or *eculeus* [rack].[155] In the crisis brought on by laughter or imminent death, objects assume a different reality; their disjunct identities and utilities merge as the hand that reaches out to seize them or the mouth that speaks them makes them anew. This is recreation, re-creation.

In the desperation of such "play," the word chopped up and strung out into different words becomes for a while the ur—word, in which all language is compressed and all being resides. The Creator's first word must have been the pun of all puns, pure nonsense, yet full of intention, and in which all words and things *in futuro* lay. The verbal compressions of joke-work are endless, attempting to get back up the butt of language, to attain the silent vortex of pure origin. Hence the story of the prison inmates incarcerated with each other so long that all they need do is call out the number of their favorite joke for everyone to laugh uproariously.[156] Yet no matter how much wit tends toward brevity, it never converges on nothing. Even a number depends on the way you tell it, even silence on right timing.

Jokes occupy grammatical space. The joins that conceal hidden meaning and hidden meaning itself are grammatical in structure. Often the joke *is* the sequence of words, where only the exact verbal formulation enacts the compression that enables the double meaning or confusion (*SE*, 8:28). Anyone who has flubbed a joke knows that if there is a strict sequence of events in a joke's narrative, there is an equally strict verbal form. In Freud's example, one Jew says to another, "have you taken a bath?" and the other replies, "why, is there one missing?" The joke would collapse if the verb "bathed" were substituted for "taken a bath" (SE, 8:49), because the pun depends on the compressed meanings within "taken." Grammatical apposition is all: what is the difference between a huntsman and his hound running ahead of him? The huntsman wears jodhpurs and the hound pants. Dialectical inflection is all: what is the difference between a bison and a buffalo? Ya can't wash yer hands in a buffalo. Homophones are all: knock knock. Who is there? Isabelle. Isabelle Who? Isabelle Necessary-On-Your-Tricycle-When-Your-Knickers-Are-Already-Wringing? "Gladly, the Cross-Eyed Bear" is a mondegreen of the hymn, "Gladly the cross I'd bear." Medieval riddles require the same precise placement that does the denotative work for two different things:

> Pourquoy sont par coustume les hommes plus sages que les femmes?
> Pour tant que ung homme a deux testes et la femme n'en a que une.[157]
>
> [Why is it so that men are wiser than women? Because a man has two heads (testes) and a woman only one.]

Dreams create similar oneiric cryptograms: A dream about a crab turns out to be a dream about *cancer* [L. crab]. Memory works in the same way. One rhetorical treatise prescribes how to remember a certain defense speech as a punning visual image of a ram's testicles [*testiculi*], which serve as *aide-mémoire* for the witnesses [*testes*] to the crime.[158] The pun on balls and witnesses enables the speaker to remember both the topic [*res*] and the very words [*verba*] of his case. It all boils down to a precise alignment of sounds and letters that spark recognition and jog the memory. The pun enables joke-work, dream-work, memorization, and knowledge itself, for it makes dissimilar things similar. Without grammar, we could not laugh, play, or recognize.

Flatus of the Voice

But whither the purpose of these grammatically whole locutions? All this struggle to achieve meaningful utterance leaves us how much closer to reality? Medieval philosphers exercised themselves greatly over the relationship between the (linguistically articulated) idea and the thing it denotes, over whether ideas existed independently of the things they designated. The ideas spoken of here are universal ideas, often referred to in the treatises as *genera et species*, in that they denote a nature common to similar things, for example, *homo* [man] is a universal idea of Socrates, Maria, you and me. The philosophical debate is referred to as that between realism and nominalism, and it is extreme nominalism, associated with the teaching of Roscelin (c.1045-c.1120) we wish to consider here.

Extreme nominalism holds that universal ideas exist *post rem* [after the thing]. Whatever conceptual existence the species *homo* may have for the purposes of logic, the word is just breath, a certain sound, and the essential nature of man resides only in actual individuals. At the other end of the argument is extreme realism, most associated with William of Champeaux (c.1070–1121), according to whom universal ideas preexist individual things, *ante rem* [before the thing]. Socrates, Mary, you, and I all share the same essential nature, *homo*, the existence of which is independent of the individual existence of Socrates, Mary, you, or me. Two other positions are associated with the debate. Moderate realism, which usually describes the position of Aquinas on the matter, holds that universal ideas exist simultaneously with and therefore *in rem* [in the thing]. Moderate nominalism, ascribed to Abelard, posits that universal ideas, although not possessing an extramental reality, nonetheless correspond to the world of things, *juxta rem* [alongside the thing]. For Abelard, the universal idea as logical concept and the breathing sound that is its sign are contiguous realities.

Unfortunately, Roscelin's ideas survive only in secondhand accounts, primarily those of Abelard, John of Salisbury, and Anselm, all of whom disagreed with Roscelin's position. According to Anselm, Roscelin held a universal idea to be mere *flatus vocis*, a term that is easy enough to translate but difficult to understand. *Flatus vocis* usually translates as a pleonasm—"breath of the voice"—thereby acquiring a pejorative sense that still prevails: "empty speech," "mere word."[159] But let us consider it more closely. From Priscian's categorizations of *vox*, we can probably assume, since the debate is about words such as *homo*, that Roscelin means meaningful, scriptable vocal emissions [*voces articulatae literatae*], namely, words proper.

What does *flatus* mean? In Latin the word means a "blowing" or "breathing," and applies more broadly than English "flatus," which just means "fart," although in verbal form—"sufflate," "inflate," "deflate"—it denotes more generally. In Roland the Farter's "saltus, flatus, et bombulum," the word means "whistle." In musical contexts, *flatus* can mean a toot on a wind instrument, and for St. Jerome, the term equates to *bombulum*, suggesting the image of Roland whistling at both ends. For Pope Innocent III, a meaningful distinction holds between *ventus*, the kind of terrestrial wind that blows around us,[160] and *flatus*, anal wind.[161] Flatulence, as the word suggests, comes from *flationes*.[162] Given the breadth of the term in Latin, we frequently find *flatus* in conjunction with some specifier, for example, *flatus ventorum* [the blowing of the winds]. Qua fart, *flatus* usually occurs with the qualifier *ventris*, and variations on the theme include *strepitus ventris*, more often, *crepitus ventris*.[163] "Voice-fart" for *flatus vocis* is a possible if tendentious translation, though no one has yet opted for it. However, given what is clearly a derogatory undertone by Anselm, who refers to those "heretical logicians who consider universal substances to be the mere wind of the voice," "voice-fart" should not be utterly discounted. Furthermore, considering the regular usage of *flatus ventris* [belly wind], *flatus vocis* sounds like a deviated fart that issues from the mouth instead of the bottom. *Flatus vocis* is not a common expression—its occurrence seems only to be in reference to Roscelin's quote; Anselm seems to have deliberately coined a new phrase that evokes an association with farting.

> Illi utique nostri temporis dialectici (*imo* dialectice haeretici, qui non nisi flatum vocis putant esse universales substantias). . .[164]
>
> [Therefore, those modern logicians (rather, the heretical logicians who think that universal substances are mere wind of the voice). . .]

Imo, more often *immo*, in context means "rather," but carries the whiff of something more insulting, being reminiscent of the ablative of *imum*, meaning "the bottom of something," and quite often, "the bowels"; in his reference to fartists, Augustine's phrase *ab imo* means "down there," more explicitly, "from the asshole."[165] A feudal tenant *in imo* in postconquest England was an inferior tenant, who paid for his land with base labor.[166] Another way of translating Anselm's sentence to capture the insulting allusion is, "Therefore, those modern logicians, *at bottom* those heretical logicians, who think that universal substances are just grammatical wind." "Wind," derogatory enough to imply bodily gas and words devoid of meaning, may prove the best translation of *flatus*. Grammatical wind makes one think of things like belching the alphabet. Anselm's dismissive tone reduces Roscelin's arguments themselves to voice-farts, and the same kind of imagery used by a chronicler of the twelfth century in speaking of one of Roscelin's followers suggests a similar perception. Herman of Tournai speaks derisively of Raimbert of Lille, who taught only about words, while Odo of Orléans, teaching at the school in Tournai, taught about things; Raimbert provided only windy chatter, Odo substance. A wise deaf-mute, being asked one day to judge between Raimbert's and Odo's teachings, gestured toward Odo and drew his finger across his palm, as if cleaving the earth with a plow, and indicating that his was the correct doctrine. Then, pointing toward Lille, from where Raimbert hailed, the deaf-mute blew [*exsufflare*] on his hand, implying a reduction of Raimbert's teaching to a fit of gas.[167] The theological resonance of *exsufflare* cannot have escaped this chronicler-monk and his clerical audience. Herman had also read Anselm on Roscelin's *flatus vocis*. Anselm, says Herman, describes Roscelin and his ilk as "those who consider universal substances to be nothing but wind" [qui nonisi [*sic*] flatum universales putant esse substantias], which means, he paraphrases, that "people with this sort of learning ought to be blown away" [eos de sapientium numero merito esse exsufflandos].[168]

Why was everyone picking on Roscelin? His basic argument seems to be that universal essences (man, wisdom, whiteness) have no autonomy, existing only in the local fact of individual utterance. The choice of *flatus vocis* to describe universal ideas conveys the sense less of a pleonasm than of an oxymoron. *Flatus* and *vox* stand as contraries: formlessness and shapeliness; meaninglessness and signification; butt and mouth. Roscelin draws a contrast between the immateriality of a universal essence and the materiality of *vox*, of gutterals and sibilants, and of physical organs. The spoken word of *flatus vocis* is sonorous but evanescent, like a fart, fleeting in contrast to the perceived permanence of the universal idea. The coincidence of and tension between conceptual opposites, permanence and transience, abstractness and concreteness, transcendence and immediacy show Roscelin's radical reduction of cerebration to physical process, reminding us that Greek *analysis* contains within it the meanings of evacuation and ejaculation. Ideas themselves prove to be inextricable from a certain sequence of words, from a determinate squeezing of muscles, and puffings of the larynx along with spits and gurgles. Even universal ideas need a particular verbal form, a bubble of their own to inhabit. Accessing Roscelin's ideas solely through the writings of men who disparaged them, we can only guess at the nuances of his position, and how far it overturned a tyrannous reality posited as metaphysical principle to which concrete *realia*, individual speech, and local historical condition must conform blindly. Realism insists on the direct intuition of the whole idea without interception of the individual *res* or *verbum*, without the noise of language, or the partialness of dialect and vernacular. Just as the joke depends entirely upon the arrangement of grammatical sounds in a certain way, so, says Roscelin, the concepts in which philosophy and theology trade depend for their "existence," at bottom, upon the scratching of someone's quill on parchment and the grammatical wind that blasts out of a mouth to hit an earhole. Classical and medieval philosophy had always agreed about some things: that ideas were nonphysical (and therefore nonhistorical) representations of objects; and that language, precisely because it was corporeal and historical, could transcend animal chatter to attain meaning only insofar as it could be made to approximate ideas. There was no question of linguistic noise actually constituting knowledge and thus reality itself. Neither ideas nor language consequently partook in the contingencies of historical reality and material causation. But Roscelin's *flatus vocis* hints at how tightly and covertly metaphysics might really grip the sphincter of the moment. Small wonder Anselm and the others wrinkled their noses and waved his ideas away as voice-farts.

DIE AFTERWISSENSCHAFT [END-KNOWLEDGE, PSEUDO-SCIENCE, BUTTHOLE-SCHOLARSHIP]

The Mystery[1] of Roland

Many have heard about the wizard of wind, Joseph Pujol, who delighted throngs of Parisian men and women at Le Moulin Rouge during the 1890s. Pujol, born in 1857 in Marseille, had, as a young boy, while swimming, "breathed" in huge quantities of water through his backside.[2] Subsequently experimenting with wind, he found his ability far exceeded vulgar farting, for his backside could make music, and without any smell. Musical at the other end also, Pujol began to realize his gift on stage, calling himself "Le Petomane." Emboldened by provincial triumph, he set his sights on the sails of Le Moulin Rouge, at which his opening night made him a star. His son and biographer describes:

> During the initial silence my father coolly began a series of small farts, naming each one "This one is a little girl, this the mother-in-law, this the bride on her wedding night (very little) and the morning after (very loud), this the mason (dry—no cement), this the dressmaker tearing two yards of calico (this one lasted at least ten seconds and imitated to perfection the sound of material being torn) then a cannon (Gunners stand by your guns! Ready—fire!) the noise of thunder, etc."[3]

Pujol then proceeded to "smoke" a cigarette placed in a yard of rubber tubing with the other end stuck up his butt, to play "Au Claire de la lune" on a flute, and to extinguish several gas jets in the footlights. The audience went wild, crying with laughter, and many women fainted.[4] After resonant success both in Paris and abroad, Pujol's fortunes foundered on contractual obligations, for Le Moulin Rouge sued him for breach of contract because of his impromptu performances at a local gingerbread stall.[5] Poor but free as the wind, Pujol continued his career independently until the Great War.

Fewer know that the Irish were doing it over a millenium earlier. An eighth-century Irish document spelling out the legal entitlements of retainers refers to "farters [*bruigedoire*], that is, they perform the farting [*bruigedoracht*] from their rears."[6] The reference suggests that farting was a service like any other, worthy of remuneration, which in one source is identified as the "fat of the shoulder" from the hunted prey[7]—no mean cut if not the choicest. In addition, the *Tech Midchúarda*, a twelfth-century diagram of the banqueting hall of Tara where the High King of Ireland resided, depicts a group of farters [*braigetori*] along with other entertainers, such as the king's jester, hornblowers, and jugglers.[8] This inclusion of farters among court entertainer sheds light on lines of William Langland, in which Activa Vita laments:

> Ac for I kan neiþer taboure ne trompe ne telle no gestes,
> Farten ne fiþelen at festes, ne harpen,
> Iape ne iogele ne gentilliche pipe,
> Ne neiþer saille ne saute, ne synge wiþ þe gyterne.[9]
>
> [I don't know (how to play) the tambourine or trumpet or to tell stories, to fart or play the fiddle at feasts, or play the harp, or jest, or juggle, or pipe skillfully, or dance or play the psaltery or sing with the giterne.]

Despite clear evidence of farting as recognized entertainment, it inevitably is omitted from the usual roster of formal skills:

> The precise repertoire of the professionals must remain conjectural, but probably most of the traditional skills were represented—acrobatics, clowning, mimicry, miming, dancing, music-making, singing, jesting, along with specialized arts such as conjuring, sword-swallowing, fire-eating, and juggling.[10]

Some kind of games, however, seemed to have featured farts, at least if their name is anything to go by. Consider the game of "Farte Pryke in Cule," in which two opponents are bound in squatting position with a stick wedged across the back of their knees, and another in their hands, which they attempt to stick in their opponents' butts.[11]

The appeal of medieval performance farting as court entertainment extends beyond England and Ireland. An illustrated scroll set from the Japanese Kamakura period (1185–1333) depicts the story of how Fukutomi, who performed fart dances for the entertainment of the aristocracy, trumped his neighbor Tōda who tried to mimic the master farter, but soiled himself instead.[12] Allen Edwardes claims musical performance-farting as an Arabic rite: "Simojeh-el-Hewweh (Breaker of Wind) was the appellation granted an Egyptian bean-eater who could break wind in tune, a favorite accomplishment of *fellaheen* [peasant] boys."[13] Niebuhr cites a jolly fart contest among the domestics of and sponsored by the then Shaikh of the al-Montafij tribe, who crowned the victor.[14] We have already considered Augustine's reference in his *City of God* (14.24) to butt-singers, which raises the possibility of such practice as far back as Roman culture. In his sixteenth-century glosses on Augustine's opus, Juan Luis Vives notes that he had himself witnessed such a one "that can breake winde back-ward so artificially, that you would thinke they sung." A German in the retinue of Maximilian I, Holy Roman Emperor (1459–1519), and his son Philip le Bel, "would haue rehearsed any verse whatsoever with his taile [*podex*]."[15]

There are enough of these isolated references to indicate that nobility across the world cherished performance farts. Breaking wind before dignity is ordinarily disgraceful but in special contexts the occasion of laughter.[16] That Emperor Claudius should have considered passing an edict to allow someone before him at table to fart quietly or noisily [*flatus crepitusque ventris*] attests to the offense of passing wind before one's superiors.[17] Augustine remarks that even blowing at the image of emperor was criminal, a point that illustrates the connection between farting and exsufflation, which, says sixth-century theologian John the Deacon, insults the devil.[18] Even among common folk, farts were impolite. When the rogue Gautiers in the bucolic farce *Le Jeu de Robin et Marion* suggests passing wind to pass the time—

> Faisons un pet pour nous esbatre
> Je n'i voi si bon.[19]
>
> [Let's entertain ourselves by cutting a fart
> I can't think of anything that's such fun.]

Robin is angry at such an inappropriate suggestion [*si grant vilanie*] being made in front of his lady. Churchmen also expressed their disapproval, John of Salisbury doing so vociferously:

> Quorum adeo error inualuit ut a praeclaris domibus non arceantur etiam illi qui obscenis partibus corporis oculis omnium eam ingerunt turpitudinem quam erubescat uidere uel cinicus. Quodque magis mirere, nec tunc eiciuntur quando tumultuantes inferius crebro sonitu aerem foedant et turpiter inclusum turpius produnt.[20]
>
> [The error (of these buffoons) has so taken hold that they are not barred from the residences of illustrious men, those indeed who heap up unsightliness with their bodies' shameful members in front of everyone, so that even a cynic blushes to see it. Still more unbelievable, the buffoons are not thrown out even when the uproar of their bottoms befouls the air with repeated noise, more shamefully emitting what is shamefully held in.]

Joseph Pujol farted without smell, and gave himself an enema every day to ensure against mishap[21]; Augustine also mentions that the people he witnessed singing out of their backsides were able to do so *sine paedore ullo* [without any stink]. The twelfth-century performers were either less fastidious or less skilful. John of Salisbury was contemporaneous with Henry II of England, who confirmed the alienation of Roland's estate. Could John have witnessed Roland in the act one Christmas day during the 1150s prior to both the alienation of the land and the publication of *Policraticus* in 1159? Were Roland's farts *cum* or *sine paedore*?

Roland, it would seem, was some kind of court minstrel. Minstrelsy was a highly diverse occupation in the Middle Ages with well-paid court performers whose services were required any time night or day to minister to royalty's needs: after bleeding, during insomnia, or while partying.[22] Such were those who were on the actual payroll: players of the harp, vielle, psaltery, and so on. More transient kinds of entertainers, for example, acrobats, had more ad hoc form of employment, and less stable rank. Minstrels were not a unique or exclusive group, but often regular members of households[23]; their musical employment might be for a brief period of their working life or a paying hobby.[24] Records indicate a high level of coming and going.[25] In his entire book on the king's serjeants, whose duties were often menial, Round does not consider the king's minstrels and entertainers, lending credence to the belief that minstrel services were generally part-time.[26] With no permanent seat of government, the royal court moved frequently, and Christmas could be celebrated each year in different places such as Winchester and Windsor; it is possible that Roland belonged permanently to the king's household, at least until his tenure of land, at which point his court appearances perhaps became seasonal (December and January being the least active months for working the land). Royal accounts indicate regular and substantial "tipping" of court minstrels, in the form of gold, clothes, and land,[27] and it seems a reasonable guess that Roland acquired his serjeanty in this way.

Minstrel stunts are often of the same ilk as Roland's act. On June 19, 1313, Edward II watched a show in Pontoise, France, which was recorded in the accounts: "To Bernard, the Fool, and 54 of his companions coming naked before the King, with dancing revelry [*nudis. . .cum tripudio*]."[28] Edward I was particularly fond of a *saltatrix* [acrobatic dancer] called Matilda Makejoy, who is believed to have performed her jumps in the nude.[29] Matilda's status as acrobat, about which profession little is known, sets her in a category peripheral to the court. We cannot tell whether Roland was just such an acrobat—a dangerous skill requiring rigorous training from childhood—or a regular court minstrel. A well-trained acrobat can control his farts, in contrast to Brun, the not-very-bright bear of the

Roman de Renart, whom Renart the fox persuades to somersault before the king and queen. He does so, but with such difficulty that his "butthole opens and unfastens" [le pertuis eslesse et desserre] and he farts so loudly that the hall reverberates, much to the amusement of the court.[30] As Tōda, contender to Fukutomi, also discovered, not everyone can achieve intestinal control. A remarkably close analogue to Roland's hat trick occurs when Panurge gives "a fart [*un pet*], a leap [*un sault*], and a whistle [*un sublet*]," and joyously cries out " 'Long live Pantagruel!' "[31] Pantagruel immediately tries to do the same thing but shits himself instead. The maneuver displays skill, and may well have been the medieval prototype of the eighteenth-century "hop, step (or skip), and jump," an exercise performed by althletes to see who could cover the most ground (*OED*, s.v. *hop*, n.[2]).

Much of such entertainment is mere buffoonery, as the sixteenth-century depiction in John Derricke's *The Image of Ireland* of the rude, mooning Irish suggests,[32] but butt-humor also sustains satire. In the *Tech Midchúarda*, the farters sit beside the king's jester,[33] and a late-eleventh-century Irish tale recounts how Mac Con Glinne "began clowning for the host . . . and satirizing and farting and singing songs."[34] Roland's routine may have been exclusively acrobatic, but may also have included satiric discourse. Farting is insulting in itself, as the Latin verb *oppedere* [to insult] demonstrates, for it literally means "to fart at."[35] Something of the spirit of the verb is caught in the early modern tract by the fictional Jack of Dover,[36] who, embarking on a "Privy Search for the veriest foole in England," tells of a humorous knight in Cornwall who called together a great assembly of knights, squires, and gentlemen to hear his public speech. However,

> He in a foolish manner (not without laughter) began to use a thousand jestures, turning his eyes this way, then that way, seeming alwayes as though he would have presently begun to speake: and at last, fetching a deepe sigh, with a grunt like hogge, he let a beastly loude fart, and tould them that the occasion of this calling of them together was to no other ende, but that so noble a fart might be honoured with so worthy a company as there was.[37]

Fart discourse of the late medieval and early modern periods shows an interest in the connection with classical oratory and in exposing scholastic logic as hot air.[38] Fart satire of the earlier Middle Ages seems more associated with acrobatics, and more pointedly political, more antiecclesiastical.

Roland was on duty on Christmas day. One of the great feastdays along with Easter and Pentecost, Christmas was the occasion for a number of special tenurial obligations: counting the king's chess pieces and returning them to their box after he has finished playing; carving before the king; offering him a handbasin and towel.[39] Christmas most notoriously was marked by lewd revelry, the Festival of Fools, the carnivalesque upending of values.[40] The election of late medieval and early modern lords of misrule to preside over festivities in university halls, colleges, and manors took its origin in earlier arrangements such as Roland's tenure. At Merton College, Oxford, the lord of misrule elected for Christmas tide went by the name of king of beans [*rex fabarum*],[41] in whose name also Edward III distributed gifts to his minstrels.[42] The titles are oxymoronic: where "lord of misrule" juxtaposes the governance of "lord" and chaos of "misrule," *rex faborum* juxtaposes the wealth of kingship with the poverty of the bean; something of little value can be counted not worth "a bene" (*CT*, 4.1854), though the title may also allude to the legume's direct effect—farts.

Another tenurial custom of the season reminiscent of bodily wind is recorded from the seventeenth century, in which the lord of the manor of Essington delivered a goose to the lord of the manor of Hilton in Staffordshire, drove it at least three times around the fire "whilst Jack of Hilton is blowing the fire." Thus paraded, the goose was dispatched to the kitchen, destined for the dinner plate.

> This Jack of Hilton is an image of brass, of about twelve inches high, kneeling on his left knee, and holding his right hand upon his head, and his left upon pego or his viretrum, erected, having a little hole at the mouth, at which being filled with water, and set to a strong fire, which makes it evaporate like an æolipile, it vents itself in constant blast, so strongly that it is very audible, and blows the fire fiercely."[43]

An aeolipile would scarcely have been owned as a domestic object in the twelfth century, and the tenure is either late or originally used bellows rather than the Jack of Hilton, but the technological possibilites of steam for bellows nonetheless were much on the mind of medieval and classical inventors. Vitruvius speaks of the figures of Aeolus, *aeolipilae*, punctured vessels filled with water, which, when still cold, have no breath [*spiritus*], but, once brought to the boil, emit a violent blast or whistle [*vehemens flatus*].[44] Albertus Magnus in the thirteenth century speaks of a similar contraption, a *sufflator* [blower], usually fashioned in the form of a man.[45] Witness to festive obscenity as a constant, Roland's whistle, recorded as *flatus* in Latin and *suflet* in French, speaks to an early comic rendering of the human body as steam-pressured.[46]

We have already considered the relation between the petard, a type of early cannon, and the *pet* [fart]. Maybe Roland's *saltus* mimicked the trajectory of a human cannonball, in likeness of the *trebuchet*, a sling-beam used in warfare in Europe during the twelfth century.[47] *Bombulum*, the Latin word used for Roland's fart, derives from Latin *bombinare* [to buzz], from which also came the *bombarda*, introduced in the fifteenth century, a new word for "cannon."[48] Of the word *la bombe*, and on account of the noise a bomb makes, Furetière claims its etymology from Latin "bombus, crepitus, aut sibilus ani" [whistle from the anus]. The onomatopoeic or "echoic" suggestiveness of the word in part explains its ubiquity across languages.[49] Although Roland's *bombulum* is too early to coincide with wartime bombards, since cannon do not appear in Europe until the fifteenth century,[50] instances of a "handgun" that shoots Greek fire date back from as early as the eleventh century.[51] By the sixteenth century, the kinship between exploding guns and butts was second nature. Gill of Brentford, seized with a gripping pain, "lift vp her buttok somewhat a wry / And like a handgun, she let a fart fly."[52]

We will probably never know the exact nature of Roland's party piece, but it must have had theatrical buildup, since, from the phrase *simul & semel* in Blount's description of Roland's performance (Fartprints, §6), he does his jump, whistle and fart all at the same time and only once, so the moment can only have lasted a few seconds. The *Summoner's Tale* gives us a hint at the kind of dramatic context that may have attended Roland's *saltus, flatus, et bombulum*. The resolution of the *impossibile* by means of the fartwheel at the end of Chaucer's *Summoner's Tale* bears the characteristics of such organized entertainment: the public occasion, the manorial (or courtly) venue, and the prearranged time all savor of the kind of buildup we presume made Roland's acrobatic bombination so spectacular.

Whatever its exact buildup, Roland's performance is some kind of a jumping dance. One of the Latin words used to refer to such dances is *tripudium*, and occurs with reference to Bernard the Fool and his fifty-four companions who appeared in the nude before the king, dancing [*nudis. . .cum tripudio*].[53] The word occurs elsewhere as a punishment.

Charta 27.Sept.an.1398. pro loco de Breuil in Burbon. Ex Camera Comput. Paris. Item in & super qualibet uxore maritum suum verberante unum tripodem. Item insuper qualibet filia communis, sexus videlicet viriles quoscunque cognoscente de novo in villa Montis Lucii eveniente 4.den aut unum Bombum, sive vulgariter Pet, super pontem de Castro Montis Lucii solvendum.[54]

[Document: 27 September, 1398, for the land of Breuil in Burbon, from the Chamber of Accounts, Paris. Likewise, in addition, in any way, for a wife who beats her husband, one dance. Likewise, in addition, in any way, for a young woman of common sex (i.e., a prostitute), evidently knowing (i.e., carnally) any man, and newly arriving at the town of Montluc, four denarii or one bottom-blast, vulgarly known as a fart, to be paid on the bridge of the castle of Montluc.]

Possibly the *tripudium* was some kind of fart-caper, and the fart-toll included a dance, for such public shaming rituals had theatrical flair and entertainment value: adulterers promenade naked through the streets, the woman holding a lead attached to the man's genitals; a prostitute [*une femme publique*] rides naked back-to-front on a donkey through the streets.[55] Both husband-beating wife and prostitute abuse their sex, and must pay for their shame in kind. Whether by a fart or four denarii, the prostitute has to pay through the nose.[56] Structure of the limen, the bridge, as locus of the prostitute's fart-toll, both connects bodies of land and holds them apart, just as the diaphragm, whence laughter originates, divides heart and lung from liver, spleen and kidneys.[57] In consideration of its sacredness, a sacrifice would often mark the erection of a bridge.[58] Prostitutes also inhabit a threshold within the social body, as does a fart within the body physical. In this fart, performed by a creature from the margin, on the physical margin of the community, one acknowledges the presence of otherness within the midst. The margin or border is the place where one jests. Medieval marginalia makes the "border" of a book the place where one makes a joke [OF *bo(u)rde*]. The pun is quite literally enacted in the iconography by a joust [OF *borde*], or drone instrument [OF *bordon*].[59] The jokester [OF *bordeor*] who farts in the margin of the *Romance of Alexander* (plate 3) turns into a rebus, visually punning on his place in the border. And a prostitute [OF *bordeliere*] who farts on a bridge to make the town laugh enacts a comic counterstep, a *contrepas*, a Dantesque *contrapasso* as she dances her shame at a place where justice and laughter intersect. *Bordage*, a Middle English word borrowed from Old French, was a feudal tenure, one of the baser ones, by which the bordar held his cot or humble dwelling in return for servile labor. Roland owned a lot more than a cottage, but his Christmas *bourde*, base in its own way, resonates at many levels.

Fartprints of Roland

Here follow the earliest known references to Roland the Farter, listed chronologically.

> §1. *Liber Feodorum* is an account of knights' fees and serjeanties largely dating from the long reign of Henry III (1216–1272), although earlier entries also exist. Fixing the actual date of tenures is especially difficult because much of the material was transcribed as late as the fourteenth century from earlier rolls. A fifth entry (e) records a similar serjeanty for the Norfolk and Suffolk area in the name of Egidius [Gilles] de Wachesham, modern-day Wattisham in Suffolk.

(a) Bosemere:[60] 1212: Alexander de Brumton tenet serianteriam Rodlandi in capite[61] de rege in Hemingeston per saltum et siflum etc. (*Liber feodorum*, 1:136)

[Bosmere: 1212: Alexander of Brumton holds the serjeanty of Roland in chief from the king in Hemingston by means of a jump and whistle, etc.]

(b) 1226–1228: Lodding, Norf. De seriantiis, dicunt quod Rollandus, le Pettus tenuit in villa de Langham[62] seriantiam faciendi saltum, siffletum, pettum, et valet per annum c.s. (*Liber feodorum*, 1:386)

[1226–1228: Lodding, Norfolk. With reference to serjeanties, they say that Roland the Farter held the serjeanty in the manor of Langham by making a jump, whistle, and fart, and it is worth a hundred shillings a year.]

(c) Suffolk 1250: Seriantia que quondam fuit Rollandi le Pettour in Hemingeston in comitatu Suff', pro qua debuit facere die natali Domini singulis annis coram domino rege unum saltum et siffletum et unum bumbulum, que alienata fuit per particulas subscriptas. (*Liber feodorum*, 2:1174)

[Suffolk 1250: The serjeanty, which formerly was held of Roland the Farter in Hemingston in the county of Suffolk, for which he was obliged to perform every year on the birthday of our Lord before his master the king, one jump, one whistle, and one fart, was alienated in accordance with these specific requirements.]

(d) Comitatus Suffolk': Hemmingeston 1250: Seriantia Rolandi le Pettur in Hammingeston', pro qua debuit facere die Natalis Domini coram rege unum saltum, etc. alienata est. (*Liber feodorum*, 2:1218–19)

[County of Suffolk: Hemingston 1250: The serjeanty of Roland the Farter in Hemingston, for which he had to make on the birthday of our Lord in front of the king one jump, etc., is alienated.]

(e) 1244: [E]t Egidius de Wachesham xxx. acras in Wachesham, et est ista seriantia faciendi unum saltum, siffletum, et pettum. (*Liber feodorum*, 2:1151)

[1244: Giles of Wattisham thirty acres in Wattisham, and this serjeanty is (held) by making one jump, whistle, and fart.]

§2. Assize Roll 827, m. 15, quoted in Kimball, *Serjeanty*, pp. 59–60. This record sheds some light on the cessation of Roland's tenure, presumably long after it had remained in name only on the books. The Assize Rolls dealt with ejectments and possessary claims, suggesting either that legal occupancy of the land was in dispute or that money rents were outstanding.

> Dicunt quod Dominus Henricus Rex pater domini Regis nunc [Edward I] iam triginta annis elapsis eo quod servicium predictum indecens fuit seriauntiam illam arentare fecit ut predictum est.
>
> [They say that our lord King Henry (III) father of our lord the King now (Edward I), thirty years having already elapsed, on account of the aforesaid service being indecent, he caused that service to be rented out as was said before.]

§3. This entry, dated 1331 in the *Calendar of Close Rolls*, is the only one that directly associates Roland with a named sovereign, Henry II, who ratified the alienation of Roland's tenure, possibly suggesting that Roland performed for an earlier sovereign, probably Henry I. (Bullock-Davies, *Register*, p. 174).

> To William Trussel, escheator this side Trent. Order not to intermeddle further with 40 acres of land in Hemmington, Arsk and Gosebek, and to restore the issues thereof, as the king learns by inquisition[63] taken by Robert Selyman, his late escheator this side Trent, that the said 40 acres, [part] of the messuage[64] and 99 acres of land in the towns aforesaid, that Roland le Fartere held of the King's progenitors [ancestors of Edward III] by the service of making a leap, a whistle and a fart (*saltum, siflum et pettum*), were alienated long before the time of [legal] memory[65] to divers men, which alienations King Henry, the son of the Empress Matilda, confirmed by his charter and that the justices late in eyre in Co. Suffolk, because it was presented before them that the said 40 acres were thus alienated and that the service aforesaid had been withdrawn for a long time, caused them to be arrented at 15s., with which sum the prior of Buttele, Ralph de Bockyng', and other tenants of the said 40 acres are charged, and that the 40 acres are worth yearly in all issues 13s. 4d., and that they were taken into the King's hands for the alienation aforesaid.

§4. *Calendarium Inquisitionum Post Mortem*, 4 Edw. III, 44, 2:34. The *Calendarium Inquisitionum Post Mortem* or the Escheat Rolls was compiled from the reigns of Henry III to Richard III. An estate would "escheat" when it reverted to the lord on the tenant dying without having left a successor authorized to inherit under the conditions of the original feudal grant. The records were published during 1806–1828 in an effort to "methodize" what was "wholly unarranged, undescribed, and unascertained," as it claims in the prefatory material in volume 1 of the series. The record of Roland, from the fourth year of Edward III's reign, seems, like the *Liber feodorum* above, to incorporate older records without ascribing their original dates.

> Roulandus le Fartere
> Hemynggeston & Gosebeck terr' & ten'   Suff'

§5. (Camden, *Britain*, p. 464). Camden does not cite his sources, and his information differs from all the other records in one important respect: the name of the tenant, Baldwin, rather than the Roland to whom all other sources refer. Camden's narrative is a chorographic description of Britain, and as one reads the chapter on Suffolk, a rubric in the margin, "farter," catches the eye:

> Upon the same river are seene two little Mercat townes, Stow and Needham, and not far from the banke, Hemingston: in which Baldwin le Pettour (marke his name well) held certain lands, by Serjeanty, (the words I have out of an old booke) for which on Christmas day, every year before our soveraigne Lord the King of England he should performe one *Saltus*, one *Suffletus*, and one *Bumbulus*, or as we read elsewhere, his tenour [tenure] was *per saltum, sufflum, & pettum*, that is, if I understand these tearmes aright, that he should daunce, puffe up his cheekes making therewith a sound, and besides let a cracke [breaking of wind] downeward. Such was the plaine and jolly mirth of those times. And observed it is, that unto this Foe [Fee], the Manour of Langhall belonged.

§6. (Blount, *Antient Tenures*, pp. 10–11). Blount does indeed mention his source (Pla. Cor. 14 Ed. I. rot. 6 dorso *Suff.*), which presumably refers to the Placita corone membranes of the Assize Rolls (Kimball, *Serjeanty*, p. 255), and thus corroborates the Assize entry (§2), which mentions the commutation of the service into a money rent.

> Roland le Sarcere, held one hundred and ten Acres of land in Hemingston in com. Suffolk, by Sergeanty, for which on Christmas Day, before our Sovereign Lord the King of England he should perform *simul & semel* [at the same time and only once], *unum saltum, unum sufflum, & unum bombulum*, or as we read elsewhere in French, *un saut, un pet, & un suflet, simul & semel*; that is, he should dance, puff up his Cheeks, making therewith a sound, and let a Crack, *Et quia indecens servitium, ideo arrentatur* (sayes the Record) *ad xxvi s. viij d. per annum ad Scaccarium Regis*. [And because the service is indecent, it is rented out for that reason at 26 shillings and 8 pence to the King's Exchequer.]

References to Roland are frequent in the nineteenth century, but they all recycle the same material. Henry Thomas Buckle (d. 1862) makes some "Contributions to the History of the Pet," and relies for his information about Roland on Thomas Blount (*Common Place Books*, §1116, 2:472). John Bourke's *Scatalogic Rites* (1891) is more thorough, although his citations can be frustratingly short on bibliographical detail. Jacques-Antoine Dulaure (*Histoire Abrégée*, pp. 314–15), whose own source is Du Cange, also mentions Roland.

M. Roland le Pettour
Hemingstone
Suffolk

What makes Roland's case unusual is the articulation of a fart as land tenure, and the recurrent citation of his obligation throughout the medieval period and after suggests the unusualness of his tenure, although the recurrence of the jump, whistle, and fart in relation to a separate serjeanty (Fartprints, §1e) hints at a practice of such feudal arrangements. The clustering of analogous fart occasions in France—Rabelais's exact repetition of the jump-whistle-and-fart routine, and the prostitute's toll-fart—points to Gallic provenance. Revisiting the fartman of the *Roman d'Alexandre* (plate 3), we might well ask what the occasion is that gives rise to his public act. One possibility is that the man is a vassal who completes his dues of a fart before his seigneurial lord.[66] Certainly, the dress of the man behind the table bespeaks a nobler class than the rude apparel of fartman, and the table suggests the collection of monies. The contraption on the table is, however, hard to identify. The editor of the manuscript facsimile suggests a cup and ball,[67] but the geometrical shapes also look as if it is some kind of measuring instrument. A medieval fartometer? Are we back to the perennial question of the division of the fart? According to one source, of doubtful authority it must be said, a feudal tenure not far from Caen required the annual delivery of one and a half farts from the tenant.[68]

In the feudal economy, tenured relationship to the land largely defined social status, and the idea of absolute property right was foreign. Although statutes such as the *Quia emptores* of 1290 helped loosen restrictions on the conveyance of land, it was not until the seventeenth century that free alienation, the hallmark of modern property law, became a basic right. The classic shape of feudalism is that of a gigantic household; the entire kingdom being the *oikonomia* of the king, within which each subject holds some function from great to menial. Since all land in theory belongs to the king, everyone save the king is a tenant of some sort. By the process of subtenancy called subinfeudation, the exact same piece of land, which was notionally owned by the king, could be held by a great lord, who was tenant-in-chief of the king, by a lesser member of the gentry, vassal of a vassal, who was obligated to the tenant-in-chief and all the way down to the unfree bondman, villein, who owned only the right to work the land for his own subsistence in return for labor on his lord's private demesne.

Tenancy agreements for free men came in various shapes and sizes. The best known is the knight's fee (*feodum militis*), which represents the agreed amount of land deemed sufficient to support one knight. In return for the land, the knight was obligated to fight for his king for a designated number of days a year, if summoned by his lord. The size of a knight's fee varied greatly with no evident attempt to standardize it, but has been roughly gauged by modern historians at five hides or carucates, each hide being a hundred or a hundred and twenty acres (Roland thus owning about one hide of land).[69] A great baron, tenant-in-chief to the king and holder of thousands of acres, would thus be required to weigh in with a substantial militia in time of war.

Usually considered less prestigious than the knight's fee, serjeanty was a hard service to define so miscellaneous were its services. Old French *sergant* means "servant"; thus a serjeant is a servant who provides some personal service for his lord or king.[70] Although the tenure no doubt originated as such, personal service does not define its function in the long term, for personal links break with successive heirs. Serjeanty seems to be a ragbag of obligations, acquiring its nomenclature well after the actual services were in place.[71] Categories were not neatly separated and tenants often held a variety of tenures: sometime before 1142, Richard de Brai held his land by a combination of the service of riding messenger and one-sixteenth of a knight's fee, most likely rendered as scutage, the substitution of cash for military obligation.[72]

Serjeanty appears to have been a Norman rather than Anglo-Saxon custom, and although some services claim to date from the Conqueror, the bulk of English serjeanty tenures originate from the twelfth century.[73] Henry II is the earliest king named in connection with Roland, but since he confirmed the cessation of Roland's personal obligation, the tenure may have been granted by an earlier monarch; possibly Roland's act "so delighted Henry I that he rewarded him with a house and 99 acres in Suffolk."[74] Henry I certainly had a proclivity for raising "from the dust" the *novi homines* who served him with lands that had escheated to him,[75] and if Roland's tenure did originate with him, Roland must have been rather wheezy by the time Henry II ascended the throne in 1154, Henry I having died in 1135.

The combined sources measure Roland's estate as somewhere between 110 and 139 acres of land, stretching across three neighboring villages in Suffolk, and with an additional manor in Norfolk. The region is easy enough to identify: Hemingstone, Gosbeck, and Ash(-Booking) exist today, lie within a few miles of each other, and are mentioned as far back as the eleventh-century Domesday Book. Such division of a holding into discrete blocks of land across different villages was common practice, and gave rise to the frequent farming out of smaller units within the entire estate to different tenants; certainly, this is the picture drawn of Roland's estate by the entry from the *Calendar of Close Rolls* (Fartprints, §3), which shows the land rented variously.

Measurement of land went more by usability than by fixed area. One bovate (the amount of land ploughable by one ox), equivalent to one half-virgate (the amount of land ploughable by one horse), represented roughly ten–fifteen acres of arable land, depending on quality. One bovate or half-virgate seems to have been roughly the size of holding for a villager of middle income in the thirteenth century.[76] A *husbond*—a farmer wealthy enough to own a house—would hold on an average thirty acres in the thirteenth century. The poorer land-holders, the "cotters," because they lived in cottages, worked about five acres or less.[77] With a holding of about five virgates, Roland was thus well endowed, wealthy among nonnoble vassals. Weighing in at some hundred and twenty acres, he was master of about one-fifth of a knight's fee.

As a tenure, serjeanty subdivided into grand (*magna serjeantia*) and petty or petit (*parva serjeantia*), and although the distinction appears as early as the Magna Carta of 1215, there is no evidence of it applying in the mid-twelfth century; if it did, it must have meant little other than "big" and "small," or "major" and "minor" in the case of some tenant having a minor holding by serjeanty and main "big" estate by knights' fee (or vice versa).[78] It is not entirely clear what systematic criteria, if any, distinguished big serjeanties from small. For Bracton in the thirteenth century, a serjeanty *in capite* was large if it was worth a hundred shillings or more, but the nature of service rather than the value increasingly differentiated the two.[79] The *Liber feodorum* values the villa in Norfolk at a hundred shillings (Fartprints, §1b), although the other sources mention only lower sums. It is not clear whether Roland's serjeanty was big or small, or even thought of in such terms; and not very likely, alas, that any pun was ever intended between *petit serjeanty* and "un saut, un *pet*, & un suflet."

The reasons for the alienation of the serjeanty during Henry II's time are also unknown. Maybe Roland broke a leg doing his *tripudium*, or just ran out of steam. For whatever reason, his lands transferred to other tenants. These subsequent vassals, unable or unwilling to pay in Roland's kind, paid hard cash to the tune of 15s. We do not know whether Henry II thought Roland's act funny, although John of Salisbury's pained testimony to such carry-on might suggest that he did, particularly when one considers that he is considered to have been the "first model of the *rex facetus* [jesting king]."[80] The pious Henry III, however, was not amused. Even though

Roland's lands had been alienated, the obscene tenure must have remained on the record book, for the Assize Rolls record that Henry III caused the service to be commuted to money on account of its indecency (Fartprints, §2), and with that ended the sergeanty of Roland the Farter.[81] Apart from questions of decorum, many serjeanties created during the earlier twelfth century at a time "when land was plentiful and money was scarce,"[82] were later commuted into money rents.

Serjeanties were inalienable, and land held *in capite* from the king could not be alienated without special licence. Alienation is the feudal term for the conveyance of property by gift or sale from one tenant to another, the transfer being effected by either subinfeudation or substitution.[83] Under subinfeudation tenant B, obligated to A, creates a new tenancy held by C, who is in turn answerable to B, who himself remains obligated to A. Subinfeudation simply describes the classic feudal pyramid, in which the same piece of land was placed under a series of subtenancies, from the single tenant-in-chief near the apex of the pyramid to many humble farmers near its base. No permission appears to have been needed for subinfeudation.[84] Under substitution, however, tenant B gets out of the contract altogether, substituting for himself tenant C, who now is answerable directly to A. Substitution was basically a sale, and although it was permitted in the local instance usually because it could provide ready money to the exchequer, it flew in the face of any idealized feudal principle of a personal relationship between lord and tenant, based on land held personally by the tenant and secured by service rendered in person to the lord. The references to the alienation of Roland's land, by conveyance of property ratified by Henry II, imply that the transaction was a substitution, in effect a sale to a new tenant (Fartprints, §3). In such substitutions, the stages of conveyance broke into separate legal acts in order to place the lord at the center of the transaction: the donor surrendered the land back to the lord, who then gave it to the new tenant.[85]

The waters are muddied considerably by virtue of an historian's claims that Roland's lands succeeded to his heirs. "In the time of Rich. I. the manor was held by Jeffrey, son of Hubert de Afleton, son of Rowland, and in 1205 by Alexander de Brompton and Agnes his wife, sister and heir of this Jeffrey."[86] Beyond the evidence of the *Liber feodorum* (Fartprints, §1.a), it is not clear what Copinger's sources are for these claims; if they are correct, they raise problems for the frequent references to the alienation of Roland's land, for that legal act is different from the granting of land by the lord to the (dead) tenant's successor. Roland's serjeanty was quite likely only for life,[87] especially if the land was reserved for the king's entertainers; life-estate, however, did not prevent the land being gifted anew by the lord to the original tenant's descendant, for successive generations of Roland's family may have held tenure, but by gift rather than by hereditary right.[88] There is a difference between succession to land by the lord's gift and by abstract rule of inheritance law. On the other hand, even if the tenure were heritable, land that had been acquired in the holder's lifetime was more easily alienable than land that had been inherited.[89] Nevertheless, whichever way we look at it, it is hard to reconcile the assertions that the land was alienated and at the same time granted to Roland's heirs.[90] Possibly the land was temporarily alienated and subsequently returned to the family,[91] but there comes a point in such inquiry that guesswork turns into clutching at straws, and this may be it.

Another inconsistency in Roland's case is introduced by Camden, who refers to our hero by a different name: "Baldwin le Pettour (marke his name well)" (Fartprints, §5). Camden does not cite his sources, though there appear to have been at least two, one Latin, one French, and Baldwin was presumably mentioned by name in at least one of them. With the exception of the additional manor in Norfolk, which only some sources cite, all the records agree on the location of the fee, primarily in Hemingstone, stretching to the northeast into Ash-Booking and Gosbeck; so we are dealing with possibly two farters (flatulent father and son, brothers, or farter minstrels?) who held the same piece of land, or one farter who went by two different names. Or did Camden simply make a mistake? The inferences drawn by Copinger lead us to surmise more than one farter. "The two manors of the Domesday Survey came later into one lordship held by Rowland le Pettour or le Farcere, and also by Rowland and Baldwin le Pettour of the King by serjeanty."[92] "Rowland le Sarcere held one hundred and ten acres of land in Hemingston by serjeanty.. . .One Baldwin formerly held the lands by the same services."[93] If Roland and Baldwin were independent farters, the argument for a holding that passed from entertainer to entertainer strengthens.

A couple of stray surnames possibly point to residual identity-by-profession. In 1327 Joh'ne [Johannes] le Fartere, who lived in Aylleston, modern Aylestone, in Guthlaxton, Leicestershire, paid five shillings as a tax on all his moveable goods to Edward III to pay for the war against Scotland.[94] The tax was collected by the appointed tax collectors designating a number of honest men from the vill to pronounce the value of each inhabitant's moveable goods, excepting the very poor and very rich, the latter fighting in the wars anyway at their own expense in accordance with their knights' fee. The tax liable represented one-twentieth of each household's moveable goods. Aylleston was a middling sized vill, with sixteen inhabitants on the lay subsidy roll. Johannes and two others contributed the biggest subsidy of five shillings, which represented an estimated moveable wealth of 100 shillings. The average subsidy throughout Leicestershire was approximately two–three shillings, with the wealthiest paying up to ten shillings and occasionally up to twenty-four shillings.

Based on this profile, Johannes le Fartere did all right for himself, as did Roland two centuries earlier. Was John in the same line of business as Roland the Farter? By 1327, fiscal records were thorough, and had John been a member of Roland's trade, we would probably have heard about it. Did John inherit the name? Or did he receive it as a nickname because he was flatulent? We might ask the same of Walterus Fartere, mentioned *en passant* in the *Calendar of Close Rolls* (*MED*, s.v. *ferter*[*e*], n.).

In Blount's record, Roland is referred to as "Roland le Sarcere." Old French *sarcer* is a variation of *sarrer* [to sieve]; alternatively *sarcier* means "to darn," although neither sieving nor darning seems to rise to the level of an occupation, and hence a name. "Sarcere" could be a slip of the pen for "Farcere," from *farcier* [to jest, make fun of].[95] Each new piece of evidence both places us further down one path of discovery and opens up a labyrinth of other possibilities. The *fragmenta antiquitatis*, the few terse historical documents create more questions than answers, clues that propagate themselves into further clues. Nor should we uncritically trust the accuracy or good intentions of the inherited data. The sole source that places Roland in the twelfth century comes from the fourteenth century. The lateness and frequency of the "contemporary" records—four mentions in the *Liber Feodorum*—may suggest that even in the thirteenth century the clerks thought the tenure amusing enough to keep alive on the record books for its anecdotal interest rather than any accurate representation of current holding. It is quite likely that the original grant of Roland's land was orally transacted and never made it to parchment.[96] How then do we reconstruct his case from the shards of writing? What would constitute a complete body of evidence for Roland? Most disturbingly, did it ever exist by any modern standard of evidentiary criteria? Would a complete body of evidence, whatever that is, answer all the questions and iron out the inconsistencies? Is it really possible to become one flesh with this past? Roland-Baldwin the Pettour-Sarcere moons at us across the centuries, reminding us that in the extimate relation between past and present, the boundaries of selfhood and otherness never settle. Decide for yourself, detector, as to the mystery of Roland. Blow the roof off.

The Color of the Balloon

I rede þat in Saynt Gregorys tyme was a woman þat het Lasma and made bred þat þe pope sang wyth and howsulde þe pepul. Þen, on a day, when þis pope howsulde þe peple, he come to þis woman Lasma and sayde: "Take here Godis body." And þen she smylut. But when þe pope see hir smyle, he wythdroȝ his hond, and layd þe ost on þe auter, and turnet to þis woman, and sayde: "Lasma, why smyleste þou, when þou shuldest haue taken Godys body?" Then sayde sche: "For þou calles þat Godys body þat I made with myn owne hondys."[97]

[I read that in St. Gregory's time was a woman called Lasma, who made the bread with which the pope celebrated mass and administered it to the people. Then, one day, as the pope gave the sacrament to the people, he came to this woman Lasma and said: "Partake of God's body." And at that she smiled. But when the pope saw her smile, he withdrew his hand, laid the host on the altar, turned to the woman, and said: "Lasma, why did you smile just now when you ought to have received God's body?" To which she said: "Because what you're calling 'God's body' was baked by my own hands."]

Horrifed, St. Gregory prays for Lasma's unbelief, at which the host miraculously turns into raw bleeding flesh, and Lasma never smirked again at the sacrificial host. Some well-grammared clerk might have smiled at the philogical joke of the "breaking" or "farting" of bread, but what makes this unlearned woman's mouth twitch is the transmutation of her bodily labor into theological mystery. In the face of metaphysical dogma, she refuses to let go of truth she knows in her hands, sharing a skepticism conventionally demonstrated by the Jew. Eucharistic faith negates sensory experience; it demands that the stuff that looks, smells, feels, and tastes like bread be bleeding flesh. For preacher John Mirk, Lasma belongs with Doubting Thomas, who was content with nothing less than groping in Christ's side to believe his resurrection. For medieval iconography, it is a powerful image of unbelief. Middle English *grope* ranges in meaning from fondling someone amorously, to a physician's searching of a wound, to a priest's examination of a penitent's conscience. Friar John gropes Thomas's butt in search of money. Groping fingers, welcome or otherwise, represent both the most penetrating inquiry into hidden mystery and the most debased knowing. According to Mirk, Doubting Thomas's gropings only brought temporary belief. Subsequently refusing to believe in the Blessed Virgin Mary's bodily assumption into heaven, he was struck by a girdle that fell out of the sky.[98] Only when truth in the form of Mary's wardrobe lay in his hands could Thomas assent to it.

Lasma belongs in the tradition of Diogenes the Cynic, who complained during Plato's show-stopping lecture on tablehood [*trapezotēs*] and cuphood [*kyathotēs*] that all he could see was tables and cups[99]; or who, on another occasion, after Plato had just defined man as a biped and featherless animal, produced a plucked chicken and insisted it was human.[100] Plato got his own back by calling him a dog,[101] and thus Diogenes was henceforth named the "Cynic" from *kynikos* [canine]. What Joubert identifies as the "cynic spasm" [*spasme cynique*] is the hostile baring of the teeth that threatening dogs assume.[102] Disbelief makes us break out in a bastard smile. In sneering at pretentious behavior in all its forms, Diogenes critically deflates what is puffed up. With his sneer, he knocks the trapped wind out of bilious [*cholēn*] and flatulent [*pephysēmenous*] pretenders of knowledge.[103]

Pain and nerve damage produce the same torsions of the mouth as does pleasure; pleasure emerges from recognition, and so does pain. Knowledge, welcome or unwelcome, results in the contraction of muscles and opening of the (buccal) orifice that we call a smile or a grimace. Both result in a cracking [L. *crepitus*] of the face, and both laughter and weeping a breaking of vocal wind. Clustering around this fissure in which knowledge occurs are the names we have bestowed over the eras to an encounter with being in a different mode: *anagnoresis*, transmutation, mystery, revelation, apocalypse, epiphany, detection, unmasking, defacement, sacrifice, inspiration, dehiscence. Common to all is the action of opening, contained in our heuristic methods (etymology, ana-lysis) and signaled in bodily function: evacuation, orgasm, purging, yawning, sneezing, laughing, crying, burping, farting, sniffing, and dying. Laughter, rather than ratiocination, is the first response to wonder. The laughing, farting body measures knowledge in terms of noise and smells, objects in terms of presence and proximity, self in terms of breath, discourse in terms of noise. It is beside itself, inhabiting the space outside its own fleshly perimeter. It does not think in terms of adequation between subject and object for the "space" between the two is itself is a third, aerial "object," full of noise and smell. If it is ultimately a religious principle that the body broken open loudly and desecrated makes the transcendent immanent and reality a present perfume, then the laughing, farting body is indeed sacred even as it is profane.

Skepticism is as essential to mystery as belief. Smirking Lasma exposes the underbelly of credulity. *Credo* means "I place in my heart," from Latin *cor, cordis* [heart] and *dare* [to put]; skepticism however issues from the other end. A mystery requires that there be something hidden to be revealed. Unlike Lasma, we must believe that there is something beyond her bread held in the pope's hand. Yet we must also be skeptical and vigilant, quick to discriminate between a relic and a hog's turd (*CT*, 6.919–55). Belief in everything destroys mystery. Inquiry about the color of the balloon may register on one level an insatiable prurience for "wie es eigentlich gewesen ist"[104] [how it really was], a relentless itch for contextualizing empirical detail that no amount of scratching can soothe, but it is also a critical testing of what mother says, a piggish suspicion of maternal *auctoritas*, however sweetly it imposes its demands. Skepticism, the refusal of blind credulity, made historical study into a science. By questioning thus, we prove our sources for sound evidence, and discard onto the trash heap what is worthless—unless of course one discards what is worthy and pockets the worthless, that is, if one is Picasso . . . or a bum.

NOTES

Introduction

1. Mary Douglas, *Purity and Danger*, quoted in Jeff Persels and Russell Ganim, eds, *Fecal Matters in Early Modern Literature and Art* (Aldershot, Hampshire and Burlington, VT: Ashgate, 2004), pp. xii–xv. Also William Ian Miller, *The Anatomy of Disgust* (Cambridge, MA: Harvard University Press, 1997), pp. 43–4. This said, Douglas does not consider the fart in any systematic way, only incidentally; for example, *Purity and Danger: An Analysis of the Concepts of Pollution and Taboo* (London and New York: Routledge 1966, repr. 1996), p. 120. Waste studies is a scholarly domain in its own right. Most relevantly to medieval waste, see Susan Signe Morrison, *Excrement in the Late Middle Ages: Sacred Filth and Chaucer's Fecopoetics* (New York: Palgrave Macmillan, 2008), especially pp. 139–58.
2. John Trevisa, *On the Properties of Things: John Trevisa's Translation of Bartholomaeus Anglicus De Re Proprietatibus*, ed. M.C. Seymour, Elizabeth Brockhurst, Gabriel M. Liegey, M.H. Blechner, Ralph Hanna III, Joseph E. Grennen et al., 3 vols. (Oxford: Clarendon, 1975–1988), 7.49, 1:401.
3. Walter Benjamin, *Illuminations*, ed. Hannah Arendt, trans. Harry Zohn (New York: Schocken, 1968), p. 197.
4. At a distance, the Angel and Royal gargoyle looks like a face, but viewed from underneath, is clearly a butt. Autun's gargoyle, however, leaves no room for doubt at any angle. See Janetta Rebold Benton, *Holy Terrors: Gargoyles on Medieval Buildings* (New York: Abbeville, 1997), pp. 60–3. "Gargoyle" comes from OF *la gargole* [throat].
5. For Middle Ages as origin of the contemporary, see Umberto Eco, *Travels in Hyperreality*, trans. William Weaver (London: Picador, 1986), pp. 64–5.
6. Galen, *On the Natural Faculties*, ed. and trans. Arthur John Brock (Cambridge, MA: Harvard University Press, 1916), 3.12.
7. Laurent Joubert, *Traité du ris* (Paris: Nicholas Chesneau, 1579), 1.26, (p. 128). English translations of Joubert throughout are from *Treatise on Laughter*, trans. Gregory David de Rocher (Alabama: University of Alabama Press, 1980), p.60.
8. Julia Kristeva, *Powers of Horror: An Essay on Abjection*, trans. Leon S. Roudiez (New York: Columbia University Press, 1982), p. 69. Citing Claude Gaignebet, Flavio Cazzaro observes the abject boundary around bodily orifices. Only when bodily matter is ejected does it become dirty. "Un Perfum de scandale ou l'esthétique scatologique dans la literature française du nord du XIIe au XIVe siècle" (Lausanne: Université de Lausanne, M.A. thesis, 2003), p. 7.

9. For a detailed critique of Platonically influenced medieval musical aesthetics and an examination of the "embodied materiality" (p. 4) of abstract number, see Bruce W. Holsinger, *Music, Body, and Desire in Medieval Culture: Hildegard of Bingen to Chaucer* (Stanford: Stanford University Press: 2001). See also C.M. Woolgar, *The Senses in Late Medieval England* (New Haven and London: Yale University Press, 2006), pp. 63–83.
10. Brian O'Doherty, "Feldman Throws a Switch between Sight and Sound," *The New York Times*, February 2, 1964, p. X11.
11. Quoted in Philippe Kohly, dir., *Matisse, Picasso* DVD (New York: Museum of Modern Art, 2003).
12. Caroline Walker Bynum, *Fragmentation and Redemption: Essays on Gender and the Human Body in Medieval Religion* (New York: Zone, 1992), p. 13.
13. Ascham, *The Scholemaster*, in *English Works*, ed. William Aldis Wright (Cambridge: Cambridge University Press, 1904; repr. 1970), p. 105.
14. Malcolm Jones, "The Parodic Sermon in Medieval and Early Modern England" *Medium Aevum*, 66 (1997): 101 [94–114].
15. Bynum, *Fragmentation*, p. 25.

The Beginning

1. *Chronicle of London, From 1089 to 1483*, ed. E Tyrrell and Sir N. H. Nicolas (London: Longman, 1827; repr. Felinfach: Llanerch, 1995), p. 20.
2. Count Rainier of Boulogne "took the meaning literally, like the Jews," in Lambert of Ardres, *The History of the Counts of Guines and Lords of Ardres*, trans. Leah Shopkow (Philadelphia: University of Pennsylvania Press, 2000), p. 68. For a blindfold Synagogia who carries tablets signifying the letter of the law, see Ruth Mellinkoff, *Outcasts: Signs of Otherness in Northern European Art of the Late Middle Ages* (Berkeley: University of California Press, 1993), 2.II.36.
3. Exodus 33.3. For L. *dura cervix*, Wyclif translates "hard nol" (head, nape of neck). John Wyclif, *The Holy Bible, Containing the Old and New Testaments*, ed. Josiah Forshall and Frederic Madden, 4 vols. (Oxford: Oxford University Press, 1850), 1:272–3.
4. For Jews throwing the murdered corpse of a Christian boy in a *wardrobe* [privy], see *CT*, 7.572–3. See also the story of Abraham, a Jew, who in 1250 bought a statue of the Virgin and Child and subjected it to a daily ritual of defecation, forcing his wife to do the same; Matthew of Paris, *Matthæi Parisiensis, Monachi Sancti Albani, Chronica Majora: Vol 5, A.D. 1248 to A.D. 1259*, ed. Henry Richards Luard (London: Her Majesty's Stationery Office, 1880), pp. 114–15. No doubt there is a triangulated association between shit, gold, and Jews in respect of their money-lending.
5. Léon Poliakov, *History of Anti-Semitism, Volume One: From the Time of Christ to the Court Jews*, trans. Richard Howard (New York: Vanguard, 1965), pp. 124–5. Martha Bayless tracks the wide dissemination of the story in "The Story of the Fallen Jew and the Iconography of Jewish Unbelief," *Viator* 34 (2003): 142–56.

6. *Middle English Sermons*, ed. Woodburn O. Ross, EETS O.S. 209 (London: Oxford University Press, 1940), p. 159.
7. *Calendar of Plea and Memoranda Rolls Preserved among the Archives of the Corporation of the City of London at the Guildhall*, ed. A. H. Thomas. 6 vols. (Cambridge: Cambridge University Press, 1929–1961), 2:237.
8. *Calendar of Plea*, 4:124, 157.
9. *Calendar of Plea*, 4:135.
10. Garderobes in palaces and castles were often multiseaters, though sometimes with some minimal privacy; Lawrence Wright, *Clean & Decent: The Fascinating History of the Bathroom and the Water-Closet* (London: Penguin, 2000), p. 47.
11. Ælfric, "An Edition of Ælfric's *Letter to Brother Edward*," ed. Mary Clayton, in *Early Medieval English Texts and Interpretations: Studies Presented to Donald G. Scragg*, eds. Elaine Treharne and Susan Rosser (Tempe, AZ: Arizona Center for Medieval and Renaissance Studies, 2002), pp. 282–3 [pp.263–83].
12. For arswyspes, see *Promptorium parvulorum sive clericorum, dictionarius Anglo-latinus princeps by Fratre Galfrido Grammatico dicto*, ed. Albertus Way (London: Camden Society, 1865), s.v. *arswyspe*. The *Promptorium* is a fifteenth-century English-Latin word list; Latin equivalents are *maniperium* and *anitergium*.
13. Seneca, *Ad Lucilium epistulae morales*, vol. 2, ed. and trans. Richard M. Gummere (Cambridge, MA: Harvard University Press, 1970), 70.20 (pp. 66–7).
14. Wynkyn de Worde, *The demaundes ioyous* 1511, anon, London, 1511. For gorse as toilet paper, see William Langland, *Piers Plowman: A Parallel-Text Edition of the A, B, C, and Z Versions*, ed. A.V.C. Schmidt (London: Longman, 1995), A.5.194.
15. Georges Duby, ed. *A History of Private Life II: Revelations of the Medieval World*, trans. Arthur Goldhammer (Cambridge, MA: Harvard University Press, 1988), p. 89.
16. *Thundergust: A Kentucky Court of Appeals Decision* (Louisville, KY: Privately Printed, 1930), unpaginated.
17. John Aubrey, *Brief Lives*, ed. Oliver Lawson Dick (Ann Arbor: University of Michigan Press, 1957), p. 305.
18. Carsten Niebuhr, *Description de l'Arabie faite sur des observations propres et des avis recueillis dans les lieux mêmes* (Amsterdam and Utrecht: S.J. Baalde [Amsterdam] and J. van Schoonhoven [Utrecht], 1774), p. 27.
19. *The Book of the Thousand Nights and a Night: A Plain and Literal Translation of the Arabian Nights Entertainments*, trans. and ed. Richard F. Burton. 10 vols. (London: Burton Club [privately printed], 19–?), 5:135–7.
20. *Book of the Thousand*, 5:137.
21. *Calendar of Plea*, 2:135: on February 2, 1372, "Richard Bakere, brewer, was fined 2s [2 shillings] for casting dung into the street against the ordinance." In May 1373, the dung dumped daily in the Ward by carters from

throughout the City of London caused oppression of the inhabitants (2:156); and Dolitellane was so "stopped up with dung," that no one could perform their labors because of the "stench and filth" (2:157). Whether Do-litel-lane acquired its name before or after the work-stopping poop is anyone's guess.

22. PRO C 1/66/290.
23. Antoine Furetière, *Dictionnaire universel* (La Haye: Chez Arnout, 1694), s.v. *vesse*.
24. *The Complete Works of François Villon*, ed. and trans. Anthony Bonner (New York: David McKay, 1960), pp. xviii–xix.
25. Rosemary Woolf, "Later Poetry: The Popular Tradition," in *The Middle Ages*, ed. W.F. Bolton (London: Barrie & Jenkins, 1970), p. 280 [pp. 263–311].
26. For discussion of the passage she contests, see p. 197, fn 291.
27. *The Antwerp-London Glossaries*, ed. David W. Porter (Toronto: Publications of the Dictionary of Old English, forthcoming), 4.2027.
28. *Owl and the Nightingale*, ed. Neil Cartlidge (Exeter: Exeter University Press, 2001), ll. 115–16, 591–6, 1686. See also Margaret Laing, "Raising a Stink in *The Owl and the Nightingale*: A New Reading at Line 115," *Notes and Queries* 45 (1998): 276–84.
29. See Thomas W. Ross, "Taboo-Words in Fifteenth-Century English," in *Fifteenth-Century Studies: Recent Essays*, ed. Robert F. Yeager (Hamden, CT: Archon, 1984), p. 140.
30. *Liber feodorum, The Book of Fees, Commonly Called Testa de Nevill*: Ed. H.C.M. Lyte et al., 3 vols. (London: His Majesty's Stationery Office, 1920–1931), 2:1174.
31. William Camden, *Britain Or A Chorographicall Description of the Most flourishing Kingdomes, England, Scotland, and Ireland, and the llands adioyning, out of the depth of Antiqvitie* (London: Impensis Georgii Bishop & Ioannis Norton, 1610), p. 464. Compare Thomas Blount's introduction to his *Fragmenta Antiquitatis. Antient Tenures of Land, and Jocular Customs of Some Mannors* (London: Richard and Edward Atkins, 1679), in which he hopes that they "might not be unacceptable to the Studious, who . . . might smile at the inoffensive mirth." Nicola McDonald speaks of the simultaneous "shocking modernity" and "radical otherness" of medieval obscenity in *Medieval Obscenities*, ed. Nicola McDonald (Woodbridge, Suffolk: York Medieval Press, 2006), p. 11.
32. E.K. Chambers, *The Mediaeval Stage*, 2 vols. (Oxford: Oxford University Press, 1903; repr. [2 vols. in one], Mineola, NY: Dover, 1996), 1:412.
33. Dominique Laporte, *History of Shit*, trans. Nadia Benabid and Rodolphe el-Khoury (Cambridge, MA: MIT Press, 2002), p. 4.
34. Miller, *Anatomy*, p. 144.
35. Richard Palmer, "In Bad Odour: Smell and Its Significance in Medicine from Antiquity to the Seventeenth Century," in *Medicine and the Five Senses*, ed. W.F. Bynum and Roy Porter (Cambridge: Cambridge University Press, 1993), p. 66.
36. Guy Hocquenghem, *Homosexual Desire*, trans. Daniella Dangoor (Durham and London: Duke University Press, 1993), p. 96.

37. Jean-Joseph Goux, *Symbolic Economies after Marx and Freud*, trans. Jennifer Curtiss Gage (Ithaca, NY: Cornell University Press, 1990), p. 79.
38. Laporte, *History of Shit*, p. 46.
39. Otto Fenichel, "The Drive to Amass Wealth," in *Collected Papers*, ed. Hanna Fenichel and David Rapaport, 2 vols. (New York: Norton, 1953–1954), 2:92 [2:89–108].
40. Laporte, *History of Shit*, p. 68.
41. David LaGuardia, "Doctor Rabelais and the Medicine of Scatology," in Persels and Ganim, eds, *Fecal Matters*, pp. 24–6 [pp. 24–37].
42. Mikhail Bakhtin, *Rabelais and His World*, trans. Hélène Iswolsky (Bloomington: Indiana University Press, 1984), p. 26.
43. Bakhtin, *Rabelais*, p. 29.
44. Duby, *History of Private Life*, p. 6.
45. Duby, *History of Private Life*, p. 8.
46. M.M. Postan, *The Medieval Economy and Society: An Economic History of Britain in the Middle Ages* (London: Penguin, 1972), p. 87.
47. Duby, *History of Private Life*, p. 9.
48. An early-fifteenth-century English version of the Rule delicately phrases it as a *lytil entirval* for tending to one's *laburs*; *Three Middle-English Versions of the Rule of St. Benet*, ed. Ernest A. Kock, EETS o.s. 120 (London: Trübner, 1902), p. 15. The concept of defecation as work is reflected in modern "job" for a bowel movement, and its diminutive, "jobby."
49. Diogenes Laertius, *Lives of Eminent Philosophers*, ed. and trans. by R.D. Hicks. 2 vols. (Cambridge, MA: Harvard University Press, 1925), 6.24, 2:27. For his defecation and masturbation, see 6.69, 2:71. See also Augustine, *The City of God against the Pagans*, ed. and trans. George E. McCracken, William M. Greene, David Wiesen, Philip Levine, Eva Matthews Sanford, William Chase Greene, et al., 7 vols. (Cambridge, MA: Harvard University Press, 1957–1972; repr. 1969–1995), 14.20, 4:368–9.
50. Duby, *History of Private Life*, pp. 587–8.
51. Miller, *Anatomy*, p. 162.
52. John Boswell, *Christianity, Social Tolerance, and Homosexuality: Gay People in Western Europe from the Beginning of the Christian Era to the Fourteenth Century* (Chicago: University of Chicago Press, 1980), pp. 269–302.
53. For lepers, see *The Book of Margery Kempe*, ed. Sanford Brown Meech and Hope Emily Allen, EETS 212 (Oxford: Oxford University Press, 1940; repr. 1982), see Chap. 74 (pp. 176–7); for husband's shit, Chap. 76 (pp. 180–1).
54. Miller, *Anatomy*, p. 161.
55. Innocent III, *De Miseria condicionis humane*, ed. and trans. Robert E. Lewis (Athens: University of Georgia Press, 1978), 1.1 [pp. 94–5].
56. The *OED* cites one late-fourteenth- or fifteenth-century use of *full wast* [foul waste] as refuse matter, but it refers to bodily decomposible by-product rather than inorganic refuse. See *Lybeaus Desconus*, ed. M. Mills. EETS 261 (London: Oxford University Press, 1969), ll. 1471–2 [p. 166].
57. Michel Foucault, *The Order of Things: An Archaeology of the Human Sciences* (London: Tavistock Publications, 1970), p. xv.

58. Sir Samuel Pepys, *Works*, ed. Robert Latham and William Matthews, 11 vols. (Berkeley: University of California Press, 1970–1983), 4:333.
59. Aristotle, *De Partibus animalium*, rev. edn., ed. and trans. A.L. Peck (Cambridge, MA: Harvard University Press, 1961), p. 645a.
60. Henry George Liddell and Robert Scott, eds. *A Greek-English Lexicon*, sup. ed. (Oxford: Clarendon, 1968), s.v. *ipnos*.
61. *The Chester Mystery Cycle*, ed. R.M. Lumiansky and David Mills, EETS s.s. 3 (London: Oxford University Press, 1974), p. 91, l. 297.
62. Jones, "Parodic Sermon," p. 101.
63. John of Arderne, *Treatises of Fistula in Ano, and of Fistulae in Other Parts of the Body*, ed. D'Arcy Power, EETS o.s. 139 (London: Oxford University Press, 1910), p. 5, ll. 12–18.
64. Françoise Bulman, *Dictionnaire des Proverbes Anglais-Français, Français-Anglais* (Québec: Les Presses de l'Université Laval, 1998), p. 139, §7.
65. For a Middle English version, see *CT*, 1.4406–7.
66. Nicholas Orme, *Education and Society in Medieval and Renaissance England* (London: Hambledon, 1989), p. 102, §27.
67. Alan of Lille, *Anticlaudianus or the Good and Perfect Man*, trans. James J. Sheridan (Toronto: Pontifical Institute of Mediaeval Studies, 1973), 2.399–400 (p. 85).
68. *Promptorium parvulorum*, pp. 43, 127, 150, 202. Also Ross, "Taboo-Words," pp. 137–60.
69. *The Vulgaria of John Stanbridge and the Vulgaria of Robert Whittinton*, ed. Beatrice White, EETS o.s. 187 (London: Oxford University Press, 1932; repr. 1971), pp. 15.28, 17.14, 19.16.
70. *Mankind*, in *Medieval Drama*, ed. David Bevington (Boston: Houghton Mifflin, 1975), ll. 129–34 (p. 908).
71. Orme, *Education and Society*, p. 104, §43.
72. Orme, *Education and Society*, p. 83, §12.
73. François Rabelais, *Oeuvres complètes*, ed. Mireille Huchon with François Moreau (Paris: Gallimard, 1994), 1.11 (p. 34).
74. Orme, *Education and Society*, p. 83, §12.
75. Peter Travis, "Thirteen Ways of Listening to a Fart: Noise in Chaucer's Summoner's Tale," *Exemplaria*, 16 (2004): 343–4 [323–48].
76. *Amorous Games: A Critical Edition of "Les Adevineaux Amoureux,"* ed. James Woodrow Hassell, Jr. (Austin and London: American Folklore Society, 1974), p. 166, §722.
77. *Amorous Games*, p. 152, §642.
78. For example, *Des Trois Dames qui trouverent l'anel*, in *NRCF*, 2:215–40; *Le Bouchier D'Abeville*, in *NRCF*, 3:237–335; *Les Deus Chevaus*, in *NRCF*, 5:251–65; and *Le Jugement des cons*, in *NRCF*, 4:23–33.
79. *Les Trois Meschines*, in *NRCF*, 4:224, ll. 60–9.
80. *Amorous Games*, p. 94, §349.
81. Latin does have a verb meaning "to fart silently" [*vissire*], but the common distinction between the noisy and the silent seems to be largely conceptual, without the specially designated vocabulary of French. Suetonius recounts

that Claudius was "even said to have thought of an edict allowing the privilege of breaking wind quietly or noisily at table [*flatus crepitusque ventris*], having learned of a man who ran some risk by restraining himself through modesty [*pudor*]"; Suetonius, *Lives of the Caesars*, ed. and trans. J. C. Rolfe, rev. edn., 2 vols. (Cambridge, MA: Harvard University Press, 1997–1998), 5.32, 2:60–1. While *crepitus* [rattling] refers to a noisy fart, *flatus* has more general application, and means silent only in context.

82. Furetière, *Dictionnaire*, s.v. *vesse*. Lord Fartsucker [*le seigneur Humevesne*] appears along with Kissass [*Baisecul*]; Rabelais, *Oeuvres*, 2.11–12 (pp. 254–60).
83. Anatoly Liberman, "Gone with the Wind: More Thoughts on Medieval Farting," *Scandinavian Studies* 68 (1996): 100 [98–104].
84. Hippocrates, *Prognostic*, 11 in *Works*, ed. and trans. W.H.S. Jones, E.T. Withington, Paul Potter, and Wesley D. Smith , 8 vols. (Cambridge, MA: Harvard University Press, 1923–1995), 2:24–5 [2: 1–55].
85. Augustine, *City of God*, 14.24, 4:390–1.
86. David Munrow, *Instruments of the Middle Ages and Renaissance* (London: Oxford University Press, 1976), pp. 8–9.
87. John Gower refers to the bombard as the bass shawm: "Ther was no song that . . . was herd in thilke compaignie so lowde . . . of bombard and of clarion" ; *Confessio Amantis*, in *Complete Works of John Gower*, ed. G.C. Macaulay, 4 vols. (Oxford: Clarendon, 1899–1902), 8.2474–82, 3:453.
88. Aristophanes, *The Clouds*, ed. and trans. Jeffrey Henderson (Cambridge, MA: Harvard University Press, 1998), l. 165 (pp. 28–9).
89. Holsinger, *Music, Body and Desire*, pp. 253–8.
90. Wilhelm Fränger, *The Millennium of Hieronymus Bosch*, trans. Eithne Wilkins and Ernst Kaiser (London: Faber & Faber, 1952), pp. 84–91.
91. Leo Spitzer, *Classical and Christian Ideas of World Harmony: Prolegomena to an Interpretation of the Word "Stimmung,"* ed. Anna Granville Hatcher (Baltimore: John Hopkins Press, 1963), p. 174.
92. Aurelian of Réome, *The Discipline of Music*, trans. Joseph Ponte (Colorado Springs: Colorado College Music Press, 1968), p. 6.
93. Munrow, *Instruments*, p. 15.
94. Quoted in Munrow, *Instruments*, p. 6.
95. *The "Summa musice": A Thirteenth-Century Manual for Singers*, ed. and trans. Christopher Page (Cambridge: Cambridge University Press, 1991), p. 61.
96. *Rhetorica ad Herennium*, ed. and trans. Harry Caplan (Cambridge, MA: Harvard University Press, 1954), 3.16.28 (pp. 206–7). See also Mary Carruthers, *The Book of Memory: A Study of Memory in Medieval Culture* (Cambridge: Cambridge University Press, 1990), pp. 70, 78, 269–71, 276.
97. *Poetria Nova of Geoffrey of Vinsauf*, trans. Margaret F. Nims (Toronto: Pontifical Institute of Mediaeval Studies, 1967), ll. 87–100 (pp. 18–19).
98. *Vitruvius on Architecture*, ed. and trans. Frank Granger, 2 vols. (Cambridge, MA: Harvard University Press, 1931–1934), 10.1.3, 2:276–7.
99. Plato, *Gorgias*, ed. and trans. W.R.M. Lamb (Cambridge, MA: Harvard University Press, 1925), 463b.

NOTES FROM PP. 31–6

100. Boethius, *Fundamentals of Music*, trans. Calvin M. Bower, ed. Claude V. Palisca (New Haven: Yale University Press, 1989), 1.34 (p. 50).
101. *Summa musice*, p. 65.
102. Spitzer, *Classical*, p. 50.
103. Spitzer, *Classical*, pp. 24–5.
104. "Eructavit cor meum terbum [*sic*] bonum." Psalm 44.2.
105. "Repleti sunt omnes Spiritu Sancto." Acts 2.3.
106. "Et eructantes omnia impleverunt bonitate." Psalm 103.28.
107. Bernard of Clairvaux, Sermon 67.4–5, in *On the Song of Songs IV*, trans. Irene Edmonds (Kalamazoo, MI: Cistercian Publications, 1980), pp. 7–9; *PL*, 183:1104B–C, 1105A taking Latin Bible citations above from Bernard's text in *PL*.
108. Joubert, *Traité*, 1.7 (pp. 58–9); *Treatise*, p. 34.
109. Augustine, *City of God*, 14.24, 4: 388–91.
110. Boethius, *Fundamentals*, 1.2 (p. 9).
111. Macrobius, *Commentary on the Dream of Scipio*, trans. William Harris Stahl, 2nd edn. (New York: Columbia University Press, 1990), p. 186.
112. Boethius, *Fundamentals*, 1.2 (pp. 9–10).
113. Boethius, *Fundamentals*, 1.2 (p. 10).
114. Plato, *Republic*, ed. and trans. Paul Shorey, 2 vols. (Cambridge, MA: Harvard University Press, 1930–1935), 376e, 1:174–5.
115. Plato, *Laws*, ed. and trans. R. G. Bury, 2 vols. (Cambridge, MA: Harvard University Press, 1926), 654a–b, 1:92–3.
116. Plato, *Laws*, 653e, 1:90–3.
117. "Feast of Tottenham," l. 92, in *Sentimental and Humorous Romances*, ed. Erik Kooper (Kalamazoo, MI: Medieval Institute Publications, 2006), p. 207.
118. William Dunbar, "Ane Dance in the Quenis Chalmer," l. 41, in *The Poems of William Dunbar*, ed. Priscilla Bawcutt, 2 vols. (Glasgow: Association for Scottish Literary Studies, 1998), 1:234 [233–4].
119. *Secretum Secretorum: Nine English Versions*, ed. M.A. Manzalaoui, EETS 276 (Oxford: Oxford University Press, 1977), pp. 52–3.
120. Andrew Boorde, *The First Boke of the Introduction of Knowledge* and *A Compendyous Regyment or a Dyetary of Helth*, in "A Compendyous Regyment or a Dyetary of Helth", ed. F.J. Furnivall, EETS e.s. 10 (London: Trübner, 1870), Chap. 19, p. 279.
121. Boorde, *Compendyous Regyment*, Chap. 20, p. 281.
122. Boorde, *Compendyous Regyment*, Chap. 21, p. 284.
123. This etymology is supported by Ogilvie, "because it acts suddenly, as a charm is supposed to do" (*Imperial Dictionary*, s.v. *carminative*). It is also supported by the more recent *Concise Oxford Dictionary* (10th edition), which, the editors of *OED* affirm in an exchange of correspondence, reflects more recent understanding of medieval Latin, although the jury is still out as to whether medieval Latin *carminare* (to disperse matter or humors) "ultimately represents *carminare* (to enchant, heal by incantation), from *carmen* (song, incantation) or *carminare* (to card wool) from *carmen* (card for carding wool) in an extension of sense."

NOTES FROM PP. 36-40 191

124. *Martianus Capella and the Seven Liberal Arts: Vol 2: The Marriage of Philology and Mercury*, trans. William Harris Stahl with E.L. Burge (New York: Columbia University Press, 1977), p. 358.
125. Macrobius, *Commentary*, p. 195.
126. Tony Hunt, ed. *Popular Medicine in Thirteenth-Century England: Introduction and Texts* (Cambridge: Brewer, 1990), p. 86, §20.
127. Boethius, *Fundamentals*, 1.3 (p. 11); 5.4 (p. 166).
128. Aulus Gellius, *The Attic Nights*, ed. and trans. John C. Rolfe, 3 vols. (Cambridge, MA: Harvard University Press, 1927; repr., 1970), 4.13, 1:352–3; Capella, *Seven Liberal Arts*, p. 358.
129. Boethius, *Fundamentals*, 1.1 (p. 5).
130. Plutarch, "Advice to the Bride and Groom," in *Moralia*, 16 vols., ed. and trans. Frank Cole Babbitt (Cambridge, MA: Harvard University Press, 1927–1976), 138b, 2:298–9.
131. "The Anglo-Saxon Charms," *Journal of American Folklore*, 22 (1909): 171 [105–237].
132. "Anglo-Saxon Charms," p. 199.
133. *Book of Secrets of Albertus Magnus of the Virtues of Herbs, Stones, and Certain Beasts*, ed. Michael R. Best and Frank H. Brightman (Oxford: Oxford University Press, 1973), pp. 88, 104.
134. Leo Spitzer, "Milieu and Ambiance," in *Essays in Historical Semantics* (New York: Russell & Russell, 1948), p. 183 [pp. 179–225].
135. Boethius, *Fundamentals*, 1.3 (p. 12).
136. Boethius, *Fundamentals*, 1.8 (p. 16).
137. *Admonition by the Father of F.A. to him being a Burgesse of the Parliament for his better Behaviour therein, . . . in Miscellanea Antiqua Anglicana, or a Select Collection of Curious Tracts Illustrative of the History, Literature, Manners and Biography of the English Nation* (London: Robert Triphook, 1816), p. 108 [pp. 49–100].
138. Macrobius, *Commentary*, p. 74.
139. Jean Froissart, *The Chronicle of Froissart*, trans. Sir John Bourchier Lord Berners, 6 vols. (London: David Nutt, 1901–1903), 3:332.
140. For reference to "gunne nor bombard," see John Lydgate, *Lydgate's Fall of Princes*, ed. Henry Bergen, EETS E.S. 121 (London: Oxford University Press, 1924), l. 1312.
141. Macrobius, *Commentary*, p. 182.
142. Orme, *Education and Society*, p. 101, §17.
143. Marcus Tullius Cicero, *De Natura deorum*, ed. and trans. H. Rackam, rev. edn. (Cambridge, MA: Harvard University Press, 1951), 2.33, pp. 202–3.
144. *De Secretis mulierum: Albertus Magnus De Secretis Mulierum*. Amstelodami: apud Iodocum Ianssonium, 1643. Chap. 2, p. 48; *Women's Secrets: A Translation of Pseudo-Albertus Magnus' De Secretis Mulierum with Commentaries*, trans. Helen Rodnite Lemay (Albany: State University of New York Press, 1992), p. 86.
145. Plato, *Timaeus*, ed. and trans. R.G. Bury (Cambridge, MA: Harvard University Press, 1929), 44d–45a (pp. 98–101).

NOTES FROM PP. 40–43

146. Ernst H. Kantorowicz, *The King's Two Bodies: A Study in Mediaeval Political Theology* (Princeton: Princeton University Press, 1957), pp. 74, 70.
147. Kantorowicz, *King's Two Bodies*, pp. 78–80.
148. Ovid, *Metamorphoses*, ed. and trans. Frank Justus Miller, rev. edn. G.P. Goold, 2 vols. (Cambridge, MA: Harvard University Press, 1977–1984), 3.273–4, 1:142–3.
149. *The Life of Cola di Rienzo*, trans. John Wright (Toronto: Pontifical Institute of Medieval Studies, 1975), p. 59.
150. Mandy Aftel, *Essence and Alchemy: A Book of Perfume* (New York: North Point Press, 2001), p. 65.
151. Francis Petrarch, *The Canzoniere or Rerum vulgaria fragmenta*, ed. and trans. Mark Musa with Barbara Manfredi (Bloomington and Indianapolis: Indiana University Press, 1996), 278.4 (pp. 398–9).
152. Petrarch, *Canzoniere*, 133.14 (pp. 218–19).
153. Spitzer, *Classical*, p. 62, and "Milieu," p. 260.
154. Angus Trumble, *A Brief History of the Smile* (New York: Basic Books, 2004), p. 107.
155. That desecration of the sacred is explicitly made in another marginal from the manuscript, fol. 56 r., in which a young man shits at a nun who is praying.
156. Henry of Huntingdon, *Henrici Archidiaconi Huntendunensis Historia Anglorum: The History of the English by Henry from AC 55 to AD 1154 in 8 Books*, ed. Thomas Arnold (London: Her Majesty's Stationery Office, 1879), 8.2 (p. 257).
157. Boorde, *Compendyous Regyment*, Chap. 33, p. 295.
158. Boorde, *Compendyous Regyment*, Chap. 3, p. 235.
159. Aftel, *Essence*, p. 14.
160. Palmer, "In Bad Odour," p. 62. The cerebral pneuma are in part created in the brain by air inhaled through the nose and entering the anterior ventricles directly along the olfactory nerves. See Rudolph Siegel, *Galen on Sense Perception* (Basel: S. Karger AG, 1970), p. 4.
161. Aristotle, *On Sense and Sensible Objects*, in *Parva Naturalia*, ed. and trans. W.S. Hett (Cambridge, MA: Harvard University Press, 1957), pp. 440b–441a.
162. *Timaeus*, 66c–67a (pp. 170–1).
163. Chaucer, *Troilus and Criseyde*, 1.731; also *Middle English Sermons*, p. 166: "What savour hathe a synnefull man in prechynge? For-soth, litill or noon; no, but as a nasse hathe in pipynge." [What joy does a sinner take in preaching? Little to none; about as much as a donkey takes in flute-music.]
164. Aftel, *Essence*, p. 11.
165. Aristotle, *On Dreams*, in *Parva Naturalia*, 459a.
166. Aristotle, *On Prophesy in Sleep*, in *Parva Naturalia*, 463a.
167. Aristotle, *On Sleep*, 457b.
168. *Life of Cola*, p. 61.
169. Aristotle, *On Prophesy*, 464a.
170. *Life of Cola*, pp. 61–2.

171. *Life of Cola*, p. 58.
172. Chaucer, *House of Fame*, ll. 765–819.
173. Aristotle, *On Dreams*, 460a.
174. Lyall Watson, *Jacobson's Organ and the Remarkable Nature of Smell* (New York: Norton, 2000), p. 80.
175. Apuleius, *Metamorphoses*, ed. and trans. J. Arthur Hanson, 2 vols. (Cambridge, MA: Harvard University Press, 1989), 3.18, 1:158–9.
176. Gower, *Confessio Amantis*, in *Works*, 6.1301, 3:202.
177. See article on nauscopie in the *Albion*, NS 1.22, June 1, 1833.
178. Watson, *Jacobson's Organ*, pp. 204–5.
179. Lucretius, *De Rerum natura*, ed. and trans. W.H.D. Rouse, rev. Martin Ferguson Smith (Cambridge, MA: Harvard University Press, 1992), 4.695–7.
180. Lucretius, *De Rerum*, 3.327–30.
181. Lucretius, *De Rerum*, 3.216–23.
182. Michael Taussig, *Defacement: Public Secrecy and the Labor of the Negative* (Stanford: Stanford University Press, 1999), pp. 13, 56. Desecration and breaking possibly achieve a new level of scandal in the Cornish *Ordinalia* (l. 1200), when one of Christ's torturers exclaims that the *harlot* has cut a *bramm*, a Celtic word meaning "farting" or "breaking." The text leaves open the possibility that the *harlot* is Christ, who has farted in his pain. *The Ancient Cornish Drama*, ed. Edwin Norris, 2 vols. (Oxford: Oxford University Press, repr. London and New York: Blom, 1968), 1:316. With thanks to Victor Scherber for drawing my attention to this occurrence.
183. Plato, *Timaeus*, 66d–e.
184. Moses ben Maimon Maimonides, *Laws Concerning Character Traits*, in *Ethical Writings of Maimonides*, ed. Raymond L. Weiss and Charles Butterworth (New York: Dover, 1975), p. 43 [pp. 27–58].
185. Joubert, *Traité*, 1.4 (p. 37). *Treatise*, p. 26.
186. Lucretius, *De Rerum*, 4.687–93.
187. Thomas Norton, *Ordinal of Alchemy*, ed. John Reidy. EETS O.S. 272 (London: Oxford University Press, 1975), ll. 1967–71.
188. Jacques Lacan, *Seminar of Jacques Lacan VII: Ethics of Psychoanalysis 1959–60*, ed. J. Alain Miller, trans. Dennis Porter (New York: Norton, 1992), p. 139.
189. Pepys, *Works*, 6:120.
190. *The Babee's Book*, ed. Frederick J. Furnivall, EETS O.S. 32 (London: Trübner, 1868; repr. New York, Greenwood, 1969), p. 77, ll. 229–32.
191. Galen, *On the Natural*, 3.13.
192. Galen, *On the Natural*, 3.5.
193. Galen, *On the Natural*, 3.13.
194. Galen, *On the Natural*, 3.12.
195. Goux, *Symbolic Economies*, pp. 29–30.
196. Watson, *Jacobson's Organ*, pp. 12–13.
197. Bernardus Silvestris, *Cosmographia*, trans. Winthrop Wetherbee, 2nd edn. (New York: Columbia University Press, 1990), p. 125; *Bernardi Silvestris de*

mundi universitate, ed. Carl Sigmund Barach and Johann Wrobel (Frankfurt am Main: Minerva, 1964), 2.14.103–4.
198. Aristotle, *On Sense*, 436b.
199. *On Sense*, 440b. Aristotle's opinion is corroborated by empirical findings. Smell is essential to taste; where the tongue's taste buds can detect only five basic categories, the nose can identify thousands of distinctive odors. The flavor of a substance depends more on our ability to smell it than taste it. The olfactory epithelium is a thin layer of nerve cells situated at the base of the nose, between the eyes. Smell signals detected by neurotransmittors send messages directly to the brain, which combines them with the taste signals from the tongue's nerve bundles, commonly referred to as "tastebuds."
200. Max Horkheimer and Theodor W. Adorno, *Dialectic of Enlightenment*, trans. John Cumming (London: Verso, 1979), p. 184.
201. For the distinction between smell as fume emitted by the smelled object and smell as immattered information, see Simon Kemp, "A Medieval Controversy about Odor," *Journal of the History of Behavioral Sciences*, 33 (1997): 211–13 [211–19].
202. Norton, *Ordinal*, ll. 1985–6.
203. Aristotle, *Poetics*, ed. and trans. Stephen Halliwell (Cambridge, MA: Harvard University Press, 1995), 1448b (pp. 36–9).
204. Caroline F.E. Spurgeon, *Five Hundred Years of Chaucer Criticism and Allusion 1357–1900*, vol. 1 (New York: Russell & Russell, 1960), pp. 124–5.
205. Shakespeare, *King Lear*, I.i.15. References taken from William Shakespeare, *Complete Works*, ed. Stanley Wells, Gary Taylor, John Jowett, and William Montgomery, 2nd edn. (Oxford: Clarendon, 2005).
206. John Mirk, *Festial: A Collection of Homilies, Part 1*, ed. Theodor Erbe, EETS E.S. 96 (London: Kegan Paul, Trench, Trübner, 1905), p. 156.
207. Shakespeare, *King Lear*, III.vii.91–2.
208. St. Athanasius, *Un Témoin important du texte de la vie de S. Antoine par S. Athanase*, ed. Gérard Garitte (Brussels: Palais des Académies, 1939), Chap. 63, 69.
209. Augustine, *Confessions*, ed. and trans. William Watts, 2 vols. (Cambridge, MA: Harvard University Press, 1912), 10.32, 2:162–3.
210. Friedrich Nietzsche, *Twilight of the Idols or How to Philosophize with a Hammer*, trans. Richard Polt (Indianapolis: Hackett, 1997), p. 19.
211. Aristotle, "On the Soul," in *Parva Naturalia*, 421b (pp. 1–203).
212. Ben Jonson, *The Staple of News*, ed. Devra Rowland Kifer (Lincoln: University of Nebraska Press, 1975), III.ii.94–103.
213. Watson, *Jacobson's Organ*, p. 41.
214. Laporte, *History*, p. 86.
215. Patrick Süskind, *Perfume: The Story of a Murderer*, trans. John E. Woods (New York: A.A. Knopf, 1986), Chap. 17 (p. 93).
216. Süskind, *Perfume*, Chap. 31–2 (pp. 148–55).
217. Aftel, *Essence*, p. 101.
218. Eric Rabkin and Eugene M. Silverman, *It's a Gas: A Study of Flatulence* (Riverside CA: Xenos Books, 1991), pp. 13–14.

NOTES FROM PP. 54-9   195

219. Aftel, *Essence*, pp. 71–3.
220. *Geoponica sive Cassiani Bassi scholastici De re rustica eclogue*, ed. Henricus Beckh, 4 vols. (Lipsiae: in aedibus B.G. Teubneri, 1895), 1:2.21, 1:150–1. *Geoponica* is a collection of agricultural writings traditionally attributed to Byzantine Emperor Constantinus VII (Constantinus Porphyrogenitus) (pp. 905–59), who in fact compiled much earlier treatises.
221. Norton, *Ordinal*, ll. 755–86. Also, Geber, *The Works of Geber: Englished by Richard Russell, 1678*, ed. E.J. Holmyard (London: Dent, 1928), p. 17.
222. Gautier le Leu, *De deus Vilains*, ll. 95–8, in *NRCF*, 9:169–81.
223. Known originally as *La Farce Nouvelle et fort joyeuse du pet*. Edited as *Le Pet* in *Receuil de Farces (1450–1550)*, ed. André Tissier, vol. 10 (Geneva: Droz, 1996), pp. 21–63. This and other such farces were performed in the Parisian guild of law clerks, the Court of the Basoche, at carnival time. Howard Graham Harvey, *The Theatre of the Basoche* (Cambridge, MA: Harvard University Press, 1941), p. 19. For discussion of the play, see Jody Enders, *Rhetoric and the Origins of Medieval Drama* (Ithaca: Cornell University Press, 1992), pp. 216–21.
224. *Le Pet*, l. 8, p. 36.
225. *Le Pet*, ll. 127–33, pp. 48–9.
226. *Le Pet*, l. 171, p. 53.
227. *Le Pet*, l. 238, p. 57.
228. Aristotle, *Nicomachean Ethics*, ed. and trans. H. Rackham, rev. edn. (Cambridge, MA: Harvard University Press, 1934), 1138a (pp. 320–1).
229. *Le Pet*, l. 201, p. 55.
230. See Robert Copland, "Iyl of Braintford's Testament," in *Poems*, ed. Mary Carpenter Erler (Toronto: University of Toronto Press, 1993), ll. 160–1 (pp. 164–186).
231. Paul Freedman, *Images of the Medieval Peasant* (Stanford, CA: Stanford University Press, 1999), p. 148.
232. *Le Pet*, ll. 157–8, p. 51.
233. *Du con qui fu fait a la besche* [*About the cunt that was made with a shovel*], in *NRCF*, 4:20, l. 66.
234. Pierre Bec, ed., *Burlesque et obscénité chez les troubadours: pour une approche du contre-texte médiéval* (Paris: Stock, 1984), pp. 154–60, 165–6, 173–5.
235. Woman is conventionally depicted as of a moister complexion than man, which results from her colder disposition, having insufficient heat to dry out the organs, and thus retaining excess moisture. Ian Maclean, *The Renaissance Notion of Woman: A Study in the Fortunes of Scholasticism and Medical Science in European Intellectual Life* (Cambridge: Cambridge University Press, 1980), p. 31.
236. Augustine, *City of God*, 14.17, 4:354–7.
237. *Le Pet*, ll. 34–5, p. 39.
238. *Le Pet*, ll. 205, 246, pp. 55, 58.
239. *Le Pet*, ll. 89–90, p. 44.
240. *Le Pet*, ll. 297–8, p. 63.
241. Rabelais, *Oeuvres*, 2.15 (p. 271).

242. "Vir in coitu sentiat virgam suam attrahi & fugi quadam clausura ex parte vulvae mulieris." *De Secretis mulierum*, Chap. 7, p. 106; *Women's Secrets*, p. 121 (also p. 67).
243. Although the relationship between Villon and the prostitute la Grosse Margot (Fat Maggie) is not marital, her behavior exhibits all the intrusiveness of habitual proximity. At bedtime, she "cuts a fart for me" (me fait ung gros pet), cackles and slaps Villon affectionately, then falls fast asleep only to awake, amorous, and crush him beneath her (Villon, *Testament*, ll. 1611–20).
244. Watson, *Jacobson's Organ*, p. 51.
245. Barthélemy, "Kinship," in Duby, *History of Private Life*, p. 117.
246. Aristotle, *On Dreams*, 459b–460a.
247. *De Secretis mulierum*, Chap. 10, p. 114; *Women's Secrets*, p. 129.
248. Tertullian, *Apologeticus*, ed. and trans. T.R. Glover (Cambridge, MA: Harvard University Press, 1931; repr. 1966), 1–227.48.7 (pp. 214–15).
249. Siegel, *Galen*, pp. 184–5. I am indebted to Carol Everest for her paper at Kalamazoo 1999: "Natural Spirits: The Physiology of Farts."
250. Norton, *Ordinal*, ll. 2377–86. The health of the vital spirits is measured by the heartbeat, pulse, and respiration, and the heart is the principal organ of this system. Animal spirits are associated with mental and psychic activity, the brain being their seat of power. The natural spirits are associated with the powers of nutrition, growth, and reproduction, the liver being their principal member. Nancy G. Siraisi, *Medieval & Early Renaissance Medicine: An Introduction to Knowledge and Practice* (Chicago and London: University of Chicago Press, 1990), pp. 107–8.
251. Daniel Joseph Nodes, *Doctrine and Exegesis in Biblical Latin Poetry* (Leeds: Francis Cairns, 1993), p. 54.
252. Augustine, *City of God*, 13.24, 4:242–3.
253. Norton, *Ordinal*, ll. 2185–96.
254. Galen, *On the Natural*, 3.1.
255. Rabelais, *Oeuvres*, 1.15 (p. 45).
256. Hippocrates, *On Breaths*, in *Works*. 3.16–22, 2:230–1 (2:219–53). This said, human and animal corpses do regularly emit residual gases after death. Dead donkeys do actually fart.
257. Hippocrates, *On Breaths*, 3.3–4, 2:228–9.
258. Hippocrates, *On Breaths*, 3.4–5, 2:228–9.
259. Hippocrates, *On Breaths*, 2.2–5, 2:228–9.
260. Hippocrates, *On Breaths*, 4.1–3, 2:230–1.
261. Hippocrates, *On Breaths*, 5. 1–4, 2:232–3.
262. Rabelais, *Oeuvres*, 4.43 (p. 639).
263. C.S. Lewis, *Studies in Words* (Cambridge: Cambridge University Press, 1960), pp. 36–7.
264. Aristotle, *The Physics*, ed. and trans. Philip H. Wicksteed and Francis M. Cornford, 2 vols. (Cambridge, MA: Harvard University Press, 1929–1934), 192b, 1:106–9.

265. Martin Heidegger, *Einführung in die Metaphysik* (Tübingen, Max Niemeyer, 1953), p. 11; *Introduction to Metaphysics*, trans. Gregory Fried and Richard Polt (New Haven: Yale University Press, 2000), p. 15.
266. Tertullian, *Apologeticus*, 9.8 (pp. 48–9).
267. See also Judith Tschann, "The Mind Distended: The *Retraction, Miller's Tale*, and *Summoner's Tale*," in *Chaucer's Humor: Critical Essays*, ed. Jean E. Jost (New York and London: Garland, 1994), p. 371 [pp. 349–78].
268. *Genesis*, trans. Robert Alter (New York: Norton, 1996), p. 3.
269. Lucretius, *De Rerum*, 5.436.
270. Villon, *Testament*, ll. 392, 400, 408, 412.
271. Ovid, *Metamorphoses*, 1.57–68, 1:6–7.
272. Aristotle, *Politics*, ed. and trans. H. Rackham (Cambridge, MA: Harvard University Press, 1932), 1330a (pp. 586–7).
273. Hippocrates, *Sacred Disease*, 16, in *Works*, 2:170–3.
274. Walter Map, *De Nugis Curialium*, ed. and trans. M.R. James, rev. C.N.L. Brooke and R.A.B. Mynors (Oxford: Clarendon, 1983), pp. 102–3.
275. Aristotle, *Politics*, 1290a (pp. 288–9).
276. Pliny the Elder, *Natural History*, ed. and trans. H. Rackham, 10 vols. (Cambridge, MA: Harvard University Press, 1938–1963), 2.46.119–21, 1:260–3; Lucretius, *De Rerum*, 5.737–47.
277. Pliny, *Natural*, 2.38.102, 1:244–7.
278. Pliny, *Natural*, 2.44.114–15, 1:254–7.
279. Pliny, *Natural*, 2.81.191–2, 1:322–5.
280. Pliny, *Natural*, 2.84.197–8, 1:328–9.
281. Pliny, *Natural*, 2.95.207–8, 1:338–9.
282. Pliny, *Natural*, 2.87–8.201–2, 1:330–3.
283. Pliny, *Natural*, 2.96.209, 1:340–1.
284. Pliny, *Natural*, 2.45.116, 1:256–7.
285. Thomas Vicary, *The Anatomie of the Bodie of Man*, ed. Frederick J. Furnivall and Percy Furnivall, EETS e.s. 53 (London: Trübner, 1888), p. 9.
286. "Calor est principium motus," *De Secretis*, Chap. 8, p. 108; *Women's Secrets*, p. 123.
287. Boorde, *Compendyous Regyment*, Chap. 21, p. 284.
288. Constantine the African, *Constantini Liber de coitu*, ed. and trans. (into Spanish) Enrique Montero Cartelle (Santiago de Compostela: University of Santiago de Compostela, 1983), p. 146.
289. Rabelais, *Oeuvres*, 2.27 (p. 310).
290. Matazone de Calignano, "Dit sur les villains," ed. and trans. (into modern French) Paul Meyer, *Romania* 12 (1883): 21, ll. 83–8 [14–28].
291. Davies, *Medieval English Lyrics*, p. 52, ll. 3–11. This reading of *verteth* as "farteth" is not unanimous, and its form in some manuscripts— *uerteth*—has caused some editors to interpret it as "turns" or "cavorts." See Woolf, "Later Poetry," p. 280, and the earlier discussion in this book, p. 13.

292. Marcus Terentius Varro, *On Agriculture*, ed. and trans. William Davis Hooper, rev. Harrison Boyd Ash (Cambridge, MA: Harvard University Press, 1935), 2.1.19 (pp. 324–5).
293. Lucretius, *De Rerum*, 3.254–5.
294. Augustine, *City of God*, 13.3, 4:140–1.
295. Rabelais, *Oeuvres*, 5.16 (p. 762).
296. Rabelais, *Oeuvres*, 4.43 (p. 639).
297. Rutebeuf, *Le Pet au Vilain*, in *NRCF* 5:369, ll. 35–45.
298. Allen Edwardes, *The Jewel in the Lotus: A Historical Survey of the Sexual Culture of the East* (New York: Julian Press, 1959), p. 235.
299. John G. Bourke, *Scatalogic [sic] Rites of All Nations* (Washington, DC: Lowdermilk, 1891; repr, Johnson Corp., 1969), p. 162.
300. Mirk, *Festial*, p. 79.
301. Jacobus de Voragine, *Golden Legend: Readings on the Saints*, trans. William Granger Ryan, 2 vols. (Princeton: Princeton University Press, 1993), 1:168.
302. Suetonius, *Lives*, 5.34, 2:62–3.
303. Mirk, *Festial*, p. 131.
304. Guibert of Nogent, *A Monk's Confession: The Memoirs of Guibert of Nogent*, trans. Paul J. Archambault (University Park: Pennsylvania State University Press, 1996), 1.22, 77–8; *PL*, 156:884B.
305. Augustine, *City of God*, 3.28, 1:386–7.
306. The Middle English verb denotes both actions of spiritual and anal cleansing (*MED*, s.v. *wipen*, v.[2a,3c]). For the latter, see Cain's reference to a sheaf of corn for God to "wipe his ars withall," in the "Murder of Abel," *The Towneley Plays*, ed. Martin Stevens and A.C. Cawley, 2 vols., EETS S.S. 13–14 (Oxford: Oxford University Press, 1994), 1:18, l. 240.
307. *Mankind*, ll. 562–3, in *Medieval Drama*, p. 923.
308. *Mankind*, ll. 783, in *Medieval Drama*, p. 932.
309. John Lydgate, *The Siege of Thebes*, ed. Robert R. Edwards (Kalamazoo, MI: Medieval Institute Publications, 2001), l. 112 (p. 32).
310. *Code of Jewish Law: A Compliation of Jewish Laws and Customs by Rabbi Solomon Ganzfried*, trans. Hyman E. Goldin, 2nd edn. (New York: Hebrew Publishing, 1963), §17 (p. 61).
311. Plato, *Phaedo*, ed. and trans. Hardol North Fowler, (Cambridge, MA: Harvard University Press, 1943), 67e.
312. Plato, *Phaedo*, 67d.
313. Marcus Tullius Cicero, *Tusculan Disputations*, ed. and trans. J.E. King (Cambridge, MA: Harvard University Press, 1945), 1.30.74 (p. 86).
314. Michel de Montaigne, *Essais*, ed. Albert Thibaudet (Paris: Gallimard, 1950), 1.20 (pp. 103–4). In connection to laughter, M.A. Screech considers Renaissance commentators on Socratic practicing of dying. *Laughter at the Foot of the Cross* (London: Allen Lane, 1997), pp. 107–10.
315. "Combien a la mort de façons de surprise?" Montaigne, *Essais*, 1.20 (p. 108).
316. "Je me desnoue par tout. . . . Jamais homme . . . ne s'en desprint plus universellement que je m'attens de faire." Montaigne, *Essais*, 1.20 (p. 113).

NOTES FROM PP. 73-8

317. *Rhetorica ad Herennium*, 3.20.33–4 (pp. 214–15).This is a well known theory, although there exists no hard evidence for it in Greek or Roman law. However, the verbal similarity between *testis* and *testiculus* is clear from the passage.
318. Aristotle, *On Sleep*, 456a.
319. Winthrop Huntington Rice, *The European Ancestry of Villon's Satirical Testaments* (New York: Corporate Press, 1941), p. 84.
320. See Mary Caroline Spalding, *The Middle English Charters of Christ* (Bryn Mawr, PA: Bryn Mawr College, 1914), pp. vii–li.
321. Rice, *European Ancestry*, p. 225.
322. *Recueil de poésies francoises des XVe et XVIe siècles: Morales, facétieuses, historiques*, ed. Anatole de Montaiglon, 13 vols. (Paris: Jannet, 1855–1878), 3:79.
323. Copland, "Iyl," ll. 77, 170.
324. *Recueil de poésies*, 1:277.
325. Rice, *European Ancestry*, p. 16.
326. Copland, "Iyl," ll. 210–14, p. 174.
327. Villon, *Testament*, ll. 1984–9.
328. Copland, "Iyl," ll. 152–5, p. 173.
329. David Fein, *A Reading of Villon's Testament* (Birmingham, AL: Summa, 1984), pp. 44–5.
330. Rabelais, *Oeuvres*, 3.5 (p. 369).
331. In its special sense, a convent refers to 12 religious persons, 13 counting the superior. A "coven" of 13 witches is closely related both conceptually and linguistically.
332. See Alan Levitan, "The Parody of Pentecost in Chaucer's *Summoner's Tale*," *University of Toronto Quarterly*, 40 (1971): 236–46.
333. Gluttony traditionally induces flatulence. See Plato, *Republic*, 405d, 1:270–3; Langland, *Piers Plowman*, B.5.340–5; Innocent III, *De Miseria*, 2.18 (pp. 166–7); Parthenius the tax collector was a notorious glutton, who would take aloes to speed up his digestion so as to eat again: "Sed et strepitus ventris absque ulla auditorum reverentia in publico emittebat" (and he would even cut farts in public without any respect for those who had to listen to them); see Gregory of Tours, *Historia Francorum*, 3.36, in *PL*, 71:268B–C. Pristinus, a glutton, was put to the rack, but, because he was stuffed with food, all that could be got from him were "hiccoughs and belchings"; see Tertullian, *On Fasting*, in *The Ante-Nicene Fathers: Translations of the Writings of the Father down to A.D. 325*, ed. Alexander Roberts and James Donaldson, rev. edn. 10 vols. (Edinburgh: T&T Clark; Grand Rapids, MI: W.B. Erdmanns, 1989–1994), Chap. 12, 4:110–1.
334. Rice, *European Ancestry*, p. 14.
335. Plato, *Phaedrus*, ed. and trans. Harold North Fowler (Cambridge, MA: Harvard University Press, 1914), 244a–e (pp. 464–9).
336. Pliny, *Natural*, 2.95.207, 1:338–9.
337. Apuleius, *Metamorphoses*, 6.18, 1:342–3. See also Virgil, *Aeneid*, ed. and trans. H. Rushton Fairclough, rev. G.P. Goold, 2 vols. (Cambridge, MA: Harvard University Press, 1999–2000), 7.568, 2:42–3.

338. Tertullian, *Apologeticus*, 23.5 (pp. 124–5).
339. Homer, "Hymn to Hermes," in *The Homeric Hymns*, trans. Apostolos N. Athanassakis (Baltimore: John Hopkins University Press, 1976), ll. 294–8 (p. 39). With thanks to John Thompson for this reference. Hermes' belly message may be a belch and not a fart, and one English translation squeamishly chooses the former; but either is equally insulting and paralinguistic. There is, however, reason for understanding "stomach messenger" as a fart, for belly wind seems consistently in early literature to mean crepitation. Distinguishing between the silent fizzler (*flatus*) and the blattering fart (*crepitus*), Suetonius speaks in either case of belly wind: *flatus crepitusque ventris* (blowing and rattling of the belly) (*Lives*, 5.32, 2:260–1). Gregory of Tours in *Historia Francorum* speaks of the fart as *strepitus ventris* (rumbling of the belly) (*PL*, 71:268C). Joshua T. Katz argues not only that the sound is a fart but also that the wording suggests parodic allusion to noble spirits. "Homeric Hymn to Hermes 296: τλήμονα γαστρὸς ἔριθον," *The Classical Quarterly* 49 (1999): 315–19.
340. Michel Serres, *Hermes: Literature, Science, Philosophy*, ed. Josué V. Harari and David F. Bell (Baltimore and London: John Hopkins University Press, 1982), pp. xxxv, xxxiv (editors' introduction).
341. Augustine, *City of God*, 1.3, 1:20–1.
342. *Tales of the Elders of Ireland (Acallam na Senórach)*, trans. Ann Dooley and Harry Roe (Oxford: Oxford University Press, 1999), p. 156.
343. *Tales of the Elders of Ireland*, p. 175.
344. John D Miller, *Beads and Prayers: The Rosary in History and Devotion* (London: Burns & Oates, 2002), pp. 87–107.
345. Hugh of St. Victor, *Didascalicon: A Medieval Guide to the Arts*, trans. Jerome Taylor, 2nd edn. (New York: Columbia University Press, 1991), 2.4 (p. 65); *PL*, 176:754B.
346. *The Trial of Gilles de Rais*, ed. Georges Batailles, trans. Richard Robinson (Los Angeles: Amok, 1991), p. 120.
347. Johannes Ravisius, *Officinae epitome*, 2 vols. (Lyon: Seb. Gryphius, 1560), 1:93, interests himself in all manners of sudden death: while making love, laughing, and while in the toilet.
348. Henry of Huntingdon, *Historia Anglorum*, 6.14.
349. *The Dethe of the Kynge of Scotis*, in *Death and Dissent: Two Fifteenth-Century Chronicles*, ed. Lister M. Matheson (Woodbridge, Suffolk: Boydell, 1999), pp. 36–45.
350. Carolyne Larrington, "Diet, Defecation and the Devil: Disgust and the Pagan Past," in Nicola McDonald ed., *Medieval Obscenities* (Woodbridge, Suffolk: York Medieval Press, 2006), pp. 151–2 [pp. 138–55].
351. *The N-Town Play: Cotton MS Vespasian D.8*, ed. Stephen Spector, vol. 1, EETS s.s. 11 (London: Oxford University Press, 1991), 1.81 (p. 24).
352. *N-Town*, 2.272–3 (p. 32).
353. For medieval *garderobes*, viewed from inside and outside, see Julie L. Horan, *The Porcelain God: A Social History of the Toilet* (Secaucus, NJ: Carol Publishing, 1997), pp. 24, 26.

354. Galen, *On the Natural*, 3.2.
355. Galen, *On the Natural*, 2.8.
356. *The Visions of Tondal from the Library of Margaret of York*, ed. Thomas Kren and Roger S. Wieck (Malibu, CA: J. Paul Getty Museum, 1990), p. 41.
357. *Visions of Tondal*, pp. 48–9. For a fifteenth-century reference to shitting out one's soul (or heart), see Barbara C. Bowen, "The 'Honorable Art of Farting,' in Continental Renaissance Literature," in Persels and Ganim, eds, *Fecal Matters*, p. 2 [pp. 1–12].
358. For example, for an illumination of hell from Augustine's *City of God*, see Jeffrey Burton Russell, *Lucifer: The Devil in the Middle Ages* (Ithaca, NY: Cornell University Press, 1984), p. 109.
359. Norton, *Ordinal*, ll. 2033–6.
360. *Visions of Tondal*, p. 29.
361. *Visions of Tondal*, p. 28.
362. Voragine, *Golden Legend*, 2:234.
363. Niceta of Remesiana, "Vigils of the Saints," in *Niceta of Remesiana: Writings*, trans. Gerald G. Walsh (New York: Fathers of the Church, 1949. 55–64), p. 63 [pp. 55–64].
364. Niceta of Remesiana, "Vigils of the Saints," p. 64.
365. For Aquinas, the question is whether there's more water than foreign substance, and he recommends straining water to get rid of mud [*lutum*] (*ST* 3ae.66.4). Piddle in the baptistery does not seem to have offended God, seeing as it was all water anyway; Barbara A. Hanawalt, *The Ties That Bound: Peasant Families in Medieval England* (Oxford: Oxford University Press, 1986), p. 173.
366. *Middle English Sermons*, p. 232.
367. Russell, *Lucifer*, p. 72.
368. Athanasius, *Témoin important*, ch. 21 (p. 36).
369. Russell, *Lucifer*, p. 71.
370. Mirk, *Festial*, p. 141.
371. In the disapproving eyes of the cloistered monks, the mendicant friars, who roved the country and lived on alms, serve only their own will and love gluttony; *Three Middle-English Versions of the Rule of St. Benet*, p. 4.
372. E.P. Evans, *The Criminal Prosecution and Capital Punishment of Animals*, 2nd edn. (London: Faber and Faber, 1987), pp. 2–3.
373. Esther Cohen, "Law, Folklore and Animal Lore," *Past and Present*, 110 (1986): 25–35 (6–37).
374. Evans, *Criminal Prosecution*, p. 135.
375. Evans, *Criminal Prosecution*, p. 86.
376. Hugh of St. Victor, *Didascalicon*, 2.4 (p. 65), *PL* 176:754B.
377. St. Ambrose, *On Virginity*, trans. Daniel Callam (Toronto: Peregrina, 1980), 7.28 (p. 16).
378. Ambrose, *On Virginity*, 11.66 (p. 31).
379. Russell, *Lucifer*, p. 72.
380. "Anglo-Saxon Charms," p. 156.
381. Russell, *Lucifer*, p. 98.

382. Evans, *Criminal Prosecution*, p. 6.
383. Guibert of Nogent, *Monk's Confession*, 1.25 (p. 88); *PL*, 156:890B–C.
384. Theology asserts nonetheless the disembodiment of demons, ascribing to them dark bodies from inferior air. Dyan Elliott, *Fallen Bodies: Pollution, Sexuality and Demonology in the Middle Ages* (Philadelphia: University of Pennsylvania Press, 1999), pp. 127–56.
385. Jeffrey Burton Russell, *Satan: The Early Christian Tradition* (Ithaca: Cornell University Press, 1981), p. 174.
386. Guibert of Nogent, *Monk's Confession*, 1.22 (pp. 77–8); *PL*, 156:884B.
387. Russell, *Satan*, p. 181.
388. *Mankind*, ll. 556–64, in *Medieval Drama*, p. 923.
389. *NRCF*, 8:207–14, l.41. German *Schwanklieder* [prank-songs] tell a similar story: in the famous Violet Prank, a knight finds the first violet of spring, and covers it with his cap to alert his companions who also seek the flower; meanwhile an onlooking peasant removes the cap, defecates on the violet, and replaces the cap; when the knight returns with the entire court, he whips off the cap, exposes the turd, and is utterly disgraced; Freedman, *Images*, pp. 151–2.
390. K.P. Wentersdorf, "The Symbolic Significance of the *Figurae Scatologicae* in Gothic Manuscripts," in *Word, Picture and Spectacle*, ed. C. Davidson (Kalamazoo, MI: Medieval Institute Publications, 1984), pp. 8–9 [pp. 1–20].
391. William of Malmesbury, *De Gestis Pontificum Anglorum: Libri quinque*, ed. N.E.S.A. Hamilton (London: Longman & Co., Trübner, 1870), 5.275 (p. 438). See also Malcolm Jones, *Secret Middle Ages* (Stroud: Sutton, 2002), p. 276.
392. Russell, *Lucifer*, pp. 90–1.
393. Mellinkoff, *Outcasts*, 1:197.
394. Athanasius, *Témoin important*, ch. 39 (p. 51).
395. Dante, *De Vulgari eloquentia*, ed. and trans. Steven Botterill (Cambridge: Cambridge University Press, 1996), 1.2 (pp. 4–5).
396. Athanasius, *Témoin important*, ch. 40 (p. 51).
397. Henry Ansgar Kelly, *The Devil at Baptism: Ritual, Theology, and Drama* (Ithaca: Cornell University Press, 1985), p. 112.
398. Kelly, *Devil at Baptism*, pp. 256–7.
399. Russell, *Lucifer*, p. 126.
400. Bowen, " 'Honorable Art of Farting,' " p 3.
401. Russell, *Satan*, p. 174.
402. *Amorous Games*, p. 175, §777.
403. Athanasius, *Témoin important*, ch. 11 (p. 27).
404. Sulpicius Severus, "Life of St. Martin," trans. Bernard M. Peebles, in *The Fathers of the Church*, 7 (NY: Fathers of the Church, 1949), p. 136.
405. Trevisa, *On the Properties of Things*, 3.19, 1:115. The Latin original refers throughout the chapter to *fumus* [smoke], *fumosus* [smoky, smoked], *fumositas* [smokiness]; Bartholomaeus Anglicus, *On the Properties of Soul and Body: De Proprietatibus Libri III et IV*, ed. R. James Long (Toronto: Pontifical Institute of Medieval Studies, 1979), pp. 47–8.

406. For picture, see Elaine C. Block, "Physical and Social Inversions in the Topsy Turvy World," *Arts Profane / Profane Arts* 7.1(1998): 8–28. Also Malcolm Jones, *Secret Middle Ages*, pp. 284–5.
407. Michel Camille, *Image on the Edge: The Margins of Medieval Art* (Cambridge, MA: Harvard University Press, 1992), p. 94.
408. Plato, *Cratylus*, ed. and trans. H.N. Fowler (Cambridge, MA: Harvard University Press, 1963), 403a (pp. 70–1).
409. Ovid, *Metamorphoses*, 1.138, 1:12–13.
410. Fenichel, "Drive to Amass Wealth," 2:96.
411. Josef Schmidt, with Mary Simon, "Holy and Unholy Shit: The Pragmatic Context of Scatological Curses in Early German Reformation Satire," in Persels and Ganim, eds, *Fecal Matters*, p. 110 [pp. 109–17].
412. Bowen, " 'Honorable Art of Farting,' " p. 5.
413. Aftel, *Essence*, p. 10.
414. Nicholas Flamel's account is excerpted in Titus Burckhardt, *Alchemy: Science of the Cosmos, Science of the Soul*, trans. William Stoddart (Longmead, Dorset: Element Books, 1967), p. 180.
415. Burckhardt, *Alchemy* p. 16.
416. Geber, *Works*, p. 75.
417. Geber, *Works*, p. 56.
418. Norton, *Ordinal*, l. 1057.
419. Laporte, *History*, p. 36.
420. Burckhardt, *Alchemy*, p. 25.
421. Ben Jonson, *The Alchemist*, ed. Peter Bement (London and New York: Methuen, 1987), II.iii.131–6.
422. Michel Foucault, *The Birth of the Clinic: An Archaeology of Medical Perception*, trans. A.M. Sheridan Smith (New York: Random, 1973), p. xiii.
423. Foucault, *Birth of the Clinic*, p. 15.
424. Geber, *Works*, p. 32.
425. Geber, *Works*, p. 34.
426. Geber, *Works*, p. 40.
427. Geber, *Works*, p. 34.
428. Burckhardt, *Alchemy*, p. 67.
429. Burckhardt, *Alchemy* p. 98.
430. Aftel, *Essence*, p. 6.
431. Burckhardt, *Alchemy*, p. 159. The antiphon written for the feast of the Annunciation, "Ave maris Stella," by "changing the name of Eva" (*mutans nomen Evae*) (l. 8), reverses E-v-a to make A-v-e, which begins the angel Gabriel's salutation to the Virgin Mary. The lost Garden of Eden is regained in the hallowed womb of Christ's mother.
432. Norton, *Ordinal*, l. 2277–80.
433. Norton, *Ordinal*, l. 2440.
434. Norton, *Ordinal*, ll. 2262–72.
435. Jacques Le Goff, *Your Money or Your Life: Economy and Religion in the Middle Ages*, trans. Patricia Ranum (New York: Zone Books, 1988), p. 39.
436. Geber, *Works*, p. 34.

437. Dante consigns charlatan alchemists to the circles of the fraudulent, for having made "an ape of nature" (di natura buona scimia) (*Inferno* xxix.139).
438. Geber, *Works*, p. 17.
439. Norton, *Ordinal*, ll. 359–62.
440. Norton, *Ordinal*, l. 356.
441. Norton, *Ordinal*, l. 1994.
442. Norton, *Ordinal*, ll. 1707–8.
443. Norton, *Ordinal*, ll. 1711–12.
444. Norton, *Ordinal*, l. 1718.
445. Norton, *Ordinal*, ll. 1541–2.
446. Plato, *Timaeus*, 66d–e.
447. Norton, *Ordinal*, ll. 1947–2050.
448. For stench overcoming sweet smells, see Norton, *Ordinal*, ll. 1961–72. For the opposite, see Palmer, "In Bad Odour," p. 66.
449. Miller, *Anatomy*, p. 9.
450. Norton, *Ordinal*, ll. 1973–6.
451. Süskind, *Perfume*, Chap. 37 (p. 179).
452. Sheila Delany, "Run Silent, Run Deep: Heresy and Alchemy as Medieval Versions of Utopia," in *Medieval Literary Politics: Shapes of Ideology* (Manchester: Manchester University Press, 1990), p. 15 [pp. 1–18].
453. Lynn White Jr., *Medieval Technology and Social Change* (Oxford: Oxford University Press, 1962), pp. 90–2.
454. Timothy O'Brien, "'Ars-Metrik': Science, Satire, and Chaucer's Summoner," *Mosaic*, 23.4 (1990): 2–3 [1–22].
455. Burckhardt, *Alchemy*, p. 13.
456. Burckhardt, *Alchemy*, p. 27.
457. Norton, *Ordinal*, l. 2520.
458. Lacan, *Seminar*, p. 136.

In Between

1. David Hume, *An Inquiry Concerning Human Understanding*, ed. Charles W. Hendel (Indianapolis and New York: Liberal Arts Press, 1955), §7.2, p. 85.
2. Varro, *On Agriculture*, 1.1.1 (p. 161).
3. John Lydgate, *Life of Our Lady*, ed. J. Lauritis, R. Klinefelter and V. Gallagher (Pittsburg: Duquesne University Press, 1961), l. 1633.
4. Dante, *De Vulgari*, 1.11 (pp. 26–7).
5. Rabelais, *Oeuvres*, 2.9 (p. 248).
6. *Ancrene Wisse*, ed. Robert Hasenfratz (Kalamazoo, MI: Medieval Institute Publications, 2000), 4.240–1 (p. 221).
7. *Ancrene Wisse*, 2.434–7 (pp. 126–7).
8. Alan of Lille, *Plaint of Nature*, trans. James J. Sheridan (Toronto: Pontifical Institute of Mediaeval Studies, 1980), Prosa 7 (pp. 191–2); *PL*, 210: 469D–470C.

9. *NRCF*, 3:45–173. *Gallic Salt: Eighteen Fabliaux Translated from the Old French*, ed. and trans. Robert Harrison (Berkeley and Los Angeles: University of California Press, 1974), pp. 218–55.
10. Seneca, *Ad Lucilium*, 91.19 (pp. 444–5).
11. *Poetria Nova of Geoffrey of Vinsauf*, ll. 1685–9 (p. 76).
12. Aristophanes, *Clouds*, ll. 156–68 (pp. 26–9).
13. Priscian, *Institutiones grammaticae*, in Keil, 2:5–6; also Martin Irvine, *The Making of Textual Culture: "Grammatica" and Literary Theory, 350–1100* (Cambridge: Cambridge University Press, 1994), pp. 93–5.
14. C.L. Barber, *The Story of Language*, 2nd edn. (London: Pan, 1972), pp. 14–15.
15. Some colonial importations prove exceptions to the rule, however late and "unEnglish" they look. Their presence only highlights our difficulty in grasping Priscian's concept of the unscriptable, which is inextricably bound up with decorum and the art of shaping letters.
16. Bartholomew of Exeter, *The Penitential from Cotton MS Vitellius A.XII*, in Adrian Moray, *Bartholomew of Exeter Bishop and Canonist: A Study in the Twelfth Century* (Cambridge: Cambridge University Press, 1937), p. 188 [pp. 161–300].
17. F. de Saussure, *Course in General Linguistics*, trans. Roy Harris (London: Duckworth, 1983), p. 66.
18. Noam Chomsky, *Syntactic Structures* (The Hague: Mouton, 1957), p. 15.
19. John of Salisbury, *The Metalogicon of John of Salisbury: A Twelfth-Century Defense of the Verbal and Logical Arts of the Trivium*, trans. Daniel D. McGarry (Berkeley and Los Angeles: University of California Press, 1955), 1.15 (pp. 41–2); *PL*, 199:84A–C.
20. Alan of Lille, *Plaint of Nature*, Prosa 4 (p. 136); *PL*, 210:450A–B. See Jan Ziolkowski, *Alan of Lille's Grammar of Sex: the Meaning of Grammar to a Twelfth-Century Intellectual* (Cambridge, MA: Medieval Academy of America, 1985), pp. 13–49.
21. Compare the medical distinction between the natural and the violent in Joubert, *Traité*, 1.6 (p. 53); *Treatise*, p. 32; or in a text contemporaneous with the *Commedia*: *De Secretis mulierum*, Chap. 1 (p. 24); *Women's Secrets*, p. 76.
22. *Women's Secrets*, pp. 114–15. The text of *De Secretis mulierum* was much commented upon, and Commentary B, from which this account is taken, is not included in this particular Latin edition.
23. Priscian, *Institutiones*, 2.25; in Keil, 2:58–9.
24. *De Secretis mulierum*, ch. 6 (p. 98); *Women's Secrets*, p. 114.
25. R. Howard. Bloch, *Etymologies and Genealogies: A Literary Anthropology of the French Middle Ages* (Chicago: University of Chicago Press, 1983), p. 42.
26. Bloch, *Etymologies*, p. 36.
27. Jacques Derrida, "Archive Fever: A Freudian Impression," trans. Eric Prenowitz, *Diacritics*, 25.2 (1995): 9 [9–63].
28. Holger Pedersen, *Discovery of Language: Linguistic Science in the Nineteenth Century*, trans. John Webster Spargo (Bloomington: Indiana University Press, 1959), p. 3.

29. Plato, *Cratylus*, 404c (pp. 74–5).
30. Plato, *Cratylus*, 393d–e (pp. 40–1).
31. Benjamin Franklin, "A Letter to the Royal Academy, 1781," in *Fart Proudly: Writings of Benjamin Franklin You Never Read in School*, ed. Carl Japikse (Columbus, OH: Enthea, 1990), p. 17.
32. An asterisk placed thus before a word denotes the word's unattested status.
33. Porter, *Antwerp-London Glossaries*, 4.2027.
34. Anatoly Liberman, *Word Origins and How We Know Them* (Oxford: Oxford University Press, 2005), p. 91.
35. *Liber feodorum*, 1:386; 2:1174; and 2:1218–19.
36. *The Earliest Leicestershire Lay Subsidy Roll, 1327*, ed. W.G.D. Fletcher (Lincoln: J. Williamson, 1888), p. 94.
37. See Dunbar's *carlingis pet*, in "The Flyting of Dunbar and Kennedie Heir efter followis iocound and mirrie," l. 247, in *Poems*, 1:208 [200–18]. Although the *OED* glosses *pet* as "indulged, spoiled, or favourite, child," and the *MED* has no listing for *pet*, editor Priscilla Bawcutt glosses the phrase as "old woman's fart." See also the fourth eclogue of Alexander Barclay, *Certayne Eglogues of Alexander Barclay, Priest, Compiled by Eneas Silvius* (1570), Spenser Society, 39 (1885) (repr. New York: Burt Franklin, 1967), p. 35: "though all their cunning be scantly wurth a pet."
38. William Dwight Whitney, *The Century Dictionary: An Encyclopedic Lexicon of the English Language*. 6 vols. (New York: The Century Co., 1889–1891), s.v. *petard*.
39. Hippocrates, *On Breaths*, 2.2–5, 2:228–9. Leo Spitzer, in "On the Etymology of *pet*," *Language* 26 (1950): 533–8, argues for the derivation of "pet" in its two senses of fond endearment and fit of temper from its meaning as "fart," suggesting that an "animal or child *qui pète* is the youngest, the one who has not yet learned to control his muscles" (p. 536), and that "a fit of excitement on the part of the child can first be inferred from his failure to control his muscles" (p. 538).
40. Rabkin and Silverman, *It's a Gas*, p. 27.
41. Dante, *De Vulgari*, 1.4–5 (pp. 8–11).
42. Bernard of Clairvaux, Sermon 67.3 (p. 7); *PL*, 183.1103D–1104A.
43. Bloch, *Etymologies*, pp. 56, 54.
44. Bruce Mitchell and Fred C. Robinson, *A Guide to Old English*, 4th edn. (Oxford: Blackwell, 1986), pp. 36–41.
45. Pedersen, *Discovery*, p. 40.
46. Pedersen, *Discovery*, p. 41.
47. K.M. Elizabeth Murray, *Caught in the Web of Words: James A. H. Murray and the Oxford English Dictionary* (New Haven: Yale University Press, 1977), p. 74.
48. Pedersen, *Discovery*, p. 262.
49. For example, Verner's Law explains apparent irregularities in Grimm's Law. Mitchell and Robinson, *Guide to Old English*, pp. 41–3.
50. N.E. Collinge, *The Laws of Indo-European* (Amsterdam and Philadelphia: John Benjamins, 1985), pp. 121–5.

51. Albert C. Baugh and Tomas Cable, *A History of the English Language*, 4th edn. (Englewood Cliffs, NJ: Prentice Hall, 1993), p. 73. Mitchell and Robinson, *Guide to Old English*, p. 28.
52. For explanatory diagrams of the placing of the vowels in the mouth, whether high, low, front, or back, see Mitchell and Robinson, *Guide to Old English*, pp. 21–2.
53. Saussure, *Course*, p. 83.
54. Bill Bryson, *The Mother Tongue: English & How It Got That Way* (New York: William Morrow, 1990), pp. 22–3.
55. Saussure, *Course*, p. 2.
56. Liberman, *Words Origins*, pp. 208–9.
57. Murray, *Caught in the Web*, p. 113. For a lucid explanation of sound changes and of the usefulness of reconstructing word origins, see Jeremy J. Smith, *Sound Change and the History of English* (Oxford: Oxford University Press, 2007), pp. 1–28, 45–50.
58. Rabelais, *Oeuvres*, 2.16 (p. 274). Joseph T. Shipley also notes these examples in his discussion of the spoonerism, which in French interestingly enough is called *le contrepet*. *The Origin of English Words: A Discursive Dictionary of Indo-European Roots* (Baltimore: John Hopkins University Press, 1984), p. 310, and pp. xxi–xxii on metathesis.
59. Saussure, *Course*, p. 162.
60. Murray, *Caught in the Web*, pp. 195–6.
61. P.G. Wodehouse, *The Code of the Woosters* (1938) (repr. Mattituck, NY: Rivercity Press, 1938; repr. 1976), Chap. 1 (p. 8).
62. Saussure, *Course*, p. 161.
63. Saussure, *Course*, p. 164.
64. Saussure, *Course*, pp. 162–3.
65. Rabelais, *Oeuvres*, 3.5 (p. 369).
66. Honorius of Autun, *De Imagine mundi*, *PL*, 172:166A–B.
67. Marcus Terentius Varro, *De Lingua Latina: On the Latin Language*, ed. and trans. Roland G. Kent, rev. edn., 2 vols. (Cambridge, MA: Harvard University Press, 1951–1958), 9.103, 2:522–3.
68. Trevisa, *On the Properties of Things*, 18.114, 2:1263.
69. *Summa musice*, p. 51.
70. *Cratylus*, 406a (pp. 78–81).
71. Liberman, *Word Origins*, pp. 110, 166: "Although two sources often converge in producing a word, it does not follow that a word can have two or more etymologies." "Our inability to choose among several equally reasonable solutions should not be used as a plea for the ability of a word to have multiple etymologies."
72. *The Oxford Dictionary of English Etymology*, ed. C.T. Onions (Oxford: Clarendon, 1966), s.v. *carminative*.
73. Walter W. Skeat, *Notes on English Etymology* (Oxford: Clarendon, 1901), p. 32.
74. Liberman, *Word Origins*, p. 10.
75. Liberman, *Word Origins*, p. 163.

76. Background noise as presence in all information and communication is a founding principle of Michel Serres's work: *Hermes*, pp. 65–70.
77. *Savour* in Middle English means smell as well as taste.
78. Mirk, *Festial*, p. 261. The modern, "correct" etymology derives *god* from "the one called upon" or "the one receiving sacrifices," and does not relate to *good*. Liberman, *Word Origins*, p. 13.
79. *The Victoria History of the County of Suffolk*, ed. William Page, 2 vols. (London: Archibald Constable, 1907), 1:358. "We can only guess at the meaning of the term."
80. Augustine, *On Christian Doctrine*, trans. D.W. Robertson, Jr. (New York: Macmillan, 1958), 4.11.26, *PL*, 34:100.
81. Augustine, *On Christian*, 4.10.24, *PL*, 34:99–100.
82. "Afrae aures de correptione vocalium vel productione non judicant." Augustine, *On Christian*, 4.10.24; *PL*, 34:99.
83. Ross, "Taboo-Words," p. 157.
84. *Rhetorica ad Herennium*, 4.21.29 (pp. 302–3).
85. Augustine, *On Christian*, 3.29.40; *PL*, 34:80.
86. Augustine, *On Christian*, 4.11.26; *PL*, 34:101.
87. Priscian, *Institutiones*, 4.5; Keil, 2:120.
88. Priscian, *Institutiones*, 4.16; Keil, 2:126.
89. Priscian, *Institutiones*, 4.1; Keil, 2:117.
90. *Rhetorica ad Herennium*, 4.32.43 (pp. 336–7).
91. Richard A. Lanham, *A Handlist of Rhetorical Terms*, 2nd edn. (Berkeley: University of California Press, 1991), p. 102.
92. Pedersen, *Discovery*, p. 4.
93. Laporte, *History*, p. 7. This part of Varro's treatise is known only by secondary quotation, as it is lost.
94. Augustine, *On Christian*, 3.29.41; *PL*, 34:81.
95. *Rhetorica ad Herennium*, 4.21.29 (pp. 300–3).
96. Rabelais, *Oeuvres*, 1.16 (p. 47).
97. Rabelais, *Oeuvres*, 1.17 (p. 48).
98. Henry Thomas Buckle, *Common Place Books*, in *Miscellaneous and Posthumous Works of Henry Thomas Buckle*, ed. Helen Taylor, 3 vols. (London: Longmans, Green and Co., 1872), 2.33, §81.
99. Anthony Corbeill, *Controlling Laughter: Political Humor in the Late Roman Republic* (Princeton: Princeton University Press, 1996), pp. 57–60.
100. Corbeill, *Controlling Laughter* p. 78.
101. Liberman, *Word Origins*, p. 188, recognizes two types of word families: the aristocratic, such as Latin *pater*, Greer *patēr*, Sanskrit *pitár*, Gothic *fadar*; and one that is "plebeian and amorphous. Its members look as though they are related, but their kinship is loose, and their number hard to determine."
102. Guillaume de Lorris and Jean de Meun, *Le Roman de la Rose*, ed. Ernest Langlois, 5 vols. (Paris: Libraire de Firmin-Didot, 1914–1924), 4:241, l. 18754.
103. Aristotle, *Poetics*, 1452a–b, pp. 64–7.

104. Aristotle, *Posterior Analytics*, ed. and trans. Hugh Tredennick (Cambridge, MA: Harvard University Press, 1960), 71b (pp. 30–1).
105. Heidegger, *Introduction*, pp. 103–22.
106. Heidegger, *Introduction*, p. 112.
107. Sophocles, *Oedipus Tyrannus*, ed. and trans. Hugh Lloyd-Jones (Cambridge, MA: Harvard University Press, 1994), ll. 1074–5 (pp. 436–7).
108. Sophocles, *Oedipus*, l. 1076.
109. Aristotle, *Poetics*, 1448b (pp. 36–41).
110. Joubert, *Traité*, 1.9 (pp. 63–70); *Treatise*, pp. 36–8. Joubert's contribution to the theory of comedy is considered by Quentin Skinner, "Hobbes and the Classical Theory of Laughter," In *Leviathan After 350 Years*, ed. Tom Sorell and Luc Foisneau (Oxford: Oxford University Press, 2004), pp. 139–66. With the Renaissance came a renewed interest in and expanded definition of laughter, which till then was traditionally identified with contempt. See also Screech, *Laughter at the Foot of the Cross*, pp. 56–60.
111. Pliny, *Natural*, 7.1.2, 2:506.
112. Aristotle, *De Partibus*, 673a (pp. 280–1). Screech considers the implications of this classical premise for Christian laughter; *Laughter at the Foot of the Cross*, pp. 1–5.
113. Mirk, *Festial*, p. 78.
114. For the connection between the Oedipus complex and the dirty joke, see Samuel Weber, *The Legend of Freud* (Minneapolis: University of Minnesota Press, 1982), p. 108, and Howard R. Bloch, *The Scandal of the Fabliaux* (Chicago: University of Chicago Press, 1986), p. 128.
115. Richard Janko, *Aristotle on Comedy: Towards a Reconstruction of Poetics II* (Berkeley: University of California Press, 1984), pp. 49, 100.
116. Aristotle, *Poetics*, 1455a (pp. 86–7).
117. Aristotle, *Poetics*, 1450a (pp. 50–1).
118. Aristotle, *Poetics*, 1453b (pp. 72–5).
119. Terence Cave, *Recognitions: A Study in Poetics* (Oxford: Clarendon, 1988), p. 493.
120. Varro, *De Lingua*, 6.60, 1:226–7; also, Corbeill, *Controlling Laughter*, p. 71.
121. Aristotle, *Poetics*, 1457a–1459a (pp. 102–15).
122. Aristotle, *Poetics*, 1459a (pp. 114–15).
123. See Lowell Edmunds, *Oedipus: The Ancient Legend and Its Later Analogues* (Baltimore, MD: John Hopkins University Press, 1985) for Oedipus riddles in modern folk-culture: "He is your son, your grandson, / the brother of your husband" (p. 222); "For this woman whom I bring here / is my wife, my daughter, and my sister" (p. 119).
124. Mirk, *Festial*, p. 79. Also, the "Hanging of Judas," in *The Towneley Plays*, 1:432, ll. 1–4.
125. Voragine, *Golden Legend*, 1:167–8. The classic study is by Paull Franklin Baum, "The Medieval Legend of Judas Iscariot," *Publications of the Modern Language Association* 31 (1916): 481–632.
126. Villon, "Poems in Slang," 3.27–30.
127. Joubert, *Traité*, 1.26 (p. 128); *Treatise*, p. 60.

128. Papias, *The Didache, the Epistle of Barnabus, the Epistles and the Martyrdom of St. Polycarp, the Fragments of Papias, the Epistle to Diognetus*, trans. and ed. James A. Kleist (Westminster, MD: Newman, 1948), p. 119.
129. Joubert, *Traité*, 1.19 (pp. 110–11); *Treatise*, p. 53.
130. Aristotle, *Poetics*, 1449b (pp. 46–9).
131. Joubert, *Traité*, 1.2 (pp. 16–17); *Treatise*, p. 20.
132. Joubert, *Traité*, 1.4 (p. 39); *Treatise*, p. 27.
133. Joubert, *Traité*, 1.6 (p. 51); *Treatise*, p. 31.
134. Joubert, *Traité*, 1.12 (pp. 81–2); *Treatise*, p. 42.
135. Aristotle, *De Partibus*, 672b (pp. 278–9).
136. Joubert, *Traité*, 1.13 (p. 86); *Treatise*, p. 44.
137. Aristotle, *Nicomachean*, 1107a (pp. 102–5). For discussion of *eutrapelia*, see also Screech, *Laughter at the Foot of the Cross*, pp. 132–40, and Stephen Halliwell, *Greek Laughter: A Study of Cultural Psychology from Homer to Early Christianity* (Cambridge: Cambridge University Press, 2008), pp. 307–31.
138. Joubert, *Traité*, 1.26 (p. 127); *Treatise*, p. 59. A sixteenth-century joke refers to a colic-stricken man who laughs so hard that he farts, and is cured: Bowen, " 'Honorable Art of Farting,' " p. 3.
139. Suetonius, *Lives*, 5.30, 2:60–1.
140. Suetonius, *Lives*, 5.41, 2:72–3.
141. Diogenes Laertius, *Lives*, 7.185, 2:293.
142. Joubert, *Traité*, 3.16 (p. 347); *Treatise*, p. 132.
143. Aristotle, *The "Art" of Rhetoric*, ed. and trans. John Henry Freese (Cambridge, MA: Harvard University Press, 1926; repr. 1994), 1385b.
144. Aristotle, *Poetics*, 1452b–1453a (pp. 68–71).
145. Measuring the moral degeneration of the Roman stage compared to the Greek, Varro derives *obscaenum* from *ob* + *scaena* [stage], remarking that what is shameful should not be spoken openly "except on the *scaena*." Varro, *De Lingua Latina*, 7.96, 1:348–51. The *OED* considers this a folk etymology, however, and suggests the word derives from L. *caenum* [filth].
146. Aristotle, *"Art" of Rhetoric*, 1385b.
147. *Book of the Thousand*, 3.118. Burton notes that politer translators than he offer "fled in haste" for "farted for fear."
148. Rabelais, *Oeuvres*, 2.19 (p. 288).
149. Joubert, *Traité*, Preface to Book 2 (p. 150); *Treatise*, p. 68.
150. Aristotle, *"Art" of Rhetoric*, 1382a.
151. Aristotle, *"Art" of Rhetoric*, 1382b.
152. Aristotle, *Poetics*, 1454b (pp. 84–5).
153. Joubert, *Traité*, 1.11 (p. 76); *Treatise*, p. 40.
154. Seneca, *Ad Lucilium*, 70.20–1 (pp. 66–9).
155. Lambert of Ardres, *History*, pp. 156–7.
156. Bloch, *Scandal*, p. 117.
157. *Amorous Games*, p. 153, §646.
158. *Rhetorica ad Herennium*, 3.20.33 (p. 214).
159. Emmanuel Levinas, *Nine Talmudic Readings*, trans. Annette Aronowicz (Bloomington: Indiana University Press, 1990), p. 20.

160. Innocent III, *De Miseria*, 1.8 (pp. 106–7).
161. Innocent III, *De Miseria*, 2.18 (pp. 166–7).
162. Pliny, *Natural*, 27.68.109, 7:346–7.
163. William of Malmesbury, *De Gestis*, 5.275 (p. 438).
164. Anselm, *De Fide trinitatis et de incarnatione verbi*, Chap. 2, *PL*, 158:265A.
165. Augustine, *City*, 14.24, 4:388–9. Following some manuscript traditions, the Latin version of Augustine's text in Vives's edition reads "ab imo sine pudore" [from below without shame], but Vives corrects the text to *sine paedore* [without stink or filth]; Juan Luis Vives, ed., *D. Avrelii Avgvstini De civitate Dei* (Basle, Froben, 1522), pp. 439–40.
166. Henry Spelman, *The Original, Growth, Propagation and Division of Feuds and Tenures by Knight-Service in England*, in *The English Works of Sir Henry Spelman...Part 2*. 2nd edn. (London: D. Browne, W. Mears, F. Clay, etc., 1727), p. 10.
167. Herman of Tournai, *The Restoration of the Monastery of Saint Martin of Tournai*, trans. Lynn H. Nelson (Washington, DC: Catholic University of America Press, 1996), Chap. 2 (p. 15).
168. Herman of Tournai, *Restoration of the Monastery*, Chap. 2 (pp. 15–16, 178–81).

Die Afterwissenschaft [End-Knowledge, Pseudo-Science, Butthole-Scholarship]

1. OF *mistere* [mystery] means "trade" or "craft," presumably because of professional protection amongst the guilds of "trade secrets." The "mystery" plays take their name from the guilds' performance of biblical events, often relevant to their trade; thus in the York Corpus Christi cycle, the shipwrights perform the Building of the Ark, the mariners the Flood, the taverners the Wedding at Cana, the bakers the Last Supper, and the butchers the Crucifixion.
2. Jean Nohain, and F. Caradec, *Le Petomane1857–1945: A Tribute to the Unique Act Which Shook and Shattered the Moulin Rouge* (London: Souvenir Press, 1967), pp. 12–15.
3. Nohain, *Petomane*, p. 18.
4. Nohain, *Petomane*, p. 25.
5. Nohain, *Petomane*, p. 49.
6. Alan J. Fletcher, *Performance, and Polity in Pre-Cromellian Ireland* (University of Toronto Press, 1999), pp. 19, 24.
7. Fletcher, *Performance*, p. 326.
8. Fletcher, *Performance*, pp. 16–17.
9. Langland, *Piers Plowman*, B.13.231–4.
10. William Tydeman, "An Introduction to Medieval English Theatre," in *The Cambridge Companion to Medieval English Theatre*, ed. Richard Beadle (Cambridge: Cambridge University Press, 1994), pp. 11–12.
11. Meg Twycross, with Malcolm Jones and Alan Fletcher, " 'Farte Pryke in Cule': The Pictures," *Medieval English Theatre*, 23 (2001): 100–21. Alan J.

Fletcher, " 'Farte Pryke in Cule': A Late-Elizabethan Analogue from Ireland," *Medieval English Theatre*, 8 (1986): 134–9. Also Jones, *Secret Middle-Ages*, pp. 289–90.

12. *Tales of Tears and Laughter: Short Fiction of Medieval Japan*, trans. Virginia Skord (Honolulu: University of Hawaii Press, 1991), pp. 157–67. It was during this dynasty that the legend of the Divine Wind, Kamikaze, came into being.
13. Edwardes, *Jewel in the Lotus*, pp. 272–3.
14. Niebuhr, *Description*, p. 27.
15. Taken from the first English translation of Vives's edition. Juan Luis Vives, ed. *St Augustine, of the Citie of God: With the Learned Comments of Io. Lod. Vives. Englished by J[ohn]. H[ealey]*. (London: George Eld, 1610), p. 527. The later, purportedly complete translation made by Alban Butler (Dublin: J. Christie, 1822) omits both Vives's comment and Augustine's original reference to the farters. For the original Latin, see Vives, ed. *D. Avrelii Avgvstini*, pp. 439–40. Vives's comment is noted by Montaigne in *Essais*, 1.21 (p. 129).
16. For two sixteenth-century joke stories in which subjects accidentally fart before German aristocracy, see Bowen, " 'Honorable Art of Farting,' " p. 3. Both Countess Mathilda of Austria and Emperor Sigismund take the faux pas in good spirit.
17. Suetonius, *Lives*, 5.32, 2:60–1. Claudius was prompted by the medical problems of one subject who had squelched his farts out of shame. The story was recycled in fifteenth- and sixteenth-century joke-books: Bowen, " 'Honorable Art of Farting,' " pp. 3–4.
18. Kelly, *Devil at Baptism*, pp. 113, 116.
19. Adam de la Halle, *Adam le Bossu: Trouvère Artésien du XIIIe Siècle. Le Jeu de Robin et Marion*, ed. Ernest Langlois (Paris: Édouard Champion, 1924), ll. 485–6.
20. John of Salisbury, *Policraticus I–IV*, ed. K.S.B. Keats-Rohan (Turnholt: Brepols, 1993), 1.8. p.54.
21. Nohain, *Petomane*, p. 35.
22. Constance Bullock-Davies, *Menestrellorum Multitudo: Minstrels at a Royal Feast* (Cardiff: University of Wales Press, 1978), pp. 19–20.
23. Clifton L. Hoyt, *Professional Minstrelsy & Amateur Performance in Medieval England c. 1300–1450* (Trinity College Dublin: Trinity College, Ph.D. thesis, 1993), pp. 246–7.
24. Hoyt, *Professional Minstrelsy*, ii.
25. Bullock-Davies, *Menestrellorum*, pp. 16–17.
26. John Horace Round, *The King's Serjeants & Officers of State, with Their Coronation Services* (London: Nisbet, 1911).
27. Bullock-Davies, *Menestrellorum*, pp. 22–3. Edward II seems to have disbursed large sums for very trivial entertainment; Terry Jones, Robert Yeager, Terry Dolan, Alan Fletcher, and Juliette Dor. *Who Murdered Chaucer? A Medieval Mystery* (New York: St. Martin's, 2003), p. 38.
28. Constance Bullock-Davies, ed. *Register of Royal and Baronial Domestic Minstrels 1272–1327* (Woodbridge, Suffolk: Boydell and Brewer, 1986), pp. xiii, 9.

NOTES FROM PP. 166-9   213

29. Bullock-Davies, *Menestrellorum*, pp. 26, 55–60.
30. *Le Roman de Renart*, ed. Ernest Martin, vol. 24 vols (in 2) (Strasbourg: Trübner, 1882–1887), Branche XXIII, l. 1784, 2:327.
31. Rabelais, *Oeuvres*, 2.27 (p. 310).
32. Fletcher, *Performance*, pp. 14–16.
33. Fletcher, *Performance*, p. 17.
34. Fletcher, *Performance*, pp. 24–5.
35. Horace, *Satires*, trans. H. Ruston Fairclough (Cambridge, MA: Harvard University Press, 1926), 1.9.59–70 (pp. 10–11).
36. Jack of Dover is a mythical character in medieval and early modern England. Chaucer refers to him (*CT*, 1.4347), and the general reference seems to be to recycled food or drink passed off as new; hence, as Brewer explains in his *Dictionary of Phrase and Fable*, to "dover," because you "do over" the food.
37. *Jack of Dover, His Quest of Inquirie, or His Privy Search for the Veriest Foole in England* (London: William Ferbrand, 1604; repr. London: Percy Society, 1842), pp. 29–30.
38. Bowen, " 'Honorable Art of Farting,' " pp. 10–12.
39. Austin Lane Poole, *Obligations of Society in the XII and XIII Centuries* (Oxford: Clarendon, 1946), p. 66; Elizabeth Guernsey Kimball, *Serjeanty Tenure in Medieval England* (New Haven: Yale University Press, 1936), pp. 58–61.
40. Joseph Strutt, *The Sports and Pastimes of the People of England* (London: Chatto & Windus, 1898), pp. 308, 446–7.
41. Alan B. Cobban, *The Medieval English Universities: Oxford and Cambridge to c. 1500* (Aldershot: Scolar Press, 1988), p. 373.
42. Chambers, *Mediaeval Stage*, 1:408.
43. William Carew Hazlitt, ed. *Tenures of Land and Customs of Manors Originally Collected by Thomas Blount and Republished with Large Additions and Improvements in 1784 and 1815* (London: Reeves and Turner, 1874), p. 118. This entry appears only in Hazlitt's expanded, not in Blount's original, tenures.
44. Vitruvius, *On Architecture*, 1.6.2, 1:54–5.
45. White, *Medieval Technology*, p. 90. White says that there is no record of the *sufflator* between Roman times and Albert's comments in the thirteenth century, but from Albert's phrasing, it is clear that the device had long been popular.
46. Compare the early Lenten feast in honor of St. Blaise, whose day is celebrated as the "jour du vent ou du souffle" [day of wind or breath]. Claude Gaignebet and Marie-Claude Florentin, *Le Carnaval: Essais de Mythologie Populaire* (Paris: Payot, 1974), pp. 117–30.
47. White, *Medieval Technology*, p. 102.
48. Keith Sidwell, *Reading Medieval Latin* (Cambridge: Cambridge University Press, 1995), p. 5.
49. Liberman, *Word Origins*, pp. 32–3. Pump-, being suggestive of roundness, and hence of a bloated stomach, similarly gives us pumpernickel, on account of the flatulence it causes (p. 33).
50. Jean Gimpel, *The Medieval Machine: The Industrial Revolution of the Middle Ages*, 2nd edn. (London: Pimlico, 1988), p. 228.

51. White, *Medieval Technology*, pp. 98–9.
52. Copland, "Iyl," ll.154–5.
53. Bullock-Davies, *Register*, p. 9.
54. Charles Du Fresne Du Cange, *Glossarium ad Scriptores Mediae et infimae Latinitatis*, 6 vols. (Paris: Charles Osmont, 1733–1736), 1:1224, s.v. *Bombus*. See also Jacques-Antoine Dulaure, *Histoire Abrégée de Différens Cultes, Vol. 2: Des divinités génératrices chez les anciens et les modernes*, 2nd edn. (Paris: Guillaume, 1825), pp. 314–15.
55. Dulaure, *Histoire abrégée*, pp. 509–10.
56. Victor Hugo's *Notre-Dame de Paris* (Paris: J. Hetzel, 1862), 1.1 (p. 21), set in the fifteenth century, requires exactly the same payment of Marie la Giffarde. Hugo must have taken his material from Du Cange or maybe from the later DuLaure.

> Est-ce que vous cherchez Marie la Giffarde?
> Elle est rue de Glatigny.
> Elle fait le lit du roi des ribauds.
> Elle paie ses quatre deniers; quatuor denarios.
> Aut unum bombum.
> Voulez-vous qu'elle vous paie au nez?
> [Are you looking for Marie la Giffarde?
> You can find her in Glatigny street.
> Making the bed of the king of thieves!
> She pays her four deniers.
> Or a fart.
> Are you going to make her pay through the nose?]

57. Aristotle, *De Partibus*, 672b (pp. 278–9).
58. Bourke, *Scatalogic*, pp. 170–1.
59. Laura Kendrick, *Animating the Letter: The Figurative Embodiment of Writing from Late Antiquity to the Renaissance* (Columbus: Ohio State University Press, 1999), pp. 217–25.
60. The heading refers to the Hundred of Bosmere, in which Hemingston was situated. A "Hundred" is an administrative grouping with its own court, possibly deriving its name from its division into a hundred hides of land.
61. According to Spelman (*Original*, p. 10), a tenure *in capite* could mean either that the tenancy was held directly from the king, or that the tenure was created with the named vassal—in Roland's case, certainly the former and probably the latter. Tenants-in-chief were commonly regarded as holding by knight's service, but could also hold by serjeanty.
62. Langham belongs to the Hundred of Holt, on the northern coast of Norfolk; it is probably a confusion with Langall, Kirstead, in the Hundred of Loddon, eight miles SSE of Norwich, and in the heart of Norfolk. Certainly Camden claims the property to be the "Manour of Langhall" rather than of Langham (§5).
63. This "inquisition" is presumably that alluded to in §4, that is, an *inquisitio post mortem*, made in 1331, the fourth year of Edward III's reign (1327–1377).

One of the chief reasons for such inquisitions was to examine the situation after the death of people who held land directly of the King, typically by knight service where the tenant was "in chief." If such a tenant died without an heir, his land escheated to the lord. If there was an heir he could not take legal possession of the land until he had paid a relief, roughly equivalent to a year's rent. During any minority, the King took the revenues of the estate and could dispose of the heir or heiress in marriage. In order to exploit these important resources of revenue, special officials were appointed from the middle of the thirteenth century onwards to investigate the circumstances at the death of each tenant in chief. A writ was sent to these men, directing them to take possession of the lands of the deceased, to summon juries of local free men.
Alan MacFarlane, *A Guide to English Historical Records* (Cambridge: Cambridge University Press, 1983), p. 35.

64. Land set aside for dwelling house, outbuildings, and adjacent land for immediate use.
65. "Legal memory" was the point of time agreed upon in 1275 to mark the formal beginning of English common law: 1189, the accession of Richard I. This was the earliest date from which evidence in land disputes could be admitted, as no man living in 1275 could testify to his father's witness prior to 1189.
66. Claude Gaignebet and Jean-Dominique Lajoux, *Art profane et religion populaire au Moyen Age* (Paris: Presses Universitaires de France, 1985), p. 210: "A man of law delivers a sum of money in a purse, while the liegeman completes his dues of a fart." The table does suggest collection of monies, although what the lord holds in his hand is unclear. For land tenure, see F.W. Maitland, *The Constitutional History of England* (Cambridge: Cambridge University Press, 1955), pp. 23–39.
67. *The Romance of Alexander: A Collotype Facsimile of MS. Bodley 264*, intr. M. R. James (Oxford: Clarendon, 1933), fol. 90v.
68. *Eloge du pet: Dissertation historique, anatomique, et philosophique* (Clamecy: Nouvelle Imprimerie Laballery, 2002), p. 28: "À quatre ou cinq lieues de Caen, un particulier, par droit féodal, a longtemps exigé un pet et demi par chacun an." The author also mentions Roland, with Furetière as the source; Furetière does not appear to be the source of the Caen reference.
69. Austin Lane Poole, *From Domesday Book to Magna Carta 1087–1216*, 2nd edn. (Oxford: Clarendon, 1955), pp. 14–15.
70. Frederick Pollock and Frederic William Maitland, *History of English Law before the Time of Edward I*, 2nd edn., 2 vols. (Cambridge: Cambridge University Press, 1968), 1:287. OF *sergant* means "servant."
71. Kimball, *Serjeanty*, 12.
72. F.M. Stenton, *The First Century of English Feudalism, 1066–1166* (Oxford: Clarendon, 1932), p. 188.
73. Kimball, *Serjeanty*, pp. 9–10.
74. Rupert Willoughby, *Life in Medieval England 1066–1485* (Norwich: Pitkin Unichrome, 1997), p. 18.

75. John Horace Round, *Feudal England: Historical Studies on the XIth and XIIth Centuries* (London: Swan Sonnenschein, 1909; repr. Bowie MD: Heritage, 1994), pp. 196–7, 212.
76. Postan, *Medieval Economy*, pp. 143–5.
77. George Caspar Homans, *English Villagers of the Thirteenth Century* (New York: Norton, 1968), p. 73.
78. Round, *King's Serjeants*, pp. 35–6. Kimball, *Serjeanty*, p. 150–1.
79. Kimball, *Serjeanty*, pp. 152–6.
80. Jacques Le Goff, "Laughter in the Middle Ages," in Jan Bremmer and Herman Roodenburg eds., *A Cultural History of Humour: From Antiquity to the Present Day* (Cambridge: Polity Press, 1997), p. 44. Certainly Henry II showed a princely sense of decorum on other occasions. His contemporary and subject, Walter Map, records an incident in which the wind blew up the habit of a Cistercian monk who had tripped, exposing his bare butt. With infinite good breeding, the king looked away and pretended not to see. Walter Map, *De Nugis*, p. 67.
81. See also W.A. Copinger, *The Manors of Suffolk: Notes on Their History and Devolution*, 7 vols. (Manchester: Taylor, Garnett, Evans, 1905–1911), 2:318. Note the discrepancy between Copinger's sum of 16s. 8d. and Blount's reference to 26s. 8d. (*xxvi s. viij d.*) (Fartprints, §6).
82. Poole, *From Domesday*, p. 20. Once the tenurial service had changed to a fixed money rent, it was no longer technically speaking a serjeanty, although this particular tenure continued to be described as a serjeanty long after it was not. Kimball, (*Serjeanty*, p. 60), notes its description as a serjeanty in the Lord Treasurer's Remembrancer accounts for the reign of Edward I; the main business of the Lord Treasurer's Remembrancer, an office that developed in the late twelfth century, was to track outstanding debts, especially from fixed land revenues (MacFarlane, *Guide*, pp. 37–8). It would appear that Roland's successors were not paying up either in kind or in cash.
83. Kimball, *Serjeanty*, pp. 208–10.
84. Maitland, *Constitutional*, p. 29.
85. John Hudson, "Anglo-Norman Land Law and the Origins of Property," in *Law and Government in Medieval England and Normandy: Essays in Honour of Sir James Holt*, ed. George Garnett and John Hudson (Cambridge: Cambridge University Press, 1994), pp. 209–10.
86. Copinger, *Manors*, 2:318. Being impartible, the serjeanty could not be split between inheritors (Kimball, *Serjeanty*, p. 5), which perhaps explains why Agnes, sister of Jeffrey, succeeded to the land after her brother rather than at the same time, although he may, being male or maybe older, have stood in line of succession before her.
87. John Hudson, *Land, Law, and Lordship in Anglo-Norman England* (Oxford: Clarendon, 1994), p. 178, notes the close connection between inalienability and life-estate.
88. Hudson, "Anglo-Norman," pp. 206–7; *Land, Law, and Lordship*, p. 66.
89. Hudson, "Anglo-Norman," p. 212.

90. Hudson, (*Land, Law, and Lordship*, pp. 210–11), observes that gifts within the family were generally effected by substitution, which would resolve the apparent discrepancy between alienation and inheritance, although the lack of mention in the records of a family member being the new donee is problematic. Alienation to a new tenant by substitution and descent to a family heir by gift remain separate legal acts.
91. Hudson, *Land, Law, and Lordship*, p. 143.
92. Copinger, *Manors*, 2:317.
93. Copinger, *Manors*, 1:xiv–xv.
94. *Earliest Leicestershire*, p. 94. The tax on an individual's moveable, personal wealth rather than their land was known as a lay subsidy. The amount, ranging between one- twelfth and one- twentieth of one's wealth, was fixed by parliament, after agreed exemptions, which usually extended to the very poor and to occupational equipment, such as knight's armor.
95. Copinger refers to "Rowland le Pettour or le Farcere" (*Manors*, 2:317).
96. Hudson, *Land, Law, and Lordship*, p. 4.
97. Mirk, *Festial*, p. 173.
98. Mirk, *Festial*, p. 225.
99. Diogenes Laertius, *Lives*, 6.53, 2:54–5.
100. Diogenes Laertius, *Lives*, 6.40. 2:42.
101. Diogenes Laertius, *Lives*, 6.40, 2:41.
102. Joubert, *Traité*, 2.3 (p. 176); *Treatise*, p. 76.
103. Diogenes Laertius, *Lives*, 6.24, 2:27. For an ethical dimension to cynical laughter, see Halliwell, *Greek Laughter*, pp. 372–87.
104. Catchphrase of Leopold von Ranke, "father of historical science," whose desire was not to judge the past but simply to report it. Ernst Breisach, *Historiography: Ancient, Medieval, & Modern* (Chicago & London: University of Chicago Press, 1983), pp. 232–3.

BIBLIOGRAPHY

Primary Sources

Adam de la Halle (c.1235–c.1288). *Adam le Bossu: Trouvère Artésien du XIIIe Siècle. Le Jeu de Robin et Marion.* Ed. Ernest Langlois. Paris: Édouard Champion, 1924.

Admonition by the Father of F.A. to him being a Burgesse of the Parliament for his better Behaviour therein, . . . (1579) in *Miscellanea Antiqua Anglicana, or a Select Collection of Curious Tracts Illustrative of the History, Literature, Manners and Biography of the English Nation.* London: Robert Triphook, 1816. pp. 49–100.

Ælfric (c.950–c.1010). "An Edition of Ælfric's *Letter to Brother Edward.*" Ed. Mary Clayton. In *Early Medieval English Texts and Interpretations: Studies Presented to Donald G. Scragg.* Ed. Elaine Treharne and Susan Rosser. Tempe, AZ: Arizona Center for Medieval and Renaissance Studies, 2002. pp. 263–83.

Alan of Lille (d. 1203). *Anticlaudianus or the Good and Perfect Man.* Trans. James J. Sheridan. Toronto: Pontifical Institute of Mediaeval Studies, 1973.

———. *Anticlaudianus: Texte critique, avec une introduction et des tables.* Ed. R. Bossuat. Paris: Vrin, 1955.

———. *Plaint of Nature.* Trans. James J. Sheridan. Toronto: Pontifical Institute of Mediaeval Studies, 1980. Latin text in *PL*, 210:429A–482C.

The Albion, or, British, Colonial, and Foreign Weekly Gazette. New York: New Series, 1833–.

Alighieri, Dante (1265–1321). *Divina Commedia.* Trans. and ed. Charles S. Singleton. 3 vols. Princeton: Princeton University Press, 1970–1975.

———. *De Vulgari eloquentia.* Ed. and trans. Steven Botterill. Cambridge: Cambridge University Press, 1996.

Alter, Robert, trans. *Genesis.* New York: Norton, 1996.

"The Anglo-Saxon Charms." Ed. Felix Grendon. *Journal of American Folklore*, 22 (1909): 105–237.

Ambrose, St., Bishop of Milan (c. 340–397). *On Virginity.* Trans. Daniel Callam. Toronto: Peregrina, 1980.

Amorous Games: A Critical Edition of Les Adevineaux Amoureux. Ed. James Woodrow Hassell, Jr. Austin and London: American Folklore Society, 1974.

The Ancient Cornish Drama. Ed. Edwin Norris. 2 vols. Oxford: Oxford University Press. Repr. London and New York: Blom, 1968.

Ancrene Wisse. Ed. Robert Hasenfratz. Kalamazoo, MI: Medieval Institute Publications, 2000.

Anselm (1033–1109). *De Fide trinitatis et de incarnatione verbi* [On Faith in the Trinity and on the Incarnation of the Word]. In *PL*, 158.0259B–0284C.

The Antwerp-London Glossaries. Ed. David W. Porter. Toronto: Publications of the Dictionary of Old English, forthcoming.

Apuleius (c.125–c.180). *Metamorphoses*. Ed. and trans. J. Arthur Hanson. 2 vols. Cambridge, MA: Harvard University Press, 1989.

Aquinas, Thomas, St. (1225–1274). *Summa Theologiae*. Ed. and trans. Thomas Gilby. Oxford: Blackfriars, 1964–1975.

Aristophanes (c.448–380 BCE). *The Clouds*. Ed. and trans. Jeffrey Henderson. Cambridge, MA: Harvard University Press, 1998. 1–211.

Aristotle (384–322 BCE). *On Dreams*. In *Parva Naturalia*, pp. 347–71.

———. *Nicomachean Ethics*. Ed. and trans. H. Rackham. Rev. edn. Cambridge, MA: Harvard University Press, 1934.

——— *De Partibus animalium* [On the Parts of Animals]. Rev. edn. Ed. and trans. A.L. Peck. Cambridge, MA: Harvard University Press, 1961.

———. *Parva Naturalia*. Ed. and trans. W.S. Hett. Cambridge, MA: Harvard University Press, 1957.

———. *The Physics*. Ed. and trans. Philip H. Wicksteed and Francis M. Cornford. 2 vols. Cambridge, MA: Harvard University Press, 1929–1934.

———. *Poetics*. Ed. and trans. Stephen Halliwell. Cambridge, MA: Harvard University Press, 1995.

———. *Politics*. Ed. and trans. H. Rackham. Cambridge, MA: Harvard University Press, 1932.

———. *Posterior Analytics*. Ed. and trans. Hugh Tredennick. Cambridge, MA: Harvard University Press, 1960.

———. *On Prophesy in Sleep*. In *Parva Naturalia*, pp. 373–85.

———. *The "Art" of Rhetoric*. Ed. and trans. John Henry Freese. Cambridge, MA: Harvard University Press, 1926. Repr. 1994.

———. *On Sense and Sensible Objects*. In *Parva Naturalia*, pp. 205–83.

———. *On Sleep and Waking*. In *Parva Naturalia*, pp. 315–45.

———. *On the Soul*. In *Parva Naturalia*, pp. 1–203.

Ascham, Roger (1515/16–1568). *The Scholemaster, or Plaine and Perfite Way of Teachyng Children* (1570). In *Roger Ascham, English Works*. Ed. William Aldis Wright. Cambridge: Cambridge University Press, 1904. Repr. 1970, pp. 171–302.

Athanasius, St. (c.296–373). *Un Témoin important du texte de la vie de S. Antoine par S. Athanase*. Ed. Gérard Garitte. Brussels: Palais des Académies, 1939.

Aubrey, John (1626–1697). *Brief Lives*. Ed. Oliver Lawson Dick. Ann Arbor: University of Michigan Press, 1957.

Augustine, St., Bishop of Hippo (354–430). *On Christian Doctrine*. Trans. D.W. Robertson, Jr. New York: Macmillan, 1958. Latin text in *PL*, 34: 0015–0121.

———. *The City of God Against the Pagans*. Ed. and trans. George E. McCracken, William M. Green, David Wiesen, Philip Levine, Eva Matthews Sanford, William Chase Greene, 7 vols. Cambridge, MA: Harvard University Press, 1957–1972. Repr. 1969–1995.

———. *Confessions*. Ed. and trans. William Watts. 2 vols. Cambridge, MA: Harvard University Press, 1912.

———. *Enarrationes super Psalmos* [Expositions on the Psalms]. *PL*, 36:0067–1032, 37:1033–1967.
Aurelian of Réome. *The Discipline of Music (Musica disciplina)* (c. 850). Trans. Joseph Ponte. Colorado Springs: Colorado College Music Press, 1968.
"Ave maris Stella" (c. C.7th or 8th). In *The Penguin Book of Latin Verse*. Ed. Frederick Brittain. Harmondsworth, Middlesex: Penguin, 1962, p. 129.
The Babee's Book. Ed. Frederick J. Furnivall. EETS O.S. 32. London:Trübner, 1868. Repr. New York: Greenwood, 1969.
Barclay, Alexander (c.1475–1552). *Certayne Eglogues of Alexander Barclay, Priest, Compiled by Eneas Silvius* (1570). Spenser Society, 39 (1885). Repr. New York: Burt Franklin, 1967.
Bartholomaeus Anglicus. *On the Properties of Soul and Body: De Proprietatibus Libri III et IV*. Ed. R. James Long. Toronto: Pontifical Institute of Medieval Studies, 1979.
Bartholomew of Exeter (d. 1184). "The Penitential from Cotton MS Vitellius A.XII." In *Bartholomew of Exeter Bishop and Canonist: A Study in the Twelfth Century*. Ed. Adrian Moray, Cambridge: Cambridge University Press, 1937, pp. 161–300.
Bec, Pierre, ed. *Burlesque et obscénité chez les troubadours: pour une approche du contre-texte médiéval*. Paris: Stock, 1984.
Beckett, Samuel. *Molloy: A Novel*. Trans. Patrick Bowles. New York: Grove, 1955.
Benedict of Nursia. (480–543). *Regula, cum commentariis* [Rule, with Commentaries]. *PL*, 66:215–932D.
Bernard of Clairvaux. Sermon 67: "De Mirabili affectu dilectionis sponsae, quem eructat propter amorem Christi sponsi" ["On the Bride's Wondrous Feeling of Love, which she Belches forth on account of her Love for Christ her Bridegroom"]. In *On the Song of Songs IV*. Trans. Irene Edmonds. Kalamazoo, MI: Cistercian Publications, 1980. 4–16. Latin text in *PL*, 183:1102B–1108B.
Benjamin, Walter. *Illuminations*. Ed. Hannah Arendt. Trans. Harry Zohn. New York: Schocken, 1968.
Blount, Thomas (1618–1679). *Fragmenta Antiquitatis. Antient Tenures of Land, and Jocular Customs of Some Mannors. Made Publick for the Diversion of Some, and Instruction of Others*. London: Richard and Edward Atkins, 1679.
Boethius. *Fundamentals of Music*. Trans. Calvin M. Bower. Ed. Claude V. Palisca. New Haven: Yale University Press, 1989.
The Book of Margery Kempe. Ed. Sanford Brown Meech and Hope Emily Allen. EETS 212. Oxford: Oxford University Press, 1940. Repr. 1982.
Book of Secrets of Albertus Magnus of the Virtues of Herbs, Stones, and Certain Beasts (late C.13th). Ed. Michael R. Best and Frank H. Brightman. Oxford: Oxford University Press, 1973.
The Book of the Thousand Nights and a Night: A Plain and Literal Translation of the Arabian Nights Entertainments. Ed. and trans. Richard F. Burton. 10 vols. London: Burton Club (privately printed), 19—?
Boorde, Andrew (c.1490–1549). *A Compendyous Regyment or a Dyetary of Helth*. In *The First Boke of the Introduction of Knowledge* . . . . Ed. F. J. Furnivall. EETS E.S., 10. London: Trübner, 1870, pp. 223–304.
Bullock-Davies, Constance, ed. *Register of Royal and Baronial Domestic Minstrels 1272–1327*. Woodbridge, Suffolk: Boydell and Brewer, 1986.

Calendar of the Close Rolls Preserved in the Public Record Office. Edward III A.D. 1330–1333. London: Her Majesty's Stationery Office, 1898.

Calendar of Plea and Memoranda Rolls Preserved among the Archives of the Corporation of the City of London at the Guildhall. Ed. A. H. Thomas. 6 vols. Cambridge: Cambridge University Press, 1929–1961.

Calendarium Inquisitionum Post Mortem sive Escaetarum. 4 Vols. London: Printed by command of His Majesty King George III in pursuance of an address of The House Of Commons of Great Britain, 1806–1828.

Camden, William (1551–1623). *Britain or a Chorographicall Description of the Most fourishing Kingdomes, England, Scotland, and Ireland, and the Ilands adioyning, out of the depth of Antiqvitie. Beavtified with Mappes of the Severall shires of England. Written first in Latine by William Camden translated newely into English, by Philémon Holland*. London: Impensis Georgii Bishop & Ioannis Norton, 1610.

Capella, Martianus (fl. 410–429). *Martianus Capella and the Seven Liberal Arts: The Marriage of Philology and Mercury*. vol 2. Trans. William Harris Stahl with E. L. Burge. New York: Columbia University Press, 1977.

Chaucer, Geoffrey. *The Riverside Chaucer*. Ed. Larry D. Benson. Boston: Houghton Mifflin, 1987.

The Chester Mystery Cycle. Ed. R.M. Lumiansky and David Mills. EETS s.s., 3. London: Oxford University Press, 1974.

Le Chevalier qui fist parler les cons [The Knight who made cunts talk]. In NRCF, 3:45–173.

Chomsky, Noam. *Syntactic Structures*. The Hague: Mouton, 1957.

Chronicle of London, from 1089 to 1483; Written in the Fifteenth Century, and for the First Time Printed from MSS in the British Museum. Ed. E. Tyrrell and Sir N.H. Nicolas. London: Longman, 1827. Repr. Felinfach: Llanerch, 1995.

Cicero, Marcus Tullius. *De Natura deorum*. Ed. and trans. H. Rackam. Rev. ed.. Cambridge, MA: Harvard University Press, 1951.

———. *Tusculan Disputations*. Ed. and trans. J.E. King. Cambridge, MA: Harvard University Press, 1945.

Code of Jewish Law: A Compliation of Jewish Laws and Customs by Rabbi Solomon Ganzfried. Trans. Hyman E. Goldin. 2nd edn. New York: Hebrew Publishing, 1963.

Du Con Qui Fu Fait A La Besche [About The Cunt That Was Made With a Shovel]. In NRCF, 4:13–21.

Constantine the African (d. 1087). *Constantini Liber de coitu* [Constantine's Book about Coitus]. Ed. and trans. (into Spanish) Enrique Montero Cartelle. Santiago de Compostela: University of Santiago de Compostela, 1983.

Copland, Robert (fl. 1508–1547). "Iyl of Braintford's Testament." In *Poems*, ed. Mary Carpenter Erler. Toronto: University of Toronto Press, 1993. pp. 164–186.

Dante, see Alighieri.

Davies, R.T., ed. *Medieval English Lyrics*. London: Faber and Faber, 1963.

Derrida, Jacques. "Archive Fever: A Freudian Impression." Trans. Eric Prenowitz. *Diacritics*, 25.2 (1995): 9–63.

The Dethe of the Kynge of Scotis. trans. John Shirley. In *Death and Dissent: Two Fifteenth-Century Chronicles*. Ed. Lister M. Matheson. Woodbridge, Suffolk: Boydell, 1999. pp. 1–59.

Diogenes Laertius. *Lives of Eminent Philosophers*. Ed. and trans. R.D. Hicks. 2 vols. Cambridge, MA: Harvard University Press, 1925 (Vol. 1 republished in 1972).
Donatus, Ælius. *Ars grammatica*. In *Keil*. 4:367–402.
Du Cange, Charles Du Fresne (1610–1688). *Glossarium ad Scriptores Mediae et infimae Latinitatis*. 6 vols. Paris: Charles Osmont, 1733–1736.
Dulaure, Jacques-Antoine (1755–1835). *Histoire Abrégée de Différens Cultes. Vol. 2: Des divinités génératrices chez les anciens et les modernes*. 2nd edn. Paris: Guillaume, 1825.
Dunbar, William (c.1460–c.1520). *The Poems of William Dunbar*. Ed. Priscilla Bawcutt. 2 vols. Glasgow: Association for Scottish Literary Studies, 1998.
The Earliest Leicestershire Lay Subsidy Roll, 1327. Ed. W.G.D. Fletcher. Lincoln: J. Williamson, 1888.
Eco, Umberto. *Travels in Hyperreality: Essays*. Trans. William Weaver. London: Picador, 1986.
Eloge du pet: Dissertation historique, anatomique, et philosophique. Clamecy: Nouvelle Imprimerie Laballery, 2002.
Faral, Edmond. *Les Arts poétiques du XII*[e] *et du XIII*[e] *siècle: Recherches et documents sur la technique littéraire du moyen âge*. Paris: Champion, 1924.
"Feast of Tottenham." In *Sentimental and Humorous Romances*. Ed. Erik Kooper. Kalamazoo, MI: Medieval Institute Publications, 2006, pp. 205–10.
Fenichel, Otto. *Collected Papers*. Ed. Hanna Fenichel and David Rapaport. 2 vols. New York: Norton, 1953–1954.
Foucault, Michel. *The Birth of the Clinic: An Archaeology of Medical Perception*. Trans. A.M. Sheridan Smith. New York: Random, 1973.
———. *The Order of Things: An Archaeology of the Human Sciences*. London: Tavistock Publications, 1970.
Franklin, Benjamin. "A Letter to the Royal Academy, 1781." In *Fart Proudly: Writings of Benjamin Franklin You Never Read in School*. Ed. Carl Japikse. Columbus, OH: Enthea, 1990. pp. 13–17.
Freud, Sigmund. *Standard Edition of the Complete Psychological Works*. Trans. James Strachey. 24 vols. London: Hogarth, 1953–1966.
Froissart, Jean (c.1337–c.1410). *The Chronicle of Froissart, Translated by Sir John Bourchier Lord Berners*. 6 vols. London: David Nutt, 1901–1903.
Furetière, Antoine (1619–1688). *Dictionnaire universel*. La Haye: Chez Arnout, 1694.
Galen. *On the Natural Faculties*. Ed. and trans. Arthur John Brock. Cambridge, MA: Harvard University Press, 1916.
Gallic Salt: Eighteen Fabliaux Translated from the Old French. Ed. and trans. Robert Harrison. Berkeley and Los Angeles: University of California Press, 1974.
Gautier le Leu. *Les deus vilains* [*The Two Peasants*]. In *NRCF*, 9:169–81.
Geber (C.8th). *The Works of Geber: Englished by Richard Russell, 1678*. Ed. E.J. Holmyard. London: Dent, 1928.
Gellius, Aulus (fl. 150). *The Attic Nights*. Ed. and trans. John C. Rolfe. 3 vols. Cambridge, MA: Harvard University Press, 1927. Repr. 1970.
Geoffrey of Vinsauf (fl. 1200). *Poetria Nova*. In Faral, *Arts poétiques*, pp. 194–262.
———. *Poetria Nova of Geoffrey of Vinsauf*. Trans. Margaret F. Nims. Toronto: Pontifical Institute of Mediaeval Studies, 1967.

Geoponica sive Cassiani Bassi scholastici De re rustica eclogue. Ed. Henricus Beckh. 4 vols. (in 1). Lipsiae: In aedibus B.G. Teubneri, 1895.

Gower, John. *Complete Works of John Gower.* 4 vols. Ed. G.C. Macaulay. Oxford: Clarendon, 1899–1902.

Gregory of Tours (c.538–c.593). *Historia Francorum* [History of the Franks]. In *PL*, 71.0159–0571.

Guibert of Nogent (c.1055–c.1124). *A Monk's Confession: The Memoirs of Guibert of Nogent.* Trans. Paul J. Archambault. University Park: Pennsylvania State University Press, 1996. Latin text in *PL*, 156:0837A–0962A.

Heidegger, Martin. *Einführung in die Metaphysik* [Introduction to Metaphysics]. Tübingen: Max Niemeyer, 1953.

———. *Introduction to Metaphysics.* Trans. Gregory Fried and Richard Polt. New Haven: Yale University Press, 2000.

Henry of Huntingdon. *Henrici Archidiaconi Huntendunensis Historia Anglorum. The History of the English by Henry from AC 55 to AD 1154 in 8 books.* Ed. Thomas Arnold. London: Her Majesty's Stationery Office, 1879.

Herman of Tournai (C.12th). *The Restoration of the Monastery of Saint Martin of Tournai.* Trans. Lynn H. Nelson. Washington, DC: Catholic University of America Press, 1996.

Hilary of Poitiers (d. 367). *Tractatus Super Psalmos.* In *PL*, 9:232C–884C.

Hippocrates. *Works.* Ed. and trans. W.H.S. Jones, E.T. Withington, Paul Potter, and Wesley D. Smith, 8 vols. Cambridge, MA: Harvard University Press, 1923–1995.

———. *On Breaths.* In *Works.* 2:219–53.

———. *Prognostic.* In *Works.* 2:1–55.

———. *Sacred Disease.* In *Works.* 2:127–83.

Homer. "Hymn to Hermes." In *The Homeric Hymns.* Trans. Apostolos N. Athanassakis. Baltimore: John Hopkins University Press, 1976, pp. 31–46.

Honorius of Autun (fl. 1106–1135). *De Imagine mundi* (1133). In *PL*, 172.0115A–0188C.

Horace. *Satires.* Trans. H. Ruston Fairclough. Cambridge, MA: Harvard University Press, 1926, pp. 1–245.

Horkheimer, Max, and Theodor W. Adorno. *Dialectic of Enlightenment.* Trans. John Cumming. London: Verso, 1979.

Hugh of St. Victor (c.1096–1141). *Didascalicon: A Medieval Guide to the Arts.* Trans. Jerome Taylor. 2nd edn. New York: Columbia University Press, 1991. Latin text in *PL* 136.0739–0880.

Hugo, Victor (1802–1885). *Notre-Dame de Paris.* Paris: J. Hetzel, 1862.

Hume, David (1711–1776). *An Inquiry Concerning Human Understanding.* Ed. Charles W. Hendel. Indianapolis and New York: Liberal Arts Press, 1955.

Hunt, Tony, ed. *Popular Medicine in Thirteenth-Century England: Introduction and Texts.* Cambridge: Brewer, 1990.

Inferno, see Alighieri, Dante.

Innocent III, Pope (c.1160–1216). *De Miseria condicionis humane.* Ed. and trans. Robert E. Lewis. Athens: University of Georgia Press, 1978.

Isidore of Seville (c.560–636). *Etymologiarum sive originum libri XX*. Ed. W.M. Lindsay. 2 vols. Oxford: Clarendon, 1911.

Jack of Dover, His Quest of Inquirie, or His Privy Search for the Veriest Foole in England. London: William Ferbrand, 1604. Repr. London: Percy Society, 1842.

Jamieson, John. *Etymological Dictionary of the Scottish Language*. 2nd edn. Paisley: Alexander Gardner. 1879–1882.

Jerome, St. "Epistola 23, ad Dardanum: De Diversis generibus musicorum." In *PL*, 30.213B–215C.

John of Arderne (b. 1307). *Treatises of Fistula in Ano, and of Fistulae in Other Parts of the Body*. Ed. D'Arcy Power. EETS o.s., 139. London: Oxford University Press, 1910.

John of Salisbury (c.1115–1180). *The Metalogicon of John of Salisbury: A Twelfth-Century Defense of the Verbal and Logical Arts of the Trivium*. Trans. Daniel D. McGarry. Berkeley and Los Angeles: University of California Press, 1955. Latin text in *PL*, 199:823A–946C.

———. (Ionnis Saresberiensis). *Policraticus, I–IV*. Ed. K.S.B. Keats-Rohan. Turnholt: Brepols, 1993.

Jonson, Ben (c.1573–1637). *The Alchemist*. Ed. Peter Bement. London and New York: Methuen, 1987.

———. *The Staple of News* (1626). Ed. Devra Rowland Kifer. Lincoln: University of Nebraska Press, 1975.

Joubert, Laurent (1529–1583). *Traité du Ris*. Paris: Nicholas Chesneau, 1579.

———. *Treatise on Laughter*. Trans. Gregory David de Rocher. Alabama: University of Alabama Press, 1980.

Keil, Heinrich. *Grammatici latini*. 8 vols. Lipsiae: In aedibvs B.G. Tevbneri, 1857–1880. Repr. Hildesheim: Georg Olms, 1961.

Kristeva, Julia. *Powers of Horror: An Essay on Abjection*. Trans. Leon S. Roudiez. New York: Columbia University Press, 1982.

Lacan, Jacques. *Seminar of Jacques Lacan VII: Ethics of Psychoanalysis 1959–60*. Ed. J. Alain Miller. Trans. Dennis Porter. NY: Norton, 1992.

Lambert of Ardres (fl. 1200). *The History of the Counts of Guines and Lords of Ardres*. Trans. Leah Shopkow. Philadelphia: University of Pennsylvania Press, 2000.

Langland, William. *Piers Plowman: A Parallel-Text Edition of the A, B, C, and Z Versions*. Ed. A.V.C. Schmidt. London: Longman, 1995.

Levinas, Emmanuel. *Nine Talmudic Readings*. Trans. Annette Aronowicz. Bloomington: Indiana University Press, 1990.

Liber feodorum. The Book of Fees, Commonly Called Testa de Nevill. Ed. H.C.M. Lyte et al. 3 vols. London: His Majesty's Stationery Office, 1920–1931.

Liddell, Henry George, and Robert Scott, eds. *A Greek-English Lexicon*. Sup. edn. Oxford: Clarendon, 1968.

The Life of Cola di Rienzo (c.1358). Trans. John Wright. Toronto: Pontifical Institute of Medieval Studies, 1975.

Lorris, Guillaume de and Jean de Meun. *Le Roman de la Rose*. Ed. Ernest Langlois. 5 vols. Paris: Libraire de Firmin-Didot, 1914–1924.

Lucretius (c.98 BCE –55). *De Rerum natura*. Ed. and trans. W.H.D. Rouse. Rev. Martin Ferguson Smith. Cambridge, MA: Harvard University Press, 1992.

Lybeaus Desconus. Ed. M. Mills. EETS 261. London: Oxford University Press, 1969.
Lydgate, John (c.1370–1449). *Life of Our Lady.* Ed. J. Lauritis, R. Klinefelter and V. Gallagher. Pittsburg: Duquesne University Press, 1961.
———. *Lydgate's Fall of Princes.* Ed. Henry Bergen. EETS E.S., 121. London: Oxford University Press, 1924.
———. *The Siege of Thebes.* Ed. Robert R. Edwards. Kalamazoo, MI: Medieval Institute Publications, 2001.
Macrobius. *Commentary on the Dream of Scipio* (c. 395). Trans. William Harris Stahl. 2nd edn. New York: Columbia University Press, 1990.
Maimonides, Moses ben Maimon. "Laws Concerning Character Traits." In *Ethical Writings of Maimonides.* Ed. Raymond L. Weiss and Charles Butterworth. New York: Dover, 1975, pp. 27–58.
Mankind. In *Medieval Drama.* Ed. David Bevington. Boston: Houghton Mifflin, 1975, pp. 901–38.
Map, Walter (fl. 1200). *De Nugis Curialium* [Courtiers' Trifles]. Ed. and trans. M.R. James. Rev. C.N.L. Brooke and R.A.B. Mynors. Oxford: Clarendon, 1983.
Matazone de Calignano (fl. late C.14th). "Dit sur les villains." Ed. and trans. (into modern French) Paul Meyer. *Romania,* 12 (1883): 14–28.
Matthew of Paris. *Matthæi Parisiensis, Monachi Sancti Albani, Chronica Majora: Vol 5, A.D. 1248 to A.D. 1259.* Ed. Henry Richards Luard. London: Her Majesty's Stationery Office, 1880.
Middle English Sermons. Ed. Woodburn O. Ross. EETS O.S. 209. London: Oxford University Press, 1940.
Mirk, John (fl. 1403?). *Festial: A Collection of Homilies, Part 1.* Ed. Theodor Erbe. EETS E.S. 96. London: Kegan Paul, Trench, Trübner, 1905.
Montaigne, Michel de. *Essais.* Ed. Albert Thibaudet. Paris: Gallimard, 1950.
———. *The Complete Essays.* Trans. M.A. Screech. London: Penguin, 1991.
Niceta of Remesiana (c.335–c.415). "Vigils of the Saints." Trans. Gerald G. Walsh. In *Niceta of Remesiana: Writings.* Trans. Gerald G. Walsh. New York: Fathers of the Church, 1949, pp. 55–64.
Niebuhr, Carsten (1733–1815). *Description de l'Arabie faite sur des observations propres et des avis recueillis dans les lieux mêmes.* Amsterdam and Utrecht: S.J. Baalde (Amsterdam) and J. van Schoonhoven (Utrecht), 1774.
Nietzsche, Friedrich. *Twilight of the Idols or How to Philosophize with a Hammer.* Trans. Richard Polt. Indianapolis: Hackett, 1997.
Norton, Thomas (fl. 1477). *Ordinal of Alchemy.* Ed. John Reidy. EETS O.S. 272. London: Oxford University Press, 1975.
The N-Town Play: Cotton MS Vespasian D.8. Ed. Stephen Spector. Vol 1. EETS S.S. 11. London: Oxford University Press, 1991.
Nouveau Recueil Complet des Fabliaux. Ed. Willem Noomen and Nico van den Boogard. 10 vols. Assen, Pays-Bas: Van Gorcum, 1983–1998.
Ogilvie, John. *The Imperial Dictionary of the English Language.* Rev. edn. Charles Annandale. 4 vols. London: Blackie, 1883.
Orme, Nicholas. *Education and Society in Medieval and Renaissance England.* London: Hambledon, 1989.

Ovid. *Metamorphoses*. Ed. and trans. Frank Justus Miller. Rev. G.P. Goold. 2 vols. Cambridge, MA: Harvard University Press, 1977–1984.
Owl and the Nightingale. Ed. Neil Cartlidge. Exeter: Exeter University Press, 2001.
The Oxford Dictionary of English Etymology. Ed. Onions, C.T. Oxford: Clarendon, 1966.
Papias (c.61–c.125), Saint, Bishop of Hierapolis. *The Didache, the Epistle of Barnabus, the Epistles and the Martyrdom of St. Polycarp, the Fragments of Papias, the Epistle to Diognetus*. Trans. and ed. James A. Kleist. Westminster, MD: Newman, 1948.
Paradiso, see Alighieri, Dante.
Patrologiae Latinae, Cursus Completus. Ed. Jacques-Paul Migne. Paris: Garnier, 1844–1855 & 1862–1865. Electronic Database.
Pepys, Sir Samuel. *Works*. Ed. Robert Latham and William Matthews. 11 vols. Berkeley: University of California Press, 1970–1983.
Le Pet. In *Receuil de Farces (1450–1550)*. Ed. André Tissier. Vol 10. Geneva: Droz, 1996, pp. 21–63.
Petrarch, Francis (1304–1374). *The Canzoniere or Rerum vulgaria fragmenta*. Ed. and trans. Mark Musa with Barbara Manfredi. Bloomington and Indianapolis: Indiana University Press, 1996.
Plato. *Cratylus*. Ed. and trans. H.N. Fowler. Cambridge, MA: Harvard University Press, 1963.
———. *Gorgias*. Ed. and trans. W.R.M. Lamb. Cambridge, MA: Harvard University Press, 1925.
———. *Laws*. Ed. and trans. R.G. Bury. 2 vols. Cambridge, MA: Harvard University Press, 1926.
———. *Phaedo*. Ed. and trans. Hardol North Fowler. Cambridge, MA: Harvard University Press, 1943.
———. *Phaedrus*. Ed. and trans. Harold North Fowler. Cambridge, MA: Harvard University Press, 1914, pp. 405–578.
———. *Republic*. Ed. and trans. Paul Shorey. 2 vols. Cambridge, MA: Harvard University Press, 1930–1935.
———. *Timaeus*. Ed. and trans. R.G. Bury. Cambridge, MA: Harvard University Press, 1929.
Pliny the Elder. *Natural History*. Ed. and trans. H. Rackham. 10 vols. Cambridge, MA: Harvard University Press, 1938–1963.
Plutarch. "Advice to the Bride and Groom." In *Moralia*. 16 vols. Ed. and trans. Frank Cole Babbitt. Cambridge, MA: Harvard University Press, 1927–1976. 2:295–343.
Porcelet [Piglet]. In NRCF, 6:185–91.
Priscian. *Institutiones grammaticae*. In Keil. Vols. 2–3.
Promptorium parvulorum sive clericorum, dictionarius Anglo-latinus princeps by Fratre Galfrido Grammatico dicto. Ed. Albertus Way. London: Camden Society, 1865.
Proverbes français antérieurs au XVe siècle. Ed. Joseph Morawski. Paris: Champion, 1925.
Purgatorio, see Alighieri, Dante.
Ravisius, Johannes (1480–1524). *Officinae epitome*. 2 vols. Lyon: Seb. Gryphius, 1560.
Rabelais, François. *Oeuvres complètes*. Ed. Mireille Huchon with François Moreau. Paris: Gallimard, 1994.

Recueil de poésies francoises des XVe et XVIe siècles: Morales, facétieuses, historiques. Ed. Anatole de Montaiglon. 13 vols. Paris: Jannet, 1855–1878.

Rhetorica ad Herrenium (c. 86–82 BCE). Ed, and trans. Harry Caplan. Cambridge, MA: Harvard University Press, 1954.

Le Roman de Renart. Ed. Ernest Martin. 3 vols. Strasbourg: Trübner, 1882–1887.

The Romance of Alexander: A Collotype Facsimile of MS. Bodley 264. Intr. M.R. James. Oxford: Clarendon, 1933.

Rutebeuf. *Le Pet Au Vilain* [The Churl's Fart]. In *NRCF*, 5:359–70.

Saussure, F. de. *Course in General Linguistics*. Trans. Roy Harris. London: Duckworth, 1983.

Secretum Secretorum: Nine English Versions. Ed. M. A. Manzalaoui. EETS 276. Oxford: Oxford University Press, 1977.

De Secretis mulierum (late C.13th/early C.14th). *Albertus Magnus De Secretis Mulierum*. Amstelodami: apud Iodocum Ianssonium, 1643. For English translation, see *Women's Secrets*.

Seneca. *Ad Lucilium epistulae morales*. Vol. 2. Ed. and trans. Richard M. Gummere. Cambridge, MA: Harvard University Press, 1970.

Serres, Michel. *Hermes: Literature, Science, Philosophy*. Ed. Josué V. Harari and David F. Bell. Baltimore and London: John Hopkins University Press, 1982.

Shakespeare, William. *Complete Works*. Ed. Stanley Wells, Gary Taylor, John Jowett, and William Montgomery, 2nd edn. Oxford: Clarendon, 2005.

Silvestris, Bernardus (fl. 1147). *Cosmographia*. Trans. Winthrop Wetherbee. 2nd edn. New York: Columbia University Press, 1990.

———. *Bernardi Silvestris de mundi universitate*. Ed. Carl Sigmund Barach and Johann Wrobel. Frankfurt am Main: Minerva, 1964.

Sophocles. *Oedipus Tyrannus*. Ed. and trans. Hugh Lloyd-Jones. Cambridge, MA: Harvard University Press, 1994, pp. 323–483.

Spelman, Henry (c.1564–1641). *The Original, Growth, Propagation and Division of Feuds and Tenures by Knight-Service in England* (1639). In *The English Works of Sir Henry Spelman, Kt. Published in His Lifetime together with his Posthumous Works Relating to the Laws and Antiquities of England: Part 2*. 2nd edn. London: D. Browne, W. Mears, F. Clay, 1727, pp. 1–46.

Spurgeon, Caroline F.E. *Five Hundred Years of Chaucer Criticism and Allusion 1357–1900*. Vol. 1. New York: Russell & Russell, 1960.

Sulpicius Severus (c.360–c.420). "Life of St. Martin." Trans. Bernard M. Peebles. In *The Fathers of the Church*, 7. NY: Fathers of the Church, 1949, pp. 101–40.

The "Summa musice:" A Thirteenth-Century Manual for Singers. Ed. and trans. Christopher Page. Cambridge: Cambridge University Press, 1991.

Suetonius (c.69–c.122). *Lives of the Caesars*. Ed. and trans. J.C. Rolfe. Rev. edn. 2 vols. Cambridge, MA: Harvard University Press, 1997–1998.

Süskind, Patrick. *Perfume: The Story of a Murderer*. Trans. John E. Woods. New York: A.A. Knopf, 1986.

Tales of the Elders of Ireland (Acallam na Senórach). Trans. Ann Dooley and Harry Roe. Oxford: Oxford University Press, 1999.

Tales of Tears and Laughter: Short Fiction of Medieval Japan. Trans. Virginia Skord. Honolulu: University of Hawaii Press, 1991.

Tenures of Land and Customs of Manors Originally Collected by Thomas Blount and Republished with Large Additions and Improvements in 1784 and 1815. Ed. William Carew Hazlitt. London: Reeves and Turner, 1874.
Tertullian (c.160–c.230). *Apologeticus*. Ed. and trans. T.R. Glover. Cambridge, MA: Harvard University Press, 1931. Repr. 1966, pp. 1–227.
———. *On Fasting*. In *The Ante-Nicene Fathers: Translations of the Writings of the Fathers down to A.D. 325*. Ed. Alexander Roberts and James Donaldson. Rev. edn. 10 vols. Edinburgh: T&T Clark; Grand Rapids, MI: W.B. Erdmanns, 1989–1994. 4:102–15.
Three Middle-English Versions of the Rule of St. Benet. Ed. Ernest A. Kock. EETS O.S. 120. London: Trübner, 1902.
Thundergust: A Kentucky Court of Appeals Decision. Louisville, KY: Privately Printed, 1930.
The Towneley Plays. Ed. Martin Stevens and A.C. Cawley. 2 vols. EETS S.S. 13–14. Oxford: Oxford University Press, 1994.
Trevisa, John. *On the Properties of Things: John Trevisa's Translation of Bartholomaeus Anglicus De Re Proprietatibus*. Ed. M. C. Seymour, Elizabeth Brockhurst, Gabriel M. Liegey, M.H. Blechner, Ralph Hanna III, Joseph E. Grennen, et al., 3 vols. Oxford: Clarendon, 1975–1988.
The Trial of Gilles de Rais. Ed. Georges Bataille. Trans. Richard Robinson. Los Angeles: Amok, 1991.
Les Trois Meschines [The Three Young Girls]. In *NRCF*, 4:217–26.
Varro, Marcus Terentius. *On Agriculture*. Ed. and trans. William Davis Hooper. Rev. Harrison Boyd Ash. Cambridge, MA: Harvard University Press, 1935, pp. 159–529.
———. *De Lingua Latina: On the Latin Language*. Ed. and trans. Roland G. Kent. Rev. edn. 2 vols. Cambridge, MA: Harvard University Press, 1951–1958.
Vicary, Thomas (d. 1561). *The Anatomie of the Bodie of Man*. Ed. Frederick J. Furnivall and Percy Furnivall. EETS E.S. 53. London: Trübner, 1888.
Le Vilain asnier [The Peasant Ass-Driver]. In *NRCF*, 8: 207–14.
Villon, François (b. 1431). *The Complete Works of François Villon*. Ed. and trans. Anthony Bonner. New York: David McKay, 1960.
Virgil. *Aeneid*. Ed. and trans. H. Rushton Fairclough. Rev. G.P. Goold. 2 vols. Cambridge, MA: Harvard University Press, 1999–2000.
The Visions of Tondal from the Library of Margaret of York. Ed. Thomas Kren and Roger S. Wieck. Malibu, CA: J. Paul Getty Museum, 1990.
Vitruvius (C.1st BCE). *Vitruvius on Architecture*. Ed. and trans. Frank Granger. 2 vols. Cambridge, MA: Harvard University Press, 1931–1934.
Vives, Juan Luis (1492–1540), ed. *D. Avrelii Avgvstini De civitate Dei*. Basle, Froben, 1522.
———, ed. *St Augustine, of the Citie of God: With the Learned Comments of Io. Lod. Vives. Englished by J[ohn].H[ealey]*. London: George Eld, 1610.
Voragine, Jacobus de (c.1229–1298). *Golden Legend: Readings on the Saints*. Trans. William Granger Ryan. 2 vols. Princeton: Princeton University Press, 1993.
The Vulgaria of John Stanbridge and the Vulgaria of Robert Whittinton. Ed. Beatrice White. EETS O.S. 187. London: Oxford University Press, 1932. Repr. 1971.

Wedgwood, Hensleigh. *A Dictionary of English Etymology*. 3 vols. London: Trübner, 1859–1865.
Whitney, William Dwight. *The Century Dictionary: An Encyclopedic Lexicon of the English Language*. 6 vols. New York: The Century Co., 1889–1891.
William of Malmesbury (c.1090–c.1143). *De Gestis Pontificum Anglorum: Libri quinque*. Ed. N.E.S.A. Hamilton. London: Longman & Co., Trübner, 1870.
Wodehouse, P.G. *The Code of the Woosters*. 1938. Repr. Mattituck, NY: Rivercity Press, 1976.
Women's Secrets: A Translation of Pseudo-Albertus Magnus' De Secretis Mulierum with Commentaries. Trans. Helen Rodnite Lemay. Albany: State University of New York Press, 1992.
Wyclif, John. *The Holy Bible, Containing the Old and New Testaments, with the Apocryphal Books, in the Earliest English Versions Made from the Latin Vulgate by John Wycliffe and His Followers*. Ed. Josiah Forshall and Frederic Madden. 4 vols. Oxford: Oxford University Press, 1850.
Wynkyn de Worde. *The demaundes ioyous* 1511. Anon. Enprynted at London: In Flete strete at the sygne of the sonne by me Wynkyn de Worde. London, 1511.

Secondary Sources

Aftel, Mandy. *Essence and Alchemy: A Book of Perfume*. New York: North Point Press, 2001.
Bakhtin, Mikhail. *Rabelais and His World*. Trans. Hélène Iswolsky. Bloomington: Indiana University Press, 1984.
Barber, C.L. *The Story of Language*. 2nd edn. London: Pan, 1972.
Barthélemy, Dominique. "Kinship." In Duby, pp. 87–155.
Baugh, Albert C., and Tomas Cable. *A History of the English Language*. 4th edn. Englewood Cliffs, NJ: Prentice Hall, 1993.
Baum, Paull Franklin. "The Medieval Legend of Judas Iscariot," *Publications of the Modern Language Association* 31 (1916): 481–632.
Bayless, Martha. "The Story of the Fallen Jew and the Iconography of Jewish Unbelief." *Viator* 34 (2003): 142–56.
Benton, Janetta Rebold. *Holy Terrors: Gargoyles on Medieval Buildings*. New York: Abbeville, 1997.
Bloch, R. Howard. *Etymologies and Genealogies: A Literary Anthropology of the French Middle Ages*. Chicago: University of Chicago Press, 1983.
———. *The Scandal of the Fabliaux*. Chicago: University of Chicago Press, 1986.
Block, Elaine C. "Physical and Social Inversions in the Topsy Turvy World." *Arts Profane / Profane Arts*, 7.1 (1998): 8–28.
Boswell, John. *Christianity, Social Tolerance, and Homosexuality: Gay People in Western Europe from the Beginning of the Christian Era to the Fourteenth Century*. Chicago: University of Chicago Press, 1980.
Bourke, John G. *Scatalogic [sic] Rites of All Nations*. Washington, DC: Lowdermilk, 1891. Repr. Johnson Corp., 1969.

Bowen, Barbara C. "The 'Honorable Art of Farting' in Continental Renaissance Literature." In Persels and Ganim, eds, *Fecal Matters*, pp. 1–12.
Breisach, Ernst. *Historiography: Ancient, Medieval, & Modern*. Chicago & London: University of Chicago Press, 1983.
Bryson, Bill. *The Mother Tongue: English & How It Got That Way*. New York: William Morrow, 1990.
Buckle, Henry Thomas. *Common Place Books*. In *Miscellaneous and Posthumous Works of Henry Thomas Buckle*. Ed. Helen Taylor. Vols. 2–3 (of 3). London: Longmans, Green and Co., 1872.
Bullock-Davies, Constance. *Menestrellorum Multitudo: Minstrels at a Royal Feast*. Cardiff: University of Wales Press, 1978.
Bulman, Françoise. *Dictionnaire des Proverbes Anglais-Français, Français-Anglais*. Québec: Les Presses de l'Université Laval, 1998.
Burckhardt, Titus. *Alchemy: Science of the Cosmos, Science of the Soul*. Trans. William Stoddart. Longmead, Dorset: Element Books, 1967.
Bynum, Caroline Walker. *Fragmentation and Redemption: Essays on Gender and the Human Body in Medieval Religion*. New York: Zone, 1992.
Camille, Michael. *Image on the Edge: The Margins of Medieval Art*. Cambridge, MA: Harvard University Press, 1992.
Carruthers, Mary J. *The Book of Memory: A Study of Memory in Medieval Culture*. Cambridge: Cambridge University Press, 1990.
Cave, Terence. *Recognitions: A Study in Poetics*. Oxford: Clarendon, 1988.
Cazzaro, Flavio. "Un Perfum de scandale ou l'esthétique scatologique dans la littérature française du nord du XIIe au XIVe siècle." Lausanne: Université de Lausanne, M.A. thesis, 2003.
Chambers, E.K. *The Mediaeval Stage*. 2 vols. Oxford: Oxford University Press, 1903. Repr. (2 vols. in one), Mineola, NY: Dover, 1996.
Cobban, Alan B. *The Medieval English Universities: Oxford and Cambridge to c. 1500*. Aldershot: Scolar Press, 1988.
Cohen, Esther. "Law, Folklore and Animal Lore." *Past and Present*, 110 (1986): 6–37.
Collinge, N.E. *The Laws of Indo-European*. Amsterdam and Philadelphia: John Benjamins, 1985.
Copinger, W.A. *The Manors of Suffolk: Notes on Their History and Devolution*. 7 vols. Manchester: Taylor, Garnett, Evans, 1905–1911.
Corbeill, Anthony. *Controlling Laughter: Political Humor in the Late Roman Republic*. Princeton: Princeton University Press, 1996.
Delany, Sheila. "Run Silent, Run Deep: Heresy and Alchemy as Medieval Versions of Utopia." In *Medieval Literary Politics: Shapes of Ideology*. Manchester: Manchester University Press, 1990, pp. 1–18.
Douglas, Mary. *Purity and Danger: An Analysis of the Concepts of Pollution and Taboo*. London and New York: Routledge 1966. Repr. 1996.
Duby, Georges, ed. *A History of Private Life II: Revelations of the Medieval World*. Trans. Arthur Goldhammer. Cambridge, MA: Harvard University Press, 1988.
Eco, Umberto. *Travels in Hyper-Reality: Essays*. Trans. William Weaver. London. Picador: 1986.

Edmunds, Lowell. *Oedipus: The Ancient Legend and Its Later Analogues.* Baltimore, MD: John Hopkins University Press, 1985.

Edwardes, Allen. *The Jewel in the Lotus: A Historical Survey of the Sexual Culture of the East.* New York: Julian Press, 1959.

Elliott, Dyan. *Fallen Bodies: Pollution, Sexuality and Demonology in the Middle Ages.* Philadelphia: University of Pennsylvania Press, 1999.

Enders, Jody. *Rhetoric and the Origins of Medieval Drama.* Ithaca: Cornell University Press, 1992.

Evans, E.P. *The Criminal Prosecution and Capital Punishment of Animals.* 2nd edn. London: Faber and Faber, 1987.

Fein, David A. *A Reading of Villon's Testament.* Birmingham, AL: Summa, 1984.

Fletcher, Alan J. *Drama, Performance, and Polity in Pre-Cromellian Ireland.* Toronto: University of Toronto Press, 1999.

Fletcher, Alan J. " 'Farte Pryke in Cule': A Late-Elizabethan Analogue from Ireland." *Medieval English Theatre*, 8 (1986): 134–9.

Fränger, Wilhelm. *The Millennium of Hieronymus Bosch.* Trans. Eithne Wilkins and Ernst Kaiser. London: Faber & Faber, 1952.

Freedman, Paul. *Images of the Medieval Peasant.* Stanford, CA: Stanford University Press, 1999.

Gaignebet, Claude, and Jean-Dominique Lajoux. *Art profane et religion populaire au Moyen Age.* Paris: Presses Universitaires de France, 1985.

Gaignebet, Claude, and Marie-Claude Florentin. *Le Carnaval: Essais de Mythologie Populaire.* Paris: Payot, 1974.

Gimpel, Jean. *The Medieval Machine: The Industrial Revolution of the Middle Ages.* 2nd edn. London: Pimlico, 1988.

Goux, Jean-Joseph. *Symbolic Economies after Marx and Freud.* Trans. Jennifer Curtiss Gage. Ithaca, NY: Cornell University Press, 1990.

Halliwell, Stephen. *Greek Laughter: A Study of Cultural Psychology from Homer to Early Christianity.* Cambridge: Cambridge University Press, 2008.

Hanawalt, Barbara A. *The Ties That Bound: Peasant Families in Medieval England.* Oxford: Oxford University Press, 1986.

Harvey, Howard Graham. *The Theatre of the Basoche.* Cambridge, MA: Harvard University Press, 1941.

Hocquenghem, Guy. *Homosexual Desire.* Trans. Daniella Dangoor. Durham and London: Duke University Press, 1993.

Holsinger, Bruce W. *Music, Body, and Desire in Medieval Culture: Hildegard of Bingen to Chaucer.* Stanford: Stanford University Press, 2001.

Homans, George Caspar. *English Villagers of the Thirteenth Century.* New York: Norton, 1968.

Horan, Julie L. *The Porcelain God: A Social History of the Toilet.* Secaucus, NJ: Carol Publishing, 1997.

Hoyt, Clifton L. *Professional Minstrelsy & Amateur Performance in Medieval England c. 1300–1450.* Dublin, Trinity College, Ph.D. thesis (1993).

Hudson, John. "Anglo-Norman Land Law and the Origins of Property." In *Law and Government in Medieval England and Normandy: Essays in Honour of Sir James*

BIBLIOGRAPHY

Holt. Ed. George Garnett and John Hudson. Cambridge: Cambridge University Press, 1994, pp. 198–222.

———. *Land, Law, and Lordship in Anglo-Norman England.* Oxford: Clarendon, 1994.

Irvine, Martin. *The Making of Textual Culture: "Grammatica" and Literary Theory, 350–1100.* Cambridge: Cambridge University Press, 1994.

Janko, Richard. *Aristotle on Comedy: Towards a Reconstruction of Poetics II.* Berkeley: University of California Press, 1984.

Jones, Malcolm. "The Parodic Sermon in Medieval and Early Modern England." *Medium Aevum*, 66 (1997): 94–114.

———. *The Secret Middle Ages.* Stroud: Sutton, 2002.

Jones, Terry, Robert Yeager, Terry Dolan, Alan Fletcher, and Juliette Dor. *Who Murdered Chaucer? A Medieval Mystery.* New York: St. Martin's, 2003.

Kantorowicz, Ernst H. *The King's Two Bodies: A Study in Mediaeval Political Theology.* Princeton: Princeton University Press, 1957.

Katz, Joshua T. "Homeric Hymn to Hermes 296: τλήμονα γαστρὸς ἔριθον." *The Classical Quarterly* 49 (1999): 315–19.

Kelly, Henry Ansgar. *The Devil at Baptism: Ritual, Theology, and Drama.* Ithaca: Cornell University Press, 1985.

Kemp, Simon. "A Medieval Controversy about Odor." *Journal of the History of Behavioral Sciences*, 33 (1997): 211–19.

Kendrick, Laura. *Animating the Letter: The Figurative Embodiment of Writing from Late Antiquity to the Renaissance.* Columbus: Ohio State University Press, 1999.

Kimball, Elizabeth Guernsey. *Serjeanty Tenure in Medieval England.* New Haven: Yale University Press, 1936.

Kohly, Philippe, dir. *Matisse, Picasso.* DVD. 52 minutes. New York: Museum of Modern Art, 2003.

LaGuardia, David. "Doctor Rabelais and the Medicine of Scatology." In Persels and Ganim, eds, *Fecal Matters*, pp. 24–37.

Lanham, Richard A. *A Handlist of Rhetorical Terms.* 2nd edn. Berkeley: University of California Press, 1991.

Laporte, Dominique. *History of Shit.* Trans. Nadia Benabid and Rodolphe el-Khoury. Cambridge, MA: MIT Press, 2002.

Larrington, Carolyne. "Diet, Defecation and the Devil: Disgust and the Pagan Past." In Mcdonald, *Medieval Obscenities*, pp. 138–55.

Le Goff, Jacques. "Laughter in the Middle Ages." In *A Cultural History of Humour: From Antiquity to the Present Day.* Ed. Jan Bremmer and Herman Roodenburg. Cambridge: Polity Press, 1997, pp. 40–53.

———. *Your Money or Your Life: Economy and Religion in the Middle Ages.* Trans. Patricia Ranum. New York: Zone Books, 1988.

Levitan, Alan. "The Parody of Pentecost in Chaucer's *Summoner's Tale.*" *University of Toronto Quarterly*, 40 (1971): 236–46.

Liberman, Anatoly. "Gone With the Wind: More Thoughts on Medieval Farting." *Scandinavian Studies*, 68 (1996): 98–104.

———. *Word Origins and How We Know Them.* Oxford: Oxford University Press, 2005.

Laing, Margaret. "Raising a Stink in *The Owl and the Nightingale*: A New Reading at Line 115." *Notes and Queries*, 45 (1998): 276–84.
Lewis, C.S. *Studies in Words*. Cambridge: Cambridge University Press, 1960.
MacFarlane, Alan. *A Guide to English Historical Records*. Cambridge: Cambridge University Press, 1983.
Maclean, Ian. *The Renaissance Notion of Woman: A Study in the Fortunes of Scholasticism and Medical Science in European Intellectual Life*. Cambridge: Cambridge University Press, 1980.
Maitland, F.W. *The Constitutional History of England*. Cambridge: Cambridge University Press, 1955.
McDonald, Nicola, ed. *Medieval Obscenities*. Woodbridge, Suffolk: York Medieval Press, 2006.
Mellinkoff, Ruth. *Outcasts: Signs of Otherness in Northern European Art of the Late Middle Ages*. 2 vols. Berkeley: University of California Press, 1993.
Miller, John D. *Beads and Prayers: The Rosary in History and Devotion*. London: Burns & Oates, 2002.
Miller, William Ian. *The Anatomy of Disgust*. Cambridge, MA: Harvard University Press, 1997.
Mitchell, Bruce, and Fred C. Robinson. *A Guide to Old English*. 4th edn. Oxford: Blackwell, 1986.
Morrison, Susan Signe. *Excrement in the Late Middle Ages: Sacred Filth and Chaucer's Fecopoetics*. New York: Palgrave Macmillan, 2008.
Munrow, David. *Instruments of the Middle Ages and Renaissance*. London: Oxford University Press, 1976.
Murray, K.M. Elizabeth. *Caught in the Web of Words: James A. H. Murray and the Oxford English Dictionary*. New Haven: Yale University Press, 1977.
Nodes, Daniel Joseph. *Doctrine and Exegesis in Biblical Latin Poetry*. Leeds: Francis Cairns, 1993.
Nohain, Jean, and F. Caradec. *Le Petomane 1857–1945: A Tribute to the Unique Act Which Shook and Shattered the Moulin Rouge*. London: Souvenir Press, 1967.
O'Brien, Timothy D. " 'Ars-Metrik': Science, Satire, and Chaucer's Summoner." *Mosaic*, 23.4 (1990): 1–22.
O'Doherty, Brian. "Feldman Throws a Switch between Sight and Sound." *The New York Times*, February 2, 1964, p. X11.
Oxford English Dictionary. Online edn. Oxford University Press. http://www.oed.com/ accessed on April 18, 2004.
Oxford Latin Dictionary. Ed. P.G.W. Glare. Oxford: Clarendon, 1982.
Palmer, Richard. "In Bad Odour: Smell and Its Significance in Medicine from Antiquity to the Seventeenth Century." In *Medicine and the Five Senses*. Ed. W.F. Bynum and Roy Porter. Cambridge: Cambridge University Press, 1993, pp. 61–8.
Pedersen, Holger. *Discovery of Language: Linguistic Science in the Nineteenth Century*. Trans. John Webster Spargo. Bloomington: Indiana University Press, 1959.
Pernoud, Régine. *Joan of Arc by Herself and Her Witnesses*. Trans. Edward Hyams. Lanham, MD: Scarborough House, 1994. Original in *Jeanne d'Arc par elle-même et par ses témoins*. Paris: Éditions du Seuil, 1962.

Persels, Jeff and Russell Ganim. *Fecal Matters in Early Modern Literature and Art.* Aldershot, Hampshire and Burlington, VT: Ashgate, 2004.

Poliakov, Léon. *History of Anti-Semitism, Volume One: From the Time of Christ to the Court Jews.* Trans. Richard Howard. New York: Vanguard, 1965.

Pollock, Frederick, and Frederic William Maitland. *History of English Law before the Time of Edward I.* 2nd edn. 2 vols. Cambridge: Cambridge University Press, 1968.

Poole, Austin Lane. *From Domesday Book to Magna Carta 1087–1216.* 2nd edn. Oxford: Clarendon, 1955.

———. *Obligations of Society in the XII and XIII Centuries.* Oxford: Clarendon, 1946.

Postan, M.M. *The Medieval Economy and Society: An Economic History of Britain in the Middle Ages.* London: Penguin, 1972.

Rabkin, Eric, and Eugene M. Silverman. *It's a Gas: A Study of Flatulence.* Riverside CA: Xenos Books, 1991.

Rice, Winthrop Huntington. *The European Ancestry of Villon's Satirical Testaments.* New York: Corporate Press, 1941.

Ross, Thomas W. "Taboo-Words in Fifteenth-Century English." In *Fifteenth-Century Studies: Recent Essays.* Ed. Robert F. Yeager. Hamden, CT: Archon, 1984, pp. 137–60.

Round, John Horace. *Feudal England: Historical Studies on the XIth and XIIth Centuries.* London: Swan Sonnenschein, 1909. Repr. Bowie MD: Heritage, 1994.

———. *The King's Serjeants & Officers of State, with Their Coronation Services.* London: Nisbet, 1911.

Russell, Jeffrey Burton. *Lucifer: The Devil in the Middle Ages.* Ithaca: NY: Cornell University Press, 1984.

———. *Satan: The Early Christian Tradition.* Ithaca: Cornell University Press, 1981.

Schmidt, Josef, with Mary Simon. "Holy and Unholy Shit: The Pragmatic Context of Scatological Curses in Early German Reformation Satire." In Persels and Ganim, eds, *Fecal Matters*, pp. 109–17.

Screech, M.A. *Laughter at the Foot of the Cross.* London: Allen Lane, 1997.

Shipley, Joseph T. *The Origin of English Words: A Discursive Dictionary of Indo-European Roots.* Baltimore: John Hopkins University Press, 1984.

Siegel, Rudolph. *Galen on Sense Perception.* Basel: S. Karger AG, 1970.

Sidwell, Keith. *Reading Medieval Latin.* Cambridge: Cambridge University Press, 1995.

Siraisi, Nancy G. *Medieval & Early Renaissance Medicine: An Introduction to Knowledge and Practice.* Chicago and London: University of Chicago Press, 1990.

Skeat, Walter W. *Notes on English Etymology.* Oxford: Clarendon, 1901.

Skinner, Quentin. "Hobbes and the Classical Theory of Laughter." In *Leviathan After 350 Years.* Ed. Tom Sorell and Luc Foisneau. Oxford: Oxford University Press, 2004, pp. 139–66.

Smith, Jeremy J. *Sound Change and the History of English.* Oxford: Oxford University Press, 2007.

Spalding, Mary Caroline. *The Middle English Charters of Christ.* Bryn Mawr, PA: Bryn Mawr College, 1914.

Spitzer, Leo. *Classical and Christian Ideas of World Harmony: Prolegomena to an Interpretation of the Word "Stimmung."* Ed. Anna Granville Hatcher. Baltimore: John Hopkins Press, 1963.

———. "Milieu and Ambiance." In *Essays in Historical Semantics*. New York: Russell & Russell, 1948, pp. 179–225.

———. "On the Etymology of *pet*." *Language* 26 (1950): 533–8.

Stenton, F.M. *The First Century of English Feudalism, 1066–1166*. Oxford: Clarendon, 1932.

Strutt, Joseph. *The Sports and Pastimes of the People of England*. London: Chatto & Windus, 1898.

Taussig, Michael. *Defacement: Public Secrecy and the Labor of the Negative*. Stanford: Stanford University Press, 1999.

Travis, Peter. "Thirteen Ways of Listening to a Fart: Noise in Chaucer's *Summoner's Tale*." *Exemplaria*, 16 (2004): 323–48.

Trumble, Angus. *A Brief History of the Smile*. New York: Basic Books, 2004.

Tschann, Judith. "The Mind Distended: The *Retraction, Miller's Tale*, and *Summoner's Tale*." In *Chaucer's Humor: Critical Essays*. Ed. Jean E. Jost. New York and London: Garland, 1994, pp. 349–78.

Twycross, Meg, with Malcolm Jones and Alan Fletcher. " 'Farte Pryke in Cule': The Pictures." *Medieval English Theatre*, 23 (2001): 100–21.

Tydeman, William. "An Introduction to Medieval English Theatre." In *The Cambridge Companion to Medieval English Theatre*. Ed. Richard Beadle. Cambridge: Cambridge University Press, 1994, pp. 1–36.

The Victoria History of the County of Suffolk. Ed. William Page. 2 vols. London: Archibald Constable, 1907.

Vulgate Latin Bible. DRBO.ORG, 2004. Online Database.

Watson, Lyall. *Jacobson's Organ and the Remarkable Nature of Smell*. New York: Norton, 2000.

Weber, Samuel. *The Legend of Freud*. Minneapolis: University of Minnesota Press, 1982.

Wentersdorf, K.P. "The Symbolic Significance of the *Figurae Scatologicae* in Gothic Manuscripts." In *Word, Picture and Spectacle*. Ed. C. Davidson. Kalamazoo, MI: Medieval Institute Publications, 1984, pp. 1–20.

White, Lynn, Jr. *Medieval Technology and Social Change*. Oxford: Oxford University Press, 1962.

Willoughby, Rupert. *Life in Medieval England 1066–1485*. Norwich: Pitkin Unichrome, 1997.

Woolf, Rosemary. "Later Poetry: The Popular Tradition." In *The Middle Ages*. Ed. W.F. Bolton. London: Barrie & Jenkins, 1970, pp. 263–311.

Woolgar, C.M. *The Senses in Late Medieval England*. New Haven and London: Yale University Press, 2006.

Wright, Lawrence. *Clean & Decent: The Fascinating History of the Bathroom and the Water-Closet*. 2nd edn. London: Penguin, 2000.

Ziolkowski, Jan. *Alan of Lille's Grammar of Sex: The Meaning of Grammar to a Twelfth-Century Intellectual*. Speculum Anniversary Monographs 10. Cambridge, MA: Medieval Academy of America, 1985.

INDEX

Abelard, Peter 160
ablaut 132–3
Admonition by the Father of F.A. 191 n137
Ælfric 10
aeolipile, see *sufflator*
air 38–44, 62–6, 90, 94, 98
Alan of Lille 124
  Anticlaudianus 188 n67
  Plaint of Nature 204 n8, 205, n20
Albertus Magnus 168, 191 n133, n144
alchemy 1, 6, 52, 98–106, 137
Ambrose 30
Amorous Games (*Les Adevineaux Amoureux*) 25, 27, 188 n76–7, n80, 202 n402, 210 n157
anagnoresis 5, 146–52, 155, 156, 157, 181
anamorphosis 106–7
Ancrene Wisse 204 n6–7
Angel and Royal, Grantham 2, 106–7, 113–14, 183 n4
Anselm 160–2, 211 n164
anti-semitism 9–10, 18, 180
Apuleius, *Metamorphoses* 44, 90, 193 n175, 199 n337
Aquinas 160
  Summa Theologiae 2, 47, 85, 93, 123, 125, 144, 201 n365
Aristophanes 29, 189 n88, 205 n12
Aristotle 20, 42, 46, 47, 49, 50, 62, 63, 65, 144, 146, 148, 150, 151, 153, 154, 156, 209 n115
  and aesthetic unity 7

The "*Art*" *of Rhetoric* 210 n143, n146, n150–1
On Dreams 192 n165, 193 n173, 196 n246
Nicomachean Ethics 195 n228, 210 n137
De Partibus animalium 7, 188 n59, 209 n112, 210 n135, 214 n57
Poetics 50, 146–7, 150–1, 194 n203, 208 n103, 209 n109, n116–18, n121–2, 210 n130, n144, n152
Politics 197 n272, n275
Posterior Analytics 209 n104
On Prophesy in Sleep 42–4, 192 n166, n169
On Sense 192 n161, 194 n198–9
On Sleep 192 n167, 199 n318
On the Soul 194 n211
Ascham, Roger 7, 184 n13
Assize Rolls 171–2, 173, 177
Aubrey, John 185 n17
Aulus Gellius 191 n128
auras 39–41, 48, 90
Aurelian of Réome 189 n92
"Ave maris stella" 203 n431

Babee's Book 193 n190
Babel 87, 115, 118, 131–46, 158
Bach Johann Sebastian 39, 40
Bakhtin, Mikhail 16, 187 n42–3
Baldwin the Farter 173, 178, 179
baptism 6, 40, 77, 87, 93
Barclay, Alexander 206 n37

INDEX

Bartholomew of Exeter 205 n16
Beckett, Samuel 2
Beinecke MS 229, Yale University 110
belches 20, 22, 32, 40, 48, 66, 67, 75, 78, 84, 87, 89, 105, 116, 117, 121, 131, 153, 161, 181
Benjamin, Walter 183 n3
Bernardus Silvestris 193 n197
Bible 101
  I John 154
  Acts 77, 151, 190 n105
  Exodus 41, 79, 98, 184 n3
  Genesis 63, 66, 197 n268
  Isaiah 30
  Luke 40
  Mark 87
  Matthew 117, 122
  Psalms 32, 80, 105, 190 n104, n106
  Song of Songs 32, 35, 131
Blount, Thomas 169, 173, 174, 179, 186 n31, 213 n43, 216 n81
Boethius 31, 190 n100, n110, n112–13, 191 n127, n129, n135–6
bombard 28, 39, 169, 189 n87, 191 n140
Bonaventure 88
Book of Fees (Liber Feodorum) 14, 170, 171, 173, 176, 177, 179, 186 n30, 206 n35
Book of Secrets 37, 191 n133
Book of the Thousand Nights and a Night 11–12, 185 n19–20, 210 n147
Boorde, Andrew 41, 190 n120–2, 192 n157–8, 195 n287
Bosch, Hieronomous, Garden of Earthly Delights 29, 34, 189 n90
Bourke, John 174, 198 n299, 214 n58
Bouts, Dieric 85
Bracton 176
Buckle, Henry Thomas 174, 208 n98
bum (tramp) 1–3, 7, 8, 181
Burgess, Anthony, Clockwork Orange 36

burps, see belches
Burton, Richard 12, 185 n19, 210 n147

Calendar of Plea and Memoranda Rolls 185 n7–9, 185 n21
Calendar of the Close Rolls 129, 172, 176, 179
Calendarium Inquisitionum Post Mortem 172
Camden, William 14, 173, 178, 186 n31, 214 n62
capitalism 15, 16
carminative 35–7, 73, 115, 140, 153, 190 n123, 207 n72
Catherine of Siena 19, 71
Chaplin, Charlie, Modern Times 157–8
charms 36–7, 140
Charters of Christ 74, 199 n320
Chaucer 43, 51, 59, 116, 128, 142, 145, 148, 183 n1, 212 n27, 213 n36
  Canon Yeoman's Tale 98, 104–5
  Canterbury Tales 12, 142, 168, 181, 188 n65, 213 n36
  Franklin's Tale 26
  General Prologue 67, 116
  House of Fame 193 n172
  Merchant's Tale 61–2
  Miller's Tale 62, 130, 150, 156
  Parliament of Fowls 107
  Reeve's Tale 62
  Summoner's Tale 4, 25, 28, 45, 75, 76–8, 88, 95–7, 105, 116, 128, 141, 169, 180, 199 n332, 204 n454
  Troilus and Criseyde 148, 192 n163
Chester Mystery Cycle 188 n61
Le Chevalier qui fist parler les cons 117
Chomsky, Noam 124, 205 n18
Christmas 34, 166, 167–8, 170, 173
Chronicle of London 9–10, 184 n1
Chrysippus 154
Cicero 72, 143, 145
  De Natura deorum 191 n143
  Tusculan Disputations 198 n313

INDEX

Claudius, Emperor   70, 154, 165, 188–9 n81, 212 n17
Cola di Rienzo, biography   42–4, 62, 192 n149, n168, n170, 193 n171
Du Con qui fu fait a la Besche   195 n233
Constantine the African, *Liber de Coitu*   67, 68, 197 n288
Copinger, W.A.   177, 178, 216 n81, n86, 217 n92–3, n95
Copland, Robert, "Iyl of Braintford's Testament"   74–5, 169, 195 n230, 199 n323, n326, n328, 214 n52
courtly love   60

Dante   5, 77, 170
  Inferno   19, 29, 67, 81–6, 91, 102, 107, 116, 117–19, 121–3, 124, 135, 204 n437
  Paradiso   148
  Purgatorio   41
  De Vulgari eloquentia   116, 131, 202 n395
death   3, 6, 9, 16, 66, 68–75, 76, 80, 85, 86, 90–1, 95, 122, 125, 151, 153, 154, 158
demandes ioyous   25
Demetrius of Sumium   118
Derricke, John   167
Derrida, Jacques   205 n27
The Dethe of the Kynge of Scotis   200 n349
devil(s)   6, 12–13, 29, 54, 57, 69, 70, 74, 80, 82, 83, 85, 87–94, 95, 97, 104, 117, 121, 141, 165, 200 n350, 201 n358, 202 n397–8, 212 n18
Diogenes Laertius   187 n49, 210 n141, 217 n99–101, n103
Diogenes the Cynic   17, 122, 180
Donatus   122
Doubting Thomas   180
Douglas, Mary   4, 183 n1
Du Cange, Charles Du Fresne   174, 214 n54, n56

ducat man   94, 97, 146
Dulaure, Jacques-Antoine   174, 214 n54–6
Dunbar, William   35, 57, 190 n118, 206 n37

Edmund Ironside   80
Edward I   166, 172, 215 n70, 216 n82
Edward II   166, 212 n27
Edward III   168, 172, 173, 178, 214 n63
Edward de Vere   11
Edwardes, Allen   70, 164, 198 n298, 212 n13
Elizabeth I   11
empiricism   99, 107, 115
Engels   2
exorcism   6, 89, 92–4, 97, 121
exsufflation   93–4, 121, 161, 165
extimacy   47–8, 52, 53, 60, 85, 107, 179
etymology   1, 4, 5, 115, 127–46, 147, 151, 169, 181, 190 n123, 206 n39, 207 n71, 208 n78, 210 n145
Evagrius of Pontus   91

fabliaux   18, 26, 57, 59–62, 91, 92, 97, 188 n78
"fart pryke in cule"   164, 211–12 n11
farts, and artillery   75, 163, 168–9, 129–30
  and auras   41, 48
  and baptism   93
  and charms   36, 37, 140
  and *contrapasso*   77, 116, 170
  and creation   84, 115–16
  and dance   164, 166–7, 169–70, 173
  and death   69–74, 84, 90
  and divinity   76–80
  division of   4, 25, 27, 75, 76, 96, 141, 174
  and epistemology   3, 52–3
  and essence   44, 52, 50, 101–4
  etymology of   128–31
  and gender   11, 54–62, 69, 142–3, 169–70

240　INDEX

farts, and artillery—*Continued*
  and hermeneutics 78–9
  and illumination 3, 41
  and language 82–3, 115–46
  and lawsuit 11, 26, 55–7
  and male erections 67–8
  and Middle Ages 1–2, 12, 47, 167
  and music 27–39
  and Old Irish 79, 163–4, 167, 200 n342–3, 211 n6
  as performance 14, 35, 163–79
  Portugese 12
  and praying 70–2
  and shame 11–12, 58, 71, 72
  silent and noisy 12, 27–9, 34, 55, 56, 57, 68, 25–6
  and smell 3, 4, 41–56, 60, 62
  and stone boundaries 12
  and toilet etiquette 45–6
  wolves' farts 12
"Feast of Tottenham" 35, 57, 190 n117
Felix Faber of Ulm 18
feudal tenures 7, 14, 166–8, 170, 174–8
feudalism 17, 174
Flamel, Nicholas 98, 103
flânerie 1–3
flatus vocis 157–60
Foucault, Michel
  The Birth of the Clinic 203 n422–3
  The Order of Things 187 n57
Franco of Bologna 41
Franklin, Benjamin 128, 206 n31
Freud Sigmund 15, 19, 58–9, 95
  "The Antithetical Meaning of Primal Words" 135–6
  Beyond the Pleasure Principle 157
  "Character and Anal Eroticism" 95, 138–9, 171–2
  Civilization and its Discontents 53, 95
  Jokes and Their Relation to the Unconscious 55, 149, 155–9
  Rat Man 53, 58
Froissart, Jean 191 n139

Furetière 23, 169, 186 n23, 189 n82, 215 n68

Galen 2, 42, 48, 64, 183 n6, 192 n160, 193 n191–4, 196 n249, n254, 201 n354–5
Ganassi, Sylvestro 30
gargoyles 2, 90, 104–5
Gautier le Leu, *De Deus Vilains* 54–5, 57, 58, 195 n222
Geber 102–3, 195 n221, 203 n416–17, n424–7, n436, 204 n438
Geoffrey of Vinsauf 30, 118–19, 189 n97, 205 n11
Geoponica 54, 195 n220
Gilles de Rais 80, 200 n346
Gower, John, *Confessio Amantis* 189 n87, 193 n176
Le Grand testament de taste vin, roy de pions 74
Le Grand testament de vert janet 74
Great Revolt of 1381 139
Greek tragedy 7, 147, 150, 153, 154–5
Gregory of Nyssa 29
Gregory of Tours 199 n333, 200 n339
Grimm, Jacob 132–3
Grimm's law 7–8, 127–8, 129, 133, 137
Guibert of Nogent 70–1, 90–1, 198 n304, 202 n383, n386
Guston, Philip 3

Heidegger, Martin 65, 147–8, 197 n265, 209 n105–6
Henry I 41, 172, 175
Henry II 122, 166, 172, 175, 176, 177, 175, 216 n80
Henry III 170, 172, 176, 177
Henry of Huntingdon 41, 192 n156, 200 n348
Henryson, Robert, *Testament of Cresseid* 74
Herakleitos 20, 24

INDEX

Herman of Tournai 161, 211 n167–8
Hermes 78–9
Hilary of Poitiers 29
Hippocrates 28, 65, 67, 130, 189 n84, 196 n256–61, 197 n273, 206 n39
Holbein, *The Ambassadors* 106
Homer 3
  "Hymn to Hermes" 78, 200 n339, 210 n137
  Iliad 144
  Odyssey 64
Honorius of Autun 207 n66
Horace 55, 213 n35
Horkheimer, Max and Theodor Adorno, *Dialectic of Enlightenment* 194 n200
Hugh of St. Victor 89, 200 n345, 201 n376
Hugo, Victor 214 n56
Hume, David 115, 204 n1
humors 1, 35, 41, 62, 64, 73, 94, 125, 153, 156

Innocent III 4, 19, 160, 187 n55, 199 n333, 211 n160–1
insects 88–90
Isidore of Seville 5, 127
  Etymologies 127, 133, 141, 144, 145, 149

Jack of Dover 167, 213 n36–7
James I of Scotland 80
Japan, medieval 79, 164, 212 n12
Le Jeu de Robin et Marion 165, 212 n19
John XXII, Pope 104
John of Arderne 21, 188 n63
John the Deacon 163
John of Salisbury 5, 160
  Metalogicon 124, 137, 205 n19
  Polycraticus 165–6, 176, 212 n20
John the Deacon 165
Johnson, Samuel 47
Jonson, Ben,
  The Alchemist 98, 99, 100, 106, 203 n421

The Staple of News 52, 194 n212
Joubert, Laurent 3, 46, 148, 154, 156, 180, 183 n7, 190 n108, 193 n185, 205 n21, 209 n110, n127, 210 n129, n131–4, n138, n142, n149, n153, 217 n102
Judas 70, 77, 151–2
Jung Carl 98

katharsis 153–5
Kempe, Margery 19, 59, 86, 187 n53
Kristeva, Julia 183 n8
Kubla Khan 79

Lacan, Jacques 193 n188, 204 n458
Lambert of Ardres 158, 184 n2, 210 n155
Land of Cockaigne 146
Langland, William, *Piers Plowman* 164, 185 n14, 199 n333, 211 n9
Laporte, Dominique 13, 184, 192 n214, 200 n419, 205 n93
laughter 4, 5, 8, 12, 13, 27, 46, 64, 92, 94, 107, 138, 146–59, 165, 170, 181, 183 n7, 198 n314, 200 n347, 208 n99, 209 n110, n112, 210 n138, 216 n80, 217 n103
Levinas, Emmanuel 210 n159
Leys D'Amors 126
linguistic turn, 5
linguistics 5, 123–4, 127, 132ñ5, 137–8, 139, 142
Lucretius 44–5, 46, 66, 67, 68, 193 n179–81, n186, 197 n269, n276, 198 n293
Luttrell Psalter 28, 30, 109
Lybeaus Desconnus 187 n56
Lydgate 71
  Fall of Princes 191 n140
  Life of our Lady 204 n3
  Siege of Thebes 198 n309

Macrobius 36, 190 n111, 191 n125, n138, n141
Magna Carta 176, 215 n69
Maimonides 20, 45–6, 74, 193 n184

Makejoy, Matilda 166
Mankind 23, 71, 72, 91, 188 n70, 198 n307–8, 202 n388
Map, Walter 66, 197 n274, 216 n80
Marriage 6, 53–62, 102
Martianus Capella 191 n124, n128
Matazone de Calignano 197 n290
Matthew of Paris 184 n4
medieval grammar 5, 22, 25, 29, 37, 39, 115, 117, 118–27, 137, 143–5, 159
medieval rhetoric 4, 5, 19, 30, 115, 116, 143–4, 159
metathesis 136–7, 139
Middle Ages 1–2, 7, 12–13, 16–19, 28, 33, 37, 40, 47, 64, 74, 89, 93, 98, 100, 105, 151, 166, 167
Middle English sermons 10, 185 n6, 192 n163, 201 n366
minstrels 166–8, 178, 212 n22–4, n27–8, 213 n29
Mirk, John 51, 142, 180, 194 n206, 198 n300, n303, 201 n370, 208 n78, 209 n113, n124, 217 n97–8
misericords 94, 146
Montaigne 72–3, 198 n314–16, 212 n15
Moses 79–80
Murray, James 137, 206 n47
music 28–41, 139, 140, 160, 163–6

N-Town Play 200 n351–2
nauscopie 44, 193 n177
New Testament, *see* Bible
Niceta of Remesiana 201 n363–4
Niebuhr, Carsten 11, 164–5, 185 n18, 212 n14
Nietzsche 51, 194 n210
noise 28, 29, 33, 34, 38–9, 41, 56, 79, 86–7, 90, 101, 115, 120–1, 136, 141, 146, 181
Norton, Thomas, *Ordinal of Alchemy* 50, 103, 193 n187, 194 n202, 195 n221, 196 n250, n253, 201 n359, 203 n418, n432–4, 204 n439–45, n447–8, n450, n457
Notre Dame, Paris 2

Oderisi of Gubbio 41
Old Icelandic 28
Old Icelandic sagas 15, 81
Old Testament, *see* Bible
Ormulum 142
Oude Kerk St. Nicolas 94
Ovid, *Metamorphoses* 66, 95, 192 n148, 197 n271, 203 n409
Owl and the Nightingale 13, 186 n28

Papias 152, 210 n128
parodic sermon 8, 184 n14, 188 n62
peasants 7, 28–9, 38, 54–5, 57, 60, 68, 69–70, 76–7, 91–2, 94, 97, 103, 141, 146, 164, 195 n231, 201 n365, 202 n389
Pepys, Samuel 20, 47, 188 n58, 193 n189
perfume 6, 41, 45, 52–4, 94, 103–4, 181, 192 n150
Le Pet, 55–9, 87, 195 n223–7, n229, n232, n237–40
Petrarch 41, 192 n151–2
physis 65–6, 106, 148
Picasso 3, 181, 184 n11
Plato 3, 17, 31, 33, 35, 42, 50, 53, 147, 180, 184 n9
  Cratylus 95, 128, 137, 203 n408, 206 n29–30, 207 n70
  and ideas 49
  Laws 190 n115–16
  Phaedo 72–3, 198 n311–12
  Phaedrus 199 n335
  Republic 190 n114, 199 n333
  Timaeus 43, 191 n145, 192 n162, 193 n183, 204 n446
Pliny the Elder 67, 197 n276–84, 199 n336, 209 n111, 211 n162
Plutarch 37, 191 n130
pneuma 66, 32, 62–6, 68–9, 83–4, 116, 192 n160
Porcelet 59, 86
prayer 6, 19, 71–3, 79, 87, 91, 92, 95, 99, 116, 180, 200 n344
prime matter 100–1, 136
Priscian 5, 119–26, 205 n15

Institutiones grammaticae 119–22, 126, 143–5, 160, 205 n13, n23, 208 n87–9
privacy 16–18, 60–1, 72
privatization 15–18
privies 9–10, 13, 15, 17, 19, 21–2, 46, 61–2, 71–2, 80–2, 90, 105, 117, 200 n347, n353
Promptorium parvulorum 185 n12, 188 n68
Protestantism 14, 15, 93
Proust 42
proverbs 6, 20–4, 56, 115, 188 n64
Ptolemaic universe 33, 81, 89
Pujol, Joseph 163, 166, 211 n2–5, 212 n21
puns 4, 5, 27, 75, 124, 128, 130, 137–9, 141–6, 151, 156, 158–9, 170, 176
Pythagoras 33, 37

Quia emptores 174

Rabelais, François 16, 23–4, 27, 59, 65, 68, 69, 75, 116, 137, 138, 145, 155, 167, 174, 187 n41–3, 188 n73, 189 n82, 195 n241, 196 n255, n262, 197 n289, 198 n295–6, 199 n330, 204 n5, 207 n58, n65, 208 n96–7, 210 n148, 213 n31
Raimbert of Lille 161
Ranke Leopold von 217 n104
Ravisius, Johannes 200 n347
realism and nominalism 5, 159–62
Rhetorica ad Herennium 189 n96, 199 n317, 208 n84, n90, n95, 210 n158
Richard I 215 n65
Richard III 172
riddles 6, 10, 25–7, 93, 159, 209 n123
Robinson, Heath 157
Roland the Farter 14, 28, 33, 35, 39, 129, 160, 163–79, 214 n61, 215 n68, 216 n82

Roman de la Rose 208 n102
Roman de Renart 166–7, 213 n30
Romance of Alexander 41, 111, 170, 215 n67
Roscelin 5, 159–62
Rule of St. Benedict 16–17
 in Middle English 187 n48, 201 n371
Rutebeuf, *Le Pet au Vilain* 7, 28–9, 69, 89, 91, 92, 94, 198 n297

sacred and profane 4, 40, 45, 136, 146, 181
Saint-Lazare, Autun 2
St. Ambrose 32, 201 n377
St. Anthony 51, 87–8, 92, 94
St. Augustine 34, 51, 64, 101, 116, 144
 City of God 28, 33, 57–8, 71, 79, 161, 165, 166, 185 n49, 189 n95, 190 n109, 195 n236, 196 n252, 198 n294, n305, 200 n341, 201 n358, 211 n165, 212 n15
 Confessions 51, 194 n209
 De Doctrina Christiana (*On Christian Doctrine*) 7, 144–5, 208 n80–2, n85–6, n94
 Enarrationes super Psalmos 80
St. Bernard of Clairvaux 32, 131, 190 n107, 206 n42
St. Gregory 90, 179–80
St. Guthlac 41
St. Helen's, Brant Broughton 106, 112
St. Hugh of Lincoln 10
St. Jerome 28, 30, 160
St. John Chrysostom 116
St. Martin of Tours 94
St. Mattias 77, 151
Satan 67, 81, 84–8, 90, 93, 95, 97, 155, 202 n385, n387, n401
Saussure 133, 137–8, 205 n17, 207 n53, n55, n59, n62–4
school exercises 20–2, 37
De Secretis mulierum 60–1, 189 n144, 193 n242, 195 n286, 202 n21–2, 203 n24

INDEX

Secretum Secretorum   35, 190 n119
Seneca   158
  Ad Lucilium   185 n13, 205 n10, 210 n154
serjeanty   14, 166, 170–8
Serres, Michel   200 n340, 208 n76
Shakespeare, William
  Hamlet   129
  King Lear   51, 194 n205, n207
shit   3, 9, 19, 20–4, 48, 52, 53–4, 56, 61, 71, 73, 81–2, 86, 87, 88, 97–8, 100, 103, 135, 138, 148, 151, 154–5, 167
  and gold   15–16, 94–5
Shulḥan Arukh   72, 87, 198 n310
sight   3, 42, 43, 45, 49–53, 86
smell   3, 41–54, 57, 85, 103
Socrates   72, 78, 95, 119, 137, 139, 159–60
Sophocles, *Oedipus the King*   146–51, 154, 155, 156, 209 n107–8
soul   34, 36, 63–4, 67, 69–74, 79, 84, 85, 87, 90, 91, 94, 97, 98, 99, 100, 104, 117, 153, 154
sound laws   7–8, 120, 127–8, 132–3, 137, 139, 143
Spelman, Henry   211 n166, 214 n61
Spooner, W.A., Rev.   137
Strindberg, August, *The Father*   140
subject/object relations   3, 8, 39, 47–50, 52–3, 75, 85, 86, 181
Suetonius   188 n81, 198 n302, 200 n339, 210 n139–40, 212 n17
sufflator   105, 168
"Sumer is icomen in"   68
Summa musice   30–1, 189 n95, 190 n101, 207 n69
Süskind, Patrick, *Perfume*   42, 54, 194 n215–16, 204 n451

Tech Midchúarda   164, 167
Tertullian   64, 65, 78, 196 n248, 197 n266, 199 n333, 200 n338

Thaïs   86
Till Eulenspiegel   96
Tiresias   3, 99
touch   3, 43, 48–52, 58, 70, 90, 95
Towneley Plays   198 n306, 209 n124
  Second Shepherds' Play   45
Trevisa, John   94, 139, 183 n2, 202 n405, 207 n68
Les Trois Meschines   26, 56, 57, 188 n79
Þorsteins Þáttr skelks   81

umlaut   133–5
usury   102

Varro   144, 151, 198 n292, 204 n2, 207 n67, 208 n93, 209 n120, 210 n145
Vespasian, Emperor   88
Vicary, Thomas   197 n285
Le Vilain asnier   92
Villon, François   12–13, 74–5, 186 n24, 196 n243, 197 n270, 199 n319, n327, n329, 209 n126
Virgil   82, 84, 119, 122
  Aeneid   79, 120, 122
Vision of Tondal   84, 201 n356, n360–1
Vitruvius   31, 168, 189 n98, 213 n44
Vives, Juan Luis   165, 211 n165, 212 n15
Voragine, Jacobus de, *Golden Legend*   86, 198 n301, 201 n362, 209 n125
Vulgaria of John Stanbridge   188 n69

waste   1–8, 15, 19, 156, 183 n1, 187 n56
William of Champeaux   160
William of Malmesbury   202 n391, 211 n163
wills   18, 74–5, 77–8

wind 6, 63, 66–8, 79
Wodehouse, P.G. 137, 207 n61
Woolf, Rosemary 13, 186 n25, 197 n291
word play 137–43, 157

Wycliffe Bible 30, 32, 63, 154, 184 n3
Wynkyn de Worde 28, 185 n14

Zeuxis 154